ROMAN SOCIETY

CIVILIZATION AND SOCIETY

Studies in Social, Economic, and Cultural History

General Editor

Theodore K. Rabb, Princeton University

Consulting Editors

Thomas W. Africa, State University of New York, Binghamton
David J. Herlihy, Harvard University
David S. Landes, Harvard University
Henry Rosovsky, Harvard University
Stanley J. Stein, Princeton University
Stephan A. Thernstrom, Harvard University

ROMAN SOCIETY

A Social, Economic, and Cultural History

HENRY C. BOREN

University of North Carolina
at Chapel Hill

D. C. HEATH AND COMPANY
Lexington, Massachusetts • Toronto

This one is for Gail and Andrew

PREFACE

The author of this volume believes that in a case like Rome, a state where almost all formal and informal institutional life was thoroughly politicized, it would be almost impossible to deal successfully with social structures or even social life over the several centuries involved without providing a political backdrop for the setting. For that reason, enough political history has been included to inform the social, economic, and cultural discussions and to give them chronological structure. Topical discussions therefore recur in various periods: there are, for example, treatments of society in early Rome, in the middle Republic during a period of rapid change, in the late Republic, in the early Empire, the high Empire, and (briefly) in the later Empire. An attempt is made to bring these together into a kind of whole, even though they are separated; this results in some overlap, but it is thought to be both unavoidable and useful, serving as it does to emphasize important and continuing aspects of development. Other topics on economics and cultural matters are dealt with in similar fashion.

The author hopes that no reader finds the title misleading, and that the parts add up to a coherent whole.

Special thanks are due to Professors Thomas W. Africa, Erich S. Gruen, and Mason Hammond, who read the manuscript. Their suggestions have been invaluable and have enabled the writer to improve the work and to escape some errors. The author is of course responsible for any errors, distortions of fact, or misinterpretations that remain. Thanks are due also to the members of the fine staff of the publisher, who have done much to make the final product a more readable and attractive book.

CONTENTS

MAPS

PLATES

INTRODUCTION

The Roman experience was once and still remains a most important segment of the human story. Not only did the Roman Empire encompass much of the civilized world and endure for centuries but, more importantly, Roman institutions and legal structures, closely imitated by numerous successor states, have survived all the way down to modern times. So, too, has Rome's cultural influence. Even now, a millennium and a half after the Empire's demise, surviving elements still may be discerned and Roman history still is regarded, by numerous thoughtful persons, to be profoundly meaningful.

Today's politicians and newspaper columnists frequently refer to Rome and its history, often to pontificate on the decline and fall of that great empire and to make doleful predictions of what that sad decay may portend for our own future if our government continues on its present course. Moreover, in recent years, several scholars not historians—sociologists, chemists, psychologists—also have turned their attention to Rome's decline, advancing new theories or refining older ones to explain it. Obviously, all these pundits believe that ancient Rome was important—*is* important. Even though some of them make faulty use of the evidence to bolster their own rationalizations, such attention serves to point up the continuing significance of the study of Rome.

Although the decline and fall has attracted the most comment, at least in the two centuries since Edward Gibbon published the first volume of his monumental work in 1776, the *idea* of Rome as a great, unifying world entity has probably been more significant over the longer period. It was this vision that inspired an ostensibly Christian version, the "Holy Roman Empire," and that in our own time continues to encourage statesmen to establish broad, unifying international organizations in their quest of a *pax orbis* in imitation of the *pax Romana*.

The history of Rome is therefore more than just a summary of the past. It is a living idea with an evolution and importance apart from the events. That is, what people think about the history of Rome is important—to some, more important than the truth itself. Perhaps it is not too much to hope that those who read this formulation of Roman history will afterward have a clearer perception than before. Like every other history book this one is intended to approach the truth as closely as possible in the light of often scanty and difficult evidence. It tries to inform the reader, not only about political events and structures, since politics was a vital matter in Rome, but also about Roman society and economy as well.

One may be sure that the saga of Rome will continue to be

used as an exemplar by many persons, whether teachers, politicians, newspaper analysts, or civic club speakers. Nothing is wrong about that. Moreover, it is quite right that each individual's picture of Rome should take on some symbolic validity that goes beyond the facts. The author sincerely hopes, in fact, that every reader will find here something thought-provoking, compellingly meaningful beyond the material set forth, and spanning past and present.

ROMAN SOCIETY

If some wise prophet of, say, the middle-seventh century B.C. had been asked to predict what city or what state of the Mediterranean was destined to rule the whole area, only a touch of the divine could have induced him to pick Rome. The prophet would surely have looked to the East, for the western Mediterranean in many ways lagged behind the more civilized and richer East. Perhaps he would have suggested Saïs in grain-rich Egypt as a candidate for such domination, where a resurgent dynasty (the Saïte) was vigorously attempting to reestablish an Egyptian empire which might rival that of seven or eight centuries past. He might have named one of the flourishing cities of the Phoenician coast, or of the western coast of Asia Minor. Several Greek cities then were pressing outward with great vitality and, like the Phoenician states, colonizing widely, to the west as well as to the Black Sea area: the prophet might have identified the strongest of these, perhaps Corinth, as predestined to power.

Even if our imaginary prophet had confined his prognostications to the states of the western Mediterranean, he would have been unlikely to point to Rome. Carthage in North Africa, Greek Massilia in the south of France, Gades in southern Spain, one of a dozen Greek cities in Sicily or southern Italy, the Etruscan states in Italy to the northwest of Rome, these all then showed more promise than Rome. In the seventh century B.C. that city was not much more than a village on the Tiber even if it was, as tradition has it, a "kingdom."

In retrospect, geography often looms large. Yet Italy seems not very impressive geographically, even by ancient standards. Only in contrast to Greece does the long, boot-shaped peninsula seem well endowed. A spine of mountains, the Apennines, connects with the Alps in the northwest, angles across

BEGINNINGS

1

the upper peninsula, cutting it off from the broad valley of the Po in the north, ranges the length of the country, down to the toe of the boot, and even, with a dip at the straits of Messina, continues into Sicily. Volcanic Etna in eastern Sicily, though separately formed, connects with the range and, at more than 10,000 feet, is its highest elevation. Much of Italy along the flanks of the hills and in the valleys is cultivable. The richest areas agriculturally are the Po valley—which was not important to Rome until the late Republic—Campania to the south of Rome, and the regions of Apulia and Calabria on the east side along the Adriatic down toward the boot-heel.[1] Etruria and Latium (wherein Rome was situated) on the western side were fairly productive also, as was Umbria, as it was eventually called, across the peninsula to the northeast. Samnium, the rugged region to the east and south of Rome back from the coasts, and Bruttium in the toe of the peninsula, were too mountainous to be very rich agriculturally. Sicily, though it seems poor today, was surprisingly productive, especially in grain, throughout antiquity.

In the raw materials important to ancient technology Italy was rich, though not so rich as Spain. There was some copper, and some—but inadequate—supplies of tin, silver, and gold; there was plenty of iron. Etruria especially, but other areas also, had abundant forests, and offshore, on the little island of Elba, were found the richest deposits of iron ore. Rome faced west from a centralized location in the Mediterranean, beside a river, far enough from the sea to discourage pirates. The Tiber, happily, was navigable, though only for comparatively small ships, as far as the city; timber, farm products, and the like could float down from the north in rafts or shallow draft boats. But Romans could not easily develop a sea trade. It is always emphasized that the Tiber Isle at Rome formed the lowest point at which the stream could conveniently be forded or bridged. Because of this and the lie of the land otherwise, natural routes converged on the site, so that it was often said later that all roads led to Rome. But Rome was not the only transport hub in Italy, not even in western Italy. Capua in Campania to the south of Rome, its soil much richer than that about Rome, was also a focus for important roads. So was Naples farther on south; the latter city also was blessed with an excellent harbor, something Rome never had despite the expenditure of vast sums during the early Empire. The Etruscan city Caere (modern Cerveteri), 40 miles north of Rome, was strategically placed also. Routes, land, and resources made this a prosperous city before Rome rose to importance.

---

[1] Calabria, in modern Italy, is now the toe of the Italian "boot."

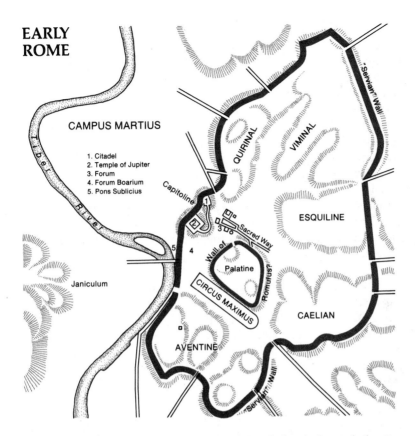

EARLY ROME

CAMPUS MARTIUS

1. Citadel
2. Temple of Jupiter
3. Forum
4. Forum Boarium
5. Pons Sublicius

QUIRINAL

VIMINAL

"Serrian" Wall

Capitoline

Sacred Way

ESQUILINE

Wall of

Palatine

Romulus?

CIRCUS MAXIMUS

Janiculum

CAELIAN

AVENTINE

"Serrian" Wall

Tiber River

    As the soil of Latium ranked far behind that of the Po valley or of Campania or Calabria, so Roman mineral and other resources were unspectacular. Caere and several other Etruscan cities to the north had better access to iron, copper, precious metals, and timber. Their technological abilities long ranked high above that of the relatively backward Romans.

    The geography of Italy, as compared with Greece, had an important advantage: the mountains did not compartmentalize the country so completely as in Greece. Moreover, if one state could manage to gain control of the whole peninsula it would have (by Mediterranean standards) a vast and fairly homogeneous population upon which to draw, with adequate agricultural and other resources at hand. The Etruscans tried to unify the whole, and failed; so did the Greeks. The Romans, from a less well-favored natural area, succeeded.

The People

Once Rome became great, generations of Roman children were taught that the determination, persistence, discipline, and endurance of her people made possible the stiff climb to dominance. There was something to this: certainly the small farmers who manned the cohorts and maniples of infantry for the Roman legions persisted doggedly even in dire adversity. Moreover, the upper classes who staffed the officer corps demonstrated a remarkably high average of ability as generals and field officers, though of course a few were egregious failures. Yet it is doubtful that the Roman soldiers were any more doughty than the men of the other Latin tribes; and certainly some of the related Italian peoples—the Samnites, for example—were man for man the equals of the Romans for centuries. Probably most of the Greeks also were as courageous and competent, though both they and the Etruscans showed some tendency to grow sophisticated and sometimes effete. We must conclude that though the simple Roman peasants made admirable soldiers, this was not unique in Italy.

The social institutions of the Romans also differed little from those of the Latins and Italians, and in some respects resembled those of the Etruscans. The highest social class, the patricians, dominated not only society, but also the army, the priesthoods, and the higher political offices. They were the largest landholders, for like their Italian counterparts, all classes in Rome were rural. In the three-class society, all other free citizens were called plebeians; beneath them were the slaves, probably not a numerous group in an early age. We shall look more closely at the social classes later in the chapter. Here we wish only to note that the Romans differed little from others in Italy.

The later Romans prided themselves on their religiosity and thought this also an important reason for their rise to power. In religion as in society and politics, however, Roman practices resembled those of the other Latins and Italians, whose racial and linguistic backgrounds were so similar to those of the Romans. All worshiped a great sky god, as did other peoples of Indo-European origin, who by then were scattered over the world from Italy to the Indian subcontinent in Asia. The Romans called this god Jupiter. They venerated a typical war god, Mars. In various locales, crossroads, rivers, fountains, streams, woods, they worshiped other deities often referred to as *numina*. They did not anthropomorphize the *numen*, but in animistic fashion thought of it only as spirit or force or power. In any case, few modern historians would think religious devotion a satisfactory explanation for the rise of Rome.

The later Romans attributed Rome's greatness in part to her willingness to learn and to borrow from others. There seems to be an element of truth here, though it is impossible to be sure whether the degree of tolerance of alien ways was really so great in Rome as to be in any sense unique. Probably most of the Latins and Italians, the Romans' kin, were equally quick to learn from their more advanced neighbors, the Etruscans to the north and the Greeks to the south. Certainly the Romans were profoundly influenced by both. Yet it is possible that the later Roman scholars were right: from the beginning Rome had a mixed population; perhaps Romans did adopt and adapt new ways more readily than other states. Romans also received foreigners much more readily than most states in antiquity. Illustrative of this is a law, traditionally ascribed to the sixth king, Servius Tullius, but retained throughout Rome's history, that gave the citizenship to emancipated slaves. In fact, for centuries, the Romans generously (by comparison, at least) awarded grants of citizenship to the peoples that they had earlier conquered.

As we shall see, Rome's ultimate success seems to relate more to political organization than to any geographic or economic determination. Romans learned, if reluctantly, to treat the conquered fairly; the lesson was first learned, perhaps, through accommodation in domestic disorders. Of course the city's central location in Italy and the peninsula's resources helped to make it all possible, once Rome had gained an initial, strong political position.

If, by comparison with others, Rome was not particularly well endowed with resources, if her men, customs, and institutions were much like those of her contemporaries, then obviously one must seek elsewhere an explanation for that first surge of accomplishment that raised the village on the Tiber above its neighbors and set it on the path to power. The credit for this surely belongs to the Etruscans. It was they who made Rome one of the most important cities in western Italy. But before giving our attention to the Etruscans and their influence, let us note briefly the rise of civilization itself in Italy.

Italy Before Rome

Archaeology constantly renews ancient history, so that often it is, in a sense, not ancient at all, but contemporary. We now know much more about ancient Italy than the Romans of Caesar's day. We have learned of a paleolithic Italy in which Neanderthal and later Cro-Magnon types of people lived. Through aerial photography we can actually see the outline-remains of hundreds of neolithic villages. We know what sorts of houses people lived in then: round or oval, dug partly into the ground, a frame supported by poles sunk even deeper, closed in with wattle and daub; the smoke from the center hearth escaping from an opening in the thatched roof. Tourists can see the holes made by framing poles in excavations on the Palatine Hill, the so-called "House of Romulus."

We have learned that the Bronze Age (beginning about 1800 B.C.) brought more complex cultures: one called Terremare in the north of Italy produced not only bronze tools, but also a distinctive pottery of high quality, houses of considerable size both round and oblong, and evidence of at least a modicum of town planning. Farther south in central Italy a culture of the same period is called Apennine, named after the mountains that range down the peninsula. It too is distinguished by its pottery —black and polished. The Apennine people buried their dead, while the Terremarans practiced cremation. Yet linguistically and ethnically, the two culture-groups may have been closely related.

The Iron Age came in around 900 B.C., a little later than in the Mediterranean East. Here too archaeologists distinguish various culture groups. Most important is a culture called Villanovan, with northern and southern variations: the northern group extended into the Po valley; the southern group reached down to the Tiber and into Latium. Villanovan culture thus blanketed ancient Etruria, the homeland of the Etruscans. Even though this culture developed in the Iron Age, the finest metal objects found in the local tombs are of bronze—swords, helmets, and the like. The Villanovans sometimes put the ashes of their dead in biconical urns covered with bronze helmets, and sometimes in little pottery urns modeled on the homes in which they lived.

Etruscan Civilization: Origins and Development

One may speak of Etruria (or Tuscany) as the homeland of the Etruscans, but whether the Etruscans were an indigenous people who there developed a high culture under the influence of the Greeks and others, or whether they came in from the East, perhaps Asia Minor, is a vexed question now as it was in antiquity. The fifth century B.C. Greek historian Herodotus said the Tyrrhenoi (as Greeks called the Etruscans) came from Asia Minor, and most other ancient scholars accepted this judgment. In the first century B.C., the historian Dionysius of Halicarnassus, after careful research based on such information as was available to him, decided that they were an indigenous people. Some scholars today, after assessing all the information available, find this view still tenable. Most, however, side with Herodotus. Dionysius objected that their language bore no resemblance to any in Asia Minor. But then, some centuries had intervened. Scattered and sparse modern finds on islands just off Asia Minor may indicate, contrary to Dionysius, that a similar language was used there in far antiquity. Certain Etruscan religious practices, an emphasis on hepatoscopy (the reading of livers of sacrificed animals), for example, and certain Oriental features of their art, along with information derived from archaeology, seem to give approximate support to the Herodotean view.

The language question is frustrating. We have a considerable number of short inscriptions, and even some gold plates found in 1964 on a temple-site at Pyrgi that are bilingual, Punic and Etruscan. Unfortunately, the Punic seems not to be an exact translation of the Etruscan. Much progress has been made, but still the language can be related to no other known tongue. Thus, what ought to tell us most about the Etruscans tells us little. On the other hand, perhaps the question of origins is not very important to the real history of either the Etruscans or the Romans. Certainly Etruscan culture developed to its height, along with Etruscan power, from a base in Etruria, and nowhere else. Yet we feel that we may understand the Etruscans better when we know more about their background as a people.

Wherever the Etruscans came from, they established themselves firmly in the area northwest of Rome named after them. Possibly they constituted only an upper class; the lower population may have been indigenous. Certainly that was the pattern in the areas to which Etruscan power gradually extended itself, into rich Campania south of Rome, then into Latium and Rome itself, and finally into the fertile and productive Po valley to the north. In Etruria they set up a loose league of twelve cities, bound together by ties perhaps more religious than political. Their *Rex* was a kind of chairman of the board of the twelve *Lucumones* at their annual meeting. This was a religious celebration at a town called Volsinii (modern Bolseno or possibly Orvieto). Other such loose federations may have been set up in Campania and the Po valley. In none of the areas did the Etruscans ever unite in any politically strong and well-organized way. The individual Etruscan city-states did not always stand together, a weakness that contributed to their ultimate political failure and subjugation to Rome.

The Etruscans developed a great metals industry, a fleet, and a strong export trade. Their imports seem to have been primarily luxury goods, as the remains of large quantities of the finest Greek pottery illustrate for the modern archaeologist. Eventually the Etruscans came into conflict with Greek immigrants in the western Mediterranean. We hear of a naval battle with Greeks near Corsica about 535 B.C. Greek fleets from Sicily and south Italy eventually defeated the Etruscans in 474 B.C. and contributed to their decline. Etruscans generally cooperated with the Carthaginians against the Greeks, as may be inferred from such evidence as the gold plates found at Pyrgi. But the relationship did not last.

Perhaps the greatest calamity for the Etruscans resulted from Celtic invasions into their northern holdings in the Po valley, a little before 400 B.C. Already weakened by trade losses —a concomitant of the naval defeats at the hands of the Greeks —and by the rebellion of the Latins, with Rome as a chief antagonist if not leader of the Latins, Etruscan power now went into swift decline. During the fourth and third centuries B.C., Rome conquered even the cities of the Etruscan homeland.

Earliest Rome

Just as our scholars today know more about bronze-age Italy than the Romans did, so also we know more about Rome in its earliest years than did the Romans of Cicero's time. Yet for all the archaeological information and ingenious comparative studies in linguistics, religion, and the like, modern scholars have had to learn humility. Heinrich Schliemann's discovery a century ago that there really was a Troy, Sir Arthur Evans' later demonstration that there was some factual basis to Greek myths bearing upon ancient Crete, a score of revelations that in some cases the Hebrew writers of the Bible were right and modern critics misled (at least) by their scholarship have taught today's historians to be a bit more respectful, not only of the historians of antiquity, but even of the myth and legend of the ancients. Indeed, some have now become too credulous.

For our early history of Rome, that is, the literary history, we are dependent upon Latin and Greek authors who lived centuries after the facts that they chronicle. So patent it is that some of their information is defective that scholars of the nineteenth and early twentieth century were inclined to discard the whole. But, once again, we have learned not to be too hasty. The most important of these ancient historians for earliest Rome were Livy, a Roman who lived until 17 A.D., and Dionysius, a Greek from Halicarnassus who lived and composed his work in Rome about the same time (beginning about 30 B.C.). Livy perhaps started earlier and continued longer than Dionysius, but apparently the works were composed in isolation from each other. Both Livy's 142 volumes (that is, rolls) *Ab Urbe Condita* (*From the Founding of the City*) and Dionysius' *Romaike Archaiologia* (*Roman Antiquities*) in 20 volumes depended upon annalistic accounts which were probably no more than a century or two older. Only about a third of Livy survives, and about half of Dionysius, including, however, in both instances, the earlier books.

Some of the information available to the two historians was older than the compilations they mainly depended on, but not much solid historical fact before about the fourth century B.C. at best was known to these authors. For the earlier period they used the motley collection of folk tale, legend, and family eulogy that passed for history. The scholarship that they brought to their task was primarily limited to choosing the most believable of two or three unlikely stories, or revising them on the basis of anachronism; sometimes they simply passed on the tales as they were received, with some indication where skepticism was in order. Both deserve some apology for the savage criticism modern scholars have given them. We must be grateful that they chose to pass on to us information which even then was seen to be untrustworthy. It helps to make our archaeological data more meaningful.

One of the things learned from archaeology is that the Aeneas story, once thought to have been invented quite late, that is, in the third or second century B.C., actually goes back to a time coeval with early Rome. Both Greek and Etruscan art employ the motif of Aeneas bearing his Father, Anchises. The tale, told by Livy but best enshrined in Vergil's *Aeneid*, linked the founding of Rome with the destruction of Troy. Anchises, son of Venus, driven by fate, arrived at length in Latium and married into a royal family. Romulus and Remus were his descendants through their mother, Rhea Silvia; their father was Mars. Romulus was, of course, the reputed founder of Rome and its first king. Varro, a scholar of the first century B.C., computing closely on the basis of tradition, set the date at 753 B.C. According to the received stories, six other kings followed, ruling until the last was driven out in 509 B.C. and the Republic was established. Archaeologists have found remains of human habitation on the Palatine Hill that antedate the eighth century B.C., but their work seems to confirm that approximate period for the founding of a true village on the site.

As the early kings are presented to us, it is apparent that they are types—even archetypes—more than real figures. Romulus was the conqueror who gave form to the state and its early institutions; his successor was Numa Pompilius (a Sabine; the Romans saw themselves as assimilators from the beginning). He was the great religious and secular lawgiver. Tullus Hostilius was another great conqueror; Ancus Marcius was much like his grandfather, Numa. The specific works attributed to each and in fact the very existence of these kings may still be doubted, in the present state of our information. As for the last three of the line of kings, the information is a bit more substantial.

Etruscan Kings Raise Rome to Regional Importance

Though the Roman sources avoid saying it outright, it is clear that the last three kings of Rome were Etruscans. Tarquinius Priscus was the first of these; Servius Tullius the second; and Tarquinius Superbus the last. The name Tarquin itself is Etruscan; the Romans also called Priscus "Lucumo" (the name for an Etruscan official) but they thought he or his family had emigrated to Etruria from Corinth. Archaeology again helps to fill in the picture for us: at about the right time to correspond with the traditional period of the Etruscan kings (616–509 B.C.), or a little later, there was a surge of Etruscan influence in Rome.

Only in this period did Rome become a real city, with pebble-paved streets and the Forum. There were, in fact, two fora; the Forum Boarium—indicating the importance of cattle in early Rome—belongs to this same early date. Under the Etruscan rulers Rome acquired important public buildings. The city's position as a natural transportation hub in the Etruscan trading area must have been the chief reason for the attention given to Rome at this time. It is notable that when, under the last Etruscan king, Tarquinius Superbus, a temple was completed to Jupiter on the Capitoline Hill, it was the largest temple in all Italy. Rome had arrived.

Etruscan tomb painting from Tarquinia. Obviously some Etruscans hoped for a joyous afterlife. (*Alinari–Art Reference Bureau*)

There is much dispute about the question of just when Rome first became dominant over the other Latin peoples. Romans of Livy's time thought their city had achieved dominance over the Latins by the second century after Rome's founding. Probably the Etruscan kings used Rome as a center from which to penetrate into other areas of Latium: in short, the Etruscans made of Rome a sort of regional capital, which means that from the date of the expulsion of the kings Rome was, as the literary tradition indicates, already a most important but not necessarily the dominant Latin city.

The Etruscan Impact

The Etruscan influence on Rome was enormous, second only to that of the Greeks. Indeed, much of the early Greek influence was transmitted to Rome by the Etruscans. The Romans learned from the Etruscans in matters religious, artistic, and political. Etruscans taught the Romans to make cult statues for their gods; they drew up the plans for the earliest important Roman temples with three rooms for a triad of deities, elaborately decorated cornices, terracotta antefixes, and other typical details. The temple of Jupiter (and Juno and Minerva) on the Capitol, reputedly completed in 509 B.C., and built by Rome's Etruscan rulers, naturally was Etruscan in style. Etruscan-style antefixes typical of major Etruscan structures have been excavated in several other locations, and attest to the breadth of the influence.

The Etruscans gave Rome much else in the area of religion, including new gods—Hera-Juno, for example—and many religious practices. These include the rites for the taking of auspices, and the Oriental practice of reading livers or scanning the sky for omens. Though these were of course pseudo-sciences, the lore required real specialization with long apprenticeship, and for centuries Romans used Etruscan experts for the reading of livers (hepatoscopy).

The functions of some of the higher officials in the Roman Republic seem to have been based on Etruscan models, as were some of the insignia as well. The lictors who preceded Roman officials, their number (twelve for the consuls) and the *fasces* (the bundle of rods enclosing a double-ax) which they carried as symbols of the magistrate's power all, it appears, were Etruscan. The Senate was probably based on Etruscan precedent. The army was organized into a phalanx in a manner that was first used in the area by the Etruscans. Gladiatorial combat and certain aspects of festival and funeral games were also borrowed from these northern neighbors.

Social and Economic Influence of the Etruscans

The most significant influence of the Etruscans on Rome is the most difficult to demonstrate because it lies in a shadowy sphere where cause and effect are mostly hidden: social and economic organization and methodology. In early Rome the social order was to be pervasively important, as one should expect. The men who dominate a society usually dominate the state and the army as well. The patron–client system at Rome, mentioned below, was probably derived from a similar Etruscan one. The Roman extension of the system into foreign affairs later during the period of expansion beyond Italy—Roman leaders acting as patrons to provinces and even to autonomous monarchies—would seem to have been unique.

It is also difficult to detail specific Etruscan economic influence on the Romans. The Etruscans emphasized manufacture and commerce in a way that Romans—at least Roman aristocrats—never did. The Roman ruling classes retained their rural outlook for several centuries. Yet other Roman citizens and people dominated by Rome—especially Greeks but also the Etruscans themselves, as well as other Italians—intensively engaged in small-scale economic production and trade. Roman armies in the period of expansion demanded large quantities of material: lumber, copper, iron, food supplies. Etruscans doubtless instructed Romans in metallurgy or did the work themselves. Without the iron industry and iron weapons from Etruria, not to mention some of Italy's best shipbuilding timber and the like, Rome would never have become a Mediterranean power. It may well be that the great slag-piles at Etruscan Populonia, marking the locations of ancient iron-smelters, symbolize better than the temple of Jupiter Optimus Maximus the most significant contribution of the Etruscans to the rise of Rome to greatness.

Rome and Greece

It has been mentioned that much Greek influence came to Rome indirectly, by way of the Etruscans who, even while fighting Greeks in the West, maintained close connections with the Greek states in the East. The Etruscan city of Caere, we happen to know, maintained a treasury at Delphi, as Athens and other Greek city-states did. But Greeks inhabited Italy also; they were so numerous in the South that the Romans called the area Great Greece (Magna Graecia).

Some direct Greek influence is seen in the early Republic, even before the Romans had completely put off the mantle of Etruscan cultural domination. The cult of Ceres at Rome, for example, established quite early, always retained Greek rites and a Greek priestess. The major temple to this goddess, built at a time when Etruscan styles were dominant in Rome, was designed in the Greek style. The altar of Hercules was constructed quite early in the Forum Boarium, and the rites solemnized there also were basically Greek. Moreover, the fact that the Latins, including the Romans, used a Greek-derived alphabet somewhat different from that adopted by the Etruscans attests to an early Greek cultural penetration of the area. There are, besides, interesting parallels between Roman and Greek practices, involving the organization of the army, the law, and the land. Another wave of Greek influence came with the Roman conquest of southern Italy in the third century B.C. Still another and continuing surge of influence came with the conquest of Greece itself a century later.

Ultimately the Romans turned primarily to Greek models in art and architecture, completely dropping the now outmoded Etruscan ways. In religion they identified their gods with those of the Greeks and adopted the Greek myths as their own. When at last they were sophisticated enough to want a philosophic undergirding to their lives and the state, they turned also, quite naturally, to the Greeks. It was first said by Horace, the Roman poet of the first century B.C., and often since, that the sophisticated Greeks conquered their barbarian conquerors; there is an element of exaggeration in the comparison, on both sides; yet it remains in a broad sense true. For Roman culture when fully developed was certainly Greco-Roman, as was the Roman state, in many ways.

Early Social Organization

In any relatively undeveloped society, the primary social structure is usually that oldest of all human institutions, the family. So it was at Rome. We know most about the workings of upper-class families, but probably the lower classes tended to follow the same patterns. However, only in situations where the extended family could serve as an economic as well as a social unit (as in a rural setting with landed families) could the family unit dominate the entire social system as it did at Rome.

It is curious that the Latin language had no term that meant exactly "family" or "nuclear family" in ordinary English usage. The word *familia* referred to the household, including slaves. The extended family was headed by the *paterfamilias*, the oldest male member. The *pater* and the *mater* were, of course, the biological parents. Perhaps the shorter length of life of that time meant that the *paterfamilias* was usually the biological parent of those under his *manus*, or control.

The *paterfamilias*, acting with the advice of a family council of some sort, had complete power over the family members, even to the right to execute those who disobeyed. This is always stressed and it is enormously significant; not that large numbers of persons were so put to death: but it shows how pervasive the family control was. Only a few actual instances of such family-ordered executions are known, and each involves a father killing his own son for some lapse that the Roman people in general might have thought worthy of death. One such example—it may be no more than legend—is that of the hero of the founding of the Republic, L. Junius Brutus, who while consul executed his own son for engaging the enemy contrary to his orders when left in command of the army.

The leaders of the aristocratic families naturally dominated areas and not merely families. By some evolution unknown to us, members of these dominant families became known as "patricians" and constituted a closed order; all other citizens were "plebeians." Together, the heads of the leading families served as a council (eventually, the Senate) of advisors to the king during the monarchy and remained as advisors to the elected officials in the Republic. But entry into the Senate came to depend upon office-holding rather than status as a family head; that is, the Senate developed into an entirely political unit. The earlier practice is doubtless reflected in the fact that senators were always called the *patres*.

The leading patricians quite naturally dominated the developing political, as well as the military, structure. The Etruscan kings may have elevated some plebeian families to political parity with the patricians. In a sense, each such regional leader represented his area in the government and was supported by the citizens of his district. Over a long period the social and economic leaders achieved political dominance by the patron–client system. Each "patron" was a man of great local influence (*auctoritas*) who sought a political role in accord with his position (*dignitas*).

The patron had both privileges and obligations in relation to his clients. He looked out for their interests in all ways, but especially in the courts. In return the clients supported their patrons; during the monarchy they probably served under them in the army; later, in the Republic, they voted in the assembly as their patrons wished. The system in many ways foreshadowed the vassal–lord relationships in feudal Europe many centuries later. The patron–client relationship came to be hereditary, passing down from father to son; and there was even a religious aspect, for the relationship was confirmed by solemn oath.

From an early period there must have been some plebeians who were client to no one; indeed, plebeians became themselves patrons when they gained great local influence. It is, in fact, well to remember that although there may have been an age when all patricians were well-to-do patrons and all plebeians less well-to-do clients, in the historic period this was never so. The group termed plebeian early began to include a broad spectrum of persons, from those of substantial means to day laborers whose lot was worse than that of many slaves. The latter, of course, were not citizens at all.

Religion entered intimately into Roman family life. In typical Indo-European fashion Romans venerated their ancestors, offering small portions of food at the hearth daily and carefully seeing to other special ceremonies. Upper-class families kept death masks of the deceased family leaders. In the later Republic and in the Empire it was mostly a matter of prestige to have these wax images—eventually, finely sculptured stone busts—on display; early, however, the practice must have been connected with ancestor worship. The gods closest to individuals were the guardians of family, house, or land. Vesta, goddess of the hearth, received regular homage. The Lares and Penates, gods of boundaries and of the storehouses, were never neglected by rural families. A woman who married and thus left her family, came under the control of her husband's paterfamilias; when first brought into her new household she was carried across the threshold so as not to offend Janus, the god of the threshold, or the other family deities. A host of other gods were important to rural families, from Ceres, a goddess of grain, to the numerous numina already mentioned, of crossroads, streams, springs, hills, and so on.

In summary, the family and family-connected ways provided the foundation for early Roman society, the economy, religion, and, to a considerable degree, the state as well. The manner in which family ways entered into the structures of the state may be seen not only in the political structure—the Senate comprising heads of important families—and in the social structure, especially the patron–client system, but also in religion. The state, like the family, had its worship of Janus, Vesta, and the Lares and Penates.

Freedom Brings Problems

Generations of Roman youngsters were taught to revere the men who expelled the Etruscan kings. Brutus and the others had saved the people from tyranny, and were venerated much as Americans have praised the fathers of the American Revolution. In truth, however, the leaders in the expulsion of the Tarquins were a small group of conservative aristocrats, and the "revolution" was not so much a blow for general freedom as it was a conservative reaction against kings who were attempting to use the lower classes against the entrenched aristocracy.

The proof that the expulsion of the kings was mostly an aristocratic reaction is inferred from the literature, a sort of reading between the lines. A comparison with neighboring states seems enlightening also. All over Italy, it appears, kings' powers were being taken over by aristocracies, even in the Etruscan cities themselves. This pattern had been established in Greece much earlier. Certain reforms attributed to Servius Tullius by the ancient writers illustrate the trend: this king is said to have reorganized the army on a centuriate pattern, and to have organized an assembly of all Roman citizens on the same basis. The army reorganization has usually been accepted by modern scholars, but the corresponding political reorganization has often been placed later, in the Republic. It is impossible to accept an army of 192 centuries in this period. However, if, as seems likely, Servius was enlarging the army—especially the heavy infantry—by his reform (this, too, was being done all over Italy), it is most likely that he would also have given to the new infantrymen added privileges, perhaps full voting rights. The larger army was a military necessity, but it should be noted that the new organization no doubt aided the tax assessor. The larger citizen body, or at least a larger group of full citizens, held their military and political rank on a

THE EARLY REPUBLIC

ANCIENT ITALY

ALPS
ALPS
VENETIA
CISALPINE
Po River
LIGURIA
GAUL
Rubicon R.
Arnus R.
UMBRIA
ETRURIA
ELBA
PICENUM
Tiber R.
CORSICA
Sabines
Veii
Adriatic Sea
Rome
Ostia
LATIUM
SAMNIUM
CAMPANIA
Capua
APULIA
Cumae
Neapolis
Cannae
Pompeii
Tarentum
Brundisium
SARDINIA
Paestum
LUCANIA
CALABRIA
MAGNA
Gulf of
GRAECIA
Tarentum
Tyrrhenian Sea
BRUTTIUM
Messina
SICILY
Syracuse
Carthage
AFRICA

0 20 40 60 80 100
Scale of miles

timocratic basis (according to wealth). This new arrangement had been an effort of Servius to broaden his popular support and to defend his own position against the attacks of the aristocracy. Perhaps it worked, but only for a short time until Tarquin the Proud, successor to Servius and the last of the kings, was expelled.

In the infant republic, the triumphant aristocrats seized the offices of the state with a stranglehold, and this led to internal dissension. There was also a critical external problem: Rome's relationship with the other Latin states. The Etruscans had made Rome a regional center. The later Roman historians thought that Rome was then the formal leader of the Latin League, but probably this is not strictly correct. These states no doubt cooperated with Rome in the struggle to keep the Etruscans from regaining control of Latium, but they did not want to see Etruscan dominance replaced with Roman dominance.

The cutting of ties with the Etruscans unfortunately brought economic depression to Rome, for her economy depended, in part, upon Etruscan trade. This economic depression is well attested by archaeology. The fine Greek pottery formerly imported now ceased to come in. The remarkable growth of the city slowed or ceased; building activity after about the middle of the fifth century B.C. almost stopped. Things did not pick up again for several decades, and even then on a limited scale. Economic stringency surely exacerbated the internal tensions.

Struggle of the Orders (494–287 B.C.)

As we have seen, the later Romans had a distorted view of the expulsion of the kings. They also to some degree misunderstood the Struggle of the Orders, but modern scholars have contributed their share of misunderstandings. Often, historians have viewed the struggle as a general uprising of the lower classes (the plebeians) against the upper class (the patricians). It was not that simple, however. The leaders of the "struggle" were plebeians, true; but they were from important families. In the later stages of the struggle, often these leaders were aristocratic heads of states that had been absorbed by Rome. These local aristocrats who attained Roman citizenship found themselves lumped in with that polymorphous group at Rome called plebeians. The term "urban plebs" did designate the lower class in the city—at the end of the Republic, many years later—but during most of the Republic the "plebs" included both upper- and lower-class individuals. The patricians comprised only some fifty or so clans (*gentes*) at the beginning of the Republic. One could become a patrician only by birth. By the middle and late Republic, only fifteen or so of these old clans remained important, while the number of plebeians had enormously increased. Patricians thus constituted only a minority of all Romans in the early Republic, and by the middle Republic they were a minority even of the aristocracy.

The lower classes were of course involved in the Struggle of the Orders; they supported plebeian leaders and benefited from some of the concessions gained. The chief winners, however, were the upper-class plebeians, for after the struggle was over these persons stood on a basis politically equal with the patricians, though perhaps not quite on their level socially.

The protests that initiated the Struggle of the Orders, according to the traditional accounts, came in 494 B.C. This crisis seems to have been the consequence of a heavy military burden and its accompanying taxation (the *tributum* or direct tax on Roman citizens was always levied strictly for military purposes). The fledgling state had to defend itself against attempts by the Etruscans to regain control, and there were troubles also with other near neighbors. Because of the economic decline, the tax burden likely hurt as much as the long military service. Some plebeian leadership came from a center on the Aventine hill. Of those involved, some may have been traders; there was a small mercantile community there. The keepers of the temple to Ceres on the Aventine, called aediles, allowed the temple to be used as a sort of cult for plebeians, kept the archives of plebeian actions there—unofficial at this time, but official later—and themselves probably assumed leadership of plebeian causes, or perhaps were chosen to the post because they were leaders. During the Struggle of the Orders the office of aedile was made an official one, ranking just below the praetorship. It is possible that some of the discontent on the Aventine came from the traders who lived there, though they seem to have been mostly Greek; at any rate they must have been affected by the economic decline that came with independence. The Roman peasants were in straits also, however. The area was heavily populated and farms were small. Freedom from the Etruscans probably meant a shrunken market for farm produce. Our admittedly undependable evidence indicates that several times in the first century of the Republic bad weather and famine struck the state, which had to import grain to relieve shortages. We hear of recurring demands for distributions of publicly owned land among the poor citizens.

In 471 B.C., according to the traditional dating, the plebeians came together in unofficial assembly and elected plebeian magistrates called "tribunes of the plebs." The people swore to consecrate to Jupiter anyone who laid violent hands on these tribunes and so conferred *sacro-sanctitas* on them. Though the patricians resisted the idea of plebeian officials, they eventually accepted the fait accompli. The two tribunes—soon increased to ten—had mostly negative powers. They could prevent the regular magistrates from carrying out punishment of plebeians, in order to protect the right of the latter. Eventually they gained the right called *intercessio*, to halt the operations of the assemblies and even of the Senate. They called together the plebeian assembly, the *concilium plebis*, for elections of their successors and of aediles; *plebescita*, measures passed by this assembly, were at first only resolutions of the plebeians but, as we shall see, by the end of the Struggle of the Orders, these attained official status as law.

The patricians did not give up all these rights and powers willingly. The plebeians applied pressure by a sort of strike; they refused to report for the army draft in time of military emergency. Once or twice they "seceded" by going out of the city and assembling nearby. Tradition has it that this occurred five times, but some of the accounts are repetitious.

The assembly that elected the tribunes of the plebs and the plebeian aediles was organized on a tribal basis, modeled on the assembly of the tribes (*comitia tributa*), which seems to have been established earlier. A distinction between the two assemblies, however, was this: While the tribal assembly was one of all citizens, plebeians and patricians, the plebeian assembly excluded the patricians, and it was presided over by the plebeian tribunes instead of the consuls. When the governing oligarchy accepted the election of tribunes of the plebs as valid, it in effect validated the *concilium plebis*, the plebeian assembly, as an official body of the state. The tribal assembly first, it seems, had sixteen tribes (residential districts); by 241 B.C. there were thirty-five, four urban and thirty-one rural. No new tribes were added after that date. As new lands were acquired within Italy and became a part of the city-state—called *ager Romanus* —they were added onto the existing tribal areas, in crazy-quilt fashion; the blocks of territory assigned to a single tribe were sometimes completely disconnected.

In the middle of the fifth century (traditional date 451–450 B.C.), the patricians acceded to yet another demand of the plebeians. The body of law, previously unwritten and in the hands of the patrician priests, was organized into a code by a special board of ten men (*decemviri*) and publicly displayed on twelve wooden tablets. The XII Tables heralded a millennium of development in the law, the beginning of what was to become one of Rome's most treasured contributions to the world. The bulk of the laws dealt with the sorts of problems that a rural people face: possession and sale of property, the control of roads and pathways, debt, theft, and other crimes, trial procedures, family relationships, inheritance. Though a written law was certainly an important gain for the lower classes, the administration of it still lay in the hands of the priests, and these were patricians—that was not changed for a century and a half. Even after that, justice might be obtained only with the help of an influential patron.

It is most interesting that the concept of popular sovereignty was embodied in the XII Tables. Though not often put to the test, it was from that time on a constitutional principle that the last enactment of an assembly of the citizens was the law. By implication, the assembly's acts could not be overturned by orders of magistrates or decrees of the Senate. However, it was also a constitutional practice that no assembly could pass laws without the prior approval of the Senate, and also in practice the edicts of the magistrates came to be an important source of new law. When toward the end of the Struggle of the Orders the Senate's check over the assemblies was removed, the concept of popular sovereignty became in theory an unrestrained principle; though potentially a very important factor in the constitution of the state, it was little applied in practice before the Gracchi (133–122 B.C.).

Tradition says that plebeian agitation for the right to hold the consulate led to the establishment of substitute chief officers, the "military tribunes with consular powers." In most years between 444 and 367 B.C., these officials—usually five to seven of them—replaced the consuls. The Roman historians thought that the purpose was to prevent plebeians from actually holding the office of consul. Perhaps the real reason was simply that Rome needed a larger number of magistrates. In 367 B.C., on the return to the use of consuls on a regular basis, it was stipulated by law that one consul should be plebeian, and a new officer, the praetor, was added. He was an important commander (praetors, like consuls, held *imperium*), but subordinate to the consul in this capacity. His primary duties were judicial. The Roman "constitution," it should be noted, consisted only of law and tradition: in consequence, changing the "constitution" or making an exception to any law—even a basic one—was only a matter of passing another law. It is therefore not surprising that after this time exceptions were made and there were years when both consuls were patrician. The successful struggle of plebeians for rights in officeholding went on until in 300 B.C. plebeians gained by law (the Lex Ogulnia) the right to be elected to the priestly colleges; that is, by 300 B.C. plebeians were eligible for all major offices.

The assemblies also gained a measure of independence

from the Senate. Although the source evidence is rather difficult to interpret, it appears that the Publilian Law in 339 B.C. gave the *comitia centuriata* the right to pass laws without prior Senate approval, and that the Hortensian Law in 287 B.C. gave the *concilium plebis* the same right. (In the sources there is some confusion between the *comitia tributa* and the *concilium plebis*.) The Hortensian Law is usually taken as the last reform of the Struggle of the Orders. Since the "struggle" lasted for two centuries, it can readily be seen that it had been long, diverse, and discontinuous.

Economic Problems and the Later Phases of the Struggle of the Orders

It must not be thought that the economic difficulties which came along with freedom from Etruscan rule lasted only a short time. The evidence is scanty but indicative of continued problems: the poor agitating for land; the necessity for new laws to supplement a provision of the XII Tables against maltreatment of debtors; the enactment of laws to reduce or even eliminate interest rates in the latter half of the fourth century B.C.

A most important series of laws were passed in 367 B.C. by the radical tribunes of the plebs C. Licinius Stolo and L. Sextius. Some of these measures were constitutional: the requirement that one consul be plebeian (it is possible that the law really only made plebeians eligible for the office) and the establishment of the offices of praetor and curule aedile. The Licinian-Sextian Laws included also a notable measure on the *ager publicus* (public land). We are not well informed regarding it: certainly our ancient sources are mistaken in some of the details they present, confusing it with later measures. The law required that the public or state-owned land must be regularly leased and it set an upper limit on the amount of such land which a single citizen could hold. Presumably more citizens now found it possible to acquire or lease parcels of public land. In the half-century after 390 B.C., many thousands of Roman citizens in one way or another obtained small parcels of it.

The Struggle of the Orders in some ways benefited all Romans, including the lower classes. Laws permitting appeal from the death sentences of magistrates and restricting the sale of debtors to satisfy debts are examples. The office of the tribune of the plebs opened an umbrella of protection, although most tribunes throughout Roman history were chosen from the ranks of upper-class plebeians and so had an upper-class outlook. The rights gained of eligibility to high office and to the priesthoods benefited mainly the well-to-do plebeians. Over the centuries, the New Men (*novi homines*), that is, men who were the first of their families to reach the upper magistracies, seem invariably to have come from the upper-class ranks just below the nobility. Access to the higher offices brought with it assimilation into an enlarged governing oligarchy; this in turn meant entrance into the nobility, for the nobility was very politicized and consisted of those families one member of which had attained the high offices. This nobility (*nobilitas*) automatically included the patricians, the older aristocrats, but gradually expanded with the addition of the newer plebeian families until, by the middle Republic there were more plebeian aristocrats or nobles than patrician ones. In the later Republic (to look ahead) the definition of nobility was further refined: it embraced, besides the politically active patrician families, those plebeian families one member of which had reached, specifically, the consulate.

The Developed Constitution in Summary: Officials

The constitutional machinery of a state ordinarily reflects the realities of social, economic, and military structures; when it does not, some sort of overturn almost inevitably occurs. The structure of government in the early Republic, with its monopoly of office for patricians, was from the beginning somewhat out of phase with the actual socioeconomic structure. After the Struggle of the Orders, however, a nobility that included the more powerful plebeians and a system that guaranteed some political privileges for all plebeians produced a more harmoniously attuned system. Every Roman, through some form of high social status, wealth, patronage, or sheer ability, might rise to hold office; no one was arbitrarily excluded from opportunity. However, the enlarged *nobilitas* monopolized the highest offices and priesthoods, and tended to become almost a closed body. Nobles also naturally dominated the Senate, making day-to-day decisions, and in time of war they led the army as well. Yet it remained possible for New Men who rose in extragovernmental circles to rise within the government also.

The two consuls, annually elected by the Centuriate Assembly, remained the chief executives and the top generals of the state. After 367 B.C. a growing percentage of the consuls were plebeians. A consul presided over the Senate and put questions to it for consideration (and ordinarily took the advice it gave); one of the consuls also presided over the Centuriate Assembly, and so could influence the major elections. A consul could preside over the Tribal Assembly as well.

By the middle of the third century B.C. there were two

praetors. One of the two was designated *praetor urbanus;* he presided over judicial proceedings involving Romans. The other, called the *praetor peregrinus,* handled cases involving foreigners. Praetors could also command armies, and in the absence of a consul, preside over the Senate or the assembly. Praetors, like consuls, were chosen in annual elections by the Centuriate Assembly. Also by the third century B.C., both praetors and consuls sometimes served beyond the year for which they were elected; that is, their terms of office were prorogued. Their official titles in such cases were proconsul and propraetor.

Two censors were elected also by the Centuriate Assembly, but only approximately every five years. They held office until they completed their work, or for a maximum of eighteen months. Their major duties were to take the census and assess property. Thus they not only determined levels of taxation and classification for army service, but also the placement of each individual in the voting centuries and tribes. They appointed men to vacancies in the ranks of the Senate and the cavalry (*equites*) and could remove them for cause. By the middle Republic among their more important functions were letting contracts for public works and leasing public lands.

The quaestors, whose numbers increased to ten in the middle Republic, took charge of the treasury and served as financial staff members for consuls, and later for praetors, proconsuls, and propraetors who governed provinces or held other important commands. They were elected annually in the Tribal Assembly. Curule and plebeian aediles also were elected in the Tribal Assembly, the former under the presidency of a consul, the latter under the presidency of a tribune of the plebs. They kept order in the Forum, supervised mercantile activity there, with judicial powers, and also superintended the major state religious festivals. The aedilate was not part of the regular order of magistracies[1] but a popular aedile often went on to higher office and so ambitious men usually sought the post. Tribunes of the plebs, elected by the Tribal Assembly presided over by a tribune (technically this assembly was the *concilium plebis*) had broad, mostly negative powers that differed little from those gained during the early Republic; but the positive side of their power had been accentuated by the Struggle of the Orders. After the Hortensian Law was passed, the *concilium plebis,* under the presidency of a tribune, could pass laws without prior approval of the Senate. Thus tribunes could now propose bills, conduct public debates, and get the bills enacted into law.

[1] The *cursus honorum*—quaestorship, praetorship, consulship—was legally fixed only in the second century B.C., but the tradition of the regular *cursus* was established earlier.

The Assemblies

Of the assemblies of all the people, the early Curiate Assembly had fallen into disuse; it still granted *imperium* to consuls and praetors, but on a purely formal basis. It was occasionally called upon for other things; for example, to register adoptions involving patricians. But only thirty Lictors, the attendants of the curule magistrates, met as delegates of the moribund assembly to transact its affairs. More important were the assemblies of the centuries and the tribes.

The Centuriate Assembly elected consuls, praetors, and censors, as we have seen. It could pass laws, though there was a tendency to use the Tribal Assembly for this; and it could serve as an appellate body in cases involving death sentences. The Tribal Assembly elected aediles, quaestors, tribunes of the plebs, and other minor officials such as the military tribunes and the decemvirs, who participated in the judicial processes or superintended religious affairs.

The voting procedures in the Centuriate and Tribal assemblies were fundamentally different. Romans were ranked in the 193 centuries according to wealth, in the manner of the earlier organization of the army. The top 18 centuries were cavalry; the first census class contained 80 centuries; the second through fourth 20 centuries each; the fifth, 30 (in the army all five classes were mostly infantry). There were four centuries of engineers and other artisans and buglers, and finally, a single century of men whose property qualification was so low as to make them totally ineligible for army service. Each century voted as a unit. Voting always started at the top and proceeded downward until a majority was reached. Thus the votes of the wealthiest citizens counted most heavily and the votes of the poorest citizens counted for almost nothing. In the Tribal Assembly, men were placed according to where they resided or held property, and the procedure was somewhat more democratic. The voting was by tribe, with the lot to determine which should vote first. The vote of the first tribe or the first century in the assemblies was always quite influential.

Though the Tribal Assembly was more democratic than the Centuriate Assembly, it should not be thought that it was genuinely democratic. In the first place, the 31 rural tribes were more sparsely populated than the 4 city ones, and the attendance in the city at the time of the convening of the assembly was even sparser. Since voting was by tribe, not by numbers, the votes of rural landholders were heavily weighted. Even if they lived in the city they could be registered in an area where they owned land. Moreover, democracy can be affected by matters not involving political structure, of course. The influence of patron over client or wealthy man over poor man was great, particularly so long as voting was open rather than secret. The aristocratic oligarchy of patricians and upper-class plebeians dominated the assemblies and thus, most of the time, the offices, the laws, and the courts.

The Senate remained a most powerful body even after it lost the right to control what legislative proposals could be submitted to the assemblies. In fact, circumstances during Rome's expansion even enhanced its power. All patricians or plebeians who reached the quaestorship were normally given a Senate seat in the next census. Membership was for life, though the censors could remove members for cause. The Senate in consequence included all of the major officials and all persons who had previously held high offices—in short, almost all the politically important and experienced men in the state. Ordinarily, several ex-consuls (consulars) would be in attendance. The body's advice, offered by decree (*senatus consultum*) in response to a question posed by the presiding officer, was not to be lightly disregarded. The membership was of manageable size—about 300 —and it could meet frequently. Its influence (*auctoritas*) was great even if its formal, legal powers apparently were not. As Rome expanded and fought numerous wars, the Senate came to control the assignments of the magistrates, the chief expenditures of the state (and thus the treasury), the provinces, once they were acquired, foreign affairs, and many other state concerns. The major policy decisions and myriad decisions of detail were settled in the debates of this body.

Early Expansion and Consolidation in Central Italy

The problems of overpopulation and economic doldrums which plagued the early Republic did more than cause internal tensions; they also gave shape to the new state's external relations. In antiquity men expected to profit from war. This was the norm: the victors got the spoils; everyone understood this and no one thought it unreasonable. Moreover, wars were in general accepted policy; it was expected that wars would be waged if there was the likelihood of victory, and it was accepted that the strong should rule the weak. Athenian orators in the fifth century B.C. (as reported by the historian Thucydides) and Aristotle a century later had stated this principle quite clearly. Few persons in antiquity would have quibbled in the least.

If Romans had to fight the Etruscans to retain their political freedom, they also expected a reward of Etruscan territory if they managed to win. And when Romans contested with the

Latins for supremacy and won, they naturally took spoils and land. It does not seem necessary to comb through the semifictional extant accounts of Rome's numerous struggles in the early Republic, which brought victories—and sometimes losses—over the Etruscans, the Aequi, the Volsci, and other peoples nearby. The pattern Rome followed after her usual victories, however, deserves recounting.

When Romans and Latins won joint victories and land was available from the conquered, the Latins usually set up separate, independent or quasi-independent states from their own citizen body. Rome seems to have joined in some Latin foundations that were intended as protectors of the frontiers. However, Rome usually settled her citizens *viritim* (individually) on the new land, and incorporated it into the Roman territory (*ager Romanus*). As a consequence Rome soon outstripped the neighboring Latin states in size of territory and in population, one quite important reason why Rome rose to dominate central Italy by the end of the fourth century B.C. Rome did later adopt the practice of establishing both citizen and allied colonies, however.

For the Romans, one crucial victory was the first successful offensive against the Etruscans. The latter had been weakened by the defections in Latium, by losses at sea to Sicilian Greeks, and, in the Po region, by an incursion of Celts (whom the Romans called Gauls). Disunity among the Etruscan states contributed to the general malaise. Rome was able to besiege and take Veii (traditional date, 406–396 B.C.), located on a valuable site north of Rome across the Tiber. The long and difficult siege was something new for the Roman army, which was unaccustomed to year-round fighting. Then, it was said, the troops were paid for the first time. Peasants might fight in midsummer without damage to their own affairs, but they needed time off from fall to spring for the plowing, seeding, and harvest. Veii provided some fine land for distribution to Roman citizens.

The next great event was disaster, not success. The Gauls moved down into central Italy, probably against the Etruscans. Rome refused a Gallic alliance, whereupon the Gauls attacked and defeated utterly the main Roman army (Allia River, 390 or 387 B.C.). Thereafter the city fell to the enemy except for the citadel on the Capitol. Eventually the Romans bought off the invaders. In the following year, under the famous dictator Camillus, the Romans got revenge on the Gauls and the threat receded. Rome was rebuilt, though there were those who wanted to move the city to the more defensible site of Veii. The city would not again be sacked by alien troops for almost 800 years.

Camillus is thought to have reorganized the Roman army

at this time, so that instead of the previous crude phalanx the army was more precisely organized and aligned for battle. In front came the skirmishers, young, light-armed *velites*. Next, in the first main battle line, were the *hastati*, or spearmen. The second main battle line was made up of prime warriors, the *principes*. The third line, a kind of last-ditch defensive force, was made up of the *triarii*, the older veterans. Perhaps by a few decades later, the standard legion consisted of about 4,000 men, drawn up in maniples of 120 each. In battle, the light-armed troopers threw their missiles and retired back through the ranks. The mainline heavy infantryman advanced, threw javelins to further harass the enemy, and then closed in to fight it out with the sword. The Greek phalanx, by contrast, depended upon the thrusting spear in close fighting. The Roman arrangement, more flexible and open, could be employed on rough terrain, unlike the close-ranked Greek phalanx. The Roman cavalry played a subordinate role; it was used on the march, on reconnaissance, and for protection of the flanks more than for combat. Alexander the Great (356–323 B.C.) made his heavy cavalry the shock-units that carried his assaults, and the successor states of the Hellenistic world imitated him. The Romans, however, continued to depend primarily upon infantry. With this army they made themselves the dominant Mediterranean power.

During a period of about two centuries, Rome broke out from her consolidated base of power in west central Italy to make the Mediterranean into Mare Nostrum ("Our Sea"). We may distinguish three major thrusts in this period of expansion: first, the swift rise to supremacy in Italy; second, victories over Carthage in the contest that decided the control of the western Mediterranean; and finally, a vigorous expansion into the Hellenistic East at the expense of the great successor states of Alexander. This chapter deals with the first phase.

Expansion into Empire: Demographic and Economic Factors

If there was a single most important factor in the seldom paralleled imperial success of Rome, it lay in the Roman people themselves. They were Rome's most dependable asset. There was a kind of rugged cohesiveness in Roman society, an ability to hang together in critical situations. (The plebeians and the patricians did indeed conflict but ground for compromise was always found.) The reasons for this cohesiveness are perhaps not entirely explicable, but have been indicated earlier. Roman society was not too diverse: distinction between rich and poor not yet great. The society was integrated ethnically, linguistically, religiously. The stresses which independence had brought had not seriously disturbed this basic stability.

Individual Romans were inured to hardship by agricultural toil and were trained to obey; yet they felt themselves involved as participants in the main political processes of the state. Roman soldiers were usually well disciplined, courageous, and persistent in the face of obstacles. Of course they were not always victorious; but they did maintain the military virtues at a consistently high level.

Numbers were important. The Latins,

CITY-STATE
TO DOMINATION
OF ITALY,
360–264 B.C.

the Samnites, and other Italians, equally tough, equally disciplined, certainly were a match for the Romans, man for man. But there were usually more Romans. In each phase of the outward struggle, Rome's manpower reserves made a difference. Rome had an advantage over the Latins because land policies made the city-state larger and more populous than any combination of the Latins. Later, in the critical struggles against the Samnites, Romans had the Latins on their side. Similarly, in the crucial struggle against the Carthaginians, most of the Latin and Italian peoples were Roman allies. The later penetration into the eastern Mediterranean was backed by an enormous reserve of manpower.

For the struggle in Italy, Rome's central location was tremendously important. In wars against a sometimes critical combination of foes—Samnites, Etruscans, Gauls—Rome's interior communications made possible more rapid movement of troops within the perimeter of the main battle arena. One cannot say quite the same thing for the importance of topography in the second and third phases of expansion considered in the next chapter. Rome did, of course, face west and this doubtless affected the order of events. The challenge to Carthage naturally preceded any advance into the eastern, Hellenistic states. But Carthage's location was also central, close to the strategic straits at the waist of the Mediterranean; Rome had no real advantage there. Later, in eastern campaigns, topography seems to have played no central role. Only the extent of Italy with its supportive, fairly homogeneous population gave Rome an edge.

Economically Rome had no advantage over her opponents in the first phase of expansion. Indeed, since the state was somewhat overpopulated until the mid-fourth centry B.C. at least, it may well have been poorer than some rivals—for example, the Etruscans. Even after Rome dominated all Latium and Roman influence reached southward into rich Campania, her people can hardly be described as affluent. But Rome then needed no large and expensive navy; draftees were paid little and provided most of their own equipment.

In antiquity as in modern times money could be the sinews of war, however. Fortunately for Rome, with expansion came increased economic potential. The conquest of Etruria brought iron mining and smelting operations that Rome needed. There was a lag, however, and Rome faced severe economic problems in the first and second wars with Carthage. In this second phase of expansion, the conquest of Sicily brought, for the first time, an annual tribute from a conquered area (collected in grain). The occupation of much of Spain during the Hannibalic war was most important of all: it assured for centuries an inexhaustible supply of precious and other metals, plus more tribute. Rome's economic resources by 200 B.c matched the city's territorial gains.

Was it through a policy of deliberate imperialism that the Roman Republic pieced together an empire? This general question should at least be surveyed. It is sometimes thought that Rome had a master plan for domination of the world, developed in the early Republic and faithfully adhered to until all the civilized world was under her sway. It has on the other hand been argued that Rome was really not imperialistic at all and that circumstances mostly fortuitous and unplanned combined to bring about the expansion. The problem is too complex for simple explanation. Romans were conditioned to war, and they took advantage of opportunity when afforded, even if without any long-range plan. They sometimes rationalized offensive operations as really defensive—as nations have done ever since. As Rome expanded it seems that different segments of the ruling class developed opposing views: some took a conservative view and opposed Roman foreign involvement, especially outside Italy. Others actively supported foreign adventures.

In antiquity as today there was more than one kind of imperialism. It is often noted that Rome hesitated to acquire provinces in the Hellenistic East even after intervening there in four major wars during the late third and early second centuries B.c. But that does not mean that Rome did not penetrate the area politically through her system of friendships and alliances, with rewards and punishments for friendly or unfriendly behavior.

The Latin Revolt (340–338 B.C.)

The Gallic sack of Rome in 387 B.c. naturally had weakened the state. Nor was the threat ended by the retaliatory victory of Camillus. Twice in mid-fourth century, in 360 and again in 349 B.c., the Romans had to meet incursions of the Gauls. Moreover, some of the Latin states attempted to contest the Roman leadership of the Latin League. A wall now completely enclosed the rebuilt city. The Romans held off the Latin challenge for the time and fought a successful war with the Etruscans. They made alliance with the Oscans (Sabellians, like the Samnites) who occupied Campania to the south, and then, as we shall see, intervened in war to help the Oscans against their cousins, the hill Samnites. The Latin states could only have looked on with dismay at the rapid growth in Roman power. They doubtless feared that Roman leadership was transforming itself into Roman domination. About 340 B.c., therefore, the Latins turned on

Rome. Despite internal tensions—the Struggle of the Orders was still in process: the Publilian Law, it will be recalled, is dated 339 B.C.—Rome managed by 338 B.C. to defeat the Latins, and to impose a settlement upon them once again.

The Settlement of 338 B.C.

It is hardly too much to say that by whatever chance, necessity, or wise policy, Rome laid the foundation for all its future success in the settlement of the Latin War in 338 B.C. Historians quite properly emphasize events that lead to change. But this treatment quite improperly .makes it seem that there is a kind of inevitability in the historical process. Sometimes we, like Livy and Vergil, think that Rome was fated to become the eternal city and mistress of the ancient world; but it was not all that inevitable. On several occasions from the third to the first centuries B.C. the Roman system might easily have collapsed—if the solid core of allied strength in Latium had not held firm. The reason why it held firm was Rome's rather generous settlement in the year 338 B.C.

Let it be admitted that at the time the defeated Latins saw nothing generous in the settlement. For them the new arrangements formalized a lost liberty. But by comparison with the sort of treatment that had been meted out to allied states by Athens or Sparta, the Roman pattern was liberal indeed. Some of the Latin states became Roman: their citizens became Roman citizens. The other states got separate treaties; they retained autonomy at home and paid no taxes directly to Rome. They did have to tax themselves to furnish army contingents to fight with Rome's army, however, under command of the Romans. And they could have no treaties with anyone else, not even with each other. This meant that Rome controlled the collective foreign policy and that the Latins had little influence upon decisions that determined when and where they might be called upon to fight. The Latin states were given trading and other privileges at Rome. Many Latins had the right to move to Rome and become voting Roman citizens, if they wished.

This liberality with the Roman citizenship makes the policy stand out as almost unique in the ancient world. Nor was it sham: new names, of men who had been Latins before 338 B.C., very quickly are seen in the *fasti*, lists of elective officials in Rome. Former Latins soon attained even the consulship. The men so honored, it must be assumed, had been aristocrats in their own states before assimilation into Rome. Now they became Roman aristocrats, though of course one must remember, they were plebeians, not patricians.

The pattern Rome was to follow in her conquest of Italy was set. Citizenship would not, in future decades, always be so liberally bestowed. In fact it would occasionally be tinged with punishment: Rome sometimes granted citizenship without the right to vote (*civitas sine suffragio*) as a means of controlling recalcitrants: such citizens were governed by officials sent from Rome. The alliance system, however, with autonomy at home, with the requirement to supply auxiliaries for the Roman army, and with monopoly relationships, would continue to be developed.

Challenge for Supremacy: The Samnite Wars

The Samnite League in mid-fourth century B.C. was perhaps the most extensive and powerful league in Italy. Its territory was not in an early period contiguous with that of the Latin League and no competition developed between Rome and Samnium until after 350 B.C. In fact, the Romans and the Samnites allied themselves against the Gauls about that time. The Roman conquest of the Volsci, however, brought them to the Samnite frontiers. Actual conflict between the two major leagues came indirectly in competition over the rich lands of Campania, on the southern border of Roman-dominated territory, and on the western border of the Samnite interests.

The Samnites first launched a drive to gain control of certain iron-bearing hills to the northeast of Campania. When the local inhabitants got the aid of the Campanians, the Samnites thrust into Campania itself. The dominant Campanians were Oscans; that is, they were Samnites; but they had long before left the hill country to occupy the rich flatlands, and their military stamina did not match that of their kinsmen. Very quickly Capua, the Oscan capital city, was put under siege.

The Oscans turned to Rome for help. Livy indicates that the Roman Senate at first refused help because of the alliance that Rome had with the Samnite League. But then the Oscans surrendered themselves and their territory completely to Rome, pointing out that the Samnites, if they gained control of their rich territory, would be extremely powerful. The Romans then decided to accept Campania as Roman territory and the inhabitants as Roman citizens, and sent armies against the Samnites. So, according to the accounts, began the first Samnite war (343–342 B.C.).

It is difficult to see why the Oscans should have preferred to be subordinated to the Romans rather than to their Samnite relatives, if it came to that choice. Perhaps the Samnites would have sacked Capua and despoiled the land; Rome was the only

Heavy-armed Samnite warrior (modern representation). Note the bronze bosses on the leathern breastplate. (*Alinari–Scala*)

state able to prevent that. Some scholars have not only doubted the Livian account but even the very fact of a first Samnite war. That, however, as the best historian of the Samnites has said,[1] seems to carry skepticism too far.

The Roman armies quickly won battles in Campania itself, though they suffered setbacks when they invaded Samnium proper. The next year brought similar action with similar results. We do not know what sort of truce or treaty ended the war, but apparently it ended with a decisive Roman advantage: Rome retained control of Campania.

For Rome there was a sequel, the revolt of the Latins, already discussed, but this, too, ended to Rome's advantage. Curiously, the Romans seem to have had the cooperation of Samnite troops in reducing the Latins. Perhaps the Samnites feared the Latins (and their possible allies) more than the Romans. Or perhaps they suspected that some of their own allies might attempt the same struggle for freedom.

The second and third Samnite wars grew naturally out of

[1] E. T. Salmon, *Samnium and the Samnites* (Cambridge, 1967), pp. 199ff. In several controverted points Salmon's views have been accepted here.

the first. In an effort to secure communications to Capua, Rome placed colonies along the Samnite frontiers. Fregellae, founded in 328 B.C. to control the Liris river valley, may actually have been placed on land that the Samnites considered theirs. The Romans sought allies to the south and southeast of Samnium, while the Samnites developed relations with Naples in south Campania and negotiated alliances on the north with the Gauls and with some of the Etruscans. Both sides prepared for a long struggle; the prize, we can now see in retrospect, would be the control of all Italy.

The first years of the second war (c. 326–304 B.C.) saw only limited skirmishing and raiding. In 321 B.C., however, the Romans attempted a major penetration of Samnium, with disastrous results. At Caudine Forks a double consular army of perhaps 16,000 men was trapped and forced to surrender. The Roman troops were sent under the yoke and went home in disgrace, without arms and equipment. For about five years (a formal truce period, perhaps, though the Roman accounts do not say so) there were no military operations of any importance. But then the war resumed and the final outcome was a definite victory for Rome. The Liris river valley, the communication corridor between Latium and Campania—when in unfriendly hands a threat to both areas—now was securely Roman. In the third war (298–290 B.C.) the Samnites finally achieved the coalition they had long worked for, as both Etruscans and Gauls joined in the struggle. In 296 B.C. a Samnite general, Gellius Egnatius, managed to effect a junction with Etruscan forces. The following year a Gallic force arrived, and the moment of decision with it. Unfortunately for the Samnites and their allies, the Etruscans were not present at the critical battle at Sentinum, 295 B.C. The fighting was desperate. One Roman consul, Decius Mus, was said to have devoted himself—and the enemy—to the infernal gods through appropriate rites; then he deliberately plunged into the enemy ranks in self-sacrifice. The Romans won, though losses were heavy on both sides. Hard fighting still remained, but Sentinum was the turning point.

In the peace, Samnium lost more of her best lands, retaining mostly the relatively unproductive mountainous regions. Moreover, the Samnites now were forced to become allies of Rome on the earlier, relatively enlightened pattern which left them autonomous at home, though in some ways subordinate. They did not have all the privileges that Latins held; nor did any receive the citizenship. Samnite troops had to fight with Roman armies for Roman objectives. The Samnites could still rebel against Rome, as we shall see, even in the first century B.C.

The Pyrrhic Wars

An extension of power both extends responsibilities and multiplies problems. The relationship Rome had cultivated during the Samnite wars with the Lucanians, who lived on the southern fringes of the Samnite territory, brought closer and often irritating contacts with the Greek states of southern Italy. Moreover, colonies that Rome had established, especially those in Apulia, had a commercial potential. For the Romans this was an incidental advantage—their purposes were strictly military—but the major Greek city in southern Italy, Tarentum, felt itself threatened economically. Tarentum decided to block any further extension of Roman power into the south, choosing as the *casus belli* the penetration into the Gulf of Taranto of a small Roman naval squadron chasing pirates. Entry into the gulf violated an old treaty with Tarentum. The Tarantines smashed the Roman fleet and refused any attempt to negotiate differences. They then brought in King Pyrrhus of Epirus with his army to conduct the inevitable land war. At sea the Tarantines would be unchallenged.

Pyrrhus, a relative of Alexander the Great by marriage, arrived with about 25,000 troops plus elephants, and in set battles twice defeated the main Roman army, at Heraclea (280 B.C.) and at Asculum a year later. Both the Macedonian superiority in cavalry and the use of elephants—the first the frightened Romans had ever seen—made the difference. The Romans claimed that Pyrrhus had won a "Pyrrhic" victory; they reported his comment that should he win another such battle he would certainly be ruined. His losses made Pyrrhus unable or unwilling to follow up with an attack on Rome itself. Besides, Pyrrhus saw other opportunities arising and had after all fulfilled his basic commitment. A weakened Rome now faced revolts of Samnite and Lucanian allies.

Pyrrhus next moved into Sicily to aid the Greeks in Syracuse against the Carthaginians, who at this point became allies of Rome. Again Pyrrhus was initially successful and again he failed to drive through to complete success. The Romans meanwhile retrieved many of their losses, and when the Greeks in Italy entreated Pyrrhus to return, the result was yet another hard-fought battle (Beneventum, 275 B.C.). Neither side won a clear victory, but the Romans this time were left in possession of the battlefield. Pyrrhus then withdrew to Greece, chiefly, it seems, to pursue his fortunes in a contest for Macedonia. It is possible that Tarentum could no longer afford his expensive services. Moreover, many Greeks in Sicily and Italy feared that Pyrrhus' ambitions in the area were personal and imperial.

Within a few years Rome had defeated Tarentum and integrated all the Greek city-states of southern Italy into her alliance system. The Greek cities furnished manned ships for Rome's small navy rather than men for her army, but otherwise the settlement followed the pattern established for the Latins and Samnites. Some Lucanian states, and the Samnites also, suffered the confiscation of part of their territories, as they were forced back into Roman alliance.

Meanwhile in these same years (280–265 B.C.) Rome was in frequent conflict with Etruscans to the northwest and Gauls to the north and northeast, and successfully reduced all organized opposition. As in the south, portions of the best lands of these old enemies went to Rome and the most productive parts of Etruria, Umbria, and Picenum were opened to Roman occupation. Forced alliances were established here also.

Colonization and Settlement as a Means of Control

Following another earlier pattern, Rome secured her position by establishing citizen and Latin colonies on the most strategic sites, especially along the coasts. To name only a few, Cosa in Etruria was established in 273 B.C., Paestum south of Naples in the same year; Rhegium, at the toe of the peninsula opposite Sicily, though not a colony, was carefully controlled after 270 B.C. On the eastern coast, Brundisium, established in 244 B.C., would become the chief port of embarkation for Greece and Asia Minor, displacing and eventually bringing about the decline of Tarentum and other Greek ports. Other colonies included several in Apulia established during the Samnite wars (Luceria and Venusia, notably), and, farther to the north, Asculum in Picenum. The citizen colonies were small, almost always on the coast, and designed for strategic military security. The Latin ones were larger. Populated by Latins and by Romans who gave up their citizenship to enter an allied state, they helped to "Romanize" the peninsula, to support Roman interests, and to prevent defections.

The lands confiscated from conquered states or from rebellious allies by this time amounted to perhaps a tenth of all Italy south of the Po valley. Some of them of course were colonized. Some of the land was leased, mostly to rich Romans, and some assigned in small lots to lower-class citizens. It is notable that one strip of state-owned land stretched eastward from Rome and effectively cut the peninsula in two. No doubt this was deliberate and designed to prevent rebellion. The Romans were systematic.

In 264 B.C., then, Rome was firmly in control of all Italy

south of the Po valley. There was now land enough to benefit all classes of citizens. Manpower resources were enormous. Mineral resources, despite the acquisition of Etruscan metal-working areas, were still minimal, however. Actual monetary wealth, too, was not great, for Rome's allies did not pay a cash tribute to Rome. Rome did profit from leasing out increased acreages of public land, but the cash flow was small. Because of wealth in land, forests, and men, however, Rome now ranked as one of the great Mediterranean powers. It would soon strive for supremacy with each of the others.

Once Rome controlled all Italy it was a great power—but only one of several others in the Mediterranean. One by one Rome eliminated the others, and in little more than a century determined the course of history throughout the area. Rome's competitors fought strongly and well; the goddess Fortuna would seem to have favored Rome in some of the confrontations. Yet one must remember that the Romans with their Latin and Italian allies generally maintained an indomitable resolve; Roman commanders led with a confidence that bordered upon arrogance; and Italy's reserves of manpower made up for occasional and inevitable disasters.

Great Power of the Western Mediterranean: Carthage

Our information on early Carthage comes mostly from Greek sources, and our knowledge of that state's conduct of the Punic Wars with Rome comes almost altogether from Roman sources. We have some background information from Phoenicia, some bits of evidence derived from coins and inscriptions, and some inferences postulated on the archaeological examination of ruins on the site of the ancient city and its dependencies. For the most part, however, we are dependent upon sources which, if not actively hostile, are indirect at best.

According to the Greeks, Carthage was founded about 816 B.C., half a century before the traditional founding of Rome. Archaeology has turned up nothing at the site quite so early, but the date may be not far wrong. The Phoenicians established numerous and varied colonies; Carthage was one of the sort which was both a trading station and a permanent settlement for numerous colonists, who developed the land for local agricultural production. Carthage retained ties with the founding city, Tyre, but when Tyre and the other Phoenician city-states weakened under the attacks of

ROME DOMINATES THE MEDITERRANEAN, 264–133 B.C.

Babylon and finally fell to Alexander the Great (332 B.C.) Carthage was looked to as the leader of all the Phoenician-occupied areas in the western Mediterranean.

Carthaginians pioneered in plantation-like farms worked by slaves. Other land about the city was mostly worked by natives. Agricultural yields made the city virtually self-sufficient in grains, vines, olives, and fruit. Whatever other produce Carthage needed could usually be obtained from nearby Sicily.

Trade, however, was the major consideration of the founders of Carthage. On the site were two harbors, one completely within the city defenses and partly artificial. The city's location at the narrowest part of the Mediterranean about a third of the way between Spain and the Phoenician coasts in the East also favored an active trade. For this trade the Carthaginians needed precious metals; gold and silver were needed also to pay the mercenaries upon whom the city depended for its imperial strength. These precious metals came mostly from Spain. Tin for use in bronze may have been brought all the way from Cornwall in southwest England. The early Phoenician traders and their descendants the Carthaginians after them, in their search for items of trade, coasted not only the Mediterranean but also the Atlantic both north and south of the Pillars of Hercules, as the ancients called the Straits of Gibraltar.

By the fourth century B.C., Carthage not only boasted a flourishing trade and held a strong political and economic position in its home territory in what is today Tunisia, but it also controlled directly or indirectly long stretches of the coastal regions in the West. All of the seaboard of North Africa from Cyrenaica to the Straits was within Carthage's sphere of influence if not actual domination. So also was southern Spain, western Sicily, and other island areas. Carthage remained a city-state but headed something of an empire.

Carthage's government, like Rome's, was an aristocratic oligarchy. At Carthage, however, there had apparently been no struggle of the orders so successful as at Rome. All citizens voted—but the Carthaginians had been very chary of extensions of their citizenship. Their Senate was even larger than that at Rome, but the real power lay in the Hundred, an inner group of senators given extensive judicial powers, and in another group, the Thirty, a sort of executive committee of the Senate; both of these were dominated by a restricted oligarchy. There were two elected officials comparable to Rome's consuls; these were called sufets. But generals and admirals were not elected. Scions of the great aristocratic families usually held these posts. Military leaders could be called to account before the Hundred.

One consequence of the policy of keeping the body of full

citizens small was that Carthage could not, like Rome, depend upon a citizen draft for military manpower needs. So far as military quality is concerned, this probably was not an important matter, contrary to what students have so often been told. Polybius, the second century B.C. Greek whose history provides us with the most dependable account of some years of the Punic Wars, was quite certain that mercenary troops were better than citizen levies. Yet in the end, military disaster meant economic difficulties which in turn made it impossible to continue to pay a large force of mercenaries. As one would expect in a trading state, Carthage's military establishment gave priority to a rather expensive navy. So long as Carthage had the funds to build and man fleets and to hire mercenaries, it would be a strong power.

One should not get the impression that the native Carthaginians totally avoided military service by hiring mercenaries. Carthaginians furnished the officer corps for both land and sea forces, and a moderate sized army unit of Carthaginians both defended the city and provided a reserve for use elsewhere in crises.

Altogether, Carthage was an antagonist worthy of Rome's best efforts; and it should be emphasized again that it was not inevitable from the beginning that the Romans would win. Indeed they very nearly lost out to this archenemy entrenched so strongly on the North African shores.

Great Powers of the Eastern Mediterranean: Macedonia

Students usually remember Macedonia, the kingdom in northern Greece, from the days of Philip II, who with a clever and effective combination of diplomacy and force succeeded in dominating all Greece in the fourth century B.C., despite the best efforts of Athens' thundering orator, Demosthenes. Even more vivid is the memory of Philip's son, Alexander the Great. He not only dominated Greece and conquered the great Persian Empire; he also initiated a new era of history, called the Hellenistic age. In the Hellenistic age, Greeks and Greek language and culture spread over the entire Near East; native influence, notably in religion, combined with the influx of Greek learning and ways to produce a distinctive new, hybridized culture. Alexander's premature death in 323 B.C. brought an untimely end to his empire, but Greek dynasties continued to rule separate large chunks of the territory that he had won, and the penetration of Greek culture continued.

Throughout the Hellenistic age, Macedonia, along with the other great powers, was sought after and fought over by the successors of Alexander. A Greek leader already mentioned,

Pyrrhus of Epirus, who fought the Romans in the third century B.C., was one of those who contended for the throne of Macedon. Two major federated leagues, formed in Greece during this period, naturally tended to contest with Macedonia for dominance of their areas. These were the Achaean League in the northern Peloponnesus and the Aetolian League just north of the Gulf of Corinth. Athens and Sparta were still important but were overshadowed by the great monarchies that characterized the age.

In earlier days the army of Macedon had played a role somewhat similar to that of Rome, being both military and political. The army voted on important matters and named or deposed the kings, at least in theory. Now, however, the Antigonids, ruling Macedonia since early in the third century B.C., made the succession hereditary. After Philip II and Alexander, the army came to include non-Macedonian, mercenary elements, somewhat like those of the other Hellenistic monarchies. The king's power tended to become more arbitrary, though Macedonian traditions acted as a brake here. Cities which once enjoyed considerable autonomy found themselves more and more subject to the king. Lands outside the core area of the older state were controlled by the monarch. Yet, as compared to the other monarchs, the Macedonian kings remained more popular national monarchs, since, after all, they ruled over their own; the other Greek dynasts used their mercenary Greek armies to dominate non-Greek natives. The Macedonian kings also put less stress on claims to divine ancestry and, unlike the other Hellenistic rulers, did not demand to be worshiped as gods.

Macedonia was self-sufficient in most agricultural commodities and in timber. Early conquests had brought control of important gold and silver mines in the northern Aegean region and in Thrace. The resulting currency helped to pay soldiers and to maintain a strong navy. These were necessary to the balance-of-power politics that sometimes brought precarious peace or more often endemic war to the Hellenistic East. The native manpower and also the quality of nearby Thracian mercenaries made it easier for Macedonia to obtain good troops than for Syria or Egypt, whose kings could not use natives at all, but must recruit troops from the Hellenic areas.

Syria

Of the great Hellenistic monarchies, Syria varied most radically during the age in both size and diversity of population. Under the founder of the dynasty, Seleucus I (hence the "Seleucid" Dynasty), or under a powerful monarch such as Antiochus III, the

Great, the polyglot kingdom included most of the former Persian Empire; under less able kings and in more troublous times, the kingdom shrank to little more than geographic Syria. The name Syria is used because Antiochus I established his capital there, at a city named after himself, Antioch, which became one of the great metropolitan centers of the Hellenistic world. Sardis in Asia Minor and Seleucia near Babylon were important regional capitals of the kingdom during much of the age.

The Seleucid monarchs strove long and hard to unify their diverse empire. The early kings established an extraordinary number of Greek colonies all over their dominion. Efforts were made, too, through emphasis on the divinity of the king, to provide a symbol of unity through religion. Rather late in the Hellenistic age, in the reign of Antiochus IV, attempts to impose this ruler-cult upon the sternly monotheistic Jews (167 B.C.) backfired. A rebellion, which was never completely put down by the Seleucids, created a precariously independent Jewish state.

This lack of real unity, of any widespread loyalty to the regime, was the Achilles' heel of the Syrian Empire. Yet there were notable strengths: a vast manpower supply, even if mostly unusable for military purposes; extensive trade in and along the fringes of the empire; and abundant, if scattered, resources in metals, timber, and the like.

Egypt

The southern neighbor and chief enemy of Syria was the third of the great Hellenistic powers, Ptolemaic Egypt. Egypt and Syria fought six major wars during the age, mostly over lands running from Sinai north along the Palestinian coast—the approaches to Egypt—a territory fought over for millennia.

Egypt was the most unified of the Hellenistic monarchies, primarily because of geography: the Nile gives to all the country an economic and social similarity and its protective geographical isolation tends to produce a sameness in the population itself. Egypt is the richest agricultural area of the Mediterranean. With irrigation, some of the "Black Land" (the ancient meaning of the word for Egypt) produces two and even three excellent crops each year. But Egypt is poor in metals and timber, and even in certain agricultural products.

The Ptolemies, following a pattern that had existed in Egypt since the beginning of the Old Kingdom nearly three thousand years earlier, held most of the land. They controlled the economy stringently, and strictly regulated exports and imports in the interest of the state and the Greco-Macedonian ruling class. The chief exports were grain and papyrus; the major imports included lumber, olive oil, and wine. The capital and chief port, Alexandria, became the greatest city of the entire Mediterranean world. The system worked rather well from every point of view except that of the natives, until the middle-second century B.C., when a disastrous series of years with very low grain prices—presumably caused by a universal overabundance of crops, with consequent low exports—dealt the Egyptian economy blows from which it never fully recovered in this period. Native unrest was a concomitant, as was rivalry between members of the ruling family for the throne, and the depredations of the kings of Syria and Macedonia against Ptolemaic holdings in southern Asia Minor.

Hellenistic Culture

In spite of the fact that the great monarchies (except for Macedonia) were ruled by foreigners who imposed upon the natives not only a military-political but even a cultural system, there was a surprising amount of influence in the other direction as well. This is most easily discerned in religion. The age was one of syncretism, of identification between gods of different regions and different names, of an emphasis upon universalism, of emphasis on likenesses rather than upon differences. Thus the Greeks identified and equated their Aphrodite with various goddesses in the Near East; in Egypt she became Isis. Isis the omnipresent, almost omniscient deity, however, was in conception, representation, and cult more Egyptian than Greek; ironically, her worship and that of other Eastern gods eventually spread to Greece, then to Rome, and thereafter over all the western Mediterranean.

Despite the continual fighting that characterized the age, progress was not limited to military matters. In trade, for example, relatively uniform practices, interchangeable systems of coinages, and a system of commercial law, much the same everywhere, developed. The later system of Roman law, so often praised as Rome's most notable contribution to Western civilization, owed much to these Hellenistic legal systems.

Each of these great powers of the Mediterranean, Carthage, Macedonia, Syria, and Egypt, Rome was to absorb after defeating them in crucial contests-at-arms. Against Carthage the Romans fought three wars; against Macedonia, four; against Syria only one but with further interference at times which might well have brought war had her rulers felt able. With Egypt, Rome quite early established a policy of friendship, apparently on the initiative of the Ptolemies. This relationship continued until the last of the Ptolemies, Cleopatra, made the mistake of casting her lot

with a Roman who turned out to be a loser: Antony. Throughout all the wars, power and influence, as well as territory, accrued to Rome; somehow that state always emerged as victor.

The Wars with Carthage (264–146 B.C.)

The long and bitter struggle between Rome and Carthage for
supremacy in the western Mediterranean will seem to have been
inevitable only to the person who believes that man is incorrigi-
bly acquisitive. Carthage was a city of merchants whose power
lay chiefly in the navy; Rome had few merchants and almost no
navy. Moreover, Carthage and Rome had been allied at various
times, most recently in their common enmity against Pyrrhus.
They made their first treaty when the Romans expelled the Tarquins, and they renewed it—perhaps twice—during the fourth
century B.C. The early pacts called on Carthage to stay out of
Italy, basically, and on Rome to recognize the Carthaginian trade
monopoly in a wide expanse of the Mediterranean—no sacrifice
for the Romans, at the time. Yet if the Romans were not traders,
their new Greek allies in south Italy were; and as sole ally,
patron, and protector, Rome must eventually make Greek interests her own.

Given the Roman necessity for looking out for the interests
of allies, and the Carthaginian propensity to interfere in eastern
Sicily whenever a sufficiently attractive opportunity presented
itself (though not manifested in recent decades), perhaps some
sort of confrontation, even if not war, was inevitable. It came at
the most sensitive spot geographically: the city of Messina, in
eastern Sicily just across the narrow straits from Italy, sought
aid from Carthage and then from Rome against King Hiero of
Syracuse. A confrontation came when both states sent aid. Thus
what both Rome and Carthage no doubt viewed as a minor
incident led to the First Punic War, as the Romans called it,
lasting from 264 until 242 B.C. The Romans felt they could not
permit the Carthaginians to control the straits, and neither side
would back down.

The war made exceptional demands upon both sides: the
Carthaginians had to hire larger mercenary forces than they
were accustomed to, chiefly for use in Sicily, but eventually to
fight off a Roman army, under the consul Regulus, which landed
in North Africa; and the Romans discovered they could not overcome the Carthaginians without a fleet, or rather a succession of
them, which they lost one by one to defeat, to inept seamanship,
or to storms. It was a titanic struggle, with manpower losses for
the Romans and their allies, of probably a quarter of a million
men. Both sides spent heavily in the war at sea. But it was the

Carthaginians who first weakened in this match of wills, after the loss of a fleet off Sicily. By the subsequent peace treaty the Romans gained Sicily plus a considerable indemnity. Three years later (238 B.C.) the Romans professed to be threatened by a Carthaginian buildup on Sardinia, which was part of a barbarous struggle between Carthage and her own rebellious mercenary troops. The Romans threatened renewed war, then demanded and obtained Sardinia and Corsica plus still more indemnity. War usually breeds war; certainly this imposed and unjust seizure sowed dragon's teeth for a second struggle.

The Second Punic, or Hannibalic war should be treated at somewhat greater length. In this conflict Rome confronted her most competent and indomitable enemy; and the alliance structure that was the basis of Rome's power bore the most severe stress. In surviving this critical test Rome took a giant stride toward supremacy in the Mediterranean world.

Carthage rebounded quickly from defeat in the first war, mainly because of the work of Hamilcar Barca, father of Hannibal, in Spain. Functioning almost as an independent ruler in his own domain, Hamilcar, through a combination of diplomacy and conquest, gained control of much of the south and east coastlands of the Iberian peninsula. He developed the Spanish gold and silver mines, making new finds that greatly increased output. After his death he was succeeded by his son-in-law Hasdrubal, and later by Hannibal, then in his middle twenties. He recruited and trained a very large army, and appeared to prepare for a war of revenge with Rome. In the time of Hasdrubal, the Romans, alarmed, made countermoves and attempted to curb Punic expansion in Spain by an agreement, accepted by Hasdrubal, to delimit the spheres of influence.

An incident in 219–218 B.C. sparked the beginning of the long conflict. This was the siege by Hannibal of Saguntum, a Roman ally, but in the Carthaginian area of influence. The resultant war came inconveniently early for the Romans. They had faced another Gallic threat from the north a few years before and had decided to pacify and occupy much of Cisalpine Gaul (the Po valley); this action was still in process. Moreover, they had intervened in Illyria across the Adriatic to suppress piracy that threatened the trade of their Greek allies in south Italy, and operations there also were not concluded when Saguntum was attacked. Therefore no help was sent to Saguntum, and at length it fell. In 218, Rome sent ambassadors to Carthage, who obtained no satisfaction, and thereon, Rome declared war.

Roman commanders planned to take the conflict to the city of Carthage by sending one army across to Africa, and to immobilize Hannibal by sending another to Spain. Hannibal seized the initiative, however—obviously he was more nearly ready than the Romans—and marched across southern Gaul (France), crossed the Alps and descended upon Italy. The march was made difficult more by the opposition of Alpine tribesmen than by the early autumn falls of snow in the Alps. He defeated the Romans in a major battle at the Trebia River, a branch of the Po, in November, then spent the winter recruiting for his depleted army, from the Gauls not yet driven out of the Po region by the Romans. In the spring he marched south, met another Roman army on the shore of Lake Trasimene, and again won a great victory. In both battles he had depended upon ambush to give him the edge.

The Romans now named Quintus Fabius Maximus dictator; he raised an army and dogged Hannibal's trail without permitting himself to be brought to battle, while Rome took emergency measures. The following year, 216 B.C., however, the Roman consul Terentius Varro felt strong enough to fight, and at Cannae, in Apulia, the Romans suffered their greatest defeat: in a single day they lost perhaps sixty thousand men to a smaller force under Hannibal. Hannibal's famous tactic was to let his center fall back, holding firm on the flanks; the Romans crammed men into the middle, where they seemed to be breaking through. Meanwhile the superior Carthaginian cavalry defeated that of Rome, and attacked the Romans in the rear. The Romans, now surrounded and packed together so tightly that most of them could not fight at all, were slaughtered. Disaster followed disaster: some Roman allies in Italy defected; King Hiero of Syracuse died and his successors left the alliance with Rome and made common cause with Carthage; King Philip V of Macedonia also joined Carthage in the struggle against Rome. Syracuse was soon taken by Rome and the Italian allies eventually were punished. By 205 B.C. a separate peace was made with Macedonia.

After Cannae, Rome returned to the tactics of Fabius: for years one or more armies, always superior to Hannibal in total manpower, stayed close to the Carthaginians, but large engagements were avoided. From beginning to end, Hannibal's strategy was to destroy Rome by breaking up its alliance system. The Roman tactics were designed specifically to prevent this. Italian allies of Rome could not declare for Hannibal without danger of immediate retaliation from a Roman army. The most interesting action of the Hannibalic War is military, and it is here that Hannibal's genius shines; but the more important battles were for the allegiance of the Latin and Italian peoples, for without these allies Rome would have sunk to the level of a minor power. Rome won this most crucial contest not just by Fabian strategy during the war, but by having forged a system a century earlier that was relatively enlightened and unoppressive. The allies that defected after Cannae were mostly Greeks and Lucanians, the most recent members of the Roman alliance system. Of the older Latin and Italian allies only one state—Capua—went over to the Carthaginians. Hannibal marked time in frustration. He could not be beaten, but he could not win.

Meanwhile, under three different Scipios, the Romans conquered Spain. In 207 B.C., a major effort was made by Carthage to reinforce Hannibal; but this army, led by Hannibal's brother, the Romans annihilated before it could effect a junction with Hannibal. Eventually Scipio, elected consul for 205 B.C., though young and not having held the usual lower offices, took an army into Africa, ravaged the country, and won over some of Carthage's allies. Carthage, in desperation, during a truce recalled Hannibal. He had been in Italy more than fourteen years. Hannibal got together a major army, only to be defeated at Zama in 202 B.C. by Scipio, who was thereafter called Africanus.

Carthage paid an indemnity of 10,000 talents, again on the installment plan, agreed to limit its navy, and agreed not to wage war without Rome's approval. Rome kept Spain, from which the Carthaginians had been completely expelled by 206 B.C. In this war, as in the First Punic War, Rome lost heavily in manpower; moreover, the depredations of Hannibal damaged heavily some of the rural areas of Italy—hurting men more than land, as we shall see. Yet Italy was still populous enough; and Spain brought Rome both tribute and income from the mines. Frequent wars with the natives there certainly reduced the net gain, but the volume of precious metals was significant. So were the installments of the Carthaginian indemnity. Rome emerged stronger than ever, and now a contender for dominance of the entire Greco-Roman world.

Carthage again managed a quick economic recovery, and as before offered to pay off far in advance the indemnity owed to Rome. But the state was no real threat any more, and the Third Punic War (149–146 B.C.), from any point of view, seems to have been unnecessary. On the Roman side it was in part the result of fear which was a legacy of the first two wars. For the Carthaginians it was a kind of irrational lashing out under the restrictions imposed on them by the peace of 201 B.C. Playing a key role in causation was a Roman ally, Masinissa of Numidia, who on several occasions took advantage of his connections with Rome and with the Scipios (patrons of his kingdom) to expand his dominions at the expense of Carthage. The famous advocacy of war by Cato the Elder, who died the year the war started at about 85 years of age, is to be explained by his conviction that the Carthaginians were no longer going to acquiesce in the Roman leadership of the West.

Irritated beyond measure at the depredations of Masinissa and despairing of justice at the hands of Roman commissions like the unsuccessful one headed by Cato, the Carthaginians raised an army and struck back at Numidia. This was illegal by the peace of half a century earlier, and Rome declared war on Carthage. The Carthaginians now reversed policy, executed some of their leaders who got them into this unwanted war, and surrendered to Rome on promise of their safety. But the Roman commander in Africa demanded that the Carthaginians evacuate their city, which was to be destroyed. Carthaginian protests were dismissed: only personal security, the Roman said, had been guaranteed. The Carthaginians had already surrendered their weapons, but they now shut the city gates, and amazingly, managed to hold off the Romans during three years of siege. All in vain at last: the city was taken and destroyed utterly by the younger Scipio Africanus, grandson by adoption of the elder Africanus (called Aemilianus because he was the son of L. Aemilius Paullus, victor over Perseus of Macedonia).

Numidia, now under Micipsa, the son of Masinissa, did not get the Carthaginian land, however; it was too valuable. The territory became the Roman province called Africa, approximately modern Tunisia. It produced for Rome a tribute in grain, oil, and wine which in a few decades grew surprisingly large. Eventually much of the land was settled by Romans. Yet the Carthaginian population was not exterminated and the Phoenician influence remained strong in the area for centuries, as archaeological excavations clearly show.

Rome Penetrates the Hellenistic East

Both the reasons for Roman intervention in the eastern Mediterranean and the methods by which this was accomplished are difficult to work out in detail, despite much scholarly investigation. In any time and place, strong powers are drawn as by magnets into weaker areas. States that feel threatened by their neighbors will seek help wherever they can find it. Allies of strong powers must be protected. Moreover, some Romans at all levels of society had much to gain by war, and became imperialists. Other Romans felt a sense of kinship with the Greeks on an intellectual level and this led them to wish to help the older city-states against Macedonia, for example. In considerable degree the Roman penetration was gradual, one step leading to another, and not at all the consequence of any long-range policy.

It was only partially a matter of military action; it involved also diplomacy and the actions of individual, powerful figures at Rome. It seems clear, however, that traders and merchants did not strongly influence the important decisions: the new imperialism was not in general economic in nature.

The Macedonian Wars

Friction between Rome and Macedonia first developed as the consequence of the Roman movement across the Adriatic to suppress piracy, shortly before the Hannibalic War. Offended minor potentates naturally looked to Macedonia for redress against Rome; and young king Philip V of Macedonia (221–179 B.C.) intervened. He also joined in alliance with Hannibal against Rome, as we have seen, after Cannae. This is termed the First Macedonian War (215–205 B.C.). Rome countered by making an alliance with the Aetolian League, an old enemy of Macedonia, and despite the manpower demands of the fight against Carthage (Rome had as many as twenty-seven legions under arms in those years) found it possible to send a few troops to Greece to keep Philip off balance. Meanwhile, Philip was far more interested in projects nearer home than in sending promised troops to Hannibal. The separate peace was drawn up before Rome carried the war against Hannibal to Africa.

The Second Macedonian War (199–196 B.C.) was brought on by Romans who resented the first war, and by Rome's Greek allies who demanded that Rome do more for them. The Roman assembly at first refused to declare war against Philip; but later, persuaded that war was inevitable and that the only question was whether it would be fought in Greece and Macedonia or in Italy after Philip invaded as Hannibal had, the people voted as requested. The war went slowly until a young consul named Titus Quinctius Flamininus in 197 and 196 B.C. made allies not only of Aetolians but also of the Achaean League, and won a decisive, hard-fought battle over Philip's phalanx in 196 B.C. at Cynoscephalae.

It was at this point that Rome had to establish some sort of general policy toward the whole Balkan area. Flamininus, a philhellene, persuaded the Senate to back him in what was thought by most Greeks and Romans to be an enlightened, even noble policy. Rome, it was announced at the Isthmian games, would not retain control of any Greek city: no Roman garrisons would replace those of Macedonia. All Greek states were to be free. The crowd at the stadium dissolved into such raptures of enthusiasm that the games did not continue. As for Macedonia itself, Rome took only 1,000 talents in indemnity, a small sum indeed, and deprived that kingdom of only small bits of Greek territory which had been conquered in recent years. These lands were mostly freed, though the Aetolian League got some. Altogether it seemed that once again the Romans had come up with the sort of brilliant policy of enlightened self-interest that had worked so well in Italy. But there were flaws: the Aetolians were furious not to have fared better at the expense of the Macedonians. And since the Romans did not forge an alliance system as they had in Italy, they had no way of enforcing their policy of freedom—which at times did indeed need to be enforced. The Romans viewed themselves as liberal patrons of their friends and clients, the Greeks. The latter hardly saw themselves as clients, and thought that they were to be left free to fight with each other as they had from time immemorial. It was inevitable that Rome would be drawn again and again into Greek affairs.

The Syrian War (192–189 B.C.)

A war waged by Rome against Antiochus III of Syria intervened between the second and third Macedonian wars. The king was called into Greece by the disenchanted Aetolians, who made an obviously anti-Roman alliance with him. Antiochus had ambitions in Europe, for he laid claim to territories in Thrace once held by Syria. He probably thought that Philip of Macedonia, now recovering from his defeat, might join in the alliance against Rome. Antiochus had already encountered Roman pressure in Egypt and in Asia Minor, where the Romans suggested that all Syrian-dominated Greek cities should be free also. And he had given grave offense to the Romans by receiving the exile Hannibal and by admitting him to councils of state.

The war was precipitated when Antiochus crossed the Aegean with a small army in 192 B.C. and spent the winter in Greece. Neither he nor the Aetolians made adequate preparations for a war with Rome; each seemed to expect the other to make the major effort. Philip stayed aloof. Rome sent an army across to Greece and defeated the combined Syrian and Greek force at Thermopylae in 191 B.C. The following year, led by L. Scipio (soon to be Asiaticus), brother of the elder Scipio Africanus, the Romans invaded Asia Minor. They had the substantial help of King Eumenes of Pergamum, who feared the power and ambitions of Antiochus. In a battle at Magnesia against the full military power of Syria the Romans and their allies were victorious.

Rome still wanted no territory east of Italy. Lands in Asia Minor were indeed taken away from Antiochus, but they were handed over to Rome's chief allies in the area, Eumenes and the Rhodians, who had furnished naval support in the war. The Romans took only spoils and money—but plenty of that: Antiochus agreed to pay 15,000 talents, 3,000 down and the rest by installments. Meanwhile, Roman soldiers garnered a rich return, not merely in spoils from the battlefields but also in "gifts" to the generals from the various cities of Asia Minor that the armies visited, persuading the local inhabitants to submit to the changed order of things. Antiochus was killed after a year or so as he was attempting to collect money for the indemnity by despoiling a temple treasury.

Third and Fourth Macedonian Wars
(171–167 B.C. and 149–148 B.C.)

When Philip V of Macedonia died in 179 B.C. he was succeeded by his son Perseus. This pleased the Romans none too well. They had favored a younger son, Demetrius, who had made friends with influential Roman aristocrats while living as a hostage in Rome. But Demetrius had been executed by his father; it was said that Perseus convinced him that the younger son was disloyal.

Perseus' policy was like that of his father: to husband his economic resources, to remain strong militarily, to cultivate pro-Macedonian factions throughout Greece, but to engage in no large and dangerous ventures. This policy, however, frightened some Greeks, who felt that the carefully groomed army of Macedon would be used against them one day. The Romans listened to complaints against Perseus. Charges made by King Eumenes of Pergamum seemed proved when a gang of toughs— said to be agents of Perseus—set upon the king and nearly killed him as he was going up to Delphi on his way home from Rome. At any rate, Rome forced an unwanted and unnecessary war upon Perseus. The king made little use of his well-filled treasury and inadequate use of his army; yet the Romans defeated him only in 168 B.C. after electing a veteran consul, L. Aemilius Paullus, and sending him to command their army in Greece. The battle, at Pydna in Macedonia, was another test of the relative effectiveness of the Macedonian phalanx and the Roman legion. As before, it was demonstrated that, while the phalanx was perhaps invincible on smooth terrain, the more flexible legion prevailed in a fight on uneven ground.

Again the Romans chose not to acquire territory. But Macedonia was broken up into four small, separate republics, which were forbidden to have even commercial relations with each other. Perseus was made to trudge along the streets of Rome, a halter around his neck, in Paullus' triumphal procession. Imprisoned, he soon died or was killed. Small states in Epirus, which had cooperated with Perseus, were punished with widespread destruction and (it was said) sale of 150,000 persons into slavery. Rome refused to permit any powerful state to exist in the Greek area, but did not accept the responsibility of leadership there. Rome did collect tribute not only from Macedonia but also from Illyria (which also had supported Perseus); the amount was small, but the Romans gave almost nothing in return.

The final Macedonian conflict came chiefly because the Romans in 167 B.C. had chopped up an area that had long been unified, not only politically, but socially and economically as well. When, therefore, a man named Andriscus claimed to be the son of Perseus and attempted to overthrow the republics he gained considerable popular support. In 148 B.C. a Roman army put down the revolt. It was led by Q. Metellus, who of course was thereafter known as Macedonicus. Now, at last, Macedonia was formally organized as Rome's first province in the East. The governor of Macedonia was charged with overseeing Illyria also.

Rome had intervened substantially in Greek affairs in various ways since the Second Macedonian War. The Aetolian League was virtually dismantled after the Syrian War. Following the war with Perseus the Romans tried to eliminate the pro-Macedonian elements in various Greek cities, especially in the Achaean League, and took numerous hostages (among them the future historian Polybius), who were released only in 151 B.C. Actions of Roman commanders in the Peloponnese after 148 B.C. tended to weaken the Achaean League. Its leaders, goaded beyond endurance by a resentment that was as much psychological as substantial, in an irrational outburst mistreated some Roman envoys. Frantically, the League prepared for the inevitable war and just as inevitable defeat. L. Mummius conducted the major operations for Rome in 146 B.C. around Corinth, which was besieged and destroyed as an object lesson. It would not be rebuilt until the time of Caesar.

It seemed a long time since the Greeks had wildly cheered Flamininus' announcement that all Greece was free. Now, Greece became a dependency of Rome under the oversight of the governor of Macedonia. Later, Augustus would make Greece into a province, called Achaea.

Penetration of Asia Minor

Rome frequently intervened diplomatically in Asia after the Syrian War; of course the threat of military action gave backing to her envoys. After the war with Perseus, Eumenes of Pergamum was threatened with loss of land because of suspected sympathy for Perseus in the late stages of the war. Rhodes, which committed the unforgivable sin of attempting to mediate between Rome and Macedonia in the war, did lose all the Carian property (southwest Asia Minor) obtained through Rome from Syria. Moreover, Rome made Delos a free port and this competition undermined the economic basis of the Rhodian state. In 167 B.C., Roman envoys, in a celebrated confrontation with Antiochus IV of Syria on the beach near Alexandria in Egypt, forced the king through mere threat to take himself and his army out of Egypt, that "friend" of Rome. Syria declined into insignificance in following decades, until its absorption by Rome in 63 B.C.

Pergamum became Rome's first province in Asia when Attalus III died in 133 B.C. after willing his kingdom to Rome. The natives put up a fight to invalidate the will but Roman arms insured receipt of the legacy. About the turn of the century Rome took action against piracy in the East. Previously the Rhodians had controlled the pirates in the area, but now weakened, they could no longer persevere. In the process of these operations Rome acquired still another province, Cilicia, along the south shore of Asia Minor (102–101 B.C.). By now the kings of Bithynia in the north and of Cappadocia in central Asia Minor were "friends and allies"—client states of Rome—which now dominated virtually the whole peninsula. For good or for ill the Romans were committed to a continuing major role in Asia, as well as in Greece and Macedonia.

Roman arms had been busy in the mid-second century B.C. The years 149–146 B.C. saw the third Punic, the fourth Macedonian, and the Achaean wars. Moreover, in Spain, Roman governors of the two provinces, Hither and Farther Spain, fought never-ending wars, and Roman troops campaigned in Illyria and Dalmatia. By the end of the second century B.C. no major competitor remained anywhere in the Mediterranean. Numbered among the provinces were Sicily, Sardinia–Corsica, Hither Spain, Farther Spain, Africa, Macedonia, Asia, Cilicia, probably Cisalpine Gaul by now, and Illyricum. Rome was unchallenged and supreme.

The period of rapid expansion beyond Italy wrought trenchant changes in Roman society and economy. For Rome's ruling classes and a small but important rising group of businessmen and bankers, the expanded dominions meant expanded opportunity. Even for the lower classes, if Fortuna smiled, or if men were clever enough to spot and seize opportunity, they might prosper. But long military service and debt crushed many lives. And the very prosperity which gilded the age for the fortunate only accentuated the poverty of the unfortunate. The gap between the rich and the poor gradually widened and finally became intolerable. In time, the whole social structure underwent a significant alteration, at length affecting politics and the state.

Along with the economic and social changes came a flood of innovations that threatened to overwhelm the old Roman mores. Broader experience and opportunity brought greater sophistication. Romans began to produce a literature that would become noteworthy. They began to examine imported philosophical concepts and to experiment with new religions. New standards of luxury for the favored classes gave rise to changing morals. To many minds the *mos maiorum* or ancestral tradition seemed to be eroding dangerously.

The young naturally embraced the changes in life style more rapidly than their elders. Just as in any period of rapid change, a generation gap was often apparent, which was most painful to conservatives, of whom there were always many at Rome. This chapter will delve into some aspects of this change, so bewildering or threatening to some Romans, so eagerly embraced by others.

CHANGING TIMES, 264–133 B.C.

Changes in the Economy

In antiquity, most wealth came from the land. The economy of Italy was based on the soil, and all else that happened did not change that basic dependency. Land ownership was coveted and respected; wealth was likely to be conceived in rural terms, even when many men made their money in banking, trade, mining, or manufacturing. This continuing rural outlook characteristic of the ruling classes should not be forgotten even in a discussion emphasizing changes associated with a developing urban culture.

One of the most basic causes of sharp alteration in state and society was the artificial stimulation of the economy—especially of the city of Rome but to a degree, of all Italy—through income from wars and the provinces. Each major war considered in Chapter 4 ended with a victory for the Romans, which brought spoils to both individuals and the state, followed either by payments of sizable indemnities over a period of years or by permanent tribute. But one must not overstate: Spain, for example, must have been unprofitable at times despite tribute and income from the silver mines because of widespread disturbances. Overall, however, vast sums by ancient reckoning came to Italy and made many Romans affluent. The city itself sprawled with new growth. It was continually bedecked with new public buildings, aqueducts, and temples. Private structures of all sorts spread outward along the Tiber and along the spurs of the hills about the city. Other Italian cities in favored locations showed similar signs of growth on a lesser scale.

The governing classes at Rome, restricted by custom and sometimes by law from certain types of business activity, necessarily left to others the wholesale and retail trade and commerce. Moneylending too was looked down upon though rich nobles sometimes got into the banking business in an indirect way. The less restricted Italians, especially the Greeks, developed a sea trade. Other Italians and lower-class Romans got into the wholesale and retail business, particularly about Rome, the largest city and the best market in the peninsula. Roman contractors called publicans (*publicani*) benefited directly from state expenditure: they supplied the armies, built ships for the navy, contracted from the censors to build roads, bridges, and public structures of all kinds. The wealth of many such Roman entrepreneurs soon approached that of the richest nobles.

Investment in Large Farms

The nobles, who accumulated capital primarily from lucrative positions in government—particularly as governors of provinces —kept their self-respect and prestige chiefly by investing in land. Rich Romans might obtain land in several ways. They could buy from those unfortunates who were ruined by long absences during military service (not all soldiers brought back spoils enough to pay off mortgages). Then, too, some unscrupulous aristocrats could find ways to force small holders off desirable acreages. But many small holders were willing enough to sell; they could go to Rome or some other city to find work or establish themselves in small shops that would mean an easier life. Mostly, however, the land available for capitalistic development was *ager publicus*, state land, which Rome had confiscated from defeated states while conquering Italy. More recently, large chunks of land had been seized during and after the Hannibalic War from states that went over to Hannibal, and added to the publicly owned land of Rome.

Ownership of land was prestigious, but the owners also wanted profit. This usually meant organizing the land in relatively large units of 100 or 200 acres or more and emphasizing cash crops. Such large acreages were organized in two different ways. A growing number were operated by slave labor. Slaves must have been available at relatively low prices at times, as for example, when Aemilius Paullus sold the 150,000 Epirotes in 167 B.C. Such slave-manned plantations in a later period were called *latifundia* ("broad acres"). These farms grew the most profitable crops possible, in contrast to the small subsistence farms; small farmers grew a little of everything a family might need. The *latifundia* were usually stock farms or orchards of olives and vines. The second method of working large holdings, less highly organized, requiring less care and supervision but probably yielding less profit, was to lease to tenants. Many a poor farmer who lost his own tiny acreage was happppy enough to be able to continue the only life he knew on rented soil.

The Small Farmer

The general prosperity in Italy did not trickle down much to the small farmers. A brisk market did indeed exist for animals, wine, olive oil, and other prized gastronomic items. But the needs were met primarily by the slave plantations or by import. In any period bulky farm products could not profitably be shipped much more than thirty or forty miles except by sea. It was the lot of most farmers to live relatively isolated lives before the advent of modern transportation. There was, similarly, no relief from the back-breaking, unremitting labor that characterized farm work until the arrival of labor-saving machinery in modern times.

In consequence of the development of the *latifundia*, the difficult life, and the alternatives available, the number of small farmers declined. This affected the military draft pool, for Rome conscripted only men who held a certain minimum of property.

During the period between the end of the Hannibalic War (202 B.C.) and the Gracchi (133 B.C.) the property requirement for army service was reduced drastically; when the inflation that came with the influx of money is taken into account, the requirement at the end of this period was perhaps no more than a tenth of the earlier amount. And still the Roman commanders filled draft quotas only with difficulty. One should not, however, think of a countryside completely dominated by slaves, although Tiberius Gracchus in 137 B.C. noted few free farmers in Etruria as he passed through. Though the total number of small farmers declined, Rome never lacked a considerable percentage of them, for one way or another their numbers were continually renewed. The number of tenant farmers seems to have increased, for army recruiting patterns indicate plenty of able-bodied men in rural areas who did not own land—but who now qualified for the military draft through ownership of personal property.

Colonization and individual (*viritim*) distributions of public land helped to keep up the numbers of small farmers. The motivation was military more than political, and economic least of all, but the effects were nonetheless economically beneficial in many ways. In the early second century B.C. most colonists went to the Po valley, where the land was incomparably better than in other areas of Italy. Army veterans especially were likely to be permitted to settle in these new colonies. By the end of the Republic, veterans almost routinely were given land even if it was necessary to confiscate it from unlucky opponents. Despite these policies, it is probable that a gradual decline continued in the numbers of family-type subsistence farm operations.

Migration to the Cities

For those farmers who were willing to leave the soil and strike out in new directions the rewards were often greater. The growing cities—Rome in particular—provided opportunity. Carpenters, masons, brick-makers, metalworkers, leather workers, potters, fullers, and other skilled and semiskilled workers were needed. Work was readily obtainable that could put more silver in a man's pocket in a month than he might see in a year on the farm. Yet real wages were low enough: an unskilled worker probably earned about half a denarius per day at the time of the Hannibalic War, rising to probably a denarius per day before the end of the second century B.C. The weight of silver in the denarius would be worth only about a quarter today. In purchasing power, however, used for barest necessities only, this wage would support a small family.

Slaves tended to displace free workers in the city also. It

was a growing practice to buy and train slaves for various tasks. By the end of the second century B.C. work for a freeman was less easy to come by for this reason and because of a general economic decline; unemployment at times plagued the city plebs. The situation at any given time depended upon the level of building and other economic activity in the city, the numbers of men coming in from the farms looking for work, and the numbers of slaves being put to the tasks freemen once were given. We cannot determine with precision these and other factors affecting the economy, but we know that together they brought about an urban crisis, as we shall see.

Some lower-class Romans came to the city with a bit of capital. It may have come from the sale of their farms or from spoils and bonuses derived from military service. A good number of these men went into business for themselves and rose in the economic scale. In Rome they founded hundreds of small shops. Both wholesale and retail establishments were needed for local products such as food and for the more expensive imported

Street scene, Pompeii. Bakery shop. (*Scala, New York/Florence*)

items. A man who sold fish or hammered out pots and pans might prosper much as the man who built a warehouse along the Tiber waterfront. Neither small businessmen nor wage earners might be listed on the census rolls as having sufficient property to be draftable, but in terms of creature comforts and varied activities they might live lives vastly preferable to those of their country relatives. The latter worked much harder to wrest a living from their tiny acreages, and for their pains were drafted into the army, often to such duty as the unprofitable, long-drawn-out guerrilla war in Spain.

Other entrepreneurs became rich. These were the men who got into the private building industry or supplied the armies or bid in contracts for roads and public buildings. Increasingly they used large gangs of free and slave labor. These rich men, though never a large group, eventually gained some political influence.

Most lower-class Romans in the city were day laborers. Their existence was likely to be more precarious than they realized. Their work was on a day-to-day basis and completely insecure. The very prosperity that enticed them to the city masked effectively the misery that would be theirs when money no longer flowed so freely. They were hardly aware that the city was becoming far too dependent upon imported food supplies. Any shortage, inevitably accompanied by hoarding and speculation, would mean high prices that hit hardest at the poor.

The Changing Social Structure: The Nobles

In part, the changes in the social classes have already been implied. It is not possible to disentangle completely for separate analysis the various strands—social, economic, political, military, intellectual—that together make up the fabric of an age. It is not even desirable to attempt to examine these different facets of life in complete isolation. We must, then, necessarily overlap a bit in our discussions.

For the upper classes in Rome the middle Republic must have been an exhilarating time. As the ruling oligarchy of the Mediterranean, they could feel with some assurance that they were the most important people in the world. Their sons took their education very seriously, knowing that they in their turn would help to determine the course of things in the Mediterranean cosmos.

Wealth came to these important Romans, as we have seen, as did prestige and power. Whether governors in the provinces, officials at home, or commanders in the field, Roman aristocrats had astonishingly unrestricted authority. For a period of time within their areas of command they ruled almost as kings. It was flattery, but not simply that, when an obsequious seeker of favor called the Senate an assembly of kings. Or, on another notable occasion, when King Prusias II of Bithynia, whose policies had offended the Romans, prostrated himself at the door of the Senate-house and hailed the senators as Savior Gods (Polybius 30. 18). Disgusting—but heady.

It is well to keep in mind what a diverse group was the nobility of Rome. A small number of patrician families formed the core. Most nobles, however, belonged to plebeian families, prominent because some of their members had held the highest offices in the state. Many such families derived from towns long before conquered by Rome; their ancestors had been the counterparts of the Roman patricians. Just below the nobles were other senatorial families. Scions of these families usually attained at least the lower rung of the *cursus honorum,* the quaestorship, and thus became eligible for appointment to the Senate. Though not all were, strictly speaking, of the nobility, all senatorial families were yet quite prestigious. On occasion a member of such a family might attain the highest rung in the *cursus* —the consulate—and so ennoble the family. A man who was the first of his family to do this was called a New Man (*novus homo;* sometimes he was so called when he merely sought the office).

It should not be thought that the nobility was vastly enlarged by reason of the growth of Rome and of the opportunities to serve. The numbers of praetors and quaestors increased as the Empire grew, but the number of consuls remained at only two. The number of New Men in the last two centuries of the Republic was not at all large. In fact, it seems that the great wealth and prestige that accrued to the nobles in the middle Republic and thereafter motivated them to form an ever more exclusive body, jealously guarding their privileges and carefully controlling the elections.

Change Threatens the Political Power of the Nobles

Though conservative in many ways, the Roman nobility nevertheless embraced with enthusiasm certain economic and social changes which were to destroy the Republic—if it is right to call such an oligarchy a Republic—dominated by them. This dichotomy may be illustrated in the life and work of Cato the Censor (234–149 B.C.), whom we have already encountered. Cato opposed much that was new, the prevailing luxury, eroding morals, effete sophistication. But in the oldest prose work in Latin still extant, his *De Agricultura,* Cato in effect advocated the investment of capital in the new slave-operated plantation-like farms. He explained how to buy land, and told what machinery and how many slaves were needed for the different types of money-making crops. And he seemed unaware that the growth of such farming operations would effectively undermine the foundations of the kind of traditional state that he desired.

The Roman aristocrats, then, owned much land and many slaves. But slaves did not vote. The declining numbers of small farmers dependent upon important Roman nobles as patrons, meant inevitably the erosion of the structure by which the nobles had maintained their political clout—the patron–client system. Many of the upper classes, moreover, moved into the city, leaving the supervision of their estates to slave or freedmen supervisors. Most did not gain much influence over the city plebs, though some of their number ultimately became demagogic or popular politicians who appealed to and used the urban elements.

The nobles of course tried to keep control of the state, and especially of the election machinery, for what seemed most important was that their sons, like themselves, should attain the highest offices. Sometime about 241 B.C.—certainly before 218 B.C. —a reform was made in the most important elective body, the Centuriate Assembly. It gave added weight to the tribal structure rather than, specifically, the centuries. At first glance the reform seems rather democratic, since the centuries were ranked according to wealth and the tribes were not, and likely to reduce the power of the richer elements in the assembly. But the number of persons in Rome on election day from the rural tribes was likely to be small, and the effect of the reform actually enabled men with control of even small numbers of votes from the rural areas to exercise greater domination of the assembly than before. The urban plebs, restricted to only four of the thirty-five tribes, was for many years unimportant.

The nobles also developed elaborate means of putting together coalitions for the elections. In the middle Republic this seems primarily to have taken the form of family combinations, which tended to endure even though constantly shifting through a period of time, perhaps even over generations. In the later Republic a greater dependence was placed on simply collecting obligations in any possible way—by doing favors and expecting favors in return, for example—all with a view to payoff only two or three times in one's life: at election to each of the major offices. Cicero made use of his oratorical ability to obligate men to himself, as did Caesar and many others; the patronage was widely used, as in all states in all ages, and men whose protégés received appointments as officers in the army or on a governor's staff, were obligated to support their benefactors. It is not proper to imply that men never supported candidates on principle or program, but the realities of political organization usually put such considerations in second or third place.

Toward the end of the Republic the political organizers began to appeal not just to the important bigwigs who could indeed still influence the vote strongly, but to lower and lower classes whose support grew more and more important. The urban plebeians never, perhaps, determined an important election by themselves, but by the end of the Republic they could greatly influence the passage of laws which had great political implications. Indeed Cicero suggests (in his speech *For Sestius* 109) that those in charge of assemblies sometimes transferred men from the city plebs to the rural tribes in order to produce a quorum or influence the outcome of a particular vote.

The Equestrian Class

As a distinct group the *Equester Ordo*, as it was termed in the later Republic, only gradually took shape. The *equites* originally were the cavalry in the army; in the Centuriate Assembly they were assigned to the top class. In the Assembly, these eighteen centuries included men retired from the cavalry, who no longer "held a public horse." (The term of military service for upper-class persons before going into public service was ten years; lower-class men served as much as sixteen years or even more in emergencies.) In the earliest age the only men rich enough to be placed in this group were the nobles, but as time went on, some plebeians whose property put them into the first census class also served in the cavalry and voted with the first class in the Assembly, but they did not necessarily aspire to a political career as sons of nobles did.

The rise of a middle group of men who were rich but neither noble nor particularly political is an important phenomenon of the middle Republic. These were the men described earlier in the chapter, who built the ships, contracted roads and buildings, engaged in trade, banking, moneylending, and tax collecting. Ultimately, by the last century of the Republic, the most important of these men were those publicans (*publicani*) who bid in the largest government contracts of various sorts, as for the collection of certain taxes. This group was not very large but became quite important.

The significant role of the *publicani* even as early as the end of the third century B.C. is illustrated in a story from Livy (25. 3. 9–11) of the activity of one of their number in 213 B.C., during the Second Punic War. Those men who owned ships and used them to supply the armies were naturally fearful of loss. The state, therefore, in effect agreed to insure each owner against loss either from enemy activity or storm. One unscrupulous publican, Marcus Postumius, bought up old ships, filled them with junk, sank them out at sea and claimed to have had valuable cargo aboard, and so collected an inflated value from the state. The scandal was brought before the Senate, but nothing was done for a time. The historian says that the Senate did not want to antagonize the publicans as a class. Presumably they were indispensable in the war effort. Yet the man was prosecuted the following year, and Livy may have been mistaken on the reasons for the delay.[1]

As a group, the Equestrian Order was legally defined only in the last century of the Republic by a series of laws, such as the one carried by Gaius Gracchus, tribune of the plebs in 123 and 122 B.C., that excluded senatorial families—that is, all the nobles plus their lesser political allies—from service on the juries of the permanent courts. Thus the nonsenatorial equestrian families gradually came to constitute a distinct class. For the most part these equestrians had an identity of interests with the senatorial families, though the issue of the degree of political influence to be permitted to the nonsenatorial equestrians in the control of the courts was long a touchy one. These equestrians for the most part did not want to displace the nobles, but they did want enough influence so as to be less dependent upon them.

So far we have only mentioned equestrians who were businessmen, bankers, and the like. There was another quite important component of this group: men from families rich enough to be included in the first class of the census, but landholders, not businessmen. In fact, most of the equestrians must have belonged to such families. Many of them were politically important in their local municipalities. The family of Cicero typifies this group well. His father was a noted man in his own town, Arpinum, about 70 miles east of Rome. He had connections with the top political figures in the capital, and doubtless as a politically minded rural citizen of importance delivered a good many votes to his Roman friends on election day. Yet neither he nor any of his ancestors had held an office at Rome until Cicero himself, who was thus a New Man.

These country gentry, to use a British term, perhaps acquiesced in the order of things; they had some status at Rome plus a modicum of local prestige. A few of them held offices in Rome, the less important ones, elective and appointive. Many

[1] See E. Badian, *Publicans and Sinners* (Ithaca, N.Y., 1972), pp. 17ff.

of these equestrians must have wished it easier to break into the closed circle of oligarchs who controlled the state. Our sources say little about them, and modern historians have too often ignored them. Many have mistakenly concluded that the middle class at Rome (to use a term subject to misinterpretation) consisted only of businessmen, publicans, and the like. But it is certain that the rural equestrians were quite numerous and that they helped to stabilize the state. In the Empire they would become more important than ever before.

The Lower Classes

The old mainstay of the state was the class of small farmers at Rome, and most of what must be said of them has already been said. Although they continued to decline throughout the Republic despite the extensive colonization and individual land distribution programs, yet they remained important in numbers, a stabilizing component of society despite their hard life on the farms and the burden of the military draft. They were important politically only as clients of the great, ordinarily. The increasing numbers (probably) of tenant farmers shared the position and fate of the small holders except that their economic position was worse.

Worst of all in the countryside was the condition of the farm laborers. Perhaps there were fewer than before, since opportunity for better things in the city beckoned. However, we read in Cato's *De Agricultura* of gangs of men—freelaborers under contract to some single agent, it appears—who moved about the countryside during the various harvest periods, to help out during these busy days. It would have been uneconomical for slave owners to purchase and house enough slaves for such seasonal activities as picking and pressing olives. These gangs of laborers, the migrant workers of antiquity, must have lived often in rather miserable circumstances as compared even to the tenant farmers, who at least had their own houses and gardens. The farm laborers' lot was often inferior to that of slaves.

For influence on Rome's future, however, the most important segment of the lower class was the urban plebs. Constantly growing, this group of wage laborers did well enough when Rome bustled and times were prosperous, even with their slum housing and poor diet. The excitement of the city with its games, theatre, races, religious festivals, and the like compensated in part for the inadequacies of house and table. Most of these plebeians did not wish to leave the city for hard work on the farms. They wanted a better life in the city. They could get it only by demanding more of the state. Once they learned this lesson they tended to give their support—it was mostly the threat of violence—to whatever leaders promised them most. But that is a subject of the next chapter.

Women's "Lib" in the Second Century B.C.

One area of notable change in Roman society was the role of women. Roman matrons from the earliest times seem to have possessed a greater personal freedom than those of Greece or the Near East. Yet at least the upper-class women were expected to be under the control of father or husband or guardian. But gradually some restrictions, as on the control of their own property, broke down; and women often were notably influential even in public affairs, though not as officeholders, of course. Cornelia, the daughter of Scipio Africanus and the mother of the Gracchi brought up her children after the death of her husband, Tiberius Sempronius Gracchus, and with great freedom maintained a kind of intellectual salon at her home.

An interesting incident of 195 B.C. illustrates one step in the legal struggle for emancipation. During the Hannibalic War the Oppian Law[2] had been passed, which restricted women in several ways: they could not possess more than half an ounce of gold, they could not wear varicolored dresses (especially purple and gold), and they could not ride about the city in carriages. Probably the hardships and economic stresses of the war account for the restrictive legislation. In 195, two tribunes proposed to repeal the law, over the substantial opposition of Cato, who was then consul, and others. We are told of women thronging the Forum, virtually picketing it, attempting to influence officials, and pressing into the assembly, even during formal session. Cato called it a sedition of women, and compared their behavior to the secession of the plebs in the Struggle of the Orders. The pressure tactics nonetheless succeeded: the law was repealed.

A Voconian law of 169 B.C. attempted to restrict the rights of women in matters of inheritance, limiting the amounts they could get. This of course indicates that women had been permitted to inherit substantial property despite the laws about being under the control (*manus*) of father, husband, or guardian. The Voconian Law, we know, was not strictly enforced. The laws giving husbands control of wives' property were evaded by use of informal wedding rites; such wives had to absent themselves from their husbands' houses three nights a year so as not to come legally under their control.

[2] Laws were named after their proposers—in this case, a man named Oppius.

Most likely it was the new affluence that made it possible for upper-class women to move about more freely: a multitude of household slaves, though requiring some supervision, simply eliminated household duties for such women. What of lower-class women? We do not know. But it is often the case in a highly structured society that lower-class women have much greater freedom than their betters.

Religious Innovation

Religion, too, changed during the late Republic. In the period when Hannibal's astounding victories terrorized Rome, anxious citizens naturally sought new ways of propitiating the gods. Women were said to have swept temple pavements with their hair. New gods and strange practices were introduced. Though Rome was relatively tolerant of religious innovation, the magistrates could be quite intolerant when they felt the security of the state was at stake. About 210 B.C. a praetor, on instructions from the Senate, forbade some of the more outlandish observances, and called for books to be brought in, apparently for burning.

Official changes were made as well, but in a more traditional way. New games were established for Apollo (the *Ludi Apollinares*) and other games were set up or lengthened. The

Denarii of the first century B.C., perhaps issued in connection with the great festival in April to the goddess Cybele, shown left with her turreted crown, and right, in her chariot drawn by lions. The goddess was especially associated with the nobility at Rome.

decemvirs on request examined the Sibylline Books and interpreted a passage to mean that success in the war would follow if Cybele, the Magna Mater, were brought from Pessinus in Asia Minor to Rome. Messengers were sent, and in 204 B.C. a meteorite symbolizing this goddess was received in Rome by representatives of two of the aristocratic families, Claudia Quinta, a vestal virgin, and Scipio Nasica, a delegate for the young men named by the Senate. In a few years a temple to Cybele was completed within the sacred boundaries of the city, on the Palatine Hill, where its remains still indicate the site. However, repelled by the gyrations and mouthings of her emasculated priests in their noisy processions, the Senate forbade any Roman citizen to serve as a priest to Cybele.

Fear of religious change may be seen in the famous investigation of the Bacchanalian cult. Cato was probably a leader in this inquisition and suppression. The affair broke out in 186 B.C. Romans were seized with panic on hearing that Bacchanalian rites were being held in and near Rome and elsewhere in Italy, and that young Romans were being initiated into the cult, believed not only to be shot through with immorality, but even to constitute a serious conspiracy against the state. The celebrants were doubtless mostly from states that had supported Hannibal in the recent war, a circumstance that may have affected the Romans' attitudes. The consul, Spurius Postumius Albinus, received certain information which he reported to the Senate. According to Livy (39.19) the consul said that "nothing is more deceptive in appearance than a false religion" and reminded the senators of past book-burnings and suppression of exotic rites. The Senate responded with a decree (which survives in an inscription found in southern Italy, the oldest lengthy Latin one extant) severely restricting the rites, though not banning them entirely. The decree, probably the first one so sweeping, led to an investigation throughout all Italy, and eventually Sardinia and Sicily as well. Thousands were reported executed, presumably for conspiracy. The whole affair remains a bit mysterious and can only be ascribed to hysteria. At about the same time, there was a "conspiracy" of shepherds along with suspicions of widespread poisonings of husbands by wives. In any event, the importation of strange religions was inhibited for a time. Not until the first century B.C. did the flood tide of religious change rise.

Moral Decline

All the ancient writers agree that Roman morals deteriorated in the last two centuries of the pre-Christian era. They all attribute it to foreign influence and to the influx of wealth, and disagree only as to the time when the decline began to accelerate noticeably. Livy seems to put it in the period of the war against Antiochus of Syria and immediately following. Polybius places it in the period after the war against Perseus of Macedonia. Sallust thought the real decay came with the destruction of that salutary enemy, Carthage. Perhaps some sources exaggerate the deterioration, but change there certainly was.

It was Cato who led the attack on declining morals and its cause, the new luxury. As censor in 184 B.C. (when the investigations into the Bacchanalian affair were still going on), Cato assessed items he considered luxurious at ten times their real value, especially young slaves purchased at high prices, presumably for their sex appeal. He dropped the brother of the great Scipio from the roll of the cavalry, and expelled from the Senate the brother of Flamininus, the victor at Cynoscephalae, for a reported moral lapse. Cato was not alone in his concern; several of the censors in the first half of the second century B.C. were as severe as he in their strictures on bad morals.

Cato and the Philosophers

Much of the lowered moral tone of society Cato blamed on Greek influence. He said that the importation of Greek literature would ruin the nation. As for Greek philosophers, he felt they taught an amoral skepticism that would erode Roman virtue. An interesting incident of 181 B.C. illustrates his view. The praetor urbanus, Q. Petilius, a political protégé of Cato, reported to the Senate that a clerk of his had dug up on the Janiculum (a hill just across the Tiber from the city) a tomb containing two stone chests. One had once contained the body of Numa Pompilius; the other contained, still in excellent condition, linen books preserved in wax, on teachings of the Pythagorean philosophy. The praetor declared that the books were subversive of religion and recommended that they be burned. A senatorial decree so ordered and Petilius consigned the books to the flames in the Forum, curiously as a kind of offering to the gods, the fire being brought by religious attendants called *victimarii*.

The whole story had to be trumped up. Even the Romans —at least in a slightly later period—knew that Numa had died long before the time of Pythagoras. This sort of public holocaust in solemn sacrifice appears to have been a stern warning to Romans who were espousing Pythagorean views. One of these may have been the poet and playwright Ennius (239–169 B.C.), one of whose extant poems expresses Pythagorean ideas such as the transmigration of souls. There might be a more personal political twist: Cato had originally brought Ennius to Rome; he was from south Italy. In 184, in Cato's censorship, Ennius had been made a Roman citizen, but in more recent years he had become a client of the Scipios, Cato's political enemies.

Cato and other conservatives continued the attack on Greek philosophy. In 173 B.C. some Epicureans were banished from Rome. In 161 B.C. all philosophers and rhetoricians were similarly banished, by decree of the Senate. (Such decrees were never enforced for long.) In 155–154 B.C. three eminent Greek philosophers including Carneades, leader of the Academy, visited Rome on an embassy. Carneades gave two well-attended lectures on justice. The first was of the sort which might warm the cockles of a conservative's heart. Justice was that which was in accord with old-established law and custom. For the Roman, that was the *mos maiorum*. But in the second lecture this skeptic demonstrated why it was that everything he had previously argued so persuasively could not possibly be right. Cato was horrified at this frivolity. He saw to it that the three philosophers completed their business and were hustled out of town.

One should not leave the impression that Cato was the ignorant country bumpkin. He knew Greek, and even—with misgivings, to be sure—sent off his son to study at Athens. His fears of foreign influence were based on moral principle rather than ignorance.

The Younger Scipio and the Philhellenes

Some Romans were capable of admiring the Greeks for their great intellectual achievements without picking up the penchant of other Greeks for luxury and sensual gratification. Of these our best example is P. Cornelius Scipio Aemilianus, who was, as we have seen, the son of L. Aemilius Paullus, victor of Pydna, adopted by the son of the elder Scipio. Scipio's home became a kind of intellectual center at Rome, partly, no doubt, because Paullus had brought back Perseus' library; it must have been the best in the city. Some writers have uncritically assigned every intellectual at Rome to the "Scipionic circle." Certainly several Greek and Roman intellectuals met there at times.

The group included Polybius, who was brought back from Greece as a hostage in 167 B.C. and who taught Scipio and became his firm friend. Polybius' history, our best source of information where extant, was highly complimentary to the Romans. He much admired Rome's constitution, which he saw as a mixed one, with elements of monarchy, aristocracy, and democracy. He also warned Romans that constitutions change, even stable ones like theirs. They could expect, he suggested, that the democratic element would demand more than its share of power, leading to instability and decline.

Another Greek who stayed in Scipio's house for several years was Panaetius of Rhodes, a Stoic philosopher. Panaetius popularized Stoicism among the Roman upper classes, emphasizing the pragmatic aspects of the philosophy, which fit in well with what the Romans already believed: the value of service to the state, personal virtue, endurance in the face of misfortune. From this time on, there were always a few prominent Romans who espoused the Stoic philosophy.

Roman members of the Scipionic circle were Scipio's friend Laelius, who became a Stoic; Terence, a playwright, who along with Plautus popularized the Greek style of comedy; and Lucilius, the first important Roman satirist. Obviously Scipio did not see eye-to-eye with Cato as to the dangers of Greek influence. Yet he believed as strongly as did Cato in maintaining the old virtues, and in fact, Cato approved of the much younger Scipio.

The Theatre at Rome

It is rather surprising that we do not hear of a vigorous attack by Cato on the developing theatre. The Romans used as models for their drama the Greek plays of their own and an earlier day. The Greek "new comedy" was often filled with dissolute characters portrayed in compromising situations. But the playwrights at Rome were cautious, and saw to it that all immoral characters and suggestive plotters were Greek rather than Roman. No Roman matron could possibly be presented as an unfaithful wife or high-class prostitute, as some of the women in these plays were.

The first production of a play at Rome took place before Cato's time, in 240 B.C. It was written by Livius Andronicus, who had been brought to Rome a captive from Tarentum about 272 B.C. Rome had seen earlier stage productions, perhaps imported from Etruria, but not true plays with plot and theme. Andronicus' plays were presented as part of one of the great games, the *Ludi Romani*. There was thus a religious connection (as in earlier Greek drama), which tended to endure: the plays were normally parts of religious festivals. Andronicus not only adapted Greek plays for the Roman stage, but he also wrote poetry long and short and, on at least one occasion, a hymn, sung through the streets of Rome as part of a religious exercise. None of his works remain. A notable successor was Naevius, who was a few years younger; he was Roman or at least Italian, possibly from Campania. Though he too wrote on themes of Greek legend, we are told that he satirized by name important Roman politicians and for his pains was exiled. He wrote an epic poem, too, a historical chronicle in verse of the First Punic War, the *Bellum Poenicum*. Ennius, mentioned previously in this chapter, was the next important playwright. Like Naevius, Ennius also wrote poetic history. His *Annales*, composed in Greek hexameters, more polished than Naevius' rough rhythms, was completed in the 170s B.C., late in his life, and apparently encompassed all of Roman history.

Plautus

The only Latin comedies to survive are those of Plautus (c. 254–184 B.C.) and Terence (c. 190–159 B.C.). By their time—after the Hannibalic war—plays were routinely presented at several of the major state festivals: the *Ludi Megalenses* (to the goddess Cybele) in April, the *Ludi Apollinares* in July, the *Ludi Romani* in September, and the *Ludi Plebeii* in November. The number of days devoted to theatre in these festivals gradually increased. It is interesting that no permanent theatre was built until the time of Pompey the Great, in 55 B.C. The Romans made do with temporary wooden structures, built for each occasion; there were not even seats until late in the second century. In 154 B.C. one of the censors started construction of a stone theatre, but he was forbidden to complete it. Perhaps the objections were rooted in religious scruple.

Most surviving Roman plays are comedies—which tells us something of the later Roman taste. Twenty of these are by Plautus. Based on models of the Greek New Comedy, they are boisterous, fun-filled, sometimes crude or obscene. They had to be fast-paced to appeal to Romans who had, perhaps, just been to the chariot races. It is not surprising that Plautus' plays seem to have had simpler plots and broader humor than those of his Greek predecessors. His plots are mostly placed in Greece: the loose women, impudent slaves, and fumbling masters could neither with propriety nor accuracy be depicted as Roman.

Perhaps as a concession to the Roman *gravitas*, Plautus produced a couple of serious comedies. In the prologue to *Captivi* (*The Captives*), the playwright had the actor say,

This play is not composed in the hackneyed style . . . nor are there in it any ribald lines unfit for utterance: here is neither the perjured procurer nor the artful courtesan, nor yet the braggart captain.[3]

And in the final lines at the close,

---

[3] All translations from Plautus are those of Henry T. Riley, in *The Bohn Classical Library* (London, 1852), with modifications.

*Spectators, this play is founded on chaste manners. No wenching
is there in this, and no intriguing, no exposure of a child, no
cheating out of money; and no young man in love here makes
his mistress free without his father's knowledge. The poets
find but few comedies of this kind [that is, in the Greek
sources], where good men might become better.*

One wonders how the Roman audience received the play; *gravitas* notwithstanding, Roman audiences enjoyed the bawdier plays.

The sexual double standard has operated in much of history, and it appears in the plays. In the *Menaechmi* (*The Twin Brothers*), an Old Man tells his daughter, a Wife,

*How often have I told you to be compliant to your husband.
Don't be watching what he does, where he goes, or what he's
about.*

The Wife replies,

But he's in love with a courtesan here close by.

The Old Man counsels the blind eye, and says,

*Do you want your husband to be your servant? You might as
well . . . bid him sit among the female servants and card
wool. . . . Since he keeps you provided for and well clothed, . . .
'tis better, madam, to entertain kindly feelings.*

Actually, in this instance, the affair is that of the unknown twin rather than the husband, but it is doubtful that that fact was intended to modify the view expressed.

It is often difficult to tell whether any particular passage significant for social mores applied to Romans as it did to the Greeks for whom the plays were first written. One passage in the *Aulularia* (*The Concealed Treasure*) on marriage between rich and poor families probably reflects Roman as much as Greek social reality: the poor man, Euclio, says,

*Megadorus, you are a wealthy man of rank; I am the poorest of
the poor; now, if I should give my daughter in marriage to you,
it suggests to my mind that you are the ox, and that I am the
ass; when I'm yoked to you, and not able to bear the burden
equally, I, the ass, must lie down in the mire; you, the ox, would
regard me no more than if I had never been born; and I should
both find you unjust, and my own class would laugh at me.*

A skit in the *Epidicus* (*The Fortunate Discovery*), satirizing women's new clothing styles, may have applied in Rome as in Greece; at least we know that there had been criticism at Rome during the Second Punic War of the dresses women were wearing. Epidicus says,

Many women go through the streets decked out with farms upon them. But when the tax is demanded, they [the men who support the women] declare it cannot be paid; while to these hussies, to whom a larger tax is paid, it can be paid. Why, what new names every year these women are finding for their clothing —the thin tunic, the thick tunic, fulled linen cloth, chemises, bordered shifts, the marigold- or saffron-colored dress, the under-petticoat or else the light vermilion dress, the hood, the royal or the foreign robe, the wave pattern or the feather pattern, the wax- or the apple-tint.

We do not have the original plays in Greek to compare with the Latin versions. But certain lines definitely were added for Roman audiences. At the end of the first act of the *Cistellaria* (*The Casket*), presented during the Hannibalic war, an actor says,

Farewell, and conquer by inborn valor, as you have done before; defend your allies, both ancient ones and new; increase resources by your righteous laws; destroy your foes; laud and laurels gather; that, conquered by you, the Poeni [Carthaginians] may suffer the penalty.

Praise in some plays for the old ways (*mos maiorum*) may well represent concessions to the gravity of the Romans (or, at least, the ruling class) also. In the *Trinummus* (*Three Pieces of Money*), an older actor advises his son not to hold any converse with profligate men, either in the streets or in the Forum.

I know this age, what its manners are. The bad man wishes the good man to be bad, that he may be like himself. The wicked, the rapacious, the covetous, and the envious disorder and confound the morals of the age. Live after my fashion, according to the ancient manners.

Later in the play, another actor bemoans the new situation ethics:

Nowadays, men pay no attention to what is proper, only to what is agreeable. Ambition now is sanctioned by usage, and is free from the laws. The public manners now have got the laws in their power; to them they are more submissive than are parents to their children!

Cato might have said that himself.

Terence

Terence wrote six plays, all extant. Composed two to three decades later than those of Plautus, they show a greater sophistication. The language is more polished, the plots and action less crude. A serious theme could govern a whole play: in the *Adelphi* (*The Brothers*), Terence depicted two sons of a farmer brought up one by the father and the other by his brother. They employed vastly different methods. The farmer brought up his son strictly, while the brother, in an urban environment, brought up the other son permissively. The latter turned out to be a fine fellow, while the son brought up under a strict regimen turned out a scoundrel. Micio, the city parent, presents the theme in the prologue:

My system, my theory, is this: he who does his duty under the lash of punishment has no dread except in the thought of detection; if he thinks he won't be found out, back he goes to his natural bent. When you link a son to you by kindness, there is sincerity in all his acts, he sets himself to make a return, and will be the same behind your back as to your face.[4]

Here one may perhaps see the influence of the Greek friends of Scipio Aemilianus. The other plays of Terence were much less relevant to anything Roman, and the historian finds little in them to shed light on contemporary Roman society.

Terence had his difficulties with his audiences. His plays had not the wide appeal of those of Plautus. In the introduction to *Hecyra* (*The Mother-in-Law*), we learn that at the first presentation a simultaneous performance of a rope dancer and rumors of a gladiatorial contest elsewhere caused most of his audience to leave, so that the performance was disrupted. Terence was criticized on a higher level because of the way in which he combined plots and borrowed characters from the Greek originals.

Tragedies also were presented at the great games, about as many as comedies, but none are extant from the period of the Republic. Pacuvius (c. 220–130 B.C.) was probably the best of the tragedians; Cicero thought so. The orator also admired his successor, Accius (c. 170–86 B.C.), who lived long enough for Cicero to have conversations with him. Cicero's interest illustrates what is probably true—that Roman intellectuals had a greater interest in tragedy than lower-class plebeians.

[4] Translation of John Sargeaunt, Loeb Classical Library.

Lucilius

The Scipionic circle included yet another Roman literary man who deserves mention as Rome's first great satirist, C. Lucilius (c. 180–103 B.C.). Satire was a genre of literature in which the Romans showed some inventiveness and independence from Greek sources. The fragments we have of Lucilius, around 1300 lines, show that he was a political partisan of the Scipionians and that he wrote with sharp, incisive, and cutting wit. His influence extended throughout Roman literary history: Horace and Martial, for example, were influenced by him.

A Developing System of Law

The growth of Rome, the broadening experience of her magistrates, increasing involvement with ever more diverse peoples brought a need for an expanded and more flexible law system. Change does not come easy: the first writing down of the law, in the XII Tables, had come only with struggle. Even after that the priests jealously guarded the operation of the courts. Actions had to be phrased precisely and only they knew the wording. The very knowledge of the days on which court could be held was kept secret until late in the third century.

Accretions to the general body of law came in several ways: by action of the Assembly, which passed *leges;* by action of magistrates, who had considerable powers both to issue edicts within their spheres and to determine what was the law; by Senate decree, which often had the force of law; and by interpretation, not only by magistrates, but also by men learned in the law, called jurisconsults. The son of Cato the Censor was one such jurisconsult; another was the consul of 133 B.C., P. Mucius Scaevola, the earliest jurist whose opinions were quoted in *Digesta* of the famed Justinian Code of 534 A.D.

The praetor was in general charge of the court system. About 242 B.C. the second praetorship was established; there were now a *praetor urbanus,* who tried cases of the *ius civile,* which technically applied only to Roman citizens, and the *praetor peregrinus,* who dealt with cases involving foreigners. The latter could function with considerable latitude, and many innovations came as the praetors dealt with men accustomed to the legal systems of Greece and the Hellenistic East. The Romans had a term for law based on widely used principles—*ius gentium,* law of nations. By the first century B.C. and under Stoic influence there was talk, too, of the *ius naturalis,* natural law.

A most important procedural change was the substitution of a new formulary system for the old system of rigidly phrased actions. This probably developed gradually, but about the middle of the second century B.C. it was specifically legalized by a law, the Lex Aebutia. After this time the praetors conducted preliminary hearings and then sent to the judges they appointed a summary of the case and the points to be decided, stated as a formula. This system was simpler. The formulas were drawn up on principles of the law to be sure, but the praetor could revise them or draw up new ones to fit the specific cases.

Provincial governors, like the praetors in Rome, drew up edicts, usually based in considerable part upon the local law. Large numbers of Roman magistrates thus gained experience in the laws of other peoples and in turn influenced legal development in Rome. Roman willingness to learn from others and to adapt foreign ways to the needs of empire was indeed, as the Romans themselves said, part of the Roman genius.

Changes in the Political System

It is sometimes suggested that the failure of the Roman oligarchy to adapt to the governance of an empire is the major reason for the decline and collapse into civil war of the Roman Republic. There is a large element of truth in this. But the degree to which Roman political institutions changed to meet the new situation is often understated or misstated.

The Roman propensity to give great power to her magistrates was at once the blessing and the curse of the government under the Republic. Men of ability had the authority they needed to solve the problems they encountered. Unfortunately, there was also latitude for shady dealings. By law, the Lex Calpurnia of 149 B.C., a permanent court was set up that made it possible for provincials (if they could get a prominent Roman to take their case as their patron) to sue for recovery of money or property extorted from their citizens. But the jurors were drawn from a panel of senators, who were disinclined to ruin the career and family of an accused fellow senator, and the procedure did little to check an increasing number of rapacious or unjust governors.

The number of governors of course grew with the increasing number of provinces. The number of praetors was increased by two after each of the first two Punic Wars, so that there would be enough propraetors and proconsuls for the governorships. By the middle-second century four of the six praetors did not serve in Rome at all but went directly as governors to provinces. The other two normally went off to govern provinces as propraetors after their year in Rome. Consuls, too, governed provinces either in the years of their consulate or as proconsuls afterward. The number of quaestors was increased to allow one for each governor and two to serve in the city.

Much political procedure in Rome was conducted on a personal basis. In that fashion, the government of Rome was to some degree responsive to the needs of Latins, Italians, and provincials. Important Romans were patrons of cities, provinces, and even allied kingdoms in a kind of extension of the old patron–client system into provincial government and diplomacy. The patron at Rome looked out for his clients' interests in the Senate. To be sure the system had its disadvantages; it was a bit haphazard and there were no checks. But on the whole it worked. The patrons were consulted on important matters in their spheres of interest and acted somewhat as state department experts now do in government. That is to say, the interests of Rome's provincial and allied cities were brought to the attention of the Roman oligarchy, which was thus less isolated, more aware of its allies' and subjects' needs, and more attentive to those needs than is often believed.

Obviously the government of the Republic did not change enough. The trouble lay primarily in the grasping and self-centered actions of too many Romans of all ranks from nobles to urban plebs, who began to struggle for the spoils of empire. At the last, even civil war was not thought too great a sacrifice in the struggle for what men considered their fair share of the profits of empire. Foremost among the avaricious politicians who must bear primary responsibility for the drift into civil conflict were many members of the closed and narrow oligarchy who jealously guarded their circle against intruders. Not enough competent "new men" from the lower ranks of senatorial families were permitted to join that close circle. Not enough attention was paid to the welfare of the Roman lower classes, from the small farmers on whose shoulders lay the increasingly crushing burden of military service to the urban plebs who were citizens of the state that ruled the world and yet had little to show for it. Even less attention was given to the plight of certain provincials. Throughout the civil war they could only yield to whichever general was in control of the local situation, wait for peace, and hope for a better tomorrow.

The kinds of changes occurring in the middle Republic naturally put numerous pressures on the Roman state and society. In any ultimate assessment, the worst strain had to originate from the unwieldy business of governing the many millions of persons living in the Roman provinces, from Spain to Macedonia. During the last century of the Republic, Rome's dominions would enlarge even more, to extend across Gaul in the West and Asia Minor and Syria in the East. It has been noted that despite enormous difficulties, the Roman oligarchy, in a sort of informal and personal way, was more responsive to the needs of provincials than sometimes believed. Yet their responses were inadequate, primarily because the oligarchs so jealously guarded their monopoly of office, power, prestige, and wealth that it became their chief preoccupation. Only a few, therefore, gave much attention to the needs of the (Republican) Empire, while most looked to their own advantage with single-minded zeal.

Since the political struggle within the oligarchy determined the course of events not only for Rome and Italy but for the Empire as well, the historian's attention both in antiquity and in modern times has been drawn to a rather narrow focus on that struggle, mostly in Rome itself. It seems unavoidable. This chapter, then, concentrates on the struggle for dominance within the closed circle of the Roman ruling class. The setting is most often at Rome. Other matters are brought in as they affect that struggle.

Long-Range Rural Problems and Short-Term Urban Crisis

The most unhealthy segment of Roman society, as we have seen, was the class of small farmers. This class also formed the backbone of the state; the problem was, then, most serious. The dwindling numbers of small holders and their declining prosperity (at least in relative terms) meant trouble. Since

FROM THE GRACCHI TO THE TRIUMVIRATE, 133–60 B.C.

only men of at least some property were eligible for service in the army, this rural group—which was still large—suffered under unreasonable demands for army service. Progressive lowering of the property requirement and even drafting quite young men did not solve the problem. The *latifundia*, slave-operated plantations, which in part replaced the small farms, did not provide men for the army nor did they produce the staple foods needed for the populace: other crops were more profitable. Rome and possibly even other Italian cities became dependent upon grain supplies brought in from the outside. In part this was in consequence of the transportation system. Bulky items could not be transported far by land and compete with similar products brought in by cheaper sea transport.

A temporary urban crisis sparked action by a young Roman politician, Tiberius Sempronius Gracchus, tribune of the plebs in 133 B.C. The crisis, with economic depression and soaring food prices, had several causes, one of which was a long-continued influx of persons into Rome, many of them small farmers or sons of small farmers. Some came in freely, happy to work for wages rather than to grub at the resisting soil. Others drifted in because there seemed nothing better to do. All did well enough by ancient standards, until an economic recession descended on the city of Rome and perhaps to a lesser degree elsewhere in Italy.

This economic downturn resulted largely from a rather sudden drop in government spending in and about Rome. The money Rome had received by way of indemnity, tribute, and spoils from the wars ending in 146 B.C. was freely spent by Roman leaders. One project, for instance, the new Marcian Aqueduct, built over a four-year period, 144–140 B.C., cost 180,000,000 sesterces (4 sestertii = 1 denarius, about a day's wage for an unskilled laborer). The two existing aqueducts were repaired at the same time. Numerous other projects were carried through. Obviously the burgeoning city demanded expanded supplies and services. But after about 140 B.C. things changed. The extraordinary expenditures ceased. No profitable wars produced great spoils. Most campaigns were like that of the younger Scipio, called Aemilianus, against Numantia in Spain between 135 and 132 B.C. Scipio called on allied states outside Italy to help with troops, since the Senate was reluctant to place any more burdens on Romans. And when the war ended successfully, his soldiers got only a few denarii as a bonus at the triumph. No longer did indemnity from Carthage or Macedonia or Syria fill the treasury. The direct tax, which had always been, specifically, a war tax, was permanently ended for Romans in Italy after L. Aemilius Paullus defeated Perseus (167 B.C.).

The lowered state income went only for "necessary" expenditures; roads, bridges, temples and other public buildings, and a host of other items could wait. In Rome there was unemployment with much distress.

For the city, caught up in the recession, the most serious immediate problem was a shortage of grain—and thus bread for the lower-class diet. This was in part the consequence of a general shortage in the Mediterranean; in Egypt, for example, prices went up enormously in only a few years. The situation was exacerbated by piracy. But most portentous for Rome itself was a slave war in Sicily (135–132 B.C.), source of perhaps half the city's grain. The rebellion, led by an interesting character named Eunus, who called himself King Antiochus, caused widespread disruption of normal agriculture in that island province. Lower-class Romans, many already without an income, could not pay the inflated prices; some must have been quite literally starving.

Tiberius Gracchus' Efforts to Solve Rome's Problems

As tribune of the plebs in 133 B.C. Tiberius Gracchus initiated a struggle that was to continue fitfully for a century. He was actuated by a desire to correct the rural problems, which affected Rome's all-important army. In the decline of the small-farmer class he saw the destruction of the *mos maiorum*, the old state. He was supported by a faction, led by his father-in-law Appius Claudius; doubtless he was also influenced by a setback his career had suffered when, as quaestor in Spain in 137 B.C., he had become involved in a scandalous military disaster. Finally, Tiberius had an adviser of Italian Greek stock named Blossius, from Cumae, who was something of a Stoic and something of a democrat. He may have encouraged the thirty-year-old tribune in some of his more radical moves.

Tiberius proposed a law not at all radical, concerning land (hence called his Lex Agraria). It involved publicly owned land (*ager publicus*) and did not touch privately owned property. By this law the amount of public land that could be leased by any one person was limited; the excess was to be recovered. This land, along with other public land not formally leased to any citizen, was to be made available for leasehold distribution in small-farm quantities to landless citizens. At one sweep Gracchus would reduce the number of slave-manned *latifundia*, increase the draft pool of small landholders (the property requirement was so low that actual land ownership was not necessary), and decrease the dependence of the city of Rome on outside grain. He surely hoped to get some Romans out of the city and onto small farms, though it is likely that when the land commission set up by the law began to operate the commissioners found it more practical and realistic to give the lots to men who were already tenant farmers in rural areas. The land distribution program, which lasted several years, had very limited success.

Tiberius Gracchus made his greatest impact on the oligarchy itself. When his rivals attempted to stop him by the veto of an opposing tribune, he conducted an unprecedented recall election and declared the man deposed. When his opponents persuaded the Senate to withhold money from the Agrarian commission, Gracchus again turned to unprecedented means: news arrived that Attalus III of Pergamum in Asia Minor had just died, after willing his kingdom to Rome; Gracchus called an assembly and by law arranged that the Pergamene treasury be used for the commission's purposes. While he was about it, he also got a provision that the new province (Asia, the Romans called it) would be organized not by the Senate as was customary, but by the assembly, with himself as agent, of course. When Tiberius announced he was a candidate for reelection, his enemies, frightened by dark rumor about his ultimate intentions, killed him. It was the first such political assassination in men's memory. His recent legislation was either voided or circumvented, except for the land law, which remained in effect.

Thus Tiberius Gracchus, while working toward conservative, time-honored goals, used means which were radical. In contemporary terminology we would say that he decided to buck the system. The manner of his use of the office of tribune, outside the control of magistrates and Senate, amounted to a declaration of war on the oligarchical system. Some of his opponents feared he wanted to make himself a tyrant. Other men had gained support for themselves through personal popularity, as he did; other tribunes had defied the system; but he did so with imaginative and daring innovation and with a considerable degree of success. He became the archetype of a new breed of imitators later called *populares*. Like him they would be scions of old families, mostly aristocrats, always upper class. None of them would be either men of low class or true democrats, but rather, men who rose to high positions through use of his methods. The traditional political leaders, opponents of the populares, would soon be calling themselves *optimates* or *boni*, the best men; these rose to power through the customary ladder of offices (though they might serve as tribunes of the plebs) and through the Senate rather than through appeals to the people by means of popular laws or programs. It is important to bear in mind that the populares and the optimates were not really political parties in the modern sense, with chosen leaders and programs. Attitudes and means separated the two amorphous groups.

The Agrarian commission set up by Tiberius' law was permitted by the Senate to continue its operations after Tiberius' murder, with Tiberius' brother Gaius a member, as he had been from the beginning, along with Tiberius' father-in-law, Appius Claudius. Licinius Crassus, Gaius' father-in-law, was appointed to replace Tiberius. The commission distributed land to at most a few thousand persons, but the urban problems eased with the end of the slave war in Sicily in 132 B.C., when presumably the grain supply returned to normal. General economic conditions, however, remained poor.

Gaius Gracchus: A Shift in Emphasis

Ten years younger than his brother, Gaius Gracchus was identified with Tiberius' program from the beginning. Only with hesitation, however, and under popular pressure did Gaius resume his brother's program. He did so, as tribune of the plebs in 123 and 122 B.C., more deliberately than Tiberius, more aware of the implications of his actions. He used no such unprecedented means as Tiberius' recall election or his challenge to senatorial authority over money and the provinces. Yet he too helped to form the mold of the "popular" politician.

Gaius shifted his attention to the lower-class city plebs. He tried to insure an adequate grain supply for them. By law he set an artificial price—below the inflated market price—for state-owned grain, but stores were inadequate and it became necessary to purchase other grain at high cost to sell at the low price. The treasury suffered and Gracchus tried to find new sources of funds. In a small way, perhaps, he continued Tiberius' land distribution. He obtained some fringe benefits for soldiers, and forbade conscription of underage youths. A colonization program—one was planned even for the site of ancient Carthage—provided large allotments of land for a somewhat higher level of the populace. Probably he hoped the beneficiaries would transport poor citizens and set them up as tenants. He attempted to detach the middle-class equestrians from the oligarchs who were his opponents, as they had been Tiberius', by giving the equestrians control of the juries for the Extortion Court, in which provincials might attempt to recover damages from unscrupulous governors—who were, of course, members of the oligarchy. Previously this court had been staffed by senators. By now, possibly other permanent courts had been established and were involved also.

In his second year, Gracchus, following the lead of a colleague, M. Fulvius Flaccus, proposed citizenship for Latins and Latin rights for Italians. The two tribunes were opposed by some of the more liberal senators, including the consul, G. Fannius, and another tribune of the plebs, M. Livius Drusus. Their counterprogram and skillful attacks on the citizenship bill, especially effective while Gaius was out of the city establishing the colony at Carthage, led to the defeat of the latter for reelection.

Early the next year (121 B.C.), Gracchus and Flaccus as private citizens tried to keep their laws from being scuttled by their opponents. A minor official was killed in a scuffle by one of Gracchus' men. In the ensuing disorder, Gracchus and Flaccus found themselves in danger of death by attainder; the Senate seems to have decreed it. They took refuge, with armed men, in a temple on the Aventine, from which they soon were driven to suffer the same fate which had overtaken Tiberius Gracchus and his followers.

The decree of the Senate under which the consul of 121 B.C., Opimius, took armed action against Gracchus and Flaccus became known as the Final Decree (*senatus consultum ultimum*). The question of the legality of such a decree—used several times in the last century of the Republic—was a hotly debated issue between the populares and the optimates in succeeding decades. In fact, almost all of the major questions of the day—wars, laws, any agitated issue—tended to develop partisan squabbling after the Gracchi.

The economic problems that the Gracchi tried to solve eased somewhat after the two brothers were gone. They would recur, however, and the social ills so acute in the ever-growing metropolis would intensify over the years. Efforts to help the urban poor invariably became entangled in politics, and mitigation of their lot—without a real solution of the underlying problems—came only with the Empire. The Gracchan programs did not either notably improve the conditions of the small farmers or substantially increase their numbers. As we shall soon see, the serious shortage of army recruits was overcome by drastically changing the army itself. Colonization programs beginning in the later Republic and continuing on into the Empire helped to maintain a small-farmer class as the backbone of the army, the state, and society. But the old order of things could never be completely restored.

The Jugurthan War (111–105 B.C.) and Marius

Since the days of Masinissa, who helped the elder Scipio defeat Hannibal at Zama, the kingdom of Numidia just to the west of the Roman province of Africa had been an ally and friend of the

Roman people, with members of the Scipio family as patrons at Rome. Jugurtha was a grandson of Masinissa and one of three sons of King Micipsa (148–118 B.C.). When Micipsa died his kingdom was divided up among his three sons, who soon were fighting over the pieces. Jugurtha defeated and killed his rivals. In the process, however, he offended some Romans and killed some Italian traders, allies of Rome from of old.

How did the question of what to do about Jugurtha become a partisan one? Two ways. First, those senators who investigated charges against Jugurtha and let him off easy were accused of having accepted bribes, as were those optimate leaders who then conducted a "war" against Jugurtha and granted him an easy peace. Second, the Roman general who finally defeated Jugurtha in the difficult guerrilla war that eventuated was something of a popularis named Gaius Marius.

Marius was a New Man; that is, none of his ancestors had previously reached the consulate. He ran for that office in defiance of his patron and predecessor in command in Africa, one of the Metelli, who though of plebeian origin were dominant members of the aristocracy for several decades. Marius for the first time enlisted lower-rank plebeians in the army in substantial numbers; these were men without the minimum property qualification. He saw that they obtained spoils in war and land distributions after their discharge. Several times he found himself in conflict with prominent optimates. Yet it is necessary to say that he was "something of a popularis" because he was his own man, no strict adherent to any partisan views, and because he was chiefly a military man and not much the politician of any stripe.

In Numidia, Marius completed the campaign that Metellus had underway and came home a popular hero with Jugurtha as his captive. He was just in time to save Rome from another peril, one of the long series of Gallic—Celtic—invasions.

The War Against the Celts (109–101 B.C.)

The Celts invaded Italy about once a century, though only two or three of the invasions seem important enough to get into the textbooks. A horde consisting of several tribes, chiefly the Cimbri and the Teutoni, moved toward Italy as early as 113 B.C. and defeated a Roman army in the passes of the Alps northeast of Italy. But then they migrated on westward instead of coming over into Cisalpine Gaul (the Po valley). In 109 another Roman army met them in Transalpine Gaul—eastern France— and again the Northmen won without following up their victory. The story was repeated once more in 107.

In 106, a consul, Q. Servilius Caepio, distinctly an optimate (for example, he attempted to restore the permanent court juries to the Senate) won a victory over some allies of the Gauls and captured some treasure. But then the treasure disappeared on its way to Rome. The following year, at Arausio (southeastern France) Caepio, now proconsul, by his failure to cooperate with the consul Cn. Mallius, a New Man, contributed to a horrible debacle in which Rome lost a reported 80,000 dead. Again Italy was saved only by the Celts' decision to turn away. They entered Spain, where they suffered heavily. Caepio seemed, to popular politicians, to embody all that was worst about the aristocracy: greed, incompetence, arrogance. Thus another war became a partisan question. Caepio eventually was prosecuted by a popular tribune and condemned to exile; all his property was confiscated. Marius was given charge of this war also, with a second consulship, in 104 B.C. His third, fourth, fifth, and sixth consulships were held in successive years until the crisis was over, in 100 B.C. The major battles in which Marius annihilated the Northmen came in 102 B.C. at Aquae Sextiae, in southeast France, and in 101 at Vercellae, in northern Italy.

Marius' most significant political action was not his standing for an unprecedented string of consulships; moreover, it was an action probably taken out of necessity without political intent at all: it was his recruitment in large numbers of propertyless citizens for his legions. This became the standard pattern for the future. Probably the recruits were as a rule drawn from the rural areas more than from the streets of Rome, but whatever their origin, they had few ties and became willing clients of their general, if only he led them well, and secured them spoils and bonuses of money and land upon discharge. Important military commands thereafter were sought by ambitious Roman politicians as the quickest and best means of acquiring the kind of power that counted.

Marius' former patron Metellus and the other optimates saw in this upstart a threat to their ascendancy in the state similar to the Gracchi. One thing that reinforced this view was Marius' alliance with the popular tribune of the plebs, L. Appuleius Saturninus. The latter, as tribune in 103 and again in 100 B.C., helped Marius obtain land for his discharged veterans, in return for the general's support. Saturninus cleverly procured the exile of Metellus; he also sold state grain for a tiny fraction of the price charged under the law of Gaius Gracchus (there was a grain shortage because of another slave war in Sicily, 103–101 B.C.); and in general Saturninus played a demagogic role. He also did not hesitate to use violence to influence elections and it was this that led to his downfall. In the election campaign for 100

B.C., he was a candidate for reelection, and a friend named Glaucia was standing for the consulate. Glaucia seemed to be running third in the contest for the two posts, when one of his opponents was murdered. He and Saturninus were implicated. The Senate passed the Final Decree, calling upon the consul to take action against Saturninus, Glaucia, and their followers. Ironically, that consul was Marius. He nevertheless took the pair and some others into custody, probably intending only to hold them for trial. But men who were probably agents of the optimates climbed up on the Senate House where the prisoners were being held, dropped roof tiles through the rafters, and killed them. After this Marius' political position deteriorated; he was accepted neither by the city plebs who gave the popular politicians their chief support nor by the optimates. He went into political eclipse for some years.

The Italian War (91–88 B.C.)

One rather unexpected effect of the work of popular politicians beginning with Tiberius Gracchus was to arouse Rome's Latin and Italian allies to bitter resentment because of their inferior status as compared to Roman citizens. The Agrarian Law of Tiberius Gracchus, it seems, benefited only citizens, and among the parcels of land distributed were large numbers held in precarious tenure by Italians. That is, this land really belonged to the Roman state by earlier confiscation. Gaius Gracchus' Grain Law aided only Romans. Colonizing schemes like those of Saturninus for Marius' veterans also seem to have been limited. In such measures, even the lowest classes of Roman citizens gained something from empire, while the Italians who had helped the Romans in their conquests got little.

The resentment, though brought out into the open only after 133 B.C., had been building for a long time. Treaties between Rome and her allies had originally been agreements between states ostensibly equals. Rome's rise in power—with the indispensable help of these allies—had upset that balance. Rome had become the hub of the world; Roman officials controlled the Mediterranean, flaunting their prestige and power. Italians remained in the background, though of course some managed to benefit in the successful wars, and some procured Roman citizenship. Even in Italy itself, beginning perhaps with the Bacchanalian Decree of 186 B.C., Romans increasingly treated Italians as provincial subjects, not allies. Doubtless most Romans treated Italians well, as civilians and as soldiers. But even occasional mistreatment breeds cankers of ill will.

The popular politicians, long before the conservative optimates, were willing to give a deserved citizenship to Latins and Italians. Fulvius Flaccus as consul in 125 B.C. and with Gaius Gracchus, tribunes together in 122 B.C., tried to pass a citizenship law. But optimates opposed such measures, fearing that they might lose control of the elections. Whoever carried a law to give citizenship to hundreds of thousands of Latins and Italians, in effect becoming their patron, would acquire enormous power.

If Roman leaders of the 1st century B.C. had shown the aptitude for compromise of their ancestors, they would have extended the citizenship and allowed new leaders to participate in the government. But the oligarchs were unwilling to permit even respected Roman equestrians to enter their circle as New Men in any numbers, let alone Latins and Italians. They continued to oppose any citizenship measure.

In the past, individual Latins and Italians had been able to attain the citizenship in several ways. Latins whose ancestors had once been citizens—expatriates who had emigrated to autonomous colonial communities—could simply move to Roman territory and register in the next census. Latins and Italians who had held important magistracies in their home states could do the same. Certain laws, such as one devised by Gaius Gracchus, which provided for prosecution of Roman magistrates guilty of misconduct, gave citizenship as a reward for conviction to Latins and Italians who brought charges. However, the rights of Latins and Italians to acquire Roman citizenship had been drastically restricted during the second century B.C., chiefly because the Italian states themselves requested restriction, complaining of depopulation and the exigencies of the military draft. Early in the first century B.C., it appears, lenient Roman censors allowed rather large numbers of Italians and Latins to come to Rome and enrol themselves as citizens. In 95 B.C. the consuls, by decree of the Senate, set up a *quaestio* (court) that expelled from the rolls all such questionable citizens. Indignant Italians began to form a conspiracy against Rome.

The Efforts of M. Livius Drusus, Jr., Tribune of the Plebs in 91 B.C.

The next major effort to obtain the citizenship for Rome's allies was the work of one of the optimates, not a popularis. M. Livius Drusus was the son of the man of the same name who was an opponent of Gaius Gracchus; the father had nevertheless proposed important benefits for Italians which, it seems, were never put into effect. And he had important Italian connections. The younger Drusus retained these relationships; he was guest-friend to one of the most important leaders in the Italian conspiracy, Pompaedius Silo. The Italians seem to have decided to give the Romans one last chance; they waited to see whether they would pass Drusus' citizenship bill.

Drusus put forward a series of measures. He wished to bring more equestrians into the Senate and to restore the courts to the control of this expanded Senate. A notorious case in the Extortion Court had brought an unjust conviction by an equestrian jury of a man named Rutilius Rufus (the uncle of Drusus), whose only sin had been to attempt, as assistant to the governor of the province of Asia, to control the agents of the publicans—equestrians just like his jurors. To garner general support for his program, Drusus proposed grain distributions at low prices and a colonial scheme as well. A majority of the Senate seems initially to have backed him, even in the scheme to enlarge that body by the inclusion of three hundred equestrians. But when Drusus went on to propose citizenship for Italians and Latins, many of his backers turned on him, suspicious of his motives and fearful that the new citizens would all be his clients. Drusus was assassinated, and the laws he had already passed were voided. The murder was quickly followed by the Italian revolt. It is often called the Social War, since the Latin term for ally is *socius*.

The Italians now set up their state, called Italia, complete with magistrates and army. In some Italian towns Roman citizens were slaughtered. Hastily recruited Roman armies more often than not lost to the similarly trained Italians in the early months of the war. Romans now passed statesmanlike laws that would have prevented the war if they had been enacted earlier. The Latins had not joined the conspiracy, nor had all Italians. Legislative action enfranchised these people, who then no longer had any reason to join the revolt. Next, a law was passed to permit even those fighting against Rome to become citizens provided they lay down their arms and appear within a prescribed period before Roman officials for registration. The conspirators, now hopelessly outnumbered, fought on; the Samnites, among the most bitter opponents of Rome, held out longer than the rest. The Romans at length beat down the last recalcitrants, but eventually gave them the citizenship also.

The assimilation of the new voters brought out partisan politics in Rome. The optimates tried to relegate the Italians into new tribes that would always vote last. Popular politicians, on the other hand, championed complete equality for the new citizens, advocating dispersion of their vote throughout all the existing tribes. After a period complicated by foreign and civil wars, the drive for equality at last succeeded.

Three *denarii* of the late Republic. Top, a boar, symbol of Hercules, on a coin perhaps issued for the Plebeian games; left, soldiers taking the military oath; this type was used by the Italians to memorialize their conspiratorial oath in 91–90 B.C. Right, the goddess Victory in two-horse chariot; coin of an ancestor of the emperor Tiberius.

The new voters were not acutely interested in elections at Rome; the optimates need not have worried. They did not appear in large numbers to register with the censors, and it is possible that they were impeded in some way. The Italians therefore did not immediately begin to play an important role in the affairs of the city of Rome and its empire. Their soldiers served now in the legions and no longer in separate units. Apparently, like the older Roman citizens, they no longer had to pay the war tax to support their troops. Only in the time of Caesar do the names of men who were Italians before 88 B.C. begin to appear in the lists as magistrates of some importance. Following Caesar's footsteps, Augustus made much more use of the former Italians—or of their sons or grandsons, for by then Italians had been citizens for more than half a century.

The Mithridatic War (88–82 B.C.)

Though the First Mithridatic War involved some hard fighting it is perhaps most significant in collateral ways: it provided the spark that finally brought civil war in Rome; and it showed the essential failure of Roman imperial governance in the eastern Mediterranean. Mithridates VI (120–63 B.C.) was King of Pontus on the south shore of the Black Sea. His territory was separated by two buffer states, Bithynia and Cappadocia, from Roman Asia and Cilicia, on the western and southern coasts of Asia Minor; the latter had become a province after a campaign against pirates based there, about 101 B.C. The kings of Bithynia and Cappadocia increasingly looked to Rome for protection against the ambitions of Mithridates, and Rome had recently forced him to evacuate parts of those kingdoms which he had occupied. The Italian war seemed to provide Mithridates a golden opportunity to even the score with Rome. He invaded Bithynia and Cappadocia and overran the inadequately defended Roman provinces as well. Everywhere in the Roman provinces he was hailed as a liberator. Roman officials were captured and disgraced. Romans, on the signal of the king, were killed: eighty thousand, it was said, in a single day. Probably there were not that many liquidated, and most of them were probably Italians. But the native feeling against Rome became painfully apparent. Greeks too saw the Romans as oppressors. Athens went over to Mithridates; her port, the Piraeus, became his chief naval base in the Aegean.

The news of the Mithridatic inroads partially explains the Roman willingness to compromise and end the Italian War. But the new war brought civil war in its wake. The Senate assigned one of the consuls of 88 B.C. to the war against Mithridates. This man was L. Cornelius Sulla. He already had an army of six legions with which he had been fighting the Samnites in late stages of the Italian War. He had served as governor of Cilicia and in that capacity had dealt with Mithridates. Earlier he had served with Marius, not altogether amicably, in the Jugurthan War. He had demonstrated his capacity in every way. And as an optimate he was a logical choice for the Senate to make.

But a tribune of the plebs had other ideas. This was P. Sulpicius Rufus, who though young was one of the leading orators of the day. No real popularis, he had prosecuted one such man earlier, and had supported the younger Drusus in 91. Perhaps the downfall of the latter had blighted his own career, or perhaps he was too liberal for the optimates. As tribune he led the attempt to give the new Italian voters justice by an equal distribution in all the existing voting tribes. The optimates who had obstructed Drusus now forcefully opposed him. Sulpicius struck a bargain with Marius. He proposed a law to give that general the command against Mithridates. No situation better illustrates the dichotomy in the Roman constitution. It was legal and usual for the Senate to name commanders, and especially one of the consuls, to take charge of a war. But it was also legal for an assembly to name such a commander by law. Technically one might say that the law should have superseded the Senate decree, for it was an established principle of the constitution that the people in assembly were sovereign. Sulpicius' supporters, however, resorted to violence. In a mêlée, the son of one of the consuls—who was also the son-in-law of the other consul, Sulla—was killed. It was argued that no law carried by violence was valid, and thus there was no clear constitutional right or wrong in the matter.

Sulla decided to settle the issue by military action. He went to his soldiers, told them his version of the circumstances, and led them on Rome, the first time a Roman general had ever invaded the city. He convoked the Senate, or at least those senators who supported him, and got several of his opponents declared outlaws, including Sulpicius, G. Marius, and his son of the same name. Sulpicius was killed, sacrosanct tribune or not, along with some others; the two Marii fled for their lives to Africa. Sulla conducted the elections; he required the two new consuls to take an oath to uphold his several measures. Then he led his army to the East to confront Mithridates.

Continued Civil Conflict

Sulla and his army were not long away from Rome before civil violence again broke out. One of the new consuls, L. Cornelius Cinna, on taking office in 87 B.C. attempted to rescind some of the legislation that Sulla had passed through threat of violence. Cinna, a patrician, like the late tribune Sulpicius, was a moderate; but the right-wing optimates had a way of making popular radicals out of aristocratic moderates. They drove Cinna out of the city and declared him deposed. He raised troops, recalled Marius from his African exile, and with him at the end of the year marched on Rome in Sullan fashion, and occupied the city. They surpassed Sulla in zealous vengefulness and slaughter of opponents. Marius, now old and embittered, probably was chiefly responsible for this. The two were now elected consuls for the year 86; Marius, designated to raise an army and replace Sulla in his command, died on January 13, in his seventh consulship, before he could organize for the expedition.

Cinna and the other magistrates attacked the numerous problems besetting Rome and Italy. The Italians were given voting rights on an equality with the older citizens. Economic matters especially demanded attention. The Italian War, the civil conflict, and the demands of the Mithridatic War caused much economic distress, and not just for the lower classes, rural and urban, who must indeed have suffered enough.

Civil war was always disastrous for upper-class debtors. Their loans were ordinarily secured with urban property or other land, and civil disturbances meant that crops and rentals might suddenly fail. Thus, the onset of civil war invariably brought a collapse of property values, which in turn meant that when loans fell due or were called in debtors could not meet their obligations. Creditors would not accept land at the valuation which was the basis for the loan. The effect was cumulative, and the results sometimes approximated a financial panic. In 86 B.C. the consuls therefore passed legislation to permit debtors to pay off their obligations at 25 percent of face value. The figure probably reflects the extent to which property values had fallen. It is not likely that creditors really suffered very much, for they would usually be paid by taking over mortgaged land, which would soon recover its value. Even if a debtor managed to get hold of coin or bullion to pay off the debt, the creditor could use it to purchase land, which would appreciate in value with the return of stability. In these years the economic situation at Rome was complicated by the appearance of a great deal of bad money, presumably forged. Means were soon developed to detect the forgeries. Stopgap measures such as these could alleviate the problems, but only a period of stability could restore economic well-being.

In the Marian manner Cinna held repeated consulships. For himself and his colleagues the most worrisome problem was, naturally, Sulla and his army. They tried negotiation and they sent a new commander with an army to replace Sulla. But neither tactic worked, and there remained only one other: to prepare as best they could for the inevitable resumption of civil war.

Sulla meanwhile methodically attacked Mithridates' bases of power. Since, as we have seen, the king had established a military presence in Greece, Sulla felt it necessary to reduce Athens and the Piraeus before attempting to cross the Aegean with his army. For Mithridates, on the other hand, it was imperative to defeat Sulla in Greece. He therefore sent armies which descended on Sulla from northern Greece. They did not arrive in time to prevent the fall of Athens, however, and Sulla, though outnumbered, defeated the two armies before the end of 86 B.C. At this point the army sent by Cinna arrived, under the command of L. Valerius Flaccus. The latter probably intended to take over Sulla's command, but this could be done only through a fight; there was none. Possibly Flaccus' men did not wish to fight Sulla's battle-tested veterans. The two men seem to have come to no accommodation, yet the armies cooperated loosely, both attacking Mithridates. Flaccus, in fact, got across the Aegean first, but in Asia Minor his legate, Gaius Fimbria, killed him and took over his army. Sulla waited for a naval victory and then invaded Asia Minor also. At the end of 85 B.C. Sulla gave Mithridates a negotiated peace on the basis of the prewar territorial arrangement, the loss of some ships, and an

This *denarius* of Gaius Marius (not *the* Gaius Marius), serrated on the edges to indicate purity, may have been issued in connection with a colonization program. On the left is Ceres, goddess of grain; right, a peasant plowing, perhaps marking out the sacred boundary of the colony.

indemnity. Then followed a confrontation with Fimbria's army; but Fimbria's troops went over to Sulla and Fimbria committed suicide. Sulla had to spend a year pacifying tribesmen in Thrace, collecting a huge sum of money—he claimed five years' back taxes at once from the unfortunate provincial natives—and arranging various settlements before he was ready to return to Italy for a third round of the civil war.

The Sullan Settlement

After a period of illness and unfruitful negotiation with the Roman Senate at long range, Sulla returned early in 83 B.C., not as a triumphant general but as a vengeful invader. At Rome popular leaders including the son of Marius made preparations to fight. Cinna had been killed the previous year by his own troops, when he attempted to lead them east. Sulla had the aid of many Romans of high standing, including the young Marcus Crassus and Gnaeus Pompeius, both of whom raised troops for him. Sulla won most of the battles and won over some troops without battle. He attempted to neutralize the former Italians, who were mostly in support of the other side, by guaranteeing optimate acceptance of their new position of equality. Yet, thousands of Samnites fought on against him, notably at the battle outside the Colline gate at Rome (82 B.C.). After this hard-fought victory Sulla killed or captured most of his enemies. Among the captives were about 6,000 Samnites, whom he summarily slaughtered.

Sulla called together the Senate and had himself named Dictator for the Reconstitution of the Republic, a new sort of dictatorship, not limited to six months' duration as in the past. While he was reconstituting the state he was also getting rid of his foes. He put up proscription lists—"enemies of the state" who were to be killed on sight and their estates confiscated. Over a period of time Sulla added names to the lists: nervous men among the upper classes could not be sure that the omission of their names from one list meant they were secure. It has been estimated that Sulla killed about 10,000 persons, including the Samnites mentioned earlier.

To eliminate the dual nature of the constitution was Sulla's prime political objective. He therefore struck down the power of tribunes of the plebs to call assemblies and pass laws independent of the Senate. Bills had to be approved by the Senate, and then went to the Centuriate Assembly. Men who held the tribunate could not go on to higher office. The Senate was enlarged by the addition of three hundred men from the equestrian class, no doubt mostly chosen from the rural aristocracy. The permanent courts were again to be staffed by this body. The office of censor was abolished. The number of praetors was raised to eight and the number of quaestors to twenty. The latter now, in the absence of the censors, automatically were enrolled in the Senate. Sulla passed a Lex Annalis which not only, like earlier laws of this type, set the ages at which one might legally hold the higher offices, but also prevented repeated consulships, by providing that ten years must elapse before a man could hold an office the second time.

Sulla laid down the dictatorship in 80 B.C., retaining the consulate, however. In 79 he retired; by the following year he was dead of a wasting disease. The new order soon was in large part scuttled; men followed Sulla's example more than his Lex Annalis, and the core optimates remained close-minded and narrow. A consul of 78 B.C., M. Aemilius Lepidus, precipitated a brief civil war when he was refused permission to run for reelection because this was forbidden by Sulla's Lex Annalis. He was defeated and slain. But tribunes regained part of their power in 75 B.C. and the rest of it in 70 B.C., when two of Sulla's erstwhile supporters, Crassus and Pompey, were consuls. Pompey defied the Lex Annalis in the election, for he was underage and had not held the required earlier offices. Why was this permitted? As it happened, both he and Crassus had armies near Rome. But we must look at some other events of this decade.

The 70s were bad years in Rome. The events at the end of

the previous decade, civil war, proscriptions, and confiscations with economic dislocation, were compounded by new wars: in Spain Sertorius, a Marian, held out still and with consummate skill; in Italy itself the gladiator Spartacus led a slave revolt; and in Asia Minor Mithridates tried yet again to overthrow Roman power in the East. After others failed to pacify Spain, Pompey took an army there and eventually, after Sertorius was killed by his own lieutenant, was able to gain control. The revolt of Spartacus (73–71 B.C.) was put down, finally, by Crassus; he (probably) killed Spartacus. The honors, however, he had to share with Pompey; the latter was returning from Spain with his army just as some of the survivors of the slave revolt attempted to flee north out of Italy. It was at this point that Pompey and Crassus approached Rome with their armies, asked permission to run for the consulate, and were allowed to do so. As for the (third) war with Mithridates, it was put into the hands of the consul of 74 B.C., a man named Lucullus, who had served as Sulla's legate in the first war. He had, at first, brilliant success, driving Mithridates out of Roman territory and then out of his own kingdom, even pursuing him into Armenia, whose king was Mithridates' son-in-law and ally. But Lucullus was unable to end the war, as we shall see.

Roman Government After Sulla

Once the more restrictive features of Sulla's constitution had been scrapped in 70 B.C., Romans might have expected that there would be some liberalization of the optimate-dominated government. There were, moreover, three hundred or so new senators, though the censors (the office was revived after the year 70) threw out sixty-four of these. Many of them must have come from families new to politics. There were hundreds of thousands of new citizens. Surely one might have expected some impact from the enlarged Senate or from the registration of these new citizens. Yet nothing at all changed: the political machinery, especially the elections, continued to be dominated by a remarkably small number of the optimate families. The reasons were inertia, entrenched position, and long experience. But there appears also to have been an increase in bribery in the elections; evidently the core oligarchs were determined to hold the line whatever the cost. Their opponents, the popular politicians, were not a charismatic lot. Pompey did not really wish to play the role; Crassus was perhaps too involved in his business affairs; other men had neither the necessary following nor the means to get it.

The work of a single tribune, little heralded, is worth

taking note of as pointing up the deficiencies within the optimate circle. This tribune of the plebs (67 B.C.) was C. Cornelius. He was no demagogic radical, it appears, but genuinely concerned with the evils that he attempted to exorcise. He tried to get the Senate to pass a law on bribery; eventually it did, but much watered down. He tried to pass laws restricting the lending of money by private citizens to foreign states—the source of much profit for rich Romans, but also great injustice, since the Romans were in so dominant a position. He tried to pass legislation forbidding the Senate from granting exceptions to the laws—a power it had arrogated to itself over a period of time. This was vetoed by a tribune with optimate sympathies. Cornelius eventually did obtain passage of a law requiring a quorum of at least two hundred men in the Senate for such action. Yet we know that this body continued casually to grant exceptions to the laws in the interest of powerful persons such as private moneylenders. When governor of Cilicia in 51 B.C., Cicero learned, for example, of several decrees permitting an illegal loan by Marcus Brutus to the city of Salamis on Cyprus, passed when Cicero had been in ordinary attendance at the Senate but of which he was nevertheless unaware. Maltreatment of provincials by Romans seems to have been on the increase. This is indicated, among other ways, by Cornelius' bills on moneylending. But Roman officials also sometimes mulcted their provinces. Cornelius applied one corrective: a law requiring provincial governors to adhere to their own laws as published in their edicts.

One of Cicero's successful prosecutions, in 70 B.C., helped him to rise rapidly to prominence as the first orator of Rome. He exposed a rapacious governor of Sicily named Verres, who went into exile to escape sentence. Cicero's Verrine orations, like some of his others, were not delivered as published, but we may nevertheless learn much from them about provincial governance. A vicious cycle had developed. To obtain high office cost a fortune; this could be recouped by a lucrative governorship. But to recoup was not enough; one also needed a gainful return for oneself. How one got it might lead one to have to bribe jurors, or at least to "hire" the best orator in town, for one might always be subjected to prosecution for extortion on returning to Rome. It was illegal for an advocate like Cicero or Hortensius to take fees but one had to pay off somehow. This was done most often by inclusion of the orators in clients' wills; meanwhile, a "loan" might be made to the orators.

In summary, the Roman ruling class was as determined as ever to remain an exclusive group, but found it ever more difficult. The struggle occupied all their efforts. They had little time and scant inclination to work out the major problems of the

Empire, to strive honestly for just government for all provincials. The provincials had no votes, no power; the Roman lower classes did, but exercised little influence on the civil war when it came. The war was, in fact, little more than a struggle among Roman upper classes for control of the Empire. Quite incidentally the end results would be ultimately beneficial for the provincials and for some Romans (and Italians, now citizens), who were at last beneficiaries of an expansion of the official oligarchy; but the enlarged oligarchy was dominated by the winner of the struggle.

Pompey's Extraordinary Commands

The Roman destruction of Carthage, the important naval power in the western Mediterranean, and the decline of Rhodes (as the result of Roman policy), the chief naval power of the East, led to a sharp increase in piracy. This uncontrolled piracy was only one instance of the failure of Rome to bear her imperial responsibilities. The fact was eventually brought home to Italy itself: cities along the coasts suffered from pirate raids; some of them in this period had to rebuild old walls. In 71 B.C. pirates bargained with Spartacus to transport his army to Thrace; they double-crossed him, but the pirate menace was now clear. When piracy threatened the food supply even of Rome itself, Romans demanded action. By law—opposed by the core oligarchs—Pompey was in 67 B.C. given an extraordinary, three-year command against the pirates, with an overwhelming force of both ships and men, and command over the whole Mediterranean littoral. The fact that his command overlapped that of other provincial governors and even, in theory, might involve sovereign states was deemed of no consequence. In well-organized action Pompey cleared the seas of pirates in just ninety days. It took somewhat longer to reduce pirate bases in Cilicia and elsewhere. Some of his troops sent to Crete clashed with those of the governor, a Metellus, and for a time it appeared that the overlapping commands might produce a debacle on that island. But Pompey let it go, for he was given a still greater responsibility. As for grain prices at Rome, they fell dramatically even before Pompey moved into action. Obviously speculators had held prices artificially high.

Pompey's new command, also given him by a tribunician law, the Lex Manilia of 66 B.C., was against Mithridates. He replaced Lucullus, whose position had been gradually undermined in the preceding years. Lucullus' story is worth noting. He had found the Roman province of Asia still suffering heavily from the economic burdens imposed by Sulla; the native towns had borrowed money from Romans (who else had capital?) to pay off the indemnity, and since interest rates were excessive, many still owed more than they had borrowed despite regular payments. Lucullus arbitrarily credited payments of interest against the principal and otherwise tried to help the provincials, an instance of one of the optimates actually demonstrating a concern for Roman subjects. But in this way Lucullus created powerful enemies among the equestrian publicans at Rome and this was one important reason for his displacement. However, Lucullus had had other problems: many of his troops were men who had been brought into Asia Minor by Flaccus in the time of Sulla; they had served longer than was required by law, and now mutinied. The men also complained of Lucullus' severe discipline, and claimed that he himself kept a disproportionate share of the spoils. Certainly he somehow became enormously rich.

Pompey brought fresh troops to his new task. Mithridates was already a beaten monarch; it was not long before he was driven completely out of Asia, to his dominions on the north shores of the Black Sea. There he was killed by his son Pharnaces, who thereafter was confirmed in this remnant of his father's kingdom by Pompey. The Roman general completely reorganized the provinces in Asia, overturning all of Lucullus' arrangements; and he reestablished relations with the various "client" kingdoms. He also, quite illegally, took over the area of Syria-Palestine to the south. The old Seleucid kingdom centered in Syria was in tatters; various native aspirants to power were struggling for control. Into this power vacuum Pompey moved without a struggle. In Palestine, where two brothers were fighting for the high priesthood and political control, the Romans had to besiege Jerusalem to persuade the natives to accept Pompey's decision as to which of the two men should rule. Thus the Jewish state also became a species of client or puppet state of Rome. The governor of Syria would in the future keep an eye on Palestine.

Cicero's Concordia: Last Chance for the Republic

While Lucullus' career was on the decline and Pompey's approached its peak, other figures who would be important in Roman history were climbing the rungs of the *cursus honorum*. These included Cicero, Caesar, and the younger Cato. Cicero was the same age as Pompey, but the latter was the son of a rich consul; Cicero's father, though not without aristocratic friends at Rome, had never run for office in the city, and was only moderately well-to-do. Cicero was thus a New Man. It was not easy for him to attain the highest offices. He rose because intense, hard work made him the best orator in Rome. He courted the populace on occasion, but he also made political allies of influential nobles, primarily by defending them in politically motivated trials. He reached the consulship in 63 B.C. at the earliest possible age. Many who supported him genuinely felt him to be a high-level statesman; others were obligated to him because of his services or supported him because they did not like the alternatives.

Cicero was no revolutionary; he wanted to reestablish the ideal, traditional state. His goal he called the *concordia ordinum* (Concord of the Orders, meaning nobles and equestrians). He hoped to broaden the oligarchy by lowering its resistance to infusions of New Men like himself, from the Equestrian Order. The resulting concord he felt would be supported by all the *boni* —good citizens of all levels. He belonged to the same category of politician as the moderates who had supported the younger Drusus.

Cicero's great opportunity came in the year of his consulship, 63 B.C. He had the broad support of the Equestrian Order, and he gained that of at least a considerable segment of the inner oligarchy. Toward the end of the year he exposed a conspiracy and revolt against the state led by a dissolute patrician named Catiline; though it was finally reduced only after a military campaign in 62 B.C., he had ensured its failure before he laid down his office. Catiline's goals are not well known, but he advocated a cancellation of debts and expected this to garner massive support, both from nobles and lower classes. Neither joined him in large numbers, but Catiline's effort surely testifies to widespread economic distress. Cicero saw the suppression of the conspiracy as a great accomplishment which should finally weld together his paternalistic coalition; the fright given to the oligarchs and the rich equestrian moneylenders, he thought, had made them aware of the necessity for unity. But he was soon to be disabused.

The aristocratic Republic could endure only if there was a de-emphasis on the powerful individual politician and strict adherence to the collegiate principle. Cicero felt it was nevertheless necessary to give recognition to outstanding individuals, to frankly allow them honor and power, but within the system. Some of the oligarchs, however, had other ideas. Lucullus and Cato among others wanted to curtail powerful individuals and to retain the narrow exclusiveness which had characterized the oligarchy in recent decades. Unfortunately for the Republic, it was their view that prevailed—and they wrecked Cicero's *concordia*.

Pompey came home from his victories at sea and in the East at the end of 62 b.c. He disbanded his army and celebrated a triumph. All he expected from the Senate was the prestige owing to a state hero, plus ratification of his arrangements in the East and a land program for his veteran-clients. Many of those arrangements were political at base: he had put his adherents into important positions. Others were economic: he had in some instances loaned money, as to the kings of Cappadocia and Bithynia. The Senate, led by Cato though he was young, refused Pompey all these things. He was furious but, for the time being, powerless.

Some important equestrians too were offended by the oligarchs: a company of publicans, no doubt depending upon government estimates, had bid too much for the collection of taxes in the province of Asia; they wanted, with some justice, a renegotiation of their contract. The Senate refused while Cicero bemoaned the breakup of his *concordia*. When Caesar returned from a governorship in Spain wanting both a triumph and the consulship, the oligarchs unnecessarily offended him by refusing to allow him both. They were to learn, at this point and again ten years later, that here was a man not to be trifled with. Caesar now put together an informal coalition of himself, Crassus, and Pompey, the so-called First Triumvirate, an antioptimate coalition that spelled the end of Cicero's hopes and those of the Republic as well. The triumvirate was made possible by the Senate's obstruction; its specific intent was to get for each of the three what the oligarchs had denied them.

Unsolved Social and Economic Problems

The fall of the Roman Republic was of course precipitated by the failure of the traditional oligarchy. The impression is often given by historians that the main lapse of the entrenched oligarchs was a failure to alter the machinery of a city-state so as to control an empire, which is what Rome had become. There is some truth in that view. However, the primary and most basic failure involved problems affecting Romans and Italians more than provincials. Moreover, many of these unsolved problems were social and economic and were political only in a secondary sense. Each such problem not solved by the oligarchs did indeed offer opportunity to "popular" politicians in the mode of the Gracchi: and these *populares*, even though usually aristocrats themselves, often were men willing to discard traditional procedures and patterns —that is, the constitution—to achieve their public and personal goals.

A few examples will underline the point. The disastrous decline of small farmers with concomitant rural distress brought no effective action from the oligarchy; but the Gracchi and their followers sought to alleviate the situation. Only Gaius Gracchus and others like him tried to do anything for the city's underemployed and often impoverished masses. The problems of a shrinking pool of potential draftees, with unhappy consequences both for the peasant-soldiers and for the quality of the Roman armies, were solved not by the oligarchs but by Marius. His solution, all unintended, did much to weaken the old order. The injustice of continuing to deny the full equality of Roman citizenship to the Italians persisted until the oligarchs were forced by rebellion to allow the change. After the citizenship was granted, only the populares among the ruling class supported legislation to spread the voting of the new citizens equitably among all the thirty-five tribes, as eventually was

FAILURE OF THE OLIGARCHY; THE RISE OF CAESAR

done. Moreover, the former Italians seem to have been discriminated against by the oligarchs even after that. In consequence, these new citizens tended to mistrust the traditionalists and to support the popular types of politicians.

The oligarchs clung to the old paternalistic, political–social pattern in which most of the rural lower classes were clients of a powerful (and surely oligarchical) patron. But society had changed. In effect, there was no longer any meaningful place in society and the state for perhaps half the population, the propertyless who were unattached to the traditional, obsolete patron–client system. After Marius' army reforms, many of the unpropertied plebeians found a place, and one of potential great influence, in the large emergency armies of the last decades of the Republic, as clients of their generals. Their votes often supported those generals who in some ways, at least, looked out for their interests.

At last the only question was how stoutly the traditionalists would or could resist those hero-generals who were also popular politicians ushering in a new order. The large number of emergency armies required in the late Republic strengthened the generals and weakened the ability of the oligarchs to resist. Yet resist they did. Under the leadership of men such as the younger Cato, they made a strong effort to control the generals and to shore up the deteriorating machinery of the state—but the oligarchs succeeded only in precipitating the wars that brought final political collapse.

One need not doubt the sincerity of the younger Cato and his political friends in their efforts to free the state from the domination of successive, powerful military figures. They wanted to restore the old collegiate principle under which aristocrats, all loyal to the group (as they saw it, loyal to the state) held the higher offices in turn. They believed that before Sulla, Marius, and the Gracchi there had been a time when individuals, even the most competent and powerful, were one and all subordinated to the state (group). But had such an age ever actually existed? The answer is a qualified yes, but long ago, in the days before Rome became an empire.

The efforts of the traditionalists peaked in the late 60s B.C. just as the younger Cato's career was getting under way. Cato and his group, as we have seen, tried to curb Pompey, Caesar, and some important equestrian tax farmers all at one time. The results they did not foresee: the creation by Caesar of an integrated opposition. The ease with which Caesar and his friends controlled the elections and garnered popular support illustrates another fact to which the oligarchs were oblivious: they had almost entirely lost touch with the people.

Caesar's Early Career

From the beginning Caesar was a popularis. A salient fact that he capitalized upon was that Marius was his uncle. While still a teen-ager he married Cornelia, the daughter of Cinna, a major opponent of Sulla. When Sulla, on his return from the East in 83 B.C and now become dictator, demanded that Caesar divorce Cornelia, the young man brashly refused. Perhaps only his youth saved him from the proscription lists. Sulla did deprive him of a priesthood to which he had been chosen and Caesar prudently decided to tour the eastern Mediterranean for a time, until Sulla's death. Caesar very early got permission of the people to move up the cursus at a younger age than allowed by Sulla's law. As aedile in 65 B.C., he borrowed heavily to put on lavish games and flamboyantly restored the banished trophies of his uncle Marius.

Meanwhile Caesar used his considerable skills as an orator to publicize his political set. For example he instigated a prosecution in 63 B.C. that was really a public attack on the Final Decree. The suit was based on the alleged participation of the accused man in the affair of Saturninus thirty-seven years before! He got himself appointed judge of the court and condemned the man. The latter appealed, however, and the consul, Cicero, undertook the defense. Nothing came of it except that Caesar built up his popular image.

Also in 63 B.C., Caesar again borrowed freely, to obtain election as pontifex maximus. The position itself was probably secondary in Caesar's mind; the contest was an indication of his growing popularity. In the same year Caesar secured election to the praetorship. At the end of the year he joined in the senatorial debate on what to do with certain prominent captives who had conspired with Catiline to overthrow the state. Caesar took a soft position, emphasizing his opposition to the Final Decree, against summary executions; let the prisoners be held until the emergency was over and then let them have fair trials. His view did not prevail—that of the younger Cato did—and Cicero as consul under the Final Decree put several conspirators to death without trial, an act he was to regret. Some Romans suspected that Caesar was himself involved with Catiline's conspiracy. Early in 62 B.C. he was actually suspended from his praetorship, but was soon reinstated. In 61, he went to Farther Spain as governor. His departure was hampered by creditors, who actually attached his baggage. He borrowed from Crassus to pay them off. In Spain, he somehow managed to profit enough from campaigns against the provincial tribesmen to recoup his financial position.

In all his public actions Caesar followed a steady course: it was to establish himself as a popular hero in the image of Marius and the Gracchi. Yet he did not at all neglect the customary methods for building a political base. He formed combinations and in every way possible put powerful men, both aristocrats and equestrians, under obligation to himself. Some of his subsequent acts as dictator suggest that in Spain even in 61–60 B.C. he was already laying a foundation for later support by the Roman citizens there. Many of the citizen associations (*conventus*) there supported him years after, in the civil war. As a reward he made them into formal colonies, which gave them preferred status. The same pattern developed in Illyria, which he also governed, later.

The So-Called "First Triumvirate"

As we have seen, Caesar returned from Spain in 60 B.C., wanting to triumph and then to stand for election to the consulate. The oligarchs, by delaying a decision on the triumph, forced him to choose between the two honors. He chose the office, but he also created the new, three-man coalition. Pompey joined with Caesar to get land for his veterans and official acceptance of his settlement in the East. Crassus (and the publicans) got a cut in the important tax contract for the province of Asia, something the Senate had refused. Thus was fashioned the informal coalition, the "first triumvirate." One Roman politician called it a three-headed monster. Cicero, who was invited to join the combination, would have none of it. Though unsympathetic with the tactics of Cato and the rest, he, like Cato, was a threat to the triumvirs.

The coalition was too strong for all its opponents. Caesar's brains, Pompey's reputation, Crassus' money, so it has been noted, added up to formidable power. Caesar naturally won election as consul for 59 B.C. and proceeded to carry out his end of the bargain. Significantly, he had to do it through friendly tribunes and the assembly, though he first tried to get action in the Senate. Ratification of Pompey's eastern arrangements left all the latter's friends secure in their posts and Pompey's loans to kings and municipalities in the area secure as well. Crassus benefited from the renegotiated tax contract. For himself Caesar wanted a lucrative post to follow upon his consulship. He chose Cisalpine Gaul and by law—not by the Senate decree—was given a five-year, extraordinary command of this territory and also Illyria. Transalpine Gaul was later added to his commands by decree of the Senate.

It was not easy for Caesar to get these laws enacted, even with tribunes as allies, and functioning through the shadow assemblies of the times, made up mostly of city plebs. The other consul, Marcus Bibulus, three of the tribunes, and of course Cato with the other core oligarchs all opposed Caesar, who used violence to override vetoes and obstruction based on claims of bad omens. Pompey did not really approve the consul's tactics but went along with him, even permitting Caesar to imply that his veterans might join in the violence. Once Caesar got his command, he immediately began to raise troops, ostensibly for use in the province, but held near Rome. It was all too much for Bibulus and the optimates. Fearing for his life—he was actually beaten once—Bibulus retired to his house and did not come out the rest of the year. Wags called it the year of the consuls Julius and Caesar.

The Conquest of Gaul, 58–50 B.C.

The acquisition of Gaul was ultimately one of Caesar's more important actions. The extension of Greco-Roman civilization into this region and beyond helped set the course for the future Roman Empire and for Western Europe. We shall not discuss the brilliant campaigns of Caesar, nor detail his frequently barbarous treatment of both soldiers and civilians among them, nor commend his rather generous and foresighted final settlement, in consequence of which the territory stayed quiet during the civil wars that followed and long afterward.

The conquest, well known to us through Caesar's own *Gallic Wars* and other sources, seems to embody all the major motives that fed Roman imperialism. There was, first of all, a threat to Roman allies and to a Roman province, Narbonensis, which Caesar called "the Province," from roving tribes, looking as usual both for plunder and a place to settle. As was often the case in Roman expansion, unsettled conditions created a sort of power vacuum just opposite territory controlled by Rome. There was the element of personal ambition—Caesar's and his staff members'.

Caesar certainly expected personal profit from Gaul; and he also expected to build up political patronage by seeing that those who served under him profited also. These expectations were more than satisfied. In fact Caesar somehow managed to bring back from Gaul enough gold alone to cause a 25 percent drop in the price of it as compared to silver. A careful reading of Caesar's *Commentaries* shows that he noted well the productivity of the land. Perhaps he thought less in terms of possible payment of tribute to Rome than of the density of population which the land could support: it could mean that a strong power might develop here next to lands dominated by Rome. Caesar always gave special attention to the richest grain-producing areas. This was partly a matter of simple military logistics, since the army needed a secure supply of grain in order to function. Yet the Roman almost instinctively felt that such economically important regions ought to be under the permanent control of the Roman state.

The question naturally arises what role Roman business-men may have played in the imperialism of the late Republic. The answer is difficult, for specific evidence is hard to come by. Though their interests seem not to have been a chief influence, there is no doubt that through tax farming and moneylending the business class had learned to exploit the provinces, especially the eastern ones. As for active trade, not very much of this was carried out by men of old Roman stock; but Italians and Italo-Greeks who gained the citizenship about 90 B.C. were great traders. Roman governors will hardly have been unaware of their interests. Caesar knew well, when he cleared some of the Alpine passes, that he was aiding Roman traders, who had been paying "tribute" to local tribal chiefs.

Even aristocrats, who were not supposed to soil themselves with such mercenary matters as trade and moneylending, never-theless did so in the provinces. M. Brutus, Shakespeare's "noblest Roman," loaned money to the city of Salamis on Cyprus. The city was suffering, along with the other municipalities on the island, from the exactions of a propraetor—Cato (Brutus' uncle) —in 58–57 B.C. Brutus loaned the money to the Salaminians at 48 percent interest. It was an illegal loan at an illegal rate of interest which required special passage of two or three special senatorial decrees permitting exceptions to the laws of the sort mentioned in Chapter 6. Brutus was discreet, of course, using agents. A few years later when payment was understandably slow, Brutus' agent got Roman troops, who collected—after starving to death six of the Salaminian Council. Except for Cicero's later governorship of Cilicia and Cyprus in 51 B.C., and report by private letter to his friend Atticus after investigation, we should know nothing of the matter. One can either suspect that such disreputable loans were quite common, or on the other hand, that this case was exceptional and not at all typical, or something in between.

Certainly Caesar must have had intimate knowledge of how valuable Cisalpine Gaul and Spain as well had become to Rome. Though he says nothing to indicate that he expected the new area to be as important as the nearby older provinces, the thought may have lurked in the back of his mind. Gaul had no deposits of precious metals such as had drawn the Phoenicians and Greeks to the Iberian peninsula centuries earlier. But Caesar would have been well aware that Spain was increasingly renowned also for horses, olive oil, wine, and other such mundane products. Emigration of Romans both to Spain and to the Province had been considerable for some years, as it had to Cisalpine Gaul even before the Hannibalic War. Such economic and demographic considerations, therefore, surely and quite naturally influenced Caesar and his fellow Romans in their movement into Gaul and other areas with great potential.

Caesar's extraordinary command was by law renewed in 55 B.C. after a revival of the triumviral coalition. His conquests in a nine-year campaign included all that today is France, with parts of Belgium, Holland, and West Germany. He made two inconclusive thrusts into Britain and probed across the Rhine. He achieved his victories through the disunity of the Gauls; this contributed to another advantage, much the better intelligence information; quick marches often brought him into a rebellious territory before the Gauls were fully mobilized, and his swift movements always kept them off balance. The superior discipline of the Roman troops—and the fighting ability of hired German cavalry and infantry—constituted another real advantage. But one cannot take away from Caesar his superior generalship. His genius was evident in organization, especially of supply; in diplomacy, including a shrewd understanding of how the masses might be made to repudiate a charismatic leader if it seemed to their advantage; in his tremendous energy and demands on the energy of his troops, not only in the forced marches but in the hard labor involved in intensive fortification and siegecraft, and in unprecedented winter campaigns; and finally, in superior tactics in battlefield situations. The campaigns were not without grim aspects: Caesar sometimes followed a deliberate policy of terror, punishing whole populations in order to make them disenchanted with particular policies and leaders; he once cut off the hands of a number of rebels as an example to others; often he permitted unnecessary killing after a battle was won. Yet on balance Caesar showed more clemency than most commanders in antiquity when faced with similar circumstances. The whole was an astonishing achievement.

The Breakdown of the So-Called Triumvirate

It is perhaps remarkable that a political coalition aligning the ambitious Caesar and the egoistic Pompey should have lasted as long as it did. In the early years Pompey and Crassus, though they reaped immediate benefits, saw Caesar accumulating wealth and a popular reputation on a long-term basis. Moreover, some of the persons who looked out for Caesar's interests in his absence irritated Pompey, to say the least. One of these was Clodius, a patrician who with the connivance of Caesar was adopted into a plebeian family and chosen tribune of the plebs for 58 B.C. In that year he got rid of two potentially troublesome politicians, Cicero and Cato. He exiled the former for putting citizens to death without trial in the conspiracy of Catiline and sent off the latter to take over the new province, Cyprus. Pompey did not like the persecution of Cicero, with whom he preferred to remain on friendly terms, and at length cooperated with those seeking his recall to end the exile (57 B.C.). Clodius seemed to delight in trying to pierce Pompey's shell of dignity or pomposity, whichever it was. Yet the marriage of Pompey and Julia, Caesar's daughter, helped to keep the two triumvirs on amicable terms; and Caesar had the good sense to patch up things in 56 B.C., by making arrangements for both Pompey and Crassus to have commands approximating his own, now extended.

The coalition soon began to break up. Crassus was killed trying to conduct a major war against the Parthians while governor of Syria (53 B.C.). Julia had died in childbirth earlier, breaking a tie between Pompey and Caesar. The traditionalists under the leadership of Cato began to make renewed efforts to win over Pompey. Some of them, at least, intended only to use Pompey to get rid of Caesar; then in his turn, Pompey would be discarded also. Pompey had command of Africa and the two Spanish provinces, but he was also given special charge of the grain supply at Rome, and therefore he could remain near the city, governing his provinces through legates.

Meanwhile Rome was degenerating into near chaos. Pompey had no authority in the city and violence prevented proper elections; organized terror was becoming a way of life. Clodius recruited a gang of toughs and ruled the political scene until a rival gang under Milo was formed to counter him. At the beginning of 52 B.C. Milo murdered Clodius and anarchy threatened the city. In this critical situation Pompey was made sole consul by the oligarchs and given authority to restore order. This he did, using the army and martial law—as was probably necessary.

Descent into Civil War

In the same year Pompey, encouraged by most of the optimates, began to move against Caesar. He had his command extended, but not Caesar's. He passed a law that no one could run for office in absentia, as Caesar wanted to do. When he was reminded that all ten tribunes had recently passed a law to permit Caesar to do just this, he replied that of course Caesar was exempt from his law; but the question of his intent remained. Another law that seemed inimical to Caesar forbade anyone who held one of the high offices from proceeding immediately to the governorship of a province. The purpose was to spread about the governorships and make the magistracies less immediately profitable. It would become more difficult to borrow in order to bribe the electorate. However, if elected to a second consulship, Caesar would afterward spend five years as a civilian, and as a civilian he could be and doubtless would have been prosecuted on one charge or another; this might have derailed his career.

The final descent into civil war revolved about the issue of whether Caesar would be permitted to hold his province until elected consul for a second time. Caesar proposed a compromise: he would lay down his command and his army if Pompey would do the same. This was rejected and the Senate not only voted to replace Caesar but also passed a decree that made him a public enemy if he refused to vacate his post. Thus threatened, Caesar decided on war, and made his fateful crossing of the Rubicon river, southernmost boundary of his province, with a few cohorts—less than a tenth of his army. He did not intend irrevocable war; he hoped even after his invasion of Italy to negotiate a compromise. But most of Pompey's optimate supporters saw Caesar as the destroyer of the traditional state, and would brook no thought of compromise. It was to be decision by war.

Objectives in war are sometimes suffused with noble purpose; but there was no noble purpose in this one. Caesar wished to maintain his own position just as the oligarchs attempted to hold theirs. Perhaps a few persons, among them Cicero and Cato, were actuated primarily by principle, beyond ambition. Cicero had been on friendly terms with Caesar in recent years and did not believe that those on the other side were really fighting for the Republic. He supported compromise; reluctantly he at last joined Pompey's side as the most constitutional one. Cato pressed for the struggle but secured passage of a Senate decree declaring that no Roman should be killed except on the field of battle, and that no city subject to Rome should be plundered. This ideal was often breached, and by those on Cato's side. On the other hand Caesar quite early earned a reputation for clemency to his defeated opponents. But as the civil war dragged on and each victory brought not an end but only a new confrontation in some different place, Caesar's clemency wore thin; in the last two major battles many persons were put to the sword who might have been spared.

The Campaigns of the Civil War

In the first year of the war, Caesar's rapid movements kept Pompey and his supporters off balance. Caesar took over Rome before a defense could be organized and got the state treasury in the bargain, no small advantage. Pompey, in imminent danger of defeat and capture, moved quickly to Brundisium, a port on the Adriatic in southern Italy, and embarked with some troops for the opposite shore. Pompey had the navy and, besides the troops with him, seven other legions in Spain. Though he had given up Italy he seemed to have the advantage.

Caesar soon made the balance more even: collecting troops that had been scattered throughout his provinces, he marched into Spain and in a swift campaign, more of maneuver than of struggle, defeated Pompey's lieutenants at Ilerda. Caesar then returned to Italy, got himself elected consul (for 48 B.C.) to regularize his position, and began to plan ways to get at Pompey, who had established himself in a base at Dyrrhachium, in Greece. The consuls and a number of other officials had gone all the way to Thessalonica. Without control of the seas Caesar was to find the going difficult.

Caesar tried to send some troops by land through Illyricum. This resulted in near disaster. Though theoretically under Roman domination for a century, the Illyrians were intractable and dangerous. Caesar—or rather, Antony—also brought troops across the Adriatic by ship during the winter, when Pompey's warships would not be on intensive patrol. It was a chancy business. Nor was the danger over: Caesar could not adequately supply his troops. The result was that, though he "besieged" Pompey at Dyrrhachium, it was his own troops who suffered most. When he attempted in the spring to penetrate the Pompeian defenses, his men were thrown back with heavy losses to one of his best legions. Caesar is reported to have said that if Pompey were not a loser he would have followed up the limited victory vigorously and all would have been over.

In early summer of 48 B.C., his army starving, Caesar moved east into Thessaly where the grain fields were ripening. He hoped for a showdown battle. Pompey wanted to delay until Caesar was further weakened and his own levies better trained. His optimate officers however, urged battle, since Caesar was outnumbered two to one. In preparation, Caesar instructed some of his best infantry in tactics for use against Pompey's superior cavalry. This group would first rout Pompey's attacking horsemen and then overwhelm his unprotected left wing. All went as planned; the battle of Pharsalus was a resounding victory for the smaller but more professional force. Caesar was said to have stopped the killing as soon as he could; he looked about the battlefield close to tears and said, "They would have it so." Pompey fled, only to be killed in Egypt by some Romans there before the pursuing Caesar arrived.

Caesar wintered in Egypt, where as everyone knows he became involved with the young queen Cleopatra, who was struggling with her brother for control of the country. The Dictator (he was given this title after his consulship expired) found himself besieged in Alexandria. Help came from allies along the eastern Mediterranean seaboard. In the spring of 47 B.C. Caesar made a quick thrust into Asia Minor, where Pharnaces, son of Mithridates, was attempting to restore the lost glories of the Kingdom of Pontus. Then, finally, he returned to Rome, a city beset by financial problems, which had begotten political and military difficulties as well. There was barely time to face these before the necessity for another major military campaign was upon him. Cato and some others had rallied all possible military resources in the province of Africa, held by a Pompeian.

Still without much of a navy, Caesar, again tempting fate and the weather gods, moved his men in the winter of 47–46 B.C. across from Sicily to Africa, established a bridgehead, and gradually built up his supplies. Brilliantly, he forced the Pompeians into the open at Thapsus in 46 B.C., and again won a complete victory. Cato, in command at Utica, was not in the fight, but won some sort of immortality by the courage and style of his suicide.

Caesar now returned again to Rome, where he celebrated four magnificent triumphs: not over Romans, of course; that would have angered even the urban plebs: over the Gauls, the Alexandrians, Pharnaces, and King Juba of Numidia, who had been unwise enough to back the losing side at Thapsus. The unfortunate Vercingetorix was led in one of the triumphs and the sister of Cleopatra in another.

The war still was not over. Caesar learned that the sons of Pompey among others, still in control of the navy, once again were rallying, this time in Spain. The battle of Munda in 45 B.C. did finally end the matter. Neither the opposing troops nor the nearby city of Corduba which had been their base was treated gently after this battle. And still, Sextus Pompey managed to get away with the fleet; from Sicily as a base, he would plague Caesar and his successors for yet another decade. Caesar could now celebrate yet another triumph (over the Spaniards, of course) and at long last begin to lay plans for the future.

Caesar was not to have much time to plan and effect his reforms. Yet he managed to complete or to get under way an astonishing number of projects. He advanced several laws to improve the structure and function of the Roman governmental system. He passed a law on bribery, the details of which are not known, but which seems to have been much needed. A colonization program provided land chiefly for civilians; there, too, the need must have been great.

The decade before Caesar's assassination, in fact, is filled with indications that Roman plebeians both city and rural were economically hard-pressed. Catiline, as we have noted, promised cancelation of debt and got the support of large numbers of the lower classes. Many were probably day laborers without land; it was these whom Caesar tried to help. The violence of the city during the period cannot be laid solely to political maneuvering, nor can the growth of the number of persons being given free grain be altogether the consequence of political pandering. There was real distress. Some of it came because of crop failures owing to bad weather conditions, which contributed to the grain shortages mentioned occasionally. It was an unfortunate cycle: cheap or free grain in the city drew in unfortunates from the country and in turn created a greater need which could only be met by increasing the cheap or free grain. Much of the popular support built up by Caesar in his last years came from his genuine efforts to help these poverty-stricken citizens.

Caesar found 320,000 persons receiving free grain in the city. He began the task of reducing the number, primarily through his huge colonization program in the provinces, both for soldiers and civilians. The number on the grain dole shrank to 150,000. Caesar was generous to his veterans: they received large bonuses at his triumphs and on discharge, besides land. He also doubled the pay of the army.

As always in civil war the economic structure was thrown into chaos, as the value of land and other property plunged. Debts were called in and there were many sellers but almost no buyers. Some of Caesar's own followers advocated the cancelation of debt during the civil wars. Caesar compromised. Creditors were forced to accept property at prewar evaluations, and all recent payments of interest on such debts were credited against the principal. We are told that the action in effect canceled about a quarter of the debt. This very moderate measure shows that Caesar did not wish to offend the powerful moneylenders.

Property belonging to defeated republicans was confiscated and sold. In his need for money Caesar seems to have been a bit ruthless about this, despite his clemency in other ways. Besides, these persons were his deadly enemies.

Several building projects in the city Caesar either completed or got well under way; others were planned. He began construction of a new and badly needed forum with a temple to Venus Genetrix. A large basilica rose across from the Curia in the older Forum. He had vowed a temple to Mars Ultor and he planned numerous other projects, including the drainage of the Pomptine marshes and of the Fucine Lake, the building of a harbor at Ostia, and construction of a new road across the Apennines to the Adriatic. It is possible that the Dictator expected these projects to provide employment for the idle poor.

One of Caesar's most important reforms was embodied in the Lex Julia Municipalis, known to us only through a fragmentary inscription. In some fashion not completely clear the law was an attempt to bring much needed order to the patchwork of local government throughout Italy. In the provinces, governors were now to serve short terms only; this measure surely was designed to prevent the rise of rivals. And his various changes in the collection of taxes in certain of the provinces probably made for greater efficiency more than for greater justice. Cuts in taxes in some of the eastern provinces after Pharsalus were probably temporary. Caesar bestowed the citizenship generously in the provinces, bringing Gauls even into the Senate, which was much enlarged. He granted citizenship liberally also to physicians and scholars.

At Rome, Caesar directed a scholar, Marcus Terentius Varro, to collect books for Rome's first public library. He

A model restoration of the Forum of Augustus at Rome. In the center is the temple to Mars Ultor (the Avenger), vowed by Caesar and constructed by Augustus as a filial act. (*Alinari–Scala*)

doubled the number of praetors to sixteen and quaestors to forty. Aediles were increased from four to six. Caesar made frequent use of prefects, appointed by himself, for important governmental posts; sometimes they displaced elected officials. For example, prefects controlled the mint in place of the *tresviri monetales*.

Caesar reformed the calendar in 46 B.C., importing for the task an Alexandrian astronomer: Egypt had used a solar calendar for almost three millennia. In order to bring the civil calendar in line with the solar calendar, Caesar added days to equal a total of 445, making this probably the longest year in history. The old Roman system of adding an intercalary month every second year to fill out the regular calendar year of 355 days had been neglected and the calendar was so badly out of correspondence with the seasons that the battle of Pharsalus was fought in August (then Sextilis) by the existing calendar, but it was actually early summer. The calendar that Caesar set up, with a sixteenth-century modification, we still use.

The most significant changes in the government were naturally those which established Caesar's own position. Early in 44 B.C. he became Perpetual Dictator, a title which appears on his coins along with his bust. He was the first living Roman whose image appeared on the coins, though the sons of Pompey had been minting coins with their dead father's image on them. The dictator was consul also. As is well known, he refused to be called king, sending the crown that Antony offered him at the Lupercal to rest on the head of Jupiter; that was the only king the Romans had, he said. He had long been augur and Pontifex Maximus as well. The Senate voted him the proconsulship for life and perpetual use of the term Imperator. He was also given the powers of a censor (*praefectus morum*) so that he could freely control the citizen lists as well as those of the equites and the Senate.

Additional honors were showered upon him (or later were falsely claimed to have been given him), some surely by men whose real motive was to bring odium upon the new autocrat: for example, it was said that a Senate decree provided that he could have as many wives as he wanted, and could sleep with whatever women he chose! Even those offered in serious vein seemed excessive: he was allowed to wear the triumphal regalia always (it was the garb of the kings of old) and the laurel wreath. He was in effect deified; a college of priests headed by Antony was set up to be in charge of the cult. His statue was placed in the temple of Romulus. Yet it is well to remember that, in the conception of most peoples of antiquity, no great chasm existed between humanity and deity. It was not Caesar

One of Caesar's most serious errors was to publicize his quasi-monarchical power, as shown on this coin, where he is portrayed (the first living Roman to be so depicted on the coinage) and described as "Perpetual Dictator." (*The Metropolitan Museum of Art, gift of Joseph H. Durkee, 1899*)

alone who claimed descent from the gods (both Venus and Mars, through descent from Iulus the ancestor of Romulus). He was not, in fact, the first of the Julii to make such a claim. Romulus himself was, for the Romans, a man-become-god, just as Hercules and others were. Yet there is no doubt that these honors were ill-advised, envied, and despised, and that the naked power so clearly displayed in all the titles and privileges—as well as in certain actions of Caesar's—caused even some of his closest supporters to waver.

One of the ways Caesar used his powers was to designate for three years in advance—it was done partly through a sort of election—all the chief magistrates, provincial governors, and the like. He was preparing to go east to fight the Dacians and the Parthians and he wanted to leave things under tight control in his absence. Such manipulation of the offices was one of his more grievous errors. Men who didn't get exactly what they wanted or expected were embittered. Others were concerned simply by the implications for the future.

About sixty upper-class Romans formed the conspiracy against Caesar; they included men whom he had forgiven for fighting the Pompeians and men who had long been close and trusted lieutenants. On March 15, 44 B.C., the great dictator who flaunted his power too openly was stabbed to death in front of a hall attached to the theater built by Pompey and near a statue of the latter. The deed, not followed through by the assassins—idealists who seemed to think one death would bring about the restoration of the Republic—would only result, after a period of wary maneuvering, in another round of civil wars.

Resumption of the Conflict

Mark Antony was consul with Caesar in 44 B.C., and another of Caesar's lieutenants, Marcus Lepidus, was Master of the Horse —that is, second in command to Caesar as dictator. Since the "liberators" (as the assassins called themselves) did not move against either and since Lepidus had a legion of troops near the city, the two quickly controlled the situation. Being realists, they soon came to an accommodation with the leading senators. All Caesar's acts both accomplished and projected were to stand; on the other side, amnesty was given the conspirators. The chief assassins nevertheless found themselves so unpopular with the urban plebs that they left Rome. Some of them had been designated to provinces; of these, two eventually decided their provinces were too insignificant.. They seized others, and ultimately the Senate gave its approval. These were Gaius Cassius, who took over Syria, and Marcus Brutus, who seized Macedonia. Decimus Brutus, a distant cousin of Marcus, had been designated by Caesar to have the strategically important Cisalpine Gaul—in fact Decimus had been made a collateral heir by Caesar —and he proceeded there.

After a time, Antony decided that he wanted Cisalpine Gaul himself. When the Senate resisted, Antony resorted to the familiar popular pattern: he had a tribune call an assembly and pass a law giving him that province. The Senate, now led by Cicero, among others, decided to oppose Antony and to support D. Brutus with arms.

Complicating the situation was the arrival on the scene of Caesar's grandnephew and chief heir, Gaius Octavius. Only eighteen years old at Caesar's death, he nevertheless left Macedonia, the site of Caesar's mobilization for the projected eastern campaign, and came to Rome determined to avenge Caesar. Once in Italy he learned that by the dictator's will he was adopted as Caesar's son and heir. Caesarian veterans hailed him Caesar and offered their help. Octavius thus recruited a considerable entourage—actually an army.

Antony not only had come to an accommodation with the assassins, but he had also seized Caesar's money and papers. He refused to give the money to Octavius as heir on the ground that it was state funds. Octavius could hardly find him a satisfactory ally. On the other hand, the leading senators including Cicero were basically anti-Caesarian. Under Cicero's urging, however, the Senate decided to try to use the young "Caesar" and his irregular army against Antony, who by now had marched several legions to Cisalpine Gaul and had D. Brutus under siege. Octavian (as he is called after the Caesarian adoption was registered, since he became Gaius Julius Caesar Octavianus) was made propraetor and sent north along with the consuls of the year 43 to fight Antony. It was hardly a secret that Cicero and the rest intended to get rid of Octavian once he had served his purpose.

In April 43 B.C., the armies of Octavian and the consuls,

Hirtius and Pansa, brought Antony to battle and defeated him. Both consuls were slain, however, and now Octavian controlled the army. Instead of pursuing Antony, he moved toward Rome and "persuaded" the Senate to make him consul—before he reached age twenty! Then at last he followed Antony to Narbonese Gaul, a province controlled by Lepidus. The three did not fight each other but instead negotiated to form a second triumviral coalition, this one later given formal status by the Senate. They made up proscription lists to get rid of their enemies; at the insistence of Antony, Cicero's name was there. The orator had indeed said many scurrilous things about Antony while trying to create an effective senatorial opposition to him. Along with numerous others, Cicero was soon killed (December 7, 43 b.c.), and his head and hands were hung from hooks in the Forum. D. Brutus had already been killed, by a Gallic chieftain who wished to please Antony.

It was not difficult for the coalition to gain control of Rome and Italy; nor was it difficult to get an assembly to legitimize them as Triumvirs for the Reconstitution of the State for a five-year period. The more difficult problems lay, first, in the East, where M. Brutus in Macedonia and G. Cassius in Syria had been scouring the whole area, collecting men and the material of war, and, second, in Sicily, now held by Sextus Pompey, who still controlled the bulk of the republican army.

By late the next year (42 b.c.) Antony and Octavian were in Macedonia ready for a military showdown with Brutus and Cassius. The first battle at Philippi was something of a draw; the second shortly after settled the matter. Cassius and Brutus were suicides. The Roman world was left to be divided up among the victorious triumvirs. Antony took the lion's share; Octavian clawed his way into second place. Lepidus, suspected of conspiracy, was soon relegated to a poor third position. Antony took as his sphere the entire East, and after some maneuvering including actual struggle, ceded to Octavian the West, except for Africa. This eventually went to Lepidus.

Reorganization and Renewed Rivalry

In the East, Antony confronted a multitude of problems. Brutus and Cassius, in combing the areas for supplies, money, and men, naturally had also put men they could trust in important positions at all levels where their authority reached. They had solicited—vigorously—the cooperation of allied states, client kings. Cleopatra, Queen of Egypt, for example, despite her earlier association with Caesar, had furnished grain to the two. Antony now called upon allies for loyalty to the new regime, overturned old arrangements and substituted new. He replaced men of doubtful reliability, and got state revenues flowing again, in the new channels.

The Parthians also presented a problem. They were seldom aggressive, mostly reacting to Roman action, but at this point a campaign seemed necessary. In good time, however. In 41 B.C. Cleopatra came in response to Antony's peremptory summons to the triumvir's headquarters in Cilicia to give account of her policy. She impressed him with her personality, flair, and companionability, and he decided to winter in Alexandria. Unresolved problems could wait.

Octavian's problems in Italy and the West, though different, were as knotty. He demobilized veterans by the thousand, and this meant he had to find bonuses and land for them. Those families that had been unwise enough to support Brutus, Cassius, and the rest he wished to punish. The two problems lent themselves to a single solution (to oversimplify): land confiscated from the republicans could be used for the veterans. A rigorous and none-too-discriminating application of the principle made the triumvir quite unpopular in some quarters. One family that suffered loss of a farm was that of young Vergil, who was to become Rome's greatest poet.

Octavian had trouble also with the consul of 41 B.C., Lucius Antonius, a brother of Antony. The dispute, abetted by Fulvia, Antony's wife, turned on the question of who was supreme in power, the triumvir or the consul; it involved the confiscated lands and the question of equal treatment for Antony's veterans. The confrontation degenerated into a real war. Thus, during the same winter when Antony was in Egypt with Cleopatra, his wife and brother were actually besieged at Perusia by the army of Octavian. The latter won, but by then Lucius was no longer consul anyway. Octavian let Lucius and Fulvia go free but took harsh measures against the Perusians—Roman citizens though they were—who had given support to the consul. He executed also some senators and equestrians who had supported Lucius and Fulvia.

A conference was arranged the next year between Octavian and Antony after Antony at length found out about the winter war. Things were patched up; Antony even married Octavia, sister of Octavian (Fulvia had conveniently died) and took her with him back to Athens and his work in the East. At this point Octavian was confirmed as ruler of all the West except Africa. By further agreement Octavian was to send him soldiers to aid in the invasion of Parthia, and Antony in turn was to send naval ships to help Octavian move against Sextus Pompey, who still occupied Sicily.

Sextus threatened Octavian and Rome in a serious way. For nearly two centuries Sicily had been a major source of grain for the city of Rome. Now this supply was lost. Moreover, Pompey's naval forces could prevent substitute imports from Africa or Egypt. In one conference, Octavian, Antony, Lepidus, and Pompey all met and came to a temporary settlement. But the power Sextus had to choke off Rome's lifeline at will seemed intolerable to Octavian, who broke the agreement and attacked Pompey. The first efforts to invade Sicily met disaster, mostly from wind and wave. Marcus Agrippa, Octavian's competent and loyal lieutenant, built a new fleet, trained new crews in an artificial harbor where they would be safe from Pompey's marauding ships, and in 36 B.C. defeated Pompey at sea. This was followed by an infantry invasion led by Octavian. Pompey fled east, only to be killed by an agent of Antony's.

Lepidus cooperated with Octavian in the attack on Sicily. As it happened, Pompey's army, after learning of the outcome of the naval battle, surrendered to Lepidus, not Octavian. Suddenly Lepidus found himself in command of enough legions to challenge Octavian. Here was heady opportunity to even the score. Octavian learned of Lepidus' incipient revolt, cautiously undermined Lepidus' position, and then in a daring nighttime maneuver persuaded the legions formerly Pompey's to come over to his side. Lepidus capitulated and was kept under virtual arrest in an Italian town until his death in 12 B.C. Probably only the fact that he had been elected Pontifex Maximus in place of Caesar saved him from execution.

Renewed Civil War: The Final Phase

The end of Sextus Pompey's strangle hold on Rome and the prospect of a surer grain supply brought jubilation in Rome and along with it somewhat greater popularity for Octavian. He was given special honors including some of the privileges of a tribune of the plebs and the date of the victory was made a holiday. However, the demobilization of so many troops brought its problems: as always they must be given land and bonuses— and this meant money. Octavian managed to find individual allotments of land in Capua for some; others he sent to colonies in Gaul.

In 36 B.C., the same year that Octavian reduced Sextus Pompey's Sicilian stronghold, Antony mounted an invasion of Parthia. He followed the strategic plan developed by Caesar, approaching through Armenia. South of Armenia, however, the Parthian cavalry attacked and destroyed Antony's siege-and-supply train. Without it, Antony's main army could not mount a major siege, and the Parthian cavalry did not allow adequate forage. It was necessary to pull out. Perhaps Plutarch was right that Antony showed his best generalship in this difficult situation, but he got back with only a fragment of his army. In 34 and 33 B.C. he was able to retrieve the situation to a considerable degree, through tactics that Octavian declared un-Roman, involving the breach of a treaty made with the King of Media. Antony even celebrated a triumph—but in Alexandria!

The historian must remember that our sources all derive from Antony's enemies. Nevertheless, it does appear that Antony's will and vigor lessened after the Parthian debacle. He became more dependent upon Cleopatra, less decisive in his moves against Octavian and the latter's skillful general, Agrippa. Too much wine and women, some said. Certainly he could still organize well and could yet command strong loyalty from his men—at least until shortly before his decisive defeat at Actium.

Toward a Final Break

Octavian maintained large armies in order to preserve a balance with Antony, though he could hardly announce this as his policy. To put a better face on things he used the troops to expand Roman dominions. In Spain, Illyria, Dalmatia, and Pannonia, up to the Danube he campaigned, sometimes leading the armies personally to enhance his somewhat shaky military reputation, and so added large territories to the Empire. The spoils pleased the army and the Roman populace as always greeted enthusiastically successes of this sort.

Marcus Agrippa masterminded most of the military successes of Octavian. He also cultivated public opinion in the city by his benefactions, especially as aedile in 33 B.C. (though he had been consul in 37). He repaired aqueducts and sewers, improved the public baths, made arrangements for gala festivals, constructed public buildings; these activities of course gave employment to thousands at Rome.

Meanwhile Octavian publicly attacked Antony on various grounds, especially for his dalliance with Cleopatra. They were the parents of twins by now, born to her, actually, while Antony was living with Octavia. He returned to Cleopatra and formally married her; it was sometime afterwards that he divorced Octavia. Octavian felt threatened by Antony's recognition of Cleopatra's oldest child Caesarion as the true son of Caesar, and he also charged Antony with virtual treason for giving Roman lands —Cyprus, for example—to Cleopatra, and for planning to give huge chunks of an expanded empire to his son by her, and others to Caesarion.

The war of words between the two triumvirs escalated throughout 33 B.C. until it was obvious that a break was imminent. Antony complained that Octavian did not share Africa with him (taken from Lepidus), did not send the aid he had promised in his Parthian campaigns, and did not send any recruits to him. Octavian of course harped on Antony's shabby treatment of the loyal Octavia, implied that Cleopatra had somehow bewitched him, and made numerous other charges.

The year 32 B.C. presented some awkward moments to Octavian. He could no longer claim to be triumvir, for the command, originally voted for five years and then extended another five, ran out at the end of 33. Of course, so did Antony's command; but somehow the latter did not worry. He continued to call himself triumvir and to exercise his imperium as if it were still valid. Both consuls were pro-Antony. Octavian attacked them and they left Italy to join Antony; about three hundred of the senators (of around nine hundred) went with them. Obviously Octavian's propaganda was not completely effective. Ultimately Octavian tried to legitimize his position by requiring all able-bodied men throughout Italy and most of the western provinces to swear personal allegiance to him—a sort of extension of the military oath.

Both Octavian and Antony pulled together money, men, arms, and ships. Octavian put on special, heavy taxes, even in Italy, which had been exempt from the war tax for a century and a quarter. Freeholders had to pay a quarter of their annual income, and freedmen were required to contribute an eighth of their capital wealth. In some places riots broke out against these exactions. We know less about Antony's efforts to raise money, but certainly he accumulated great quantities of it in order to pay and to provision his approximately thirty legions and thousands upon thousands of sailors. Cleopatra of course helped substantially, contributing money, ships, and men to the cause.

Actium

Antony and Cleopatra chose Actium, across the heel of the Italian boot in Greece for their base of operations. Its bay could accommodate their huge navy and nearby there was space for the legions. Octavian, with Agrippa as a kind of chief of staff, got together an army that was probably somewhat better than Antony's and a fleet that could rival his though without the huge ships that Cleopatra furnished.

Antony was curiously inactive at Actium during the first eight months of 31 B.C.; he allowed Octavian and Agrippa to

A "legionary" *denarius* of Antony, issued not long before the battle of Actium, 31 B.C., and showing the eagle of Legion IV plus standards. Much of Antony's coinage in this period was somewhat debased.

cross over the Adriatic and besiege his position. Octavian might have expected, earlier in the winter of 32, that Antony would himself have invaded Italy, where he had even yet a great deal of support from all classes. Some among his men blamed the deteriorating situation upon Cleopatra. As typical Roman soldiers, no doubt they superstitiously condemned bringing any woman along on the campaign, let alone having her share command.

The battle of Actium, though decisive, seemed less than climactic. Intended as a naval showdown, it appears that the struggle was scarcely joined before Cleopatra, with a contingent of the fleet, sailed southward for home. Antony, seeing her sail off, overtook her in a small boat and went with her back to Alexandria, virtually abandoning the navy and his untested legions. The army soon capitulated to Octavian.

The following year Octavian moved in force into Egypt itself. Cleopatra had been vigorously preparing to rally her forces, apparently on the Red Sea. She attempted to move her large warships across the sands on rollers, only to have them attacked and burned by desert tribesmen, who had seldom seen so delectable and vulnerable a caravan. Antony had lapsed into deep depression after Actium, but now bestirred himself as Octavian approached, but too late. He, and finally Cleopatra as well, were suicides. She had declared she would never be led in triumph at Rome.

The Mediterranean world now belonged to Octavian, soon to become Augustus.

The Urban Plebs

The term city plebs has been used by historians both of antiquity and modern times to refer to the city poor. In more precise historical usage, the "plebs" included all citizens not patrician, rich and poor. For a long time, most of the upper-class leaders of the state had been plebeians. In this period, for example, Cato, Pompey, and Cicero were all plebeians. Caesar, on the other hand, was patrician. The composition of the city plebs, the lower-class population of Rome, is worth noting, not only because politicians like Caesar appealed to it, but because its changing makeup helps to explain social, religious, and political developments during the late Republic.

The most important impulse for continuing change in the city's population related to one institution—slavery—and to a liberal policy of the Romans connected with it: slaves were often freed, and freed slaves were made Roman citizens. The first generation of freedmen retained legal obligations to their former masters and could not stand for office; in the next generation they had full privileges of citizenship. They were viewed as social inferiors by citizens of freeborn ancestry. Freedmen had become numerous enough to be a problem in the city even in the second century B.C. Scipio Aemilianus shortly before his death in 129 B.C. railed at the mobs who heckled him for his attitude toward Tiberius Gracchus and called them "stepchildren of Italy" whom he had "brought in in chains." Obviously he thought that most of the crowd were freedmen or even slaves; he could not have discriminated by their manner of dress. Votes of freedmen were restricted for a time to a single urban tribe, in an effort to neutralize their political potential. After a generation or so, sons or grandsons of freedmen could acquire land in one of the rural tribal areas and be registered in one of the politically

SOCIAL CHANGE IN THE LATE REPUBLIC

8

more important tribes even while residing in Rome, just like the upper classes of the city.

Noncitizens flocked to Rome also, drawn by the attraction of a great capital. Embassies, merchants and traders, even tourists comprised considerable percentages of the population. Probably no more than half the population of the city, slave and free, citizen and immigrant, were in Caesar's time of old Roman stock. The rest had come mostly from the Hellenistic East: they were Greeks, Syrians, Egyptians, natives of Asia Minor and other areas in the region. A Jewish community was established on the Janiculum, across the Tiber. A few Celts had come down from the north, and some Iberians from Spain. By now Rome had displaced Alexandria as the most polyglot city in the Mediterranean basin.

While Rome's population swelled with persons of foreign origin, many of the native citizens were moving up to colonies in the Po valley or elsewhere; and the Gracchan land assignations with the later similar programs took at least some native stock from the city. The proportion of citizens of foreign origin in Rome therefore continually rose.

The city's lower class formed the lowly base of the economic pyramid. Those of old Roman stock often fared less well than the freedmen, many of whom had useful connections and acquired some wealth. Rome's proletarians usually held semiskilled jobs which paid existence-level wages, about a denarius a day. For a family of four, about half that would be needed for food alone; the rest had to suffice for minimal clothing and miserable lodgings. The top floors of *insula*, large apartment buildings with no water or sanitary facilities, always in danger of fire and occasionally of collapse, or the worst of other slum structures—these furnished quarters for the poor.

After the precedent set by Gaius Gracchus the government did on occasion offer public grain at low rates. The land distribution programs provided sporadic help for some of the city plebs. Occasional largesse at the great games, bribes for votes in the electoral or legislative assemblies, and regular small gifts from patrons to clients helped further to supplement incomes. In 58 B.C., as noted earlier, the popular tribune Publius Clodius, an aristocratic demagogue who supported Caesar, for the first time provided free grain for the city poor. His motives were partly political, as is usually the case with welfare legislation, but doubtless partly compassionate. Even the conservative younger Cato had favored a similar program a bit earlier. Though Caesar reduced the number, by the beginning of the Empire about a quarter of a million of the urban plebs regularly received free grain from the government.

Many of the city's plebeians were organized into groups; some of these were comparable to guilds. *Collegia* and *sodalicia*, as they were called, had existed from early times. The older clubs, social at base, frequently had a religious aspect; many were primarily burial societies. During the first century B.C., however, there appeared large numbers of *collegia* of a new sort, formed for a primarily political purpose. They seem to have been somewhat comparable to the *hetaireia* found in certain Greek cities, and indeed the new groups may have been organized by citizens of Greek origin. Some of the clubs were more or less for hire: among other things they made it easy to organize bribery on a large scale for the elections or the legislative assemblies.

As noted in the preceding chapter, Clodius made extensive use of these new political clubs for organized violence, and the optimate side countered with a similar combination under the leadership of Milo. The two groups in general terrorized the Forum. When, after a chance confrontation outside Rome early in 52 B.C. Milo murdered Clodius, the latter's gang burned down the Senate house and miscellaneous other flammable items handy in the Forum as a suitable pyre for their dead champion and turned Rome itself into a tinderbox ready for the spark. Pompey, as we have seen, restored order; no doubt he also curbed Clodius' *collegia*. Caesar had once found Clodius' clubs useful, but after he attained power he outlawed all the local associations except the oldest.

To keep the city masses quiescent, something more was needed than cheap grain, or occasional private and public largesse, or bribes by office-seekers. That something was entertainment. Romans of all ranks went to bed early and rose early. The workday began early also, and for many workers it ended early as well. Add to this the enforced idleness of those who had no work or not enough of it, the fact that homes were unsatisfactory places to while away the hours, and it is easy to see that the city plebeians, with time on their hands, would be hungry for entertainment. If it was not provided, they might arrange it for themselves in a fashion displeasing to the magistrates. Entertainment for the masses therefore became at once a kind of necessity as well as a means by which magistrates might endear themselves to the lower classes in Rome. The state itself did not adequately finance the presentation of the games and festivals; any aedile (or sometimes other officer or future candidate for office) who wished to put on a crowd-pleasing spectacle had therefore to scrape up money however he could. Sometimes he borrowed heavily, with his future prospects as collateral, in order to entertain on a suitable scale.

By the first century B.C. there were numerous official holidays crammed with action. They tended to be concentrated in the spring—April was the month most filled with spectacles—but some were observed even in winter. The five major religious festivals were those to the Great Mother (Cybele), to Ceres, to Jupiter (the Ludi Romani), to Apollo, and to Hercules (the Ludi Plebeii). Each lasted for several days and included processions, theatre of several sorts, and other activities.

Gladiatorial games were growing in popularity but were not a part of any official, regular festival. They were presented at funeral games and by private individuals, especially future candidates for public office. Yet more popular were the chariot races in the Circus Maximus. This race track, located just below the Palatine Hill, and in recent decades excavated and landscaped in a sort of restoration of the site, still impresses the tourist. It could seat about 150,000 spectators and there were vantage points for many more. The rivalry of the various colors so characteristic of chariot racing in the Empire was only beginning. Much of the excitement doubtless related to the betting that accompanied the races. Wild animal shows also excited the mob, and already the Empire was being scoured for animals to cough out their lives before Roman audiences. Exotic species would in the future be brought in from distant countries at great expense. On occasion there was revulsion, however. Pompey once put on a spectacle of elephants; the crowd, normally bloodthirsty enough, was displeased with the butchery of these majestic and dignified beasts and let Pompey know it.

Unfortunately, theatrical performances at Rome seem to have been in qualitative decline, this in spite of the fact that in 55 B.C. Pompey gave Rome its first permanent, stone theatre, a magnificent building said to have been capable of seating forty thousand persons. It was dedicated with an elaborately overdone

Chariot race in the circus. (*Scala, New York/Florence*)

spectacle. The new polyglot population of Rome—and other major cities in the West—desired spectacles of the sort that seem depraved to the modern taste, and they showed less appreciation for the higher types of tragedy and comedy. Perhaps there is a kind of Gresham's law of entertainment, that bad shows tend to crowd out the good.

Religion and the City Populace in the Late Republic

The flood tide of religious change in Rome belongs to the period of the Empire. However, the beginning of this shift is seen in the Republic and relates in large part to the changing nature of the city's population. Immigrants, no matter how they came—as slaves or merchants or traders or ambassadors—tended to bring with them their own religions. Over a period of time, therefore, shrines and even temples began to be built in and about the city to these new deities. Merchants in particular seem to have brought their own religion with them. The worship of some Egyptian gods, for example, seems to have come to Rome by way of Delos and other trading ports. Some religious innovations were the result of the travels of Romans, especially men in the army.

Three Oriental deities important to the life of the city by the end of the Republic were Cybele, Isis, and Mithra. Cybele, as mentioned earlier, was brought in at the end of the Hannibalic war, an official import, not the bag and baggage of immigrants, even though the latter were doubtless the most involved spectators at the spring processions that marked the Magna Mater's rites. The native Roman temperament moderated the orgiastic character of the goddess's ceremonies, and visitors to Rome in the early Empire remarked on the processions, so stately as compared with those in Asia Minor, Cybele's homeland. Moreover, the ranks of the Galli—priests—continued to be augmented mainly by foreigners who showed their devotion to the goddess through public self-castration. We know of only one native Roman citizen who thus became a Gallus. Since it was illegal, this man may have forfeited his citizenship.

Isis was an Egyptian fertility goddess connected with the Nile; her history already extended three millennia backward in time. In the Hellenistic age, she was identified with Aphrodite by the Greeks who were dominant throughout the eastern Mediterranean. Isis developed into a universal goddess, omnipresent and omniscient, especially important to pregnant women and also to travelers everywhere. She was thus no longer exclusively identified with Egyptians, but was worshiped by a vast, ethnically mixed mass of people. The Senate still disapproved strongly of foreign shrines and temples within the sacred precincts of the city; five times in the middle years of the first century B.C. shrines to Isis were destroyed by Senate decree. It appears that they were usually rebuilt rather quickly. Mark Antony vowed a temple to this goddess but never had opportunity to build it. Not until the early Empire was Isis ensconced in a properly consecrated temple within the pomoerium.

The god Mithra derived from Persian Zoroastrianism as modified in the Hellenistic world, especially in Asia Minor. Roman soldiers, possibly of Sulla's army, certainly of Pompey's, brought back his worship. He was admirably suited for soldiers; he was a man's god, for women were excluded or virtually so. There were seven degrees of purification. Holy days were Sundays (we derive the name from this religion) and December 25, the birthdate of the Sun (father of Mithra; sometimes Mithra himself). Various other similarities to Christianity can be detailed but, in contrast, Mithra was distinctly a mythical, not historical character. The cult statues displayed in the great museums of the world show the beneficent Mithra killing the sacred bull, from which he created all that is. The great flourishing of this religion lay in the future: the third century A.D. saw the widest expansion of Mithraism. But some Mithrea—half-underground chambers where the god was worshiped—in Italy, as in Ostia, for example, date probably to the late Republic.

Various other eastern deities including the Jewish Jahweh (or Jehovah) also found their way into the Rome of this age. All were warmer than the more austere gods of the old Romans; all offered some personal contact with the deity; some, a system of morals; and most, a means of purification that brought hope of an afterlife. Several of them used as a purificatory rite the *taurobolium*. A bull was sacrificed on a grate; the devotees stood beneath and allowed the blood to stream over them. Much of what took place in the name of religion during the late Republic would have horrified old Cato.

Lower Classes of the Countryside

The conditions of rural society are much less well known to us than those of the city of Rome. The reason is simple enough: our chief sources of information are the writings of Cicero and others like him, who lived in Rome and who thought that city the center of the universe. Yet Cicero realized full well that what Rome was and would become depended much more on the Romans and (former) Italians of the countryside than on the urban plebs. Caesar and other generals were even more acutely aware of the relative value of the rural plebs.

The number of small farmers in Italy remained large despite both the attrition of population to the city and the continued emphasis on the slave-manned, plantation-like farms. The two basic factors that prevented the small farmer from declining into insignificance were the colonization of rich areas, especially to the north of Rome and on into the Po Valley, and the distribution of land to individuals through various programs like that of Tiberius Gracchus in 133 B.C. At the end of the third century B.C. and during the second, large colonies were sent out, particularly into the Po region; these were at first Latin. Romans who joined such colonies in large numbers gave up their citizenship for the "Latin right." The areas involved were not contiguous with land of the Roman state (ager Romanus). By the second quarter of the second century, however, Rome had begun to establish large-size citizen colonies. So many thousands of Romans migrated into the Po valley that the demographic character of the region changed entirely. The area, in fact, became a sort of conservative haven for old Roman customs as well as Roman stock.

Although individual land allotments held fewer persons than did colonial settlements, still an appreciable number of individual settlers helped offset the growth of the latifundia. The Gracchan type of program was less significant in the late Republic than the settlement of veterans on the land as a kind of discharge bonus. Veterans were given land all over Italy and eventually even in the rich areas of public land to the south, as in Campania. Some were sent outside of Italy also, especially by Caesar, who placed many thousands of veterans (and civilians) on choice pieces of provincial soil.

The continuing existence of large numbers of small holders in Italy in this period is confirmed by archaeological surveys. Even in Etruria, where the latifundia were already numerous in Tiberius Gracchus' day, the stone foundations of numerous farm huts of the period testify to the persistence of small farmers there. It is difficult to infer their economic position. It cannot have been very good: small farmers are never really prosperous; a single family, before the age of machines, was physically unable to produce much of a surplus. These farms, as always, will mostly have been subsistence operations; the goal was to attain the greatest possible degree of self-sufficiency. Little would or could have been produced for sale.

Small farmers with very little land had always supplemented their meager incomes by providing supplementary labor for the larger land holders, as at harvest time. However, the rise of the slave plantation and the use of contract labor gangs at harvest time reduced such opportunities. It seems, too, that public pasture land previously available to small farmers was increasingly swallowed up either by lessees or by squatters, who took over public land not formally leased out, in a semilegal practice called *occupatio*.

More debilitating to Italian agriculture in the long run, especially to the small farmer, were a series of bad farm practices, the consequence both of ignorance and poverty. The best Roman farmers understood the importance of allowing the land to lie fallow periodically; the recommended practice was to leave half of one's land fallow. Rudimentary crop rotation was understood as well. But the poorest farmers could not allow half their tiny holdings to be unproductive in any year; nor could they practice an ideal crop rotation whose immediate effect was lowering overall annual production of the most needed crops. Not even the larger farms had enough animal manure to keep the soil at a high level of tilth and fertility, though the importance of it was well understood. Something was known about composting also, but the practice was necessarily very limited. The result was that, in general, soil cultivated over a period of centuries gradually lost its productive capacity in spite of the best efforts of the farmers.

Similarly debilitating was the gradual deforestation of hills and uplands. This practice ravaged the land in antiquity; its effects are still noted in Greece, Italy, Spain, and elsewhere in the Mediterranean basin. The reasons for eliminating the forests were simple and practical: demand for timber for ships, lumber for building, and fuel for burning; this coupled with a need for more pasturage and cultivable soil. The inevitable long-range results were the eroding of deforested hills, the choking up of river mouths, and the conversion of lagoons (especially along the west coast of Italy) into marshes. Swamp areas brought an additional and portentous consequence: the western coast of Italy became increasingly subject to invasion by the malaria-carrying anopheles mosquito; although the disease had existed from an early time, now some areas slowly became almost uninhabitable. It must be reemphasized that declining production, deforestation, and the silting-up process were gradual. Their effects were beginning to be felt by the end of the Republic, however, and in later centuries help to explain the declining economic role of Italy within the Empire.

We have seen that the small farmers played a decreasing role in the citizen assemblies in the city, since most of them found it impossible to come in more than once or twice a year, and others did not come at all. The city residents, many of them registered in rural tribes, dominated the assemblies except on rare occasions. Nevertheless, the country poor—serving in the army—ultimately had much more to say about the Roman fate than the somewhat parasitic urban poor. Rome's generals knew that the sturdiest soldiers were not to be found on the city streets. What we know of the recruiting areas in the late Republic and in the Empire shows that the soldiers who were the final arbiters in the civil wars and who later determined (with the prodding of their leaders) who the emperors would be came from rural areas.

The slaves of the peninsula, numerous as they were, lived lives almost as varied as those of the free population. The most intelligent slaves reared from childhood were given training that made them valuable, sometimes even as managers of farms or businesses. They were allowed to accumulate money and often could purchase their freedom. Alternatively, many were rewarded for their service with emancipation, and as freedmen perhaps continued on a salary in their former posts. Some slaves, including the most attractive, served in the great households of the rich, and these too might lead relatively favored lives. (See Chapter 10 for a discussion of the slave populations of the large establishments of a slightly later time.)

Less well trained or untrainable (or intractable) slaves were routinely consigned to the rigors of the farms. Conceived of much as draft animals, they tended to receive minimal care; some, as we know, at times worked in irons and lived in infamous *ergastula* (prisons). Perhaps most rural slaves were well treated, but the labor itself, with confinement and utter boredom, made them potentially dangerous. The rebellion under Spartacus, briefly noted in Chapter 6, indicates as clearly as anything could the unhappiness of these slaves. When Spartacus' early success against the Roman militia gave them a glimmer of hope, they joined him by the thousand. The decision was not easily made, for their lives were forfeit. No wonder most of them fought with Spartacus against odds to the end rather than submit to their fate. We cannot trust the reported statistics on the number of slaves who revolted then or at other times, but Spartacus' success against even a consular army shows that his army numbered many thousands; the implications for the total size of the rural slave population are obvious.

Again in 63 B.C., when the patrician conspirator Catiline raised an army against the regime, an appeal to the slaves seems to have brought them in some numbers into his rebel force—although the numbers must have seemed disappointingly small to Catiline. It is possible to argue, of course, that the ease with which slaves escaped to join Spartacus or Catiline implies that they were not confined under very tight security, and that those in rural bondage in Italy certainly could not be described as cowed and spiritless. In any case Roman law and Roman officials invariably showed no mercy to rebellious or violent slaves. Nothing seems more portentously threatening to slave masters than news of a rebellion of their charges.

The Middle Classes in the Late Republic

The *equites* were those citizens whose possession of property qualified them in the census for service in the cavalry. After about 241 B.C. this class was apparently identical with that which furnished the first class of infantry. In the late Republic the amount of property required for a census listing in this class was a valuation of 100,000 sestertii. This probably had changed from 100,000 asses (the as was a copper coin) at about the time the denarius was revalued from ten to sixteen asses in the middle-second century B.C. (the sestertius was one-fourth of a denarius). This amount would have seemed impossibly huge for a wage earner, who might have to work a century or so to make so much money. On the other hand, to the richer Romans the amount must have seemed modest. The total number of persons in the class cannot have been very large, relatively speaking.

The *equites*, since the days of the Gracchi, and to some degree even before, had come to be sharply distinguished from the senatorial—that is to say, politically oriented—members of the same census class. The distinction was legal, involving such legislation as that which put the permanent courts into the hands of the nonsenatorial *equites*. The staffing of the juries of these courts changed with the times. In the late Republic a compromise placed both *equites* and senators on juries. Yet the separation of the group remained enshrined in law. This separation produced the *equester ordo* of the time of Cicero; and it is this equestrian class which we must notice.

There is a rather common misconception that the equestrians of Rome were practically all businessmen, moneylenders, or tax collectors. Rather, most of them, like the families of Marius and Cicero, were residents of the Italian towns and cities away from Rome. These equestrians were landholders, and many of them were politically important in their own towns. Cicero's father has previously been cited as an example; he had connections with important Romans—Marcus Aemilius Scaurus, the *princeps senatus* (the senator called on first for his opinion or vote), for example—but did not closely involve himself in politics at Rome. At Arpinum, however, he was an important person. The interests of these rural equestrians paralleled those of the ruling class at Rome. Such rural families provided a kind of reservoir from which the ranks of the Senate could, when necessary, be filled—as in Sulla's enlargment of the body.

One shortsighted weakness of the oligarchy of the later Republic was its failure to continue to admit substantial numbers of New Men from the (originally) Italian middle class into the governing elite of the state. These rural equestrians provided officers for the protagonists in the civil wars, and with the rise of Caesar found their way increasingly into the higher posts of the government. By the time of the emperor Vespasian, himself of this background, most aristocrats had ancestors who in the late Republic were merely country equestrians.

It is true, nevertheless, that the most visible and individually influential of the equestrians were those of the city. And of these the most important were the *publicani* (publicans). Associations of publicans organized somewhat like joint-stock companies bid in the contracts for the tithes and customs, leased the state-owned mines, both in Italy and (primarily) in the provinces, constructed ships, public buildings, and highways. Some were also moneylenders, businessmen, or merchants. They served on the jury panels of the permanent courts from the time of Gaius Gracchus—though they formed only a portion of the jurors after 70 B.C. In this role they exercised a degree of political influence even within the provinces, since the threat of prosecution before an unfriendly jury might serve to coerce a governor.

It was not the equestrians' participation on the juries, however, that explains their power. Often even today's historians of antiquity are unaware just how much the state needed this group of men. They provided much of the secondary organization of the government. Without their staffs of accountants, clerks, and other agents, the state out of necessity would have enormously expanded its own rather limited bureaucracy. Everyone knows about the Jews' contempt for the agents of the publican companies (these were always minor employes and not the people whom Cicero referred to as *publicani*), and one feels that in general the opprobrium may well have been merited. Yet can one really feel that if the government had directly collected the tithes and customs, built its own ships, roads, buildings, etc., the result would have been any more humane or economical? There is certainly ground for doubting that a government bureaucracy would have been as efficient. The truth is, Rome needed the upper equestrians, because their companies functioned as a kind of extension of the state.

The rich equestrians exercised an influence on politics also. They made loans to politicians like Caesar; Cicero (who was a rural *eques* before he entered the Senate) became both a spokesman for the financial group and a defender of their interests. At times he defended them even when he disapproved of their demands, simply because he knew that the oligarchy could not function without their support. Though it is difficult to detail, it seems fairly certain that equestrian dissatisfaction with the core oligarchy caused large numbers of them to support Caesar; that support in turn helped Caesar to win his victories. And later, equestrian revulsion against civil war and desire for peace, without which they could not prosper, caused them to give general support to the man who might bring enduring peace. The middle class, that is to say, helped Octavian to become Augustus, the first emperor.

Titus Pomponius Atticus (110–32 B.C.)

A most prominent equestrian of the first century B.C. was Atticus, the friend of Cicero. He was hardly typical—richer than most of his class, much too cultivated—he did not engage even in the fringe political activity, such as on juries or in public contracting, that occupied many equestrians. Yet he does serve to typify the group in some ways, particularly in his instinct for survival in difficult times; this led him and other powerful equestrians to exert their influence very judiciously and evenhandedly in the direction of order and stability.

We happen to know much more about Atticus than about other equestrians both because of Cicero's sixteen books of *Letters* to him, spanning, with some gaps, the period from 68 to 44 B.C., and because Cornelius Nepos, a contemporary biographer, left a life of Atticus. Nepos was rather too fulsome in his praise, as biographers often are. Atticus' wealth was inherited, partly from his father and, in middle life, from a rich uncle. In the middle 80s B.C., when civil war could be seen in the making, Atticus invested much of his capital in Epirus and Greece (probably) and took up residence in Athens for two decades. This, plus his remarkable facility in the Greek language, accounts for his surname.

This early decision to detach himself from the political arena grew into a fixed policy, and he always refused to be connected with any *factio* in Rome. It might easily have been otherwise. By marriage he was related to the tribune Sulpicius, who opposed Sulla and was slain by him. Nevertheless, in Greece Atticus became the close friend of Sulla, who was charmed by him, according to Nepos. Adhering to his decision, however, Atticus refused when urged by Sulla to return to Italy with him, presumably as a supporter. Atticus could certainly have had a distinguished political career had he so desired; possibly he, like his friend Cicero, could have attained even to the consulate. Instead, he chose noninvolvement in any direct way; yet he was involved indirectly, through friendship, judicious use of money, and advice.

Atticus illustrates for us also the fact that certain of the equestrians were approximately the social equals of the *nobiles*, the officeholding aristocracy. He moved in high social circles. It is notable that when Cicero refers in his letters to the richest of the core oligarchs—and their fishponds—he describes them as "your friends." Besides his family ties to the Patrician Sulpicii, his sister married Quintus Cicero, brother of the orator, and later, his daughter became the wife of Marcus Agrippa, the chief lieutenant of Octavian/Augustus and mother of the wife of the future emperor Tiberius. Though the consular nobles may have considered themselves a cut above Atticus, everyone surely recognized that only his decision to stay away from politics separated them.

Atticus used his wealth generously (and ultimately in his self-interest, of course) to support various individuals on all sides of the political arena. He did this even when, at times, it might have been dangerous to do so. For example, he helped some friends of Antony and Fulvia, Antony's wife, at a time when most persons at Rome felt that Antony's fortunes were dropping to a low ebb. This probably explains why Antony erased his name from the list of the proscribed in 43 B.C.—a list that condemned several friends of Cicero along with the orator himself. Atticus was at one point in danger from the oligarchs on the other side, however, some of whom attacked him because he remained unaligned. They felt that he should support the *boni* and oppose their "evil" opponents.

The equestrian also played the role of benefactor in literary matters. He maintained a staff of skilled slaves and freedmen who helped to research and publish works of Cicero and doubtless other authors. He himself served as Cicero's advisor and critic. He wrote himself; we know of a chronological compendium of history, much used in his time and after.

In Athens Atticus used his money as any provincial city would expect of a resident rich Roman (or citizen). He once distributed substantial supplies of grain to the Athenian citizens in a bad time, and on several occasions he either loaned money to the city or guaranteed loans, at low interest. Probably there were many other such benefactions in both Athens and Rome. Yet Atticus lived a relatively simple life. Nepos, who was his friend and claimed that he saw Atticus' daily account books, said that Atticus never spent more than an average of about 3,000 sesterces per month on his own household, even allowing for entertaining others. Nor did Atticus own even half as many villas as those Cicero acquired with only a fraction of his friend's wealth.

When finally the civil wars were over, Atticus and many other wealthy equestrians survived. Doubtless they helped to finance both sides, but they managed to stay politically uninvolved. They perhaps lost something when Caesar reduced debts, in effect, by forcing the use of prewar valuations of property used as collateral for loans, but at the end they still had much wealth. Some, Atticus among them, retained also their *dignitas* and even their integrity. The support of such persons perhaps meant most when the war was decided and funds were needed to achieve stability. In any case, the influence of equestrians like Atticus probably tilted the balance more than we know.

The Upper Class in the Late Republic

Quite a lot of what we know about Roman Society really involves only the upper classes. Or at least it involves those members of the upper classes who held important office, or who wrote literary or historical works, or who were friends of Cicero and thus are mentioned in his letters—one of the most valuable sources of social information on the last decades of the Republic.

Obviously the men of the higher levels of society had more of everything that men crave than those beneath them: money, prestige, and power. The continual expansion of the republican empire meant increased opportunity for officeholders, increased prestige for the small group of men who ruled most of the Mediterranean world. Yet the total number of top offices remained relatively few: however many provinces there might be, there still were only two consuls annually. The praetorship (there were eight praetors after Sulla, until Caesar doubled the number) was a plum worth having, especially as it usually meant a governorship. Failing those, one could still hold up his head a bit at least, if he held a quaestorship and perhaps an aedileship, and had a seat in the Senate.

The total number of persons who are the subject of this section was perhaps larger than may often be realized. One has only to browse through the lists of magistrates of the Republic to see many names which are little more than that—names—but which designate men who must have been important figures at Rome. We must always bear in mind that the accidents of survival of information do not present to us anything like a complete picture. It is instructive, for example, to look at the list of the men known to have been involved in the conspiracy to assassinate Caesar. These are men who surely were trusted as absolutely safe for the republic, that is to say, loyal to the oligarchy. Several of the names mean nothing at all to us. Yet they came from important families and certainly formed an essential part of the politically oriented upper class. Nevertheless the men who held real power in the core oligarchy were few in number: that group was pretty exclusive. A New Man like Cicero or the son of a New Man, Pompey, might somehow be quite important and yet not move within the inner circle either of society or of politics. On the fringes also were those men of secondary families who held important but lesser office. Beyond this, many equestrians who were involved neither in government and politics nor in finance or business must still have enjoyed relatively high social status because they came from well-to-do old and respected families.

The most important reason for the failure of some members of old families to play what they might secretly have thought their proper role in the state was surely the lack of money. Standards of luxury had increased rapidly for upper-class Romans. Cicero was a late-comer of a not particularly wealthy family; yet he had a town house on the Palatine in Rome which cost more than three million sesterces. Moreover he acquired seven other villas of varying value outside the city, some in resort areas. These had, of course, separate staffs and their own maintenance expenses. Most of Cicero's money came from bequests; wealthy clients, grateful for acquittals the orator obtained for them in the courts, but unable to pay a direct fee (this was illegal) left money in their wills; meanwhile Cicero's credit was good, since his future prospects were known. Also, he had income from gifts, from his wife's dowry, and from farmland and urban rental property. The really rich Romans—Crassus, Lucullus, or Pompey, for example—had a great deal more than the parvenu Cicero. Romans of this and later times were astonished how little money earlier figures of importance had. They used to come to see the small apartment Sulla had lived in as a young man and to marvel at the small rental that he then had found it possible to pay.

It is not surprising that most of the richer men of state took a very conservative stance politically and wished to see no thoroughgoing change. They enjoyed their villas, their retinues, their prestige. Cicero once remarked during the civil war of the 40s that these men were more concerned with keeping their fishponds (for their gourmet appetites) than anything else.

The upper class was much more sophisticated in Cicero's time than even a century earlier. This sophistication showed itself in religion and morals, manner of life, intellectual pursuits. The changes came mostly through interaction with the Hellenistic East. The philosophical thought of the Greeks, for example, not only influenced some Romans toward one or another of the schools of philosophy but also impinged upon their religious beliefs. They picked up the essential skepticism of Greek intellectuals almost by osmosis. They already looked upon religion as something usable for state—or personal—purposes. Romans continued to desire positions in the higher priestly colleges because of the prestige involved; and as aediles they put on ever more elaborate religious festivals. The purpose, however, had always been political more than religious, and the fact can hardly have escaped even the lowest class of citizens, when they saw Roman officials manipulate the omens before a battle or use them to block legislation they opposed. The tendency of the lower classes to seek consolation with the Oriental gods brought in by immigrants or the army surely related to this decline in basic religiosity among ruling class Romans.

It is easy to overstate the decadence of the state religion in upper-class Rome of the late Republic, however. Religion was somehow in the Romans' very bones; if with their minds educated Romans doubted the traditional gods they nevertheless embraced the whole pantheon with their hearts. Moreover, the intermingling of religion and politics was complete, the distinction made in modern times unthought of; dedication to the state religion thus was a part of essential patriotism. Thoughtful Romans saw in the neglect of certain aspects of the state religion one of the causes for the deterioration of the constitution.

Three intellectuals of the late Republic and early Empire, Cicero, Varro, and the historian Livy, all display this sort of ambiguous attitude toward religion. Cicero professed himself a follower of the Academy; by this he meant that he was a skeptic, though at times he seemed more Stoic than skeptic. His skepticism certainly extended to religion; yet he felt that religion was important, and not merely a sort of opiate of the masses. He somehow really believed that Rome's destiny was inextricably entwined with augury, auspices, and all the rest.

Philosophy, Literature, Life, and Law in the Late Republic

One of Rome's strengths over the centuries lay in the sizable number of upper-class persons who worked hard in the public service. We are familiar with the politicians and the generals. But there were others. With their usual pragmatism these Romans tended to gravitate to those pursuits that somehow related to politics: if they studied philosophy they might be especially concerned with constitutional theory and the law; if they learned rhetoric, it was to improve their performance as speakers in the Forum. In literature Romans placed great emphasis on history, which they saw as specifically useful. Even their satire often had a political tinge.

The philosophical schools that had the greatest impact on the Romans were naturally those current in the contemporary Hellenistic East: Academic skepticism, Stoicism, and Epicureanism. The sophisticated skepticism of the New Academy had come to Rome as early as 155 B.C. when the head of the Academy, Carneades, came with an embassy to the city and lectured in public. As mentioned earlier, he took both sides of the question, What is Justice, and scandalized the elder Cato, among others, by dealing so cavalierly with so serious a topic. Though Cicero professed himself an Academic, he was ambivalent in his convictions, and no Roman ever became an important teacher of this school; its subtle effects, however, are seen in the upper levels of Roman society for many decades.

Stoicism was much more directly influential. Panaetius, the house guest of the younger Scipio and a member of the so-called "Scipionic circle," popularized the teachings of the school at Rome. Among his pupils was P. Rutilius Rufus, consul in 105 B.C. and legate in the province of Asia in 97 or 94 B.C. He serves to remind us of that all too little publicized group of conscientious men of high integrity who made Roman rule—at least oftentimes—fair and palatable to provincials. Another pupil of Panaetius was the Rhodian Posidonius, whose influence on Roman thought and literature in the first century B.C. was pervasive. Stoicism powerfully influenced Cicero and the younger Cato as it did Seneca and Marcus Aurelius in the time of the Empire. Romans were not much attracted by the cosmological teachings of the Stoics, nor even by such basic principles as the fatherhood of god and the brotherhood of man. However, the emphases upon virtue as an end in itself, its own reward, upon acceptance of one's fate with equanimity, and upon duty, especially in the public service—these all appealed strongly to the Romans, whose *mos maiorum* (ancestral custom) already embraced those concepts. The Stoics merely articulated and ordered what most responsible Romans already believed.

Epicureanism in a formal sense appealed perhaps to only a few Romans, among them Julius Caesar. A basic theory was that the gods were unmindful of humans, who must seek their own pleasure. In its somewhat degenerate form, this was interpreted to mean merely a hedonistic life. This debased form of the philosophy perhaps spread rather facilely among a certain vein of the upper classes. Those who insisted, along with the founder, Epicurus, that only the virtuous man could be truly happy, were less numerous. The greatest exponent of Epicureanism among the Romans was a literary figure, Lucretius (c. 94–55 B.C.), who wrote *On the Nature of Things*. Lucretius' poem, almost evangelical in tone, preaching to and teaching its readers, is nevertheless a fine work. He expounded the atomic theory of the origins of things as Epicurus had (based on still earlier philosophic thought) and taught a kind of chance creation followed by long periods of geological and biological evolution. A prime purpose of the poet was to free his readers from the fear of death. For him, it was a comforting thought that the end of life was to be the end of everything for everyone.

A contemporary of Lucretius was Catullus (c. 84–54 B.C.), Rome's premier lyric poet. It is hard to imagine two poets more different. Lucretius was serious, contemplative, apparently rather isolated; Catullus was capable of being serious but he was more often frivolous, as he was gregarious and fun-loving. Catullus belonged to the young set that immediately comes to mind when one thinks of the charges of moral decadence in the Rome of his time. It would be a mistake, however, to conclude that the life style of this rather small upper-class group was really typical of Roman society in general.

Catullus' best lyric poems were written in celebration of one of his love affairs, with Clodia (Lesbia in his verses), beautiful if amoral sister of Clodius, the politician. She was a widow at the time. Eventually she tired of the amorous poet; his works run the gamut from ardent, wild love to doubt and finally spiteful hate when once he fully felt his rejection. The simple intensity of feeling and fine flow of words have led discriminating readers to adjudge that Catullus' works belong with the best of all lyric poetry.

Romans often turned to some form of history as a sort of respectable ancillary occupation. The elder Cato in the middle-second century B.C. published a book of history, *Origines*; his writing he felt was as important as his study of the law and his service as Rome's leading orator. In the last quarter of the same century the official records (*annales maximi*) of the office of the pontifex maximus were published by the consular, Publius Mucius Scaevola, and served as the basis for a number of works produced both at the end of the second century B.C. and later. None of the earlier ones remain. Other important historical sources too were lost, including the memoirs of several important men. Sulla's memoirs, however, were available two centuries later to Plutarch (as were some other works of the period) and we have to rely on such secondary authors.

The best known historical work that survives from the last century of the Republic is the *Gallic Wars* of Caesar. The fine, straightforward prose has caused it to be inflicted upon many a schoolchild whose interest in the topic is nil; in its own day it may have been intended as propaganda for the politician's own cause. However that may be, it stands as a valuable work of history and literature, as well as of style.

Another historian of Caesar's time, Sallust (G. Sallustius Crispus, c. 86–35 B.C.) typifies the genre of history better than does Caesar. Sallust was much imitated in his style, which he may himself have derived from an imitation of Thucydides. Besides a *History* of the period of the second quarter of the first century B.C., of which only some fragments remain, Sallust wrote a work on the Jugurthan War and another on the conspiracy of Catiline. The first, especially, portrays with exaggerated emphasis the decadence of the aristocracy. The theme is implicit also in the Catiline. Yet Sallust had some excellent sources and, despite his Caesarian sympathies, wrote well and objectively. His pessimism and emphasis on decadence set a trend—almost a fashion—for future writers, who felt called upon also to take a similar moral stance.

The student may think of Cicero primarily as a politician and orator, but he was also a literary figure of importance. He influenced the development of the Latin language more than any other single person, and his works have had a literary (and often a rhetorical or humanistic) impact on Western scholars consistently over many centuries. Orations and essays he published in his lifetime, but it is the letters—more than eight hundred of them, published only after his death—which have had perhaps the greatest influence in modern times. They have also attracted the closest attention from historians, whether their major interests involve intellectual, social, or economic conditions, or politics. These letters, polished and elegant in style, are windows through which we glimpse the Rome of Cicero's day more intimately and directly than in any other literature of any sort. Because we can also get into Cicero's mind as into that of no other Roman, scholars develop more emphatic views about the great scholar than about any other of his contemporaries except perhaps Caesar. The tendency is to love the one and despise the other or vice versa, and often in most unscholarly manner!

Most of Cicero's orations in court cases display political overtones. Characteristic of his calling as an orator, he was not an outstanding legal expert; equally characteristic, legal experts were not necessarily good orators. Those public-spirited men who studied the law intensively in order to give free, expert legal advice to all comers were called jurisconsults or jurisprudents. It would have been illegal for them to accept a fee, just as it was for the trial lawyers. The two greatest *jurisprudentes* of

Cicero. (*Alinari–Scala*)

the first century B.C. were Q. Mucius Scaevola, consul in 95 B.C., son of Publius Mucius Scaevola, consul in 133 B.C. and also a jurisprudent, and Servius Sulpicius Rufus, consul in 51. Much influenced by Stoic thought, Scaevola made a beginning of rational codification. Rufus also was a prolific writer, but none of his works have survived. The law at this time was in process of rather rapid change, largely because of Rome's expanding responsibilities. All Roman magistrates had the right to make law to a degree through their edicts. The urban praetors were most influential in this respect. The so-called formulary system, introduced some time earlier, was still in process of replacing the older, much more rigid action system. Through the use of *formulae* the praetors could fit the law to the specific case much more exactly; a *formula* was, essentially, an instruction, given by the praetor after a sort of preliminary hearing to the judge who was to preside over the case, indicating that if the circumstances were found to be such and such then the decision should be such and such. In certain sorts of cases equity was being emphasized: determination on the basis of what was fair rather than on specific law.

Another group of Romans made themselves expert in religious matters, as for example in the taking of auspices and omens. This seems rather unimportant in retrospect, but at the time it was a more significant matter.

146 SOCIAL CHANGE IN THE LATE REPUBLIC

Such public figures as these, many of the jurisprudents, and all of the orators had multiple motives: they wished to obligate important men to themselves, to build up a clientele in usual fashion that would carry them to high office. Yet it remains remarkable that so many of Rome's upper classes were willing to work so long and hard in service to the state for the sake of recognition. The tradition was to continue under the Empire, though the rewards then came from the emperor more than from the people. The upper classes of the late Republic, following the picture painted by Sallust, are often portrayed as morally bankrupt and decadent; a more accurate sketch will depict also those numerous jurists, scholars, and orators who, for the rewards of respect and recognition, dedicated themselves to the public service.

In neither ancient nor modern times have men disputed Augustus' greatest achievement: it was peace. People in his own time had lived through the civil war years with all their misery, uncertainty, and fear. To them peace, even at the price of restricted freedom for some, was as welcome as sunshine after long rain. A leader who could not only bring peace but also maintain it ranked in their eyes as a savior of humanity. Modern admirers of the first emperor, looking backward from a perspective of many centuries, have been most impressed by the length of time—two and a half centuries, except for brief episodes —that the pax Romana endured.

Peace became a consciously developed theme of the regime. The gates to the temple of Janus, closed only on the rare occasion when there was no war at all, were shut three times during Augustus' years, with public celebration. The Altar to Peace (Ara Pacis), constructed on the Campus Martius in the middle years of Augustus' reign, elaborated the theme in fine high-relief sculpture, as the Augustan poet Vergil sang the theme in verse. The poet saw in Augustus the embodiment of the Roman destiny, which was to put an end to chaos and to fashion a new golden age of peace and law. Many of the panels of the Ara Pacis may still be seen in a little museum on the Tiber opposite the remains of the mausoleum Augustus built; they convey with powerful feeling the serenity of the age. Peace was also a theme of the *Res Gestae*, the document Augustus left as a kind of summary and defense of his career. It has been largely preserved in inscriptions (in particular one found in Turkey and called the Monumentum Ancyranum). Here the theme is indirect: the victories that brought peace are emphasized. But this was the Roman view of things. Even Vergil saw peace as something that Romans imposed upon others.

Peace alone was not enough, of course:

THE EARLY EMPIRE: AUGUSTUS AND TIBERIUS, 27 B.C. – A.D. 37

A relief from the *Ara Pacis* (Altar to Peace) at Rome. Erected by Augustus to elaborate the theme of peace. (*Alinari–Scala*)

in civil war rivals may be only temporarily subdued. For Augustus it was a great advantage, to be sure, that most Romans were weary of war. But any peace that could endure had to be based on *clementia, iustitia,* and *libertas;* the victor in the wars was wise enough to see that. These virtues, as also *pietas,* were, along with peace, themes of the new age. Augustus did indeed show clemency for many of his defeated rivals—such of them as survived, at any rate! He may also properly be called just— evenhanded—in his treatment of Roman and provincial, upper class and low. Liberty he saw in the *Res Gestae* as the good which resulted from his defeat of the "tyrant," by whom he meant Antony; but he also attempted to restore at least a measure of that elusive commodity to the former ruling class by giving them an important role in the new order. As for the Roman lower classes, peace probably meant more freedom of action and opportunity than any electoral process had provided in the past. However, their voting rights did gradually disappear, both in the electoral and in the legislative spheres; thus it could be said that the price they paid for security was their free institutions. But had they ever been really free?

The pattern was essentially repeated in the provinces. There Rome had generally granted the city-state units self-governing institutions that primarily benefited a rather restricted ruling class. As for the lower-class provincials, quite likely many of them enjoyed more personal freedom under the Romans than before, under their own rulers. Lower-class freedom then, both at Rome and in the provinces, existed under the Empire in significant senses, but was not defined in terms of the privilege of participation in governmental processes.

The "Restoration of the Republic"

In 27 B.C. Augustus announced the restoration of the *res publica*, a term which usually translates—transliterates, actually—somewhat imperfectly into English as Republic. Augustus certainly meant to restore many of the traditions of the old Republic and to continue the important offices, which would be held by men elected in the citizen assemblies. However, the Republic had been dominated by great individuals since the time of Sulla and earlier; even such a republican as Cicero had come to doubt that it could endure without a great figure at the helm. It is therefore hardly right to charge Augustus with a totally cynical hypocrisy, as some have done, in this announced restoration. It seems probable that he was consciously following Cicero's view, though in the matter of ultimate power for the dominant leader (himself) he certainly went beyond the great orator's ideal type of the patron of the state.

It must be admitted that no institution of the new state, not even the Senate, could be really free when confronted by the arbitrary power Augustus held in his grasp, even if in velvet glove. Yet it is doubtful that Augustus fully understood this (in 27 B.C. he was still only thirty-five); at any rate, most Romans were satisfied with the imitation of freedom that could be projected by a *princeps* (first citizen) who displayed tolerance and clemency. Augustus and at least a majority of his successors for two centuries were *principes* of that sort.

For Augustus and for all Romans, *res publica* meant much more than the political structure of the oligarchy of the Republic. The term embraced all public aspects of state, society, and culture, which were firmly rooted in the traditions of the past. A closely parallel expression was *mos maiorum*, the customs of the ancestors. In many ways Augustus did try very hard to restore the old ways. He reconstituted priesthoods, some of which had long deteriorated; he rebuilt temples, restored the historic sacrifices and festivals. He attempted to restore the old morals, and passed several laws in the attempt. Sumptuary legislation, in the pattern of earlier laws stretching back a couple of centuries, attempted to limit how much individuals might spend in banqueting and the like. Conspicuous consumption and ostentation the princeps also dampened somewhat by his own modest manner of life. New laws against adultery he applied even against his own daughter Julia, and her daughter of the same name as well: both were banished.

Adultery threatened the social fabric of the state; it damaged the family, that most important constituent unit. Especially in the upper strata of society the family had lost cohesiveness under stress of prosperity and the freer sexual mores of the late Republic. Paradoxically, the new affluence made it difficult for many upper-class families to raise more than a minimum number of children. Child-rearing cost a great deal, especially because each girl required a dowry and each boy an inheritance, if the children were to take their proper places in society at the level these families tried to maintain. Augustus often gave large presents of money to heads of families in distress. As a rule the man involved was about to lose his rank—usually senatorial—because he could not meet the minimum property requirement, a million sesterces; but Augustus' motives were not solely political.

The princeps made it clear that the normal life style of the upper class should include marriage and children: he hoped the upper classes would increase in numbers. He taxed unmarried persons of marriageable age, even widows and widowers; and he permitted men with children to hold office earlier than childless candidates. He even allowed men and women—except those of the senatorial order—to enter into formal marriage with freed persons, ex-slaves. Yet these measures to maintain the great families largely failed. Many such families in the next several decades disappear from history. In part this may reflect only the withdrawal of the scions of great families from political activity (did they consider it all a charade or did they just shirk the army and provincial service ordinarily required?) and thus from the records remaining to us from which we fashion history. However, it is likely that most such families simply died out.

The Augustan emphasis on family and the ancient mores is best comprehended in the term *pietas*. Piety for Romans meant loyalty and devotion both to the family and to the state. This basic concept of course weakened along with the family. No longer did the great families venerate illustrious ancestors— at least many sons of the leading families seem to have made little effort to emulate the great deeds of their forebears. Since their ancestors had become great through service to the state, the attitude portended a corresponding decline in patriotic enthusiasm for public service.

In Vergil's *Aeneid* the Trojan Aeneas is an archetype of *pietas*. After his best efforts to save the state fail, Aeneas flees the burning city carrying his aged father on his shoulders. In sculpture even in quite early times, in painting, and in coin

A renaissance sculptor's conception of Aeneas bearing his father, Anchises, from Troy. Used as a theme by Caesar and Augustus, symbolic of piety. Perhaps by Bernini. (*Alinari–Roma, Museo della Villa Borghese*)

types the portrayal of Aeneas carrying his father symbolizes this ancient virtue. The Aeneas symbol appears on one of Caesar's coin types. Augustus and the Romans remembered, of course, that Caesar claimed descent from Aeneas and thus from Venus, his mother. The Dictator planned a temple to Venus in his new forum. The temple to Mars which Augustus later constructed in another new forum was in a way a work of piety: Caesar had vowed it; moreover, he had claimed descent from that god also, since in the myth Romulus was both the descendant of Aeneas and the son of Mars. Augustus' emphasis on the deified Caesar, seen particularly on his early coinage, represents thus a form of *pietas* which had the further advantage that it forged a strong link between the princeps and his popular father by adoption. Augustus also built a temple to the Divine Julius in the Forum, with similar dual benefit. The second princeps, Tiberius, in turn performed such acts of filial piety for the dead Augustus, and paid him the further compliment of following his stated policies in almost every conceivable way. This in spite of the fact that he surely felt more a stepson to a stepfather than a legitimate son and successor.

Power: The Government

The major bases of power in any government lie in the army, in finance, and in the chief offices. We have already seen that Augustus followed a deliberate policy of dominance in the pattern of the great figures of the late Republic. He learned from Caesar's fate that one's power should not be too open, and chose to adhere more closely to the traditional forms than Caesar had. In Augustus' early years by and large, the people, as in the Republic, continued to elect the chief officers of state. These performed mostly in duties assigned in traditional manner by the Senate, which also controlled the old treasury, the Aerarium Saturni. A part of the army was commanded by these elected officials. However, Augustus was for some years always one of the consuls. Later, in 23 B.C., when he ceased to hold annual consulships, he was given what was called *maius imperium*. This meant that his *imperium*, or right of command outranked that of any other official. Moreover, most of the army was under his command and he controlled all recruitment and retirement. Further, he had a great deal of income at his disposal which did not filter through the Saturn treasury at all. He had in addition the powers of a tribune (*tribunicia potestas*), which meant that he could convoke the assembly; and occasionally he exercised the old powers of a censor without actually reviving the office.

Augustus preferred to mask this great power. Whereas Caesar had been dictator, Augustus liked the title princeps, of republican origins. The title "Augustus," conferred by the complaisant Senate, implied a personage of great influence, dignity, and semidivine qualities. Later on he was styled *pater patriae*, Father of his Country, by the Senate and stressed it on the coinage. His behind-the-scenes power affected the elections: he did not always specify favored candidates, but when he did, sometimes openly canvassing for his choices, so far as we know they always won.

The Senate was hardly a free body despite the carefully maintained appearance of freedom. The most powerful senators were always somehow tied to the regime. Those who wished full careers could advance most rapidly, or perhaps could advance at all, only if they had the good will of the princeps. The positions conferring the greatest prestige—especially in the command of troops—were those held by the princeps' deputies or legates. These were appointed by him, not elected; the Senate neither gave them their assignments nor allocated them funds.

Yet in some ways the Senate was technically more powerful than during the Republic. Its decrees gradually acquired the formal force of law: the emperors enforced them, since the Senate rather than the assemblies enacted the measures they desired. The most important matters recommended to it were first screened by the princeps, with the assistance of a kind of cabinet, at first unofficial, the *consilium principis;* this body always included some of the chief senators. In the last half of Augustus' reign, attendance dropped at elective assemblies, which began to consist more and more only of residents of the city. Certain voting units called prerogative centuries, now composed entirely of senators, voted first in the elections; since the other centuries followed like sheep, the senators decided the votes. Tiberius (probably) eliminated the pretense; in effect, elections became simply a function of the Senate.

The body also acquired new judicial power, both over its own members and over others in cases involving high crimes. In addition it served in some instances as an appeals body. By the reign of Tiberius, it seems the Senate was fulfilling these judicial functions somewhat haphazardly. Tiberius tried to raise standards by sitting in on some trials with the Senate. The historian Tacitus, an old senatorial conservative in sentiment, declared this was good for justice but bad for freedom. He meant the Senate's freedom, of course.

Certainly the Senate did not behave like a free institution under Tiberius, though he began his reign with an appeal to senators to share the heavy burdens of his post. The worthies tended to make decisions on the basis of what they felt the princeps might wish rather than on any independent judgment. Thus in the later years of Tiberius many persons were tried and condemned for *maiestas*—treason—against the emperor, on trivial charges. Earlier Tiberius several times personally quashed such charges, but he should have stopped these trials altogether. The procedure was inherently bad: the Romans had never had public prosecutors and always depended upon private citizens to bring charges against those guilty of political crimes (among others). The accusers or informers (*delatores*) were rewarded from the estates of persons condemned. Though *delatores* might also be punished for false accusations, some men seem virtually to have made a career of informing. The atmosphere created was repressive in the extreme.

The emperors put some of the most important and sensitive administrative posts in the government into the hands of officials called prefects, mostly drawn not from the aristocracy but from the equestrian order. Such men often owed all to the princeps and thus were likely to be more loyal than the nobles. The highest ranking prefects included the governor of Egypt (other imperial provinces were governed by legates); the praetorian prefect, who commanded the Praetorian Guard, the prefect of the grain supply at Ostia, Rome's port, the prefect of the *vigiles* (police/fire units) at Rome, and the urban prefect, who governed the city of Rome for the emperor. The latter was a senator. Equestrians also supplied the imperial procurators, who looked after the financial matters of the principes all over the Empire, commanded the fleet, and governed small provinces.

Power: Imperial Finance

Although the old treasury in the temple of Saturn survived, and the Senate in time-honored fashion continued to appropriate from it for the traditional purposes, most of the Empire's wealth gradually came under the control of the principes. One new treasury was established, the *aerarium militare;* supported by a new sales tax levied in Italy and by an inheritance tax, it was designed to ensure bonuses and retirement benefits for soldiers. Of course it was totally controlled by the emperor. Most of the imperial provinces that required legionary forces produced no net income for the Empire; this meant that the monies raised in those provinces through taxes remained within the provincial treasuries (*fisci*) for expenditure locally. Naturally the governor (that is, the emperor) or his representative controlled these funds, and doubtless rendered account on paper at Rome.

Only one of the new provinces yielded a considerable surplus—primarily of wheat—and that was Egypt. This province was somehow different from the rest and under the special care of the emperor. As we have seen, it was governed by an equestrian prefect, and senators were not allowed to visit it without special imperial approval: history had demonstrated clearly how a leader with an army could turn the country into an easily defended, independent kingdom. The income from this rich province was of course under imperial control.

The emperor's property itself, the *patrimonium*, came to be so large that it too was an important element in the imperial financial structure. The early emperors accumulated property rapidly. Every important person felt it an obligation, if not an actual honor, to include the princeps in his will. Properties confiscated from upper-class persons condemned of high crimes seem usually to have remained in the control of the emperor.

Emperor Augustus in
ceremonial armor and
commanding pose.
(*Alinari–Roma, Museo
Vaticano*)

Gifts added to the whole. Possibly income from Egypt swelled
the total. It is doubtful that the freedman (probably) who kept
the accounts for the imperial household thought it important
to distinguish property of the Empire from that of the princeps.

Procurators looked out for the emperor's financial interests
even in senatorial provinces. As every reader of the New Testament knows, some played a role in the smaller provincial areas
indistinguishable from that of governors. In addition, certain of
the prefects appointed by the emperor controlled important
funds or financial operations. Whatever overall financial planning was done took place in the imperial offices (we do not
know anything in detail about it, however). Thus in indirect
but quite open ways, Augustus and Tiberius set a trend that was
to continue until virtually all important public funds were controlled by an official appointed by the emperor and responsible
only to him. By the second century A.D. there had evolved, probably out of the office originally in charge of the *patrimonium*,
a central treasury at Rome, the *fiscus*, which became *the* treasury
of the Empire.

The emperors also closely controlled the coinage. Coins
were struck to meet current expenditures; there was no con-

ception of manipulation of the money supply to control the economy. The coins were issued in gold, silver, bronze, and copper. (The bronze and copper coins usually have the inscription S.C., indicating they were authorized by the Senate, but that authorization seems to have been only formal.) The gold coin, aureus, weighing about forty-two to the Roman twelve-ounce pound, was tariffed at twenty-five denarii. The latter, struck at the old standard, eighty-four to the pound, were the standard silver coins, and were issued in huge quantity. The sestertius, one-quarter the denarius in value, was usually brassy in appearance and often a beautiful coin; larger than the gold and silver it gave the engraver freer scope for his art. The dupondius, as, and other smaller coins were struck in copper. Enough has been remarked of coin types to indicate what was true, that the coinage was used for propaganda as well as for purely monetary purposes. It is not certain, of course, that the types were personally approved by the emperors, but in general the emphases seem to correspond to those known from the literary sources, inscriptions, art, and architectural monuments.

Power: The Military

Emergency armies, only loosely controlled by the central government, each soldier sworn to obey his commander, had helped to bring down the Roman Republic. Augustus therefore decided not only to keep a standing army of such size that rarely would it be necessary to recruit emergency armies, but also to control all recruiting and retirement arrangements. Troops took an oath of loyalty to the princeps rather than to the men who eventually exercised the actual command in the field. Obviously Augustus also served as official commander-in-chief of most of the legions, since through his legates, he governed the provinces in which most of them were stationed. Not all: some still were commanded by proconsuls appointed by the Senate—as, early in Augustus' reign, in Macedonia, which was a senatorial province, and in Africa.

Augustus managed to rule his dominions, to hold off threats to the frontiers, and even to extend them vastly, with an army of only 28 legions, later 25, plus auxiliaries. Toward the end of his reign, the legions were distributed as follows: in Spain, once the conquest of the peninsula was completed in 19 B.C., a reduction to three; in Gaul, none, small units only; in Germany, along the troublesome Rhine frontier, eight; along the Danube and in Macedonia, six or seven; in Syria, three or four; in Egypt, three; and in all the rest of North Africa, only one, with other units.

That this army, totaling not much more than a quarter of a million (about half legionaries, half auxiliaries) should have been equal to such tasks indicates how few troops were required within the center of the Empire and how effective the legions were out on the frontiers. Such an army seems extremely small for an empire so far-flung, made up of a population of many millions (just how many is extremely uncertain; perhaps, say, more than fifty million but less than one hundred million) of such diverse groups, and with frontiers so long and exposed. Yet this was about the maximum number the Empire could support without adverse effects on the economy. When at the famous battle of the Teutoburger forest in Germany the Roman general Varus and three whole legions fell to the German Arminius (9 A.D.), Augustus did not feel he could reconstitute the lost legions. He simply called off any expansion into Germany, consolidated the frontier on the Rhine, and managed with fewer legions.

Part of his problem may have been recruitment rather than finance. The legionaries were Roman citizens only, drawn mostly from Italy. Were there too few citizens willing to go into the still arduous army service? There were advantages. Wherever the legionaries served they constituted a privileged class. For one thing, they were citizens; in most provinces there were still few such. Moreover, they were representatives of the dominant power. Also, their pay compared favorably with the local wage scales, and they could look forward to a generous retirement. For some few persons the army could become the steppingstone to a distinguished career. Men who became centurions often displayed such abilities as to mark them as candidates for higher posts in the government. *Primi pili* (the chief centurions of legions) often advanced to rather important military tribunates and then, occasionally, to procuratorships or prefectureships.

Auxiliaries were drawn from the noncitizen classes all over the Empire. Though paid less than the legionaries, required to serve longer, and qualifying for lesser bonuses on retirement, the army career attracted many in the provinces. One reason was that on retirement they received the citizenship. Both auxiliaries and legionaries often were settled in colonies that received the Italic Right—that is, its residents were free of taxes and other usual obligations. Such communities in the provinces naturally were Latin-speaking and although the cultural level was not high, they became quite important as centers of Romanization. Such colonies, most likely to be placed in the less settled of the provinces, served an acculturization role most significantly in the western areas and along the Danube. Army service tended to become hereditary, the sons of retired soldiers enlisting in their turn. The role of the Italians in the army gradually declined, perhaps in part because of the availability of citizen-recruits from the colonies or elsewhere in the provinces and in part because of an increasing disinclination of Italians to commit themselves to twenty years of army service.

Augustus established a new and prestigious branch of the armed forces, the Praetorian Guard. Commanders had long used praetorians to guard their headquarters, the *praetorium*. Though not a personal bodyguard, the Guard in a sense served the traditional function and thus was based on precedent. However its size (nine cohorts, one double-size) was extraordinary. Moreover, the fact that their commander usually stayed in Rome meant that these cohorts were stationed in Italy—and later, by Tiberius, just outside Rome itself. The troops therefore served to prevent outbreak of any sort against the regime. They could be and occasionally were used as a sort of reserve for emergency service in critical situations in the provinces. Mostly, however, they acted simply as an elite guard, superloyal to the princeps. Praetorians were citizens, and for two centuries were drawn only from Italy. They served a shorter period than the legions (usually sixteen years) and received both higher pay and larger bonuses on retirement. The Guard also served as a means of social mobility, for praetorians of promise might be promoted to officer rank in the legions.

Freedmen, too, found opportunity in the imperial military service. They made up the ships' complements of the fleet. Augustus established two major naval bases, both in Italy: one at Misenum, and the other on the Adriatic side, at Ravenna. The most competent freedmen, however, surely stayed out of the navy; they found more lucrative careers in small business and industry, at least in Italy.

Freedmen also served in another new organization of a semimilitary nature, the *vigiles* of the city of Rome. These seven cohorts functioned both as firemen and police in the city, which in the late Republic suffered from the lack of such units. Augustus formally organized Rome into fourteen *regiones* and into smaller units called *vici;* each cohort of a thousand men was responsible for two of the regions.

Augustus used his army rather vigorously for some years. He, or rather, his chief lieutenant and son-in-law, Agrippa, campaigned in Spain until the entire peninsula was more or less under Roman control, by 19 B.C. At the same time he was bringing under Roman dominion the vast areas in the northeast which the Romans called Noricum, Pannonia, and Maesia; here the Danube became the frontier, except that Thrace for the time remained an independent, client state. Exploratory thrusts eastward across the Rhine into Germany at first went well but came to a sudden halt after the disaster that overtook Varus' army in 9 A.D. At the same time a rebellion had to be put down on the extended northeastern frontier. Augustus thereupon, as we have seen, made the Rhine and the Danube his frontiers and followed a generally passive policy during the last years of his life.

Tiberius, who in most ways tended to follow the policy of Augustus, took the same route. He had to restrain Germanicus, his nephew, who as commander in Germany seemed determined to seek Varus' fate. In the East, the Parthians to some degree occupied the attention of both Augustus and Tiberius. Augustus felt it necessary to regain the three eagles captured by the Parthians in 53 B.C. when they overwhelmed Crassus' ill-fated expedition in the desert. But he recovered the eagles through diplomacy backed by the threat of force. Tiberius too avoided a major confrontation. Peace in the last half of the reign of Tiberius helped to make it possible for him to accumulate a substantial surplus in the treasury.

Partners in Prestige: The Upper Classes

It is a tribute to Augustus' wisdom that he shared with the Roman nobles the facade of power but not its reality. It frustrated some of them who were not satisfied with prestige alone. The historian Tacitus reflects well that frustration. But most accepted the situation. Tiberius continued the policy but, characteristically, with less finesse and, consequently, with more resentment on the part of some of the upper classes.

Augustus' early attitude contrasts somewhat with that of the last half of his reign. He did not, apparently, trust or make use of the scions of the old aristocratic families in his earlier years. He chose rather to elevate relative unknowns. Often these were descendants of Italian families, citizens only since the Italian war of 90–89 B.C. Once assured of his position, however, the princeps tended to give more important posts to old-line aristocrats—such of them as had survived the civil wars. And he made several marriage compacts involving his relatives and the great families. His own marriage with Livia had brought connections not only with Livii, but with the patrician Claudii. His granddaughter Julia was married to an Aemilius Paullus; his nieces, the daughters of Mark Antony by Octavia, to a Claudius and a Domitius; another niece, Octavia's daughter by Marcellus, he married to an Aemilius Lepidus. To some extent Augustus was simply doing the natural thing, making the best marriages for his relatives, but he seems deliberately to have sought a kind of reconciliation with the old aristocracy. The Roman nobles, who had lost much in the new order, conciliated in this and other ways, were for the most part content to bask in the warmth of their secondary place in the sun.

The emperors also supported the upper classes in the provinces, here following what had been the steady policy of the government of the Republic. Local government functioned with a considerable degree of autonomy in the city-states that made up the fabric of the provincial system. But what Rome encouraged was a much used form that meant little oligarchies, not democracies, with popular assemblies that elected officials from among a restricted class of eligible persons. The upper classes of the provincial cities were often on terms of friendship with Roman nobles. Provincial aristocrats might be rewarded for their good service in local government by seats on the provincial council, where there was little power but much prestige. And they might even be rewarded with Roman citizenship.

In the West Augustus and Tiberius were less generous to the native stock. Tribal organizations were set up in the less settled areas in place of the city-state forms in the East. Though Julius Caesar had given not only citizenship but even, to a few Gauls, Senate appointments, Augustus chose, not precisely to reverse the policy, but at least to apply it with great deliberation. Yet in the West as well as in the East the primary effort to tie provinces to the central government with bands of loyalty involved the upper classes, not the common people.

For citizens, the most precise definition of the highest rank was political rather than social. The senatorial class thus is most often mentioned in the sources. The nobles were primarily those descended from the older *nobilitas*, though sometimes the term seems synonymous with the senatorial class. The class wore the broad stripe (*latus clavus*) on the toga; sons of senators wore the stripe by right also, as they were expected to follow in their fathers' footsteps. Occasionally the princeps granted the right to wear the senatorial symbols, perhaps to someone who sought a senatorial career, or to a man who deserved special distinction. There was also a census qualification of one million sesterces in property.

The equestrian order was, it seems, a bit more amorphous. In one sense it included all citizens who met the technical census qualification, now four hundred thousand sesterces in property, whether they lived in Italy or in some provincial city. The term also might refer to a more restricted portion of the order: those men who at some time in their lives actually served in the cavalry—"held a public horse"—and who ordinarily went on to a political career. Sons of senators were normally included in this group, until they were elected quaestors and entered the Senate. For this group Augustus revived the old practice of an annual parade or review, a ceremony of dignity and honor. Occasionally the term refers to the still smaller group of those who actually held one of the offices open to equestrians.

The equestrians wore the narrow stripe (*angusti clavus*). Their sons began their political careers with a lower office than the sons of senators, and could not normally aspire to the highest ranks. The highest posts available to men of this class were the prefectureships already discussed. The prefectureship of Egypt was most prestigious: it compared to the senatorial *legatus pro praetore*, for the Egyptian governor commanded three legions and controlled property of great value. The post of praetorian prefect at Rome grew in power and importance so that by the middle-first century its importance rivaled that of the Egyptian prefecture.

Many of those who qualified for the equestrian census, especially those away from Rome itself, will have been businessmen. Many of these put much of their wealth into land as the most stable and sure investment. Moreover, some who remained equestrians, as for example Augustus' friend Maecenas, moved in the highest social circles. The number of equestrians in the empire cannot be determined; it was not large relative to the total population, but the number must have increased in the early Empire. Augustus and his immediate successors created conditions under which trade could flourish, with peace, little governmental interference, and reasonable levels of taxation. Only in connection with the grain supply did the government intervene and exercise restrictive controls.

It still meant something to be a patrician, though no political distinction remained. Acting on a precedent established by Caesar (through a law), the early emperors on occasion created new patrician families. This was done only because of the disappearance of the older ones. The class was not distinguished politically from the senatorial families.

Literary Figures of the Early Empire

As everyone knows, artists and writers in some ways reflect their own times. Not even a Lucretius lives in a vacuum. And so it was during the Augustan period, in which literature flourished so richly that this is usually called the Golden Age of Latin literature.

The historian Livy (Titus Livius, 59 B.C.–A.D. 17 or 64 B.C.–A.D. 12) approved of Augustus and his general aims and yet felt a strong nostalgia for the great days of the past. He helped generations of Romans—and of others since—not merely to understand but to feel the crises their ancestors surmounted through the simple virtues. How profoundly Livy impressed the Roman mind by his *History of Rome* in his own day is illustrated by the story—told by the younger Pliny—of the Roman citizen resident in Spain who came to Rome solely to lay eyes on the great historian and having seen him, paid no attention to anything else in the resplendent world capital but returned home immediately.

Livy's strong attachment to the old ways and his admiration for the great figures of the Republic might have seemed dangerous to a more paranoid princeps than Augustus. The emperor, in fact, once called Livy a Pompeian; and it is possible that Livy did not take his history further—it came down, in 142 books, to about 9 b.c—because of the sensitivity of the material. Still, Augustus seems to have been wholly tolerant of the historian and of others of similar view; after all both of them saw many things alike, and Livy must have approved wholeheartedly of the princeps' attempts to restore old virtues and mores. As for the historian's failure to go further, the enormity of his task is sufficient explanation for that. Indeed, his toil was heavy enough to excuse many of the weaknesses of his work, which include occasional contradictions and failures to make use of the most basic source materials. His achievement has stood high enough not only to survive but even to triumph over all criticism.

The way in which the premier poet Vergil (P. Vergilius Maro, 70–19 b.c.) reflected some of the ideals and aspirations of the new age has been well enough indicated already. In a sense, he narrated in verse what Livy did in prose—the rise of Rome to become, through the strivings of virtuous men, the ruler of the Mediterranean. But whereas Livy was pessimistic about his own times in contrast to the greater past, Vergil felt that a new era, a Golden Age, had come through the Julii. That was his mature view, in the *Aeneid,* which he left unfinished at his death. Earlier he may well have shared Livy's uneasiness, but not his despair; for his earlier works, the *Eclogues* and the *Georgics,* are romantic, almost escapist works. Intellectuals often turn to rural themes, to the idealization of the sturdy, virtuous farmer when the troubles of their times seem to defy solution.

Horace (Quintus Horatius Flaccus, 65–8 b.c.), writing flawless and facile lines, dwelled on themes somewhat more petty than those exalted ones of Vergil. His *Epodes, Satires, Odes,* and *Epistles* deal with everyday joys and concerns or with the faults and foibles of ordinary humans. Though Horace was the son of a freedman from Apulia, he got a good education at

Rome. He was in Athens when Brutus organized opposition to the triumvirs; caught up in republican enthusiasm he fought on the losing side at Philippi. He was basically apolitical, however, and not only was forgiven but soon became a supporter of Octavian/Augustus. Several of his *Odes* and *Epodes* deplore the carnage of civil war and laud Augustus as one who restored peace along with all the neglected virtues: piety, patriotism, justice, restraint, modesty.

It was Maecenas, the trusted lieutenant of Augustus and patron of the arts, who brought Horace to the good graces of the emperor. Descended from a reputedly royal Etruscan line, Maecenas was a bit too voluptuous in his tastes for Augustus, and did not formally hold high office, but he was enormously useful nevertheless. He encouraged Vergil and gave aid to Horace. The latter seems to have lost property (as Vergil's family lost a farm in north Italy) because he embraced the losing cause. But Maecenas got for him a fine farm in the Sabine country not far from Rome. It gave Horace a living and the independence he required.

These three major writers reflected in their works the upper-class viewpoint. This may seem surprising since none of them came from a noble background. Horace, especially, of a freedman father, one might expect to retain lower-class views. But education, as it often does, brought with it an upper-class outlook. And it is worth noting that Roman upper-class society would freely accept such a person, because of his literary achievements. Horace sneered at the upstart rich military tribune, though he also poked satirical fun at nobles and equestrians. And as has often been noted, both Vergil and Horace played the part, even if sincerely, of propagandists for the Augustan regime. Horace became a sort of court poet. When Augustus put on the great Secular games in 17 B.C. (celebrated each *saeculum*, a century or 110 years), it was Horace who wrote the *Carmen Saeculare*, including in it fulsome praise for the emperor. Yet any fair appraiser must admit that Augustus' considerable achievements, coming as they did after so much war and destruction, deserved recognition in the contemporary literature.

Though less important to the political historian, the Augustan poet Ovid (Publius Ovidius Naso, 43 B.C.–A.D. 17) casts light on a dissolute social scene in the capital. This poet came of an old equestrian family and might have been expected to climb the political ladder or at least to have joined Maecenas' circle near the center of power. Instead he chose to drop politics after a small beginning; he stood apart from the regime as a member of a loose set whose behavior and morals undercut Augustus' public policy on these matters. One of his best known and probably most read poems was his *Ars Amatoria*, the Art of Love or perhaps more exactly, the Art of Seduction. He married well—three times—and moved in some of the same circles as the emperor's own daughter Julia, who was later exiled for adultery. Ovid himself was exiled in A.D. 8 for some undisclosed offense, perhaps somehow involving Augustus' granddaughter Julia, to Tomis on the Black Sea, and there he lived out his remaining years, constantly appealing to return and complaining about his miserable fate.

Ovid's important works include not only the works on love but also the *Metamorphoses*, a valuable compilation mostly of somewhat romanticized Greek mythology, and the *Fasti*. The latter is a calendar of activity at Rome—the first six months of the year only, unfortunately. From it we learn much of the religious and other festivals. As poetry it lacks the quality of Ovid's other works, but for the social historian it brings understanding of various aspects of the Roman religion. Yet it somehow does not convey Roman feelings toward religion and the gods as well as do the works of Livy or Vergil or Horace.

Farms and Farmers

Vergil and Horace, like many another poet before and since, portray rural life not merely as pleasant and beautiful but as idyllic, somehow ministering to man's deepest needs. Almost everyone has of course been similarly moved, especially in spring. But throughout the history of the West, there seems to be a recurring intellectual, romanticized glorification of life on a farm coupled with a desire to return to the soil. In application, however, the feeling, brought on by the beauties of spring and the excitement of the first growth of plants, often peters out

Mosaic depicting pastoral scene. (*Alinari–Scala*)

under the hot July sun when the weeding needs to be done. One must remember that in ancient times farming was not only hard but sometimes brutish, and that Horace and Vergil wrote as absentee landlords.

Some Roman and provincial farmers obviously prospered and sent their sons to be educated in the city—perhaps even to Rome or Athens. But more of them struggled hard, prospered little, put little store in education *per se*, were provincial, suspicious of foreigners, narrow in their views. Moreover, rural life had its perils from bands of robbers, disease, drought, flood, and the like. Every farmer needed a sharp lookout, two or three strong dogs, and high walls to enclose house, barn, and yard against night prowlers.

Our sources indicate that the problems in Roman agriculture seen during the Republic continued into the early Empire: a decline in small holders, further increases in the plantation-like farms, and a continuing trend toward more tenant farming, with all the evils that go with absentee landlordism. We have seen that these reports may be exaggerated, since the colonization programs, especially for veterans, in the Republic and in the Empire, certainly reestablished thousands of small holders, many of them permanently, in the Italian countryside. Slaves were harder to come by, and thus more expensive, in the peace of the early Empire, and this must also have been something of a deterrent to the continued growth of the large latifundia. As for absentee landlordism, we may well believe in the continued spread of this unfortunate system.

Southern Italy seems even in the early Empire to have begun the decline that has endured to our own day. The countryside of Apulia is described as deserted by Seneca; the Greek cities no longer flourished. A combination of deforestation and perhaps climatic change may have been factors. In the central areas of Italy farmers seem to have been doing well. They did not grow much grain, of course; that was imported, at least into Rome and the coastal cities. An increasing number of fine wines fermented in vats fed by the vineyards of the area; olives remained important. Close to the cities truck gardening probably was most profitable. In some areas herds of pigs, cattle, poultry, and sheep (whose wool naturally was in demand) multiplied.

In the west central region, from Rome southwards, in all the most pleasant areas of the Alban Hills and particularly all about the Bay of Naples, the rich built villas both as stopping places for themselves and their friends when traveling and for annual respite from Rome's summer heat and daily grind. These villas took much land out of cultivation and produced little except for some truck gardens tended by local slave staffs. Increasingly such estates included fishponds, to tempt the palates of their owners. The north of Italy and especially the Po valley flourished. There the rich soil produced an abundance of grains, fruits, and animals. Wool was high in quality and relatively cheap. Augustus gave greater security to the area. He cleared several of the passes over the Alps; in one campaign in the vicinity of the Great and Little St. Bernard passes he killed thousands of native Salassi and sold other thousands into slavery. To protect the passes he planted a colony called Augusta Praetoria, now Aosta. The Brenner pass, debouching into Verona, had been clear for some years. Greater security meant a greater prosperity for the entire area, as trade through the passes stimulated the growth of towns such as Verona. Other communities of the region burgeoned, nourished by the strong agricultural base. Cremona, Padua, Mediolanum (now Milan) and other towns grew into cities.

Rural life in the provinces is less well known to us than that in Italy. The prosperity and stability of the new age certainly had a general reflection everywhere. If prosperity did not trickle down to all, there was the opportunity to enlist in the *auxilia* of the Roman army. As we have seen, various privileges including Roman citizenship after twenty-four years of service attracted many provincial young men to military service.

In the province of Africa (gradually extended east to Cyrenaica) great emphasis was placed on the production of grain and oil. The climate of course made these suitable crops, but the primary reasons for the emphasis were transportability and Roman needs; this policy surely restricted farmers in their freedom to grow the most advantageous crops for the local markets. Moreover, absentee landlordism seems especially to have afflicted this province, and a few families—Romans— gained control of vast acreages. Nevertheless, the archaeology of the area indicates a general prosperity continuing into the next century and even later.

Egypt, like Africa, was required to provide much grain for the needs of the city of Rome; presumably it continued as it had for centuries on end to be the chief source of grain also for many areas in the Mediterranean east. The Roman control, while in some ways less restrictive than that of the Macedonian dynasty of the Hellenistic age, yet largely continued the Ptolemaic arrangements. The lot of the lower classes there was the same as always: to produce for landlords (often absentee) whether owners, renters, or the state, while living themselves the barest existences.

Elsewhere in the eastern Mediterranean, Greece moldered gently but still produced grain in the Thessalian plains, along with oil and wines. Art objects were important. Asia Minor had not recovered fully from the economic burdens that had come with the Mithridatic wars and continued during the civil wars. Each successive war had seen the entire eastern Mediterranean stripped of money and supplies. A lack of capital caused by debt to Roman bankers slowed recovery. Farther south, Syria and Palestine too had suffered in intestine problems and the Roman civil wars. The area soon revived to a degree and exported dried fruits, nuts, and manufactured products including notably, purple-dyed fabrics mostly sent to Rome.

To the west, Spain and the Gauls prospered well. The rich farmland in Gaul produced abundant crops of grain, and increasingly, also of vines, along with lesser products. Spain still furnished Rome with most of her precious metals, and also was beginning to export to Rome and elsewhere a superior quality of olive oil along with some wines, horses, and products such as drugs and other metals.

Industry

Italy was for most of this period a strong exporter of certain manufactures. Arretine pottery, a glossy red ware, usually made in relief-molds, dominated the market for ceramics in the West. Glassware and some bronzeware produced in the Naples area were widely sought after. Bricks were produced in great abundance, especially about Rome, but of course were not exported. Bronze- and copperware were fabricated especially at Capua; Puteoli now (rather than Etruria) smelted much of the iron needed in Italy and for export. However, already by the end of this period small industries had sprung up in the western provinces, especially the Gauls. Workmen imitated the Arretine pottery and Italian metal goods and competed with the Italian manufacturers. The costs of transportation from Italy, labor costs, and other factors put the Italian products at a disadvantage, despite the somewhat lower quality of provincial wares. The major consequences of this unequal competition, however, belong to a later period.

No really large industry developed in Italy or anywhere else in the Empire. We know of some potteries that were quite large, it is true. At Arretium north of Rome, the center of Arretine production, it is reported that one pottery had a mixing vat that would hold ten thousand gallons; it must have employed scores if not hundreds of persons, but it was exceptional. It is, in fact, rather puzzling why something more like mass production did not evolve. The typical production unit was and remained the small workshop—salesroom. Even lead water pipe,

Cast of an Arretine bowl; symbolic scene of the harvest, vintage, Dionysian festival. (*Courtesy, Museum of Fine Arts, Boston*)

which in the cities might easily have been standardized in size and in manufacture, was always expensively custom-made by each plumber-installer. As for textiles, spinning and weaving remained mostly a household activity. In the cities, materials were sent out to professional fullers for finishing.

The failure to develop more economical means of production may be explained partly by the lack of capital. Trade was more profitable than manufacture if the gods of storm and sea looked on one's ships with favor. For greater security and prestige, even if with a smaller return, capital was put into land. But somehow the small, family-controlled workshop–salesroom seemed most satisfactory to the artisan–businessman of the ancient world. He did not usually aspire to more than a comfortable income, and he prized his independence of action. If he accumulated extra capital he was more likely to invest it in land than to expand his production facilities.

The consequence of this attitude was a failure of the empire, even in a period of long peace and general prosperity, to develop a sizable middle class. There was such a class, to be sure, but it was far too small to play any important role anywhere. Its members were the men who entered the world of trade and commerce or who took up banking and moneylending. There was also a middle group of landholders neither poor nor rich; but these held an identity of interest with the landed upper class. This group furnished the manpower for the middle positions in government and the army. They were occasionally rewarded with upward political and social movement. What was lacking in the Empire was a class whose first concern was large-scale manufacture, whose members ardently sought to increase production through the continual application of capital in the development of increasingly efficient methods. It must be admitted, however, that almost everyone in the modern world, misled by the present easy availability of fossil fuels, has an overly simplistic view of how quickly and easily the processes of manufacture can be improved.

Economic Policy in Tiberius' Later Years

Though some Romans might have called Tiberius stingy, it is no doubt fairer to say he was thrifty, and he was so throughout the Empire. He could, however, be generous on rare occasion because of his accumulated reserve. When in A.D. 17 an earthquake in Asia Minor devastated Sardis and other cities of the area, he remitted their taxes for five years and made substantial grants of money also. He deposed and brought to trial a rapacious governor of Asia. Another governor who was overly eager in the collection of taxes he warned to "shear his sheep," not "skin them."

In Italy Tiberius was able to cut in half the sales tax that supported the military treasury. During a grain shortage at Rome a couple of years later (19 A.D.) he spent liberally from the treasury to bring emergency supplies. In a monetary crisis in 33 A.D. he made 100,000,000 sesterces available from the treasury for low-rate loans. And when fire ravaged the Aventine and adjoining areas in 36 A.D. he made a similar sum available for rebuilding the burned-out areas. Some of his generosity was made possible by the continuing growth of the personal wealth of the emperor. Yet Tiberius lived a comparatively unostentatious life in imitation of his predecessor. And he sometimes refused inheritances when there was a legitimate heir.

Tiberius' policy of thrift, which was to leave 2,700,000,000 sesterces in the treasury at his death, in some ways and places depressed the economy. This is especially notable at Rome, which of course was the city most sensitive to changes in the levels of state expenditure. Absent from Rome for the last decade of his reign, Tiberius put on many fewer games and festivals in the capital and spent less on those staged. The consequence was felt not merely in the boredom of the lower classes but also in the pocketbooks of the people. In any economy that uses precious metals as currency almost exclusively, the consequence of thrift—saving—by both public and private persons can easily have a depressive effect on the economy. Bullion thus withdrawn from circulation decreases the money supply unless there is an equivalent production of the precious metals through mining. (Actually, at Rome the production of metals would also have had to compensate for attrition through normal loss of coins, through export of them in the Empire's usual adverse trade balance with the East, and through use of precious metals in jewelry, statuary, and the like.) Thus Tiberius' accumulation of this relatively huge sum in the treasury was probably a major factor in the financial crunch of 33 A.D. As we have seen, he did take measures to relieve the crisis.

The End of Tiberius' Reign

In 23 A.D., Drusus, Tiberius' son, died (perhaps from poisoning); after 26 A.D. Tiberius withdrew from Rome altogether; he took up residence on the island Capri and ruled almost entirely through his praetorian prefect Sejanus. The sources present Sejanus as an unscrupulous and ambitious man who engineered the deaths of Drusus and two of the sons of Agrippina and Germanicus so as to eliminate claimants to the succession in preparation for his own takeover. Some scholars have suspected that Sejanus was merely Tiberius' tool; but we cannot effectively second-guess the ancients in such matters. In 31 A.D. Tiberius belatedly learned of Sejanus' machinations and, from Sejanus' former wife, that he had even made away with Drusus. Moving cautiously, Tiberius had the prefect deposed and executed. The remaining six years of Tiberius' life were embittered. The treason trials marred those years and Romans felt neglected. There were stories of depraved sex orgies, the old emperor as voyeur, in the imperial palace on Capri. The provinces were little affected and in general seem to have been well governed throughout Tiberius' reign. But men rejoiced when the old recluse died— smothered in his bedclothes by his new praetorian prefect Macro —in 37 A.D.

The Roman state as constituted by Augustus endured for several centuries, but slowly changed character. The old traditions held over from the Republic faded in influence. The ruling classes gradually if grudgingly accepted a role subordinate to and in some ways merely an extension of the office of the princeps. How graciously each generation of aristocrats acquiesced in their reduced role depended primarily upon the personality of each emperor and how gracious his attitude toward them. Unfortunately, in this period several of the emperors proved inept in the delicate social and political relationships involving scions of the great families.

It is not surprising that a good many conspiracies were hatched, even against the better emperors. For a century or more of the early Empire men hoped and plotted to restore the oligarchy called the Republic. As everyone knows, those conspirators who managed to assassinate an emperor did not succeed in bringing back the Republic. Most conspiracies were nipped in the bud by the executioner's sword. Such executions depleted the ranks of the old families. The growing subservience in the Senate is partially explainable simply by the changing composition of the ruling classes; the new families all owed their positions to the emperors, and this made a difference. These gradual changes at Rome, however, meant little outside Italy.

A Political Sketch: Gaius (37–41 A.D.)

Even though Augustus had forced Tiberius to adopt Gaius' father, Germanicus, and apparently intended him to succeed his stepson, there was little reason for Gaius to hope for the throne until late in Tiberius' reign when Drusus, son of Tiberius, died (or was murdered) and Sejanus' hopes aborted. Thus Gaius was both young (in his middle twenties) and politically inexperienced when he acceded to power. Nevertheless, he seems

THE STATE AND SOCIETY FROM GAIUS TO DOMITIAN, 37–96 A.D.

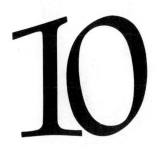

10

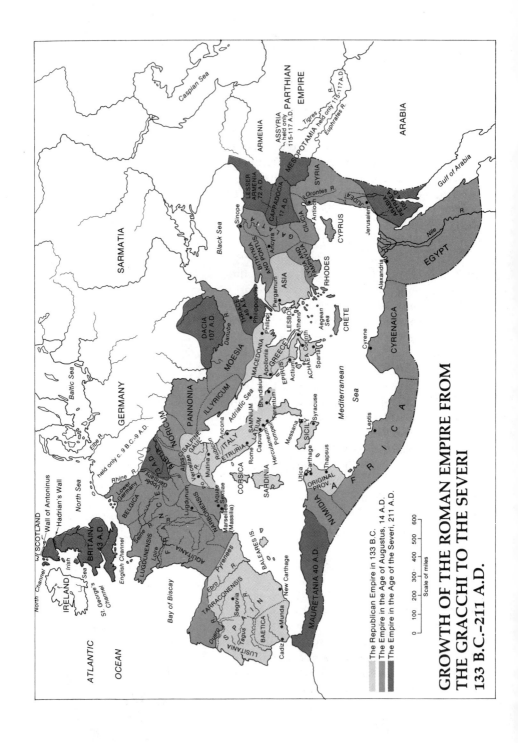

GROWTH OF THE ROMAN EMPIRE FROM THE GRACCHI TO THE SEVERI 133 B.C.–211 A.D.

The Republican Empire in 133 B.C.
The Empire in the Age of Augustus, 14 A.D.
The Empire in the Age of the Severi, 211 A.D.

Scale of miles

0 100 200 300 400 500 600

to have had definite ideas about his position. The trouble was that these did not correspond to general expectations. His father, Germanicus, had been personable and popular. As a child Gaius had traveled about with him—it was in Germany that he got the nickname Caligula (Little Boot)—and thus he came to be identified with him. Both Gaius' father and grandfather, Drusus, brother of the Emperor Tiberius, were thought to have had republican leanings; but not Gaius. Nothing was further from his mind.

Gaius' mind was, to some extent, unhinged, possibly by serious illness early in his reign. It is impossible to explain away all his acts that seem factually established so as to make his conduct seem totally rational. Yet one must allow for exaggeration and hostile reporting. Moreover, a theory has been advanced that may explain some of his deeds that, to his contemporaries, seemed inexplicable or sinister. It is quite plausibly conjectured that he did not like the strait jacket of expectations that he inherited, and that he intended instead to rule in the manner of the Hellenistic monarchs, a pattern familiar to any educated Roman. Thus is explained his insistence on deification and worship; Augustus had resisted this, though he allowed worship of himself along with Roma in the provinces, and he was deified formally only in death. Tiberius, as in almost all things, followed the Augustan pattern. Gaius' different attitude may at first have engendered little more than amusement in the capital, along with sardonic comment; but in the provinces there was little objection to the emperor as god. Except in one: but for Gaius' assassination there would have been rebellion among the Jews. It was only the resistance and procrastination of the governor, Petronius, at the risk of his own life, that kept the lid on. Gaius had ordered his image set up in the Temple, as a god, and Petronius, fearing a rebellion, delayed the work for many months. Only the death of the emperor prevented his own execution.

How does an apologist explain Gaius' great expedition north to the English channel where, the sources say, he eventually lined up his troops, told them to gather seashells, and then returned home to celebrate a triumph as if they had indeed invaded Britain as he planned? It is noted that one major purpose of the expedition was to put down a conspiracy by one of his generals in Germany—dangerous because of the large legionary force under the general's control—and it is suggested further that the secondary objective, the invasion of Britain, was aborted because of the complete unwillingness of the troops to venture out into what they considered the shadowy limits of the inhabited world.

But the building of a bridge of ships about three miles

long across the Bay of Naples is simply not susceptible of any rational explanation. Did Gaius want to impress a visiting Parthian embassy by building a bridge like that of Darius the Great but longer? Perhaps. Was his bizarre sense of humor concocting a huge practical joke? One of the sources suggests he did it because someone important once said that he had about as much chance of being emperor as of riding his horse across the Bay of Naples. It was in any case an enormously expensive whim.

One may choose simply not to believe that Gaius really said he intended to get his horse elected consul, to show his contempt for the Senate; it surely is best to discount as mostly gossip or rumor the stories of his sexual vagaries, including incest with his three sisters. But there is no way to exonerate him of extravagance: he found a full treasury; in three years of tax cuts, games, gifts, and general carousing he managed to empty it. Confiscation of the estates of those judged guilty of conspiracy helped to refill it, but not enough. Still one must admit that his spending did no real damage; in fact, piling up bullion in the manner of Tiberius was likely more injurious to the general economic welfare. And, to repeat, the provinces—except Judea—were little affected one way or another.

Gaius was murdered in a conspiracy between a prefect and several tribunes of the praetorian guard.

Claudius (41–54 A.D.)

That Claudius, the uncle of Gaius and the brother of Germanicus, would accede to power was even less expected than that Gaius would. Afflicted with some sort of paralytic disability which made him ungainly, Claudius had been an embarrassment to both Augustus and Livia, Claudius' grandmother. They had kept him in the background; he had a good education, however, and displayed an intellectual bent. He studied and wrote history (dealing with the Etruscans and the early Empire) and was interested in linguistics. The great Livy seems to have advised and consulted with him. He had held no important office until Gaius let him be consul for a couple of months.

It was the praetorians, afraid because Gaius had been slain by one of their own officers and looking out for themselves, who put Claudius in power. One source says that the praetorians encountered him accidentally as they rampaged through the palace following Gaius' assassination. Claudius, hardly a free agent, agreed to serve. However it was, a very bad precedent was set: not only was an emperor installed by soldiers without even the consent of the Senate (which meanwhile was debating

how to achieve a restoration of the Republic); but the guardsmen also demanded and got from Claudius what amounted to a
huge reward—15,000 or 20,000 sesterces per guardsman. The
money must have come from Claudius' own personal fortune.

The sources say that Claudius was too much influenced by
women and freedmen, and there is some truth to the assertion.
There is no doubt, however, that in important matters of state
policy he was his own man; and as a matter of fact he seems to
have thought through matters well. Some rulers mindful of
history and transfixed by past traditions have adopted a stub-
born conservatism. Not Claudius. He accepted Livy's view of the
Republic, that Rome rose to greatness because of a willingness
to learn from others and to accept others on an equal basis into
full citizenship and participation in the state. He avowed an
intention to follow in the steps of Augustus, but he seems to
have followed Caesar rather more. Twice Caesar had briefly
invaded Britain; Claudius acquired it as a province. Caesar
wanted to build a port at Ostia; Claudius did it. Caesar wanted
to drain the Fucine lake; Claudius did it, with less than complete
success. Caesar rather liberally extended the citizenship to Gauls
as he made Cisalpine Gaul part of Italy, and even admitted some
into the Senate; so did Claudius, in the case of some Transalpine
Gauls.

The motivation for the conquest of Britain, as for any
major imperialist expansion by the Romans involved a mixture
of reasons. Romans thought the Britons stirred up dissatisfaction
among their subjects on the continent, and conquest would presumably take care of that. But reasons more purely economic,
such as opportunities for Roman businessmen, may have existed.
Moreover, the historian Tacitus implies that one major objective
was the gold and silver mines in Britain. Other known mineral
wealth on the island included lead, tin, and coal. Cornwall's
tin, it is thought, had drawn Phoenicians to Britain centuries
earlier. It is doubtful that the Romans ever mined these minerals
in sufficient quantity to profit from the conquest. There wasn't
a great quantity of gold; some silver, copper, and tin were mined,
however, along with much lead. And the coal was extensively
used, mostly for heating, as by Roman troops stationed along
the walls built in the north, in the next century. There was too
much sulfur in the coal to make it desirable for the smelting of
iron ore, which was also found in some quantity in Britain. The
Spanish mines long continued to furnish most of Rome's silver,
copper, and lead. If the invasion of Britain was mounted in the
hope of economic gain, the gain was not realized: in spite of the
income from the numerous state-owned mines (regularly leased

to private persons or companies), or from trade or agricultural production, the outlay for the legions required there must have put the governors' books into the red.

Claudius reorganized the civil administration of the government. The earlier emperors had quite naturally followed the usual aristocratic familial procedures, whereby freedmen of their households acted as civil administrators of the Empire. Claudius formalized and extended the system. It is often fashionable to decry the growth of administrative bureaucracies, and it surely is true that the men who staff them in every age tend to become as interested in their own personal situations as in the affairs of state. Yet such a service is absolutely necessary. Surely Claudius' rational ordering of the services ought to be accounted a positive good.

Four of Claudius' talented if grasping freedmen headed up major departments with clearly defined areas of responsibility. Here was the origin of the charge that freedmen too much influenced the emperor. Two of these freedmen, Pallas, the financial department head, and Narcissus, head of correspondence (and thus of routine provincial matters) became both powerful and rich. The great power delivered into the hands of such freedmen, and at times, similarly, even into the hands of imperial slaves, made them very important figures. Their social position was therefore much enhanced; a senator might even wish to be seen walking along the street with one of them. Other aristocrats who would not so demean themselves resented the situation and transferred their hate to the emperor.

It is not surprising that there were conspiracies against Claudius, though it is difficult to credit the figures given in the sources of the number of grandees this emperor is said to have executed—tens of senators and scores of equestrians. At any rate, it is certain that the gradual disappearance of the older families for one reason or another continued; others replaced them.

Claudius had a rather morbid fascination with the bloodier combats at the games and pandered to the public demands for such displays. In spite of the impressive number of good things that may be said about his reign, it is easy to focus on Claudius' faults, on his freedmen, and on the two women who were his wives in this period, Messalina and Agrippina.

There seems no reason to doubt the accounts of Messalina's extravagant parties and her affairs with various men. She offended Claudius' freedman Narcissus. When she developed an infatuation for a man, Silius, who was a possible candidate for the throne in event of a sudden vacancy and reportedly "married" him at a party in Claudius' absence, Narcissus persuaded Claudius to order her execution. Thus left wifeless Claudius, whose sexual appetite was said to have been unimpaired by his physical disability, cast about for a suitable replacement. He eventually settled upon the younger Agrippina, his own niece, sister of the previous emperor. It is doubtful whether it was his idea or hers. The outcome was significant: Claudius' own son by Messalina, called Britannicus, was displaced and murdered by Agrippina's child, Nero, after his accession. Nero was born Lucius Domitius Ahenobarbus (Agrippina's previous husband); Claudius Nero was his name after adoption by Claudius. Through his mother he was Augustus' great-great-grandson.

Nero (54–68 A.D.)

In the popular mind Nero has become a sort of classic archetype of the tyrant; this is partly the consequence of his short, sharp, and probably localized persecution of Christians, whom he (with the advice of others, presumably) decided to use as scapegoats for the great fire of 64 A.D. This was indeed tyrannical enough and cowardly besides since, as everyone knows, his enthusiasm for rebuilding the city, with a vast new palace and grounds for himself, had made him suspect of having set the fire to create the opportunity. The fire or rather fires may have been set, but by whom is still a mystery. Surely not by Christians or by Nero either, though he may have been moved to dramatic declamation by the lurid and grandiose sight. About half the city burned. Nero provided funds to help private persons rebuild and set up a kind of fire code requiring building setbacks and such to make the reconstructed city safer from fire. Yet his "golden house" took up about a quarter-square-mile of the most valuable land in Rome.

Nero was less bloodthirsty than his adoptive father Claudius; he favored the Greek style of game and tended to neglect the depraved spectacles the city crowd increasingly demanded. Though he became suspicious and executed some persons who probably had not actively joined in any conspiracy, he did so only because real conspiracies taught him to fear. The most notable conspiracy against Nero was headed by the reputable noble Calpurnius Piso in 65, and involved several high personages. It was discovered and came to nothing. Piso and others committed suicide. Some of those done to death by Nero in connection with this and other conspiracies are familiar and respected names: Seneca, the Stoic but nevertheless rich man who had been his tutor and had served him well in the government for several years; Petronius, writer and critic of the regime; Lucan the poet; and Corbulo, the most renowned general of his time.

Certainly Nero was a megalomaniac who vastly overrated his own abilities and accomplishments. A hundred-foot-plus statue of himself attired in the accouterments of Apollo was placed in the vestibule of his new palace. It is often forgotten that a large statue of Augustus, though only about half the size, was placed in a similar very richly decorated propylaeum adjoining Augustus' palace on the Palatine. Nero became obsessed with art and in particular with his own singing, lyre-playing, and the like. He gave public performances at which it was dangerous even to be inattentive, much less go to sleep as the future emperor Vespasian once did. The latter got off with a rebuke, since he was both a good general and a social nobody. Nero felt he was really among his own when he made a tour of Greece, participating in the great games—all held during the same year out of the usual order in honor of the royal participant. The emperor seems to have won almost all the laurels—the ancient equivalent of first-place gold medals—more than 1800 "victories," for everything from lyre-playing to chariot racing. In return he made Greece free from tribute; since he was near the end of both power and life the award was short-lived.

As an administrator, Nero's record was not so dismal. He chose good men for important jobs in the provinces, the best examples being Vespasian for the Jewish rebellion and, earlier, Corbulo for a general command against the Parthians, where the struggle involved the control of Armenia, as so often was the case. Partly by war and partly by diplomacy Corbulo achieved a satisfactory compromise settlement. Nero had no drive for martial glory, the bloody route that most megalomaniacs in high places pursue. He should probably not be blamed for the rebellion in Britain under Boudicca, a native queen, though his minister Seneca may have helped perpetrate it through huge loans there at predatory rates of interest. The rebellion in Judea that broke out in 66 A.D. was primarily the result of long-standing hatred between Jews and gentiles in the area. The precipitating incident involved Jew-baiting in the Roman provincial capital, Caesarea, and also Nero's recent decision not to permit Jewish participation in the local government. Yet it seems less Roman misgovernment than the complete impossibility of governing to everyone's satisfaction that caused the revolt.

Nero did depreciate the coinage (see later the section on economics); and though he was personally extravagant, there is little evidence of irresponsible economic policy in general. Still, if a fraction of the stories recounting the persecution of innocent

Nero. (*E. Richter–Roma*)

Christians are true, if indeed men like Seneca and Corbulo were guiltless of crime, and if, finally, one bears in mind that Nero killed his own mother Agrippina in 59 for trying to retain influence over him—even if she may have been an actual threat to him—then perhaps one must admit that Nero deserves his popular reputation as a personal tyrant.

"Year of the Four Emperors" (69 A.D.)

Nero's artistic public appearances, his preoccupation with the construction of his Golden House, his trip to Greece with all its peccadillos, and in particular his alienation of powerful army officers, partly by neglect and partly through his treatment of Corbulo, who was suspected of conspiracy and forced to commit suicide, caused the emperor's fall. Generals in the provinces began the rebellion; the last straw was the defection of the praetorian guard. Nero committed suicide in the summer of 68 A.D., still only 31 years old. The Senate had already declared him deposed and sentenced him to die. Since Nero was the last of the Julio-Claudians, the Senate and the praetorians accepted the man who led the revolt as the new princeps, Galba.

The new emperor was an elderly man in his 70s, an aristocrat of an old family. With his own army from Spain, where he had been a provincial governor, the support of some troops in Gaul and of one of the powerful Rhine armies, plus the backing of the Senate and the Praetorian Guard, he seemed to have a solid base. One would not have guessed that there was to be a succession of ephemeral emperors.

Galba quickly committed a number of errors. He alienated some of the upper classes when he attempted to reverse many of Nero's arrangements; he lost the backing of the guardsmen and many others as well by his choice of a successor; and he refused to pay what had been promised in his name to the Praetorian Guard. Besides, the other armies had learned how easily a new emperor could be created and how profitable the deed might be.

In January 69 A.D. the legions of Lower Germany were persuaded to renounce their annual oath of allegiance and a short time later to acclaim as emperor their general, Vitellius. Before the news arrived in Rome the praetorians had already killed Galba and elevated their choice, Otho; thus the stage was set for civil war. The Vitellian commanders managed to get their troops through the Alpine passes before spring fairly arrived—no doubt sooner than Otho anticipated. The latter energetically marshaled his forces into the Po valley, near Cremona. If he had waited his army would have been augmented by a strong contingent from the Danubian frontier; but with bad judgment he chose to fight immediately—and lost; in April he committed suicide.

Vitellius punished some of his captured opponents, executing a good many centurions, a distinct error which only caused many army officers to look to their interests elsewhere. In his short reign, if his ancient biographers are right, he seems to have been more concerned with his gourmet meals than anything else. He was said to have spent fantastic sums on exotic foods. Meanwhile, other army officers were ambitious also; and other legions disliked the way the German legions had taken over. Though Vitellius did not pay the legionaries large bonuses because of the state of the treasury and his own extravagance, they profited by treating Italy to some degree as conquered territory to be despoiled.

The governor of Syria and the prefect of Egypt, both commanders of substantial armies, got together to nominate as emperor the commander of a third army in the East, Titus Flavius Vespasianus, who was engaged in suppressing the Jewish rebellion. He had by this time overrun the northern areas of the country and was mounting a siege of Jerusalem itself. Vespasian may have been influenced by a Jewish captive, one Josephus (the historian), who had prophesied to Vespasian that the general would one day be emperor. July 1, when the first troops took oath to him, was always used by Vespasian as his accession date, but it was October before the decisive battle took place —again near Cremona in the Po valley—and it was about a year after that before the new emperor actually arrived in Rome.

The battle for Vespasian's ascendancy was fought by Danubian troops; disappointed earlier not to have arrived for the first battle of Cremona against Vitellius, they hurried to Italy without waiting for the contingents from the Syrian or Egyptian forces. They took the disorganized army of Vitellius by surprise and in a hard-fought and bloody battle that lasted many hours, the Danubian troops at last won a complete victory. They, too, moved south to Rome, of course living off the country as they went. Meanwhile a separate little civil war devastated the capital. Vitellius agreed to abdicate, but in December his troops attacked Flavian supporters on the Capitoline Hill, where the great temple of Jupiter Optimus Maximus burned once again. When the Vespasianic troops came from the north they killed Vitellius. Rome, Italy, and the rest of the empire, having tasted the evils of chaos and civil war, now were ready to let the latest emperor have a chance to reestablish order.

Vespasian (69–79 A.D.)

Despite some remaining embers of civil war, as well as other problems, the military was soon fully under control. Vespasian had been accounted a good general; and most other possible military claimants to the throne were gone. The rest had chosen not to enter into competition. The war against the Jews the new emperor left in the hands of his oldest son Titus, who sacked Jerusalem in 70 A.D. Contrary to Titus' intention, the temple Herod had rebuilt and embellished went up in flames. Thousands of Jews died in the fighting and more in the long siege; and other thousands were sold into slavery. Some went to Rome and helped to build the Flavian Amphitheatre, popularly known as the Colosseum; it rose on the spot where Nero had placed a reflecting pool for his Golden House.

Along the Rhine a rebellion of Gauls and Germans took on the proportions of a war of liberation. A Romanized Batavian named Civilis, under suspicion of sedition before the war began, led an uprising when in the absence of the great Rhine armies the Roman frontiers were left thinly defended. Trying to make it a general rebellion, he persuaded some free Germans and some Gauls already serving in the Roman auxiliary forces to join with him. But most of the Gauls refused to aid him, even when news of the burning of the Capitol gave hope to enemies that Rome's end was approaching. By reinforcing the Rhine the Roman commander Cerialis, a relative of the new emperor, split the rebel territory in two. He soon accepted the former auxiliaries back into Roman loyalty. Next, in 70, he reduced Civilis' headquarters at the captured Roman camp of Vetera, and finally he made peace on easy terms with the Germans. Perhaps the failure of most of the Gauls to join in the struggle indicates that they had become too civilized and soft: but it is in any case a tribute to the original settlement of Caesar and to subsequent Roman policy that the tribes were not eager to take up arms for freedom.

In the second year of his reign Vespasian closed the doors of the Janus temple as a sign of peace; there were, however, still pockets of resistance in Judaea. The most celebrated of these was atop the rocklike fortress of Masada, on the Dead Sea. Not until 73 did the Roman circumvallation and laboriously engineered assault reduce that desperately defended outpost.

Vespasian, though a military man, did not increase the number of permanent legions, but returned to the former number as soon as possible. He did strengthen the naval flotillas on the Rhine and the Danube. The milestones uncovered by archaeologists and happenstance proclaim him a great road builder. One of his more important roads connected the Rhine and Danube frontiers through a newly acquired territory in south Germany. The route had obvious military significance. It is noteworthy that Italy no longer supplied the majority of legionary recruits. That peninsula now furnished men mostly for the Praetorian Guard and other special units. Most legionaries were now recruited from the citizen population of the provinces. The change had been gradual, and the fact says something both of Italy and of the increasing percentage of citizens in the provinces.

Vespasian asked the Senate to confirm to him the powers Augustus held, demonstrating in this and other ways his intent to restore the old partnership, to play the role of princeps, not tyrant. Inevitably his middle-class background affected his outlook, as it did his choices for the depleted ranks of the Senate. Into the Senate and into the lower governmental ranks as well he ushered many new persons, mostly from old Italian families, some from provincial backgrounds. That he chose well is indicated by the fact that the great emperors of the next century derive from families who were brought into the aristocracy under Vespasian. Naturally the low-born emperor had difficulty with some old-line aristocrats, who resented both him and his new men. This resentment took forms we will discuss in a later section of this chapter.

Perhaps Vespasian's greatest problem was economic. He

found the treasury bare; yet immense sums were required not only for the routine expenses of empire but also for reconstruction in Rome and other cities. The temple of Jupiter on the Capitol, in ruins, was only the most conspicuous example of this need. Cremona, once a flourishing city, had been destroyed; and in many other places the devastation and spoliation had reduced Italian cities and towns to a depressed state. Vespasian met the economic needs by heavier taxation, even in the capital. When he put a tax on urine collected from the public latrines by fullers for use in bleaching cloth, his son Titus protested this was going too far. Vespasian, who was noted for his dry sense of humor, held a denarius under his son's nose and said, "This doesn't stink, does it?" Doubtless the provinces groaned under the added tribute. Vespasian instituted a complete survey of privileged communities all over the empire, probably with the intent of revoking some undeserved privileges and increasing revenues. Greece was again made subject to tribute. Some estates given away by his predecessors were taken back, for the patrimonium. But Vespasian also economized; he embarked on no new expansive ventures, except that he did resume the conquest of Britain. Before the end of his reign he reduced taxation to its former levels and still left the treasury in a healthy state of solvency.

Titus (79–81 A.D.)

Vespasian had been practical, hard-working, effective—and a bit parsimonious. He died with the humorous comment that he was on the point of becoming a god—referring to the usual practice of deifying dead emperors. His eldest son Titus was tremendously popular, and there was great rejoicing when he assumed power. There had been no doubt of the succession: Vespasian had made it quite clear, despite criticism, that he intended to establish a dynasty. Titus was associated with him in the government almost from the beginning, at times serving with him as consul. All the Flavians served as consuls on an almost annual basis, unlike the Julio-Claudians. Titus' own popularity naturally helped to ensure that there would be no difficulty with the succession.

In spite of his desire to please everyone and his tendency to spend more freely than his father, Titus might have been a good princeps if he had lived; his reign lasted less than two and a half years. Unfortunately, it is remembered more for disasters —no fault of his—than for any other thing. The year 79 saw another destructive fire at Rome followed by plague; and most important for us today, a violent eruption of Mt. Vesuvius, near

Naples, which buried Pompeii and Herculaneum, partially preserving them for rediscovery by the world in excavations that continue today.

In 80, Titus dedicated the great Colosseum with games lasting more than three months, tremendously pleasing to the Roman mob but excessive, even by Roman standards. He also made into public baths a part of Nero's Golden House. Other sections of the House were simply abandoned. It was a symbol of Nero's extravagance and of the belief that he had caused the burning of Rome. Covered over by fill for the baths, part of the palace was preserved and may still be seen by tourists.

Domitian (81–96 A.D.)

On the untimely death of Titus, his younger brother Domitian came to power without difficulty. Our sources portray this emperor with venom as an unfeeling tyrant, a characterization which Domitian doubtless deserved to some degree. Yet perhaps his most heinous offense was that he stripped off the facade of the principate, exposing the Senate and the upper classes for what they had become—dependents and servants of the emperor. He kept his own counsel for the most part, trusted no one fully, and through a less-than-winning personality presented to the world an image that was easy to despise. Stories of his cruelty help to explain this revulsion further. Like the emperor Gaius, he was deified in life, and he was addressed as "dominus et deus," Lord and God. He had reason to be mistrustful, even fearful: he snuffed out several conspiracies before the successful one that finally took his life.

It is possible that a bit of charm, an outgoing personality, a diplomatic and deferential attitude toward the Senate, a greater effort to please the crowd, these may have been all that Domitian required to be accounted one of Rome's better principes. He was hardworking and conscientious in his responsibilities. The men he chose for high position seem mostly to have been excellent people. He was not extravagant, but made good use of public funds.

Along the Danube frontier where the most serious problems with outside invaders arose Domitian was, however, not totally successful. Ultimately he made the most troublesome leader, Decebalus, King of the Dacians (Dacia was approximately modern Rumania), a Roman friend and ally by granting him an annual subsidy—as had at times been done earlier in the case of the King of Armenia. Then he strengthened the Danube army and built permanent forts at strategic points. He also recalled

Agricola (Tacitus' father-in-law) from Britain, and called off any effort to expand into Scotland. To the more jingoistic of Roman critics these actions seemed reprehensible: Rome, they thought, had always been greatest when expanding. In his policy, however, Domitian followed the example of Augustus, who learned from a long and expensive series of campaigns that expansion was not always the wisest course. Trajan, as we shall see, was to change that policy. And Trajan is accounted the greater ruler; but in these matters at least it is possible that Domitian was right.

Local Government: Italy and the Provinces

Rome was doubtless the most interesting and exciting city in Italy, but in matters of self-government the cities and towns away from the capital had a great advantage over the metropolis. The situation in the city of Rome was somewhat comparable to that of Washington, D.C. today, where the federal government overshadows and to a considerable degree displaces local institutions.

That local government was alive and well in the Italian cities is clearly indicated in the inscriptions painted everywhere on the walls of Pompeii. Support for candidates was solicited by individuals, neighbors, and religious groups ("all the worshipers of Isis urge you to vote for. . . ."). In particular, the members of the various craft and service occupations were active in the elections. Mule drivers, fruit sellers, dyers, garlic dealers, goldsmiths, perfumers, barbers, fishermen, and many other groups all proclaimed their candidates.

As for the candidates themselves, they too must have wanted to serve, for not only were they unsalaried, they were expected to spend their own funds, perhaps to present shows or to build or repair a public building or to donate free oil for the public baths. In many towns such obligations were specific and required. We do hear of times when prominent citizens had to be urged to put their names forward, but usually the local aristocrats who held the top offices felt sufficiently paid off in honor.

Most Italian towns had four top officials, *duumviri*—a board of two men—with judicial authority, and usually two others called *aediles*, who were in charge of finance and the treasury as well as the marketplace, temples, and festivals. Lesser posts were sometimes held by men who did not rank high on the social scale. Every five years the *duumviri* took a local census and performed other tasks analogous to those of the censors at Rome in the days of the Republic. Every city supported a variety of priests also, some of whom by now ministered to the imperial cult. The *Augustales*, formed in the reign of Augustus and devoted to the cult of the reigning emperor, were rich freedmen, who thus gained a modicum of status despite their rank.

The major institutions of the cities were the assembly of all citizens, which elected the officials, and a kind of senate made up of ex-officials like the Senate at Rome. This organization, ordinarily called the curia, usually contained one hundred members, or decurions. Election day could be a lively time: we hear of riots during elections at Pisa in this period. When such irregularity occurred, it was apparently the emperors' custom to intervene and to appoint prefects to govern the offenders for a time.

In most of the provinces—though there was naturally wide variation—a similar sort of oligarchical self-government existed, with officials and a town council comparable to the Italian curia, all drawn from the upper classes, and a body of citizens who served as an elective assembly. In the western provinces tribal organization sometimes played a role. But even there Roman policy encouraged urbanization and thus the establishment of similar institutions. Though they ruled an empire, Romans still considered the city-state the proper unit for local affairs.

Local officials and decurions in the provinces often were awarded Roman citizenship, and this naturally added to the luster of their positions. Yet obligations accompanied the honors; local tradition invariably required high officials to provide public benefactions (λειτουργοι) at their own expense. In addition, Rome used local officials as instruments of central policy. In a general way the local oligarchy was expected to keep things under control for Rome. More specifically, the local governing class supported the imperial cult and aided in the collection of taxes and in the raising of auxiliaries to serve in the Roman army. These obligations perhaps lay lightly enough upon the shoulders of the leading citizens of provincial cities in this period; but in times of trouble, such as lay in the future, responsibilities like these would weigh heavily indeed. Other local obligations normally not too irksome included the upkeep of some roads, usually by adjoining property owners, and bridges. Main roads were as a rule built at imperial expense.

In Italy as in the provinces there was a tendency for the cities to mimic Rome in many ways. Citizens almost everywhere wanted aqueducts, basilicas, temples, theatres, and arenas. The remains of these structures, still to be seen all over the area of the defunct empire, testify to the economic health of the times as well as to the efforts of the provincial citizens to make their cities into miniature Romes.

The Economy of the Empire in the First Century

The greatest single blessing for the economic life of the Empire was the era of peace that Augustus secured. The devastation of the civil wars of 68–69 was confined mostly to Italy, though the contemporary struggles in Judaea and Gaul of course disrupted the economies of those areas. Everywhere else the single political administration, coinage system, safe sea routes, and a continually improved road system all contributed to a healthy economic structure throughout the empire.

The road network, finely conceived and engineered, helped to hold the empire together politically and militarily. Its importance in trade must not be overstressed. Farmers of course found the roads useful in getting their products to local markets. But only objects of high unit value could profitably be transported more than a few miles overland. No bulky items would normally be sent, for example, from Italy to northern Gaul (or vice versa) through the Alpine passes overland. It is instructive to note that grain could be transported from almost any seaport in the Mediterranean to Rome by ship cheaper than an equivalent amount could be transported overland as much as seventy-five miles by cart or by pack-donkey.

Neither must it be thought, though there was internal peace, that the roads and the seas were completely secure. Local officials had the general charge of security along the roads and they did not always suppress the highwaymen who infested some areas. Nor were the seas always completely safe from piracy. On balance, however, conditions remained favorable for traders. Except for the grain trade, which was government controlled at Rome and to some extent at other cities, commerce was neither closely controlled nor excessively taxed. Port dues and customs were no real impediments to the trader; he was harassed more by pirates, but his worst enemy was the weather. The large number of ancient ships found by modern underwater archaeologists—only the tiniest fraction of the total number lost—testify to that.

The trader who risked his capital in ships rather than placing it in the much safer and more prestigious investment, land, did not usually content himself with bringing oil and wine from Spain or the like; he wanted to deal with oriental spices, fruitwood furniture, especially prized and expensive salted fish from the Black Sea, dried fruits from the eastern areas, valuable products of that sort. And then, once he made his pot of gold he usually wanted to put it in a safe place—once again, likely in land—rather than to continue taking risks. Thus in trade as in small industry (as emphasized in the preceding chapter) little effort was made to employ capital to effect continuing improvements in organization and facilities.

There was considerable progress, nonetheless. In the building industry, for example, astonishingly complex and useful cranes were invented for the hoisting of heavy stone; and in the harbors ingenious devices aided in loading and unloading of vessels. Yet it remains true that the very concept of the continual application of capital in the interest of laborsaving efficiency and profitability which is so integral a part of the modern business world never developed in ancient times.

The Structure and Importance of Public Spending in the Empire

The effect of state spending on the economic prosperity of the various regions of the empire has not often been noticed. Income was drawn fairly evenly from all parts of the empire in proportion to local productivity, but certain geographic regions saw a great deal of government expenditure, others very little; and the economic consequences were considerable. The effects of monies coming into the capital city itself have been noted well enough: it is often said that Rome imported tribute and exported government. However, other areas, too, benefited from a disproportionate share of state spending.

The income of Rome came mostly from two taxes, a poll tax and a property tax (*tributum capitis, tributum soli*). Italy and provincial towns with the Italic right were exempt from these but like other areas paid customs duties, sales tax, and miscellaneous other taxes such as the charge for manumitting slaves. On the other side of the ledger, expenditures were for goods and services, salaries of civil service and other government officers, building, and the military. Military spending for salaries of the soldiery, equipment, troopships, warships, and the like, and military bases, surely constituted by far the largest single cost category of the state, exceeding all other outlays combined. Proportionately large sums thus went to the areas where military bases were located.

It should be pointed out also, that no elaborate credit structure existed, as in the modern world, whereby the state could increase or decrease the supply of money in given areas according to some perceived economic need. Thus the supply of money in any region might depend heavily upon government expenditure in that region. Total expenditures were limited by the total received from all forms of taxation plus income from government-owned property, the mines (the most productive were in Spain) being especially important in this connection.

To reiterate, though Rome drew funds from all over the Empire, she spent most of them either at Rome and the vicinity or on the frontiers, at the fringes of the Empire, because that was where the legions were. The legions thus tended to bring prosperity to certain provinces—of course at the expense of others. Provinces such as Greece or Asia—even Italy itself apart from the Po valley and the region from Rome south to the Bay of Naples—suffered a constant net drain of funds, a situation somewhat analogous to that of estates owned by absentee landlords who took as much as they could in profit, returning very little in continuing capital investment. Partly because of this situation, by the end of the first century, some of the older, interior provinces were characterized by stagnant or declining economies while the newer provinces prospered.

We have seen the disposition of Augustus's twenty-five legions. Under Claudius the Romans invaded Britain, and most of the time until the abandonment of the province in the early fifth century three legions were there. The process of enlarging the province and at the same time putting down rebellions continued until the reign of Domitian. On the other hand, by now, one legion instead of the former three sufficed for Spain. Domitian reinforced the Danube frontier. Through the whole period the greatest concentration of troops was on the Rhine (four legions each in upper and lower Germany) and on the Danube (six to eight legions in the four, later five provinces involved). Under Vespasian two legions were stationed in Cappadocia. Elsewhere, one legion was maintained in Judaea, Syria had three legions, Egypt now only two, and Africa only one.

Though the Gallic provinces had few troops, the Gauls nevertheless benefited greatly from military expenditure, because of the road system—the supply routes—and because the bulk of the supplies for the German legions came from the Gauls. In any case the Gauls and Spain as well seem to have been productive enough, mainly in agricultural products, to remain economically healthy; Spain was not seriously affected by the withdrawal of two of its three legions. The Danubian provinces suffered from the incursions of tribes across the river, especially in the latter part of the period, so that any economic benefit from a favorable balance of state funds hardly mattered. In Egypt the expenditure for the two or three legions there will not have balanced the heavy flow of money and goods—particularly wheat and paper—to Rome. In grain alone, Egypt furnished enough to feed all of Rome's several hundred thousand persons—perhaps as many as one million—for one-third of each year.

In Italy the prosperity from Rome radiated outward to some degree. Despite Claudius' tremendously expensive effort to build a harbor at Ostia much of Rome's shipping came in to Puteoli on the Bay of Naples and proceeded north via the Appian Way to Rome. Moreover, much of the coast south from Rome to Sorrento on the south side of the Bay of Naples was prized as resort territory; many rich Romans owned one or more villas in the region. These contributed less to the real economy of the area than is sometimes supposed, but nevertheless did something to spread the wealth.

The Coinage in the First Century

As in the Republic, coin types to some degree reflect official policy and thus are useful to the historian. Augustus displayed on his coins his favorite titles—for example, *pater patriae*, father of his country; and he called attention to events he considered important, as when he regained from the Parthians the legionary eagles lost by Crassus and marked the achievement with a coin type labeled *signis receptis*. Coinage in precious metals, the standard silver denarius and the gold aureus, worth twenty-five denarii, Augustus apparently controlled himself. For the sake of propriety he minted them all at Lugdunum (Lyons), in one of his provinces. The brass or bronze sestertius (four to the denarius) and the other smaller copper coins were nominally under the control of the Senate and usually marked S.C., "by decree of the Senate." However, the emperors later in the first century began to mint in Rome and the S.C. legend on the lower coinage

A *denarius* of the princeps Augustus, displaying one of the titles he was given by the Senate and which he obviously liked to flaunt: *pater patriae* (father of his country).

or the occasional absence of it, probably meant little or nothing.

Nero's money is especially interesting both for the coin types and for the fabric of the coinage. Early on, soon after Claudius' death, the power of Agrippina is indicated: she appears with Nero, in the dominant position, on the obverse of the major coins. Later she and Nero get equal billing, appearing face to face. Then Agrippina's bust is relegated to the reverse of the coin, leaving Nero to dominate the obverse in the manner customary since Caesar. Finally the queen-mother is banished from the coins altogether, reflecting the decline of her power over her son.

Nero was also the first of the emperors to devalue and debase the coinage. The denarius had been minted to a standard which varied little from about the end of the Second Punic War. Nero reduced it in weight from about eighty-four to the pound to about ninety-six to the pound, and he also debased the silver content from virtually pure metal to about 90 percent silver. Thus the new denarii contained only about three-fourths the weight of silver of the old ones. The gold aureus, though not debased, was reduced in weight to a standard of about forty-five or forty-six to the pound as compared to the earlier forty to forty-two.

The meaning of the debasement is not as simple as might appear. It is easy to say that an extravagant Nero needed money and decided to ease the strain on the treasury in this way. But there remains the problem of the smaller devaluation of the gold as compared to the silver: there must have been some change in the relative value of gold and silver, the latter having increased in comparative value. Further, inflating of the currency by later emperors seems to have been done in part because of an appreciation in the value of silver. The reasons for the increased values of gold and especially silver relate to loss of coins through attrition, through an adverse balance of trade with the East, and through other uses of precious metals; but the chief cause was simply a problem of inadequate supply, owing to a decline in production from the major mines and an increasing demand for currency: that is to say, the supply of bullion— the only currency—being too low, the value of the coins appreciated.

It is thus possible to argue on the one hand that Nero merely took measures to increase the money supply in a time of need. Or it may be suggested that since gold changed value less than silver the Empire now went on a gold standard, and that the debasement of the denarius was thus relatively unimportant. This latter view, however, assumes that it was always possible to take twenty-five denarii to the treasury (or somewhere) and obtain for them one gold aureus; and this is unlikely. On balance, what happened may be explained by a combination of these views: there probably was a shortage of currency and it probably caused both gold and silver to rise in value, silver the more; but Nero probably devalued the currency more than these circumstances required, to gain a temporary advantage for the treasury. And thus he set a bad precedent which would often be followed by future emperors.

Upper-Class Intellectuals: Uncertain Loyalties

Anyone connected with a university in the twentieth century probably realizes well how very important intellectual or "academic" freedom is in the search for better ideas and better ways of doing things; the very process involves criticism of the status quo and a consideration of junking it in favor of something else. In first-century Rome such freedom of thought and action existed only at the will and good nature of the emperor. This in turn meant that sometimes there was little restriction and sometimes, depending upon the personality—or whim—of the reigning princeps, there was a great deal of restraint, whether active or indirect.

Even in the age of Augustus and even when authors favored the regime there could be awkward situations. Historians especially, of any age, may feel the lack of untrammeled freedom, for their works will be read with a view to the present: the manner in which the past is treated will often imply criticism or approval of the present situation. It has been suggested, for example, that the historian Livy took his work no farther than he did because of his mixed feelings about Augustus. Another great historian whose works are unfortunately altogether lost, Asinius Pollio (76 B.C.–A.D. 4) though he had been one of Caesar's commanders, had supported Antony, and in general Augustus as well, yet tread on shaky ground as he asserted a critical independence; even those who attended his salons perhaps sometimes feared they were exceeding bounds. The poet Horace, addressing one of his *Odes* to Pollio, spoke graphically of the situation:

Thou are treating of civil strife . . . a task full of dangerous hazard—and art walking, as it were, over fires hidden beneath treacherous ashes.[1]

Pollio's major work, covering the years of the civil wars from about 60 to 42 B.C., was much used by later writers.

[1] Horace *Odes* II, 1. Translation of C. E. Bennett, Loeb Classical Library (New York: 1929).

Pollio is also noted for having established the first really public library for the city of Rome. That of the Antigonids, brought back from Macedonia by Aemilius Paullus in the second century B.C., had perhaps been available for most scholars, as also another similarly brought from Greece by Sulla; but Pollio's was regularly and widely available much as a public library is today. The number of such libraries increased during the first century until there were five; but one of these may have suffered damage in the Neronian fire and another burned in the fire of 80 A.D.

The dilettante historian Velleius Paterculus (19 B.C.–30? A.D.), who had served as an army officer under the future emperor Tiberius, could hardly have offended anyone, even though he did manage to admire a broad spectrum of the great figures of the late Republic. His work—mostly extant—was a mere sketch of the history of the state, for one thing: for another, he saved his greatest admiration for the emperor Tiberius himself. At any rate the tone of his work helps to offset the later works of the historian Tacitus and the biographer Suetonius; the former hated Tiberius and cleverly vilified him, while the latter, though he treated Tiberius much more objectively, yet incorporated unbelievable stories of his perverse sexual behavior as an old man in secluded semiretirement on the island of Capri.

More courage was demanded of Aulus Cremutius Cordus, a historian who lived and wrote under Augustus and Tiberius. He praised republican heroes Cicero, Cassius, and Brutus and resolutely refused to flatter Augustus. Sejanus seems to have instigated his prosecution for treason: the unfortunate man committed suicide in 25 A.D., and his books were burned. His daughter courageously reissued them at some later date. They too no longer exist for our firsthand judgment.

The most important works of the minister of Nero, the younger Seneca (c. 4 B.C.–65 A.D.), are essays and letters reflecting his Stoic views. The philosopher rises to a more lofty ethical plane in his writings than he managed to reach in his personal life. For example, he extols the simple life—but he became enormously rich and loaned out his money at high rates. It is interesting, in fact, that by then moneylending had become so usual that Seneca need not keep it secret, as M. Brutus did in the late Republic.

Seneca also wrote tragedy of a peculiar one-dimensional type which reads as if it was intended for presentation through reading at a literary salon—as it probably was—rather than for performance. Yet because of its availability, perhaps, his work strongly influenced the great Elizabethans in the most flourishing period of English drama. One tragedy of this period once ascribed to Seneca but written by an unknown author soon after Nero's death is the *Octavia*, which sympathetically sets forth the plight of the daughter of Claudius whom Nero married then rejected and ultimately executed. One lesser work, generally thought to have been Seneca's, may have been ultimately damaging to him. It was a scathing satire, the *Apocolocyntosis*, written soon after the death of Claudius. A fantasy, it lampooned the efforts of the dead emperor, recently proclaimed a god in usual fashion, to join the other deities. No doubt the young Nero read it and laughed heartily. But how did the mature Nero feel about it? Did he perhaps suspect that Seneca would as easily write satire upon him also? Did he possibly suspect that this little work best reflected Seneca's real feelings about the whole institution of the principate? After all, Seneca had also written bad things about Gaius and indeed about the principate itself. Perhaps it helped convince Nero that Seneca was involved in the Pisonian conspiracy. Similarly, Petronius' work might be seen to embody an implied criticism—some modern scholars find it there. At any rate, both he and Seneca were invited to commit suicide.

A poet who wrote on a historical theme, Lucan (39–65 A.D.), the nephew of Seneca, found first restriction and then, also, death for his pains. His epic work, the *Pharsalia*, on the civil war between Caesar and Pompey and Cato, glorified republican heroes and themes. Nero—it is thought that it was partly owing to simple jealousy—forbade the young poet to read his works in the salons which Asinius Pollio had made so important a part of the intellectual world. Lucan later joined the Pisonian conspiracy and thus inexorably came to the hour when he had to take his own life.

Even a second-rank poet, the Stoic Persius (34–62 A.D.) may have offended Nero by his austere and obscure satires. Probably he would have joined in a conspiracy too if he had not died prematurely a few years earlier. Possibly both Lucan and Persius suffered in the Emperor's esteem because their Stoic teacher Cornutus had dared to suggest that Nero's plan to write an epic poem on Roman history was too grandiose; Cornutus had been banished for his temerity.

The Stoic Focus of Disloyalty

High-level opposition to the Caesars of the first century was mostly seen in a rather small but closely knit group of Stoics. A few Cynic philosophers joined in the disapprobation. The basis for their opposition apparently lay both in a sentimentalized view of the Republic and in a concept, less philosophical than political, that government should be in the hands of the best men (or the best man), which of course to them meant the old oligarchy, naturally led by themselves.

The republican heroes of these dissidents were Cato the Younger, Marcus Brutus, and Gaius Cassius. Lucan made Cato a kind of Stoic martyr to the cause of freedom. A Stoic senator of Nero's time, Thrasea Paetus, wrote a life of Cato; we do not have it, but we can perhaps see his attitude in the life of Cato by Plutarch, who used Thrasea. Cicero, who understood Cato's shortcomings well, would scarcely have recognized the man he knew. The veneration of Cato became almost cultic; groups of people gathered secretly to celebrate his birthdate. Thrasea irritated Nero most, it may be, by his silence. He walked out of the Senate when that body basely congratulated the emperor on his "escape" from his mother's conspiracy—really it approved of his matricide. Later he withdrew again, and he stayed out of the Senate for three years. A remark of Juvenal (Satire 5, 35ff.) may indicate that Nero and other emperors after him who moved against the Stoics had reason to suspect real conspiracy. He says that Thrasea and his son-in-law, Helvidius Priscus, used to celebrate the birthdays of the Cassii and the Bruti with garlands on their heads (as one might wear for sacrifice). Thrasea was accused of treason and chose to forestall the inevitable by his suicide.

Nero was the more fierce in his tyrannical behavior because he was frightened by the extent of the Pisonian conspiracy, which had included several high officers in the Praetorian Guard as well as many of the upper aristocracy. If the assassination had been planned for a time a few days earlier it would surely have succeeded, and the history of the Empire might have been very different.

Helvidius, along with Arulenus Rusticus and his brother, Junius Mauricus, after Thrasea's death headed up the opposition—once Helvidius returned from the exile into which Nero had sent him. They and others of their way of thinking not only vexed Vespasian but perhaps actually conspired against him as well. We are not as well informed about this as we are of the Pisonian plot against Nero, but Vespasian was goaded into reluctant reaction: about 75 A.D. Helvidius Priscus was executed—we are told that Vespasian tried to reverse the order but not in time—and other philosophers were expelled from Rome. Domitian, with characteristic heavy-handedness, in 89 not only expelled philosophers from Rome, as his father had, but even from Italy; three or four years later he executed a man who eulogized Helvidius as well as the son of Helvidius and he banished others, Arulenus Rusticus among them.

Such blanket expulsions of philosophers naturally injured completely innocent men. Among those sent away from Italy by Domitian was Epictetus, who had risen from slavery to become a freedman Stoic philosopher both blameless and harmless; his *Discourses* emphasize attainment of happiness through action of the will regardless of anything external. Another whose banishment was Rome's loss was Dio Chrysostom, friend of Vespasian and later, under Trajan, enthusiastic supporter of the Empire. Yet another exile, Appollonius of Tyana, was less of a loss to Rome. Part philosopher, part mystic, he was a man who gained a reputation through reputed miracles. Future pagan admirers would set him up as a kind of rival to the Christians' Jesus.

A remarkable group of women connected with the philosopher-resistors of the regime ought to be mentioned, particularly because the usual student view of first-century Roman women is shaped by the likes of Messalina and Agrippina. Perhaps one should begin with the elder Arria, wife of one Caecina Paetus, who was caught in a conspiracy against Claudius. He hesitated at the actual plunge of the dagger in the suicide he had determined upon; Arria took the dagger, gave herself a mortal thrust, and handed it back to Paetus, saying, "Paetus, it doesn't hurt." Nor was she only intending to follow her husband in a sort of wifely martyrdom: she had been a part of the whole thing. It was their daughter, also named Arria, who was the wife of Thrasea Paetus. Like her mother she shared her husband's feelings and like her wished to follow him in death, but was dissuaded. Their daughter, Fannia, was wife to Helvidius Priscus; she shared his exile and almost shared his death. She was later exiled herself, and her property confiscated, for encouraging men who tried to carry on the tradition of opposition. Seneca's mother Helvia, had also been a remarkable woman; though the elder Seneca was a rhetorician of repute, it was she, not her husband, who gave young Seneca his love of philosophy.

Connected with this list only by chronology and sex is another worthy woman, Domitilla, niece of Domitian and wife of Flavius Clemens. Her son might well have been chosen by the emperor as his successor if she and her husband had elected to give him blind support. But she and Clemens were attracted to monotheism—Jewish or Christian, it is uncertain which—and suffered the penalty for "atheism": death for Clemens, banishment for Domitilla.

Senatorial Supporters of Empire

By no means all thinking men and women of the upper classes turned against the first-century rulers. The elder Pliny (23–79

A.D.), for example, found it possible to serve the state and follow the path of the scholar as well. His compendious *Natural History* by its very nature was less likely to give offense than history or political philosophy, dealing as it did with topics such as astronomy, mining and metallurgy, and the like. Pliny was commander of the fleet at Misenum when Vesuvius erupted in 79. He took some ships close to Pompeii, partly from scientific curiosity and partly to help fleeing refugees if possible, only to die himself, asphyxiated by volcanic gases.

Agricola, father-in-law of the historian Tacitus, found it possible to advance to high office even under Domitian. His most important service was as governor of Britain, where he advanced both imperial boundaries and civilized settlement. It was rumored, however, that at the end of his career his life was in danger from a capricious Domitian. All of our information is slanted, especially that coming from Tacitus (see Chapter 12), whose *Annals* and *Histories* suggest that several emperors of the first century were some species of monster.

The greatest support for the regime came from the formerly obscure persons raised to important posts by the various emperors, particularly the Flavians. This group, lacking any family traditions of power and independence, were deeply obligated to the emperors who chose to elevate them. As the Senate came to be filled with such men, the very concept of freedom tended to change among senators. No longer did it mean a really independent Senate as in the Republic. Republicanism was now—and quite logically–all but dead. Freedom to most senators of this age meant no more than the right to be respected, consulted, and permitted to do and say what they pleased within reasonable limits. A restricted concept of freedom indeed, but the system could now offer nothing more.

This is not to say that the new families enrolled among the upper classes did not provide a needed balance; out of their rural, colonial, or provincial origins often emerged the solid virtues, the frugal habits, and something of the spirit, extolled by Tacitus (*Annals* 3. 55), that had made Rome great. And Tacitus was a severe critic. He tells us, moreover, that Vespasian did much to set the same tone.

Lower-Class Worlds: The Slaves

At least until Nero, the emperors lived in constantly increasing luxury and affluence, with the great families imitating royalty so far as their means could permit. The Pax Romana created a general prosperity, as we have seen, which tended to be concentrated at the center of empire; on some lesser scale, it permeated to the cities of the provinces as well, and to a small degree radiated out to the countryside. Unfortunately, one form of the new prosperity was the development of ever larger domestic slave establishments among the wealthy.

Slavery was debilitating to ancient society, quite aside from the degrading human dimension. Slaves were used everywhere possible: on farms, in small industry—even a cobbler might have several, as memorial inscriptions show. Slaves might be trained as skilled accountants, educators, physicians or midwives, managers. It probably is true, as modern scholars have argued, that slaves and free men were rarely in direct competition in any cost-cutting sense. However, it is also true that certain occupations, which might have been desirable and remunerative for free persons, were dominated by slaves or freedmen, thereby greatly restricting opportunities for free men. Similarly, slavery tended to make it difficult to establish a small business enterprise and rise to a comfortable situation. Rich people were not likely to spend very much patronizing small contractors or caterers of any sort: they simply acquired enough slaves to take care of all or almost all of their needs, so that the large households were in many ways almost as self-sufficient as a medieval manor. The enormous amount of capital tied up in the institution of slavery might easily have been used in more productive ways.

Above all, slaves were used as personal servants, sometimes for a kind of conspicuous show of wealth and luxury. The remains of ancient cemeteries have taught us much about the enormous slave establishments in the large houses. In the eighteenth century a few miles south of Rome on the Appian Way was discovered the *columbarium* (repository of the ashes of the cremated dead) of Augustus' household, mostly slaves. The total number of persons buried there was not less than six thousand. Some of these had died young, which makes it difficult to extrapolate the normal size of the imperial slave establishment, but certainly it was large. Of the total number, about a tenth, or six hundred, had been personal servants of Livia. There was a whole corps of persons whose responsibilities related to Livia's personal needs: hairdressers, persons in charge of her bath, perfumers, keepers of jewelry, no less than eight goldsmiths (though one must remember, these are burials; she may not have had that many all at one time). Those who saw to her clothing had very detailed tasks: there was a slave for just her dresses of the royal purple; another for morning dresses; still another for clothing worn on state occasions. One slave kept— probably made—her sandals: she presumably had two or three others for her different types of shoes.

Other *columbaria* of great households have been found and tell a similar story. The Statilia family, important in the reign of Augustus and later—Messalina, wife of Claudius, was a Statilia—had a comparably huge retinue of slaves and freedmen. One of the notable things we learn of this family is that all phases of the making of clothes from the carding of wool to weaving and sewing was done in the house. This might have been expected in a country estate, but is surprising in an urban house, and illustrates the earlier point about self-sufficiency of the great households. Several of Statilius' servants were keepers of horses: he was a racing enthusiast and kept many of Spanish breed. Thus some household slaves were used in economically productive ways, but most were not.

Away from the great houses, slaves performed more socially useful tasks. Slaves and freedmen even held important managerial posts, not only in small businesses, but in contracting corporations; at Rome, for example, slaves usually managed the huge complexes of warehouses along the Tiber; in the suburbs they ran brickyards, tileyards, and the like; in the rural areas they often managed farms, vineyards, and orchards.

Most production slaves, however, were ordinary laborers, who lived under miserable circumstances and who were worked as hard as possible on as little food and clothing as might keep them alive and in condition to function satisfactorily. Slaves who worked the mines and quarries had perhaps the bleakest outlook; ordinary farm laborers, who sometimes worked in chains, were not much better off. Free day laborers without land worked when they could on others' farms, and were only marginally better off, if at all, than agricultural slaves. Slaves were often called as court witnesses in cases involving some member of the household, and Romans routinely tortured them before taking their evidence. Even worse, when any slave murdered his master, all the slaves of the household—in the larger ones this meant several hundred—were killed even when the culprit was identified. It was the law.

As we have seen, however, Roman law was in some ways more lenient to slaves than were the legal systems of other states in antiquity. It was relatively easy for Romans to free slaves on payment of a small tax, and moreover, freedmen automatically became citizens. Romans allowed their slaves to accumulate personal property; many of them were able to save enough to purchase their freedom. The law protected them more or less in certain other ways. Masters did not have unrestricted right to mistreat slaves (at least not to kill them). Marriages, though unofficial, were in several ways recognized and protected in law. A free man could free a woman slave and make her his legal wife, unless he was of the highest social and political class; however, the reverse was not true.

Many court cases involving slaves concerned the question of whether they were slave or free. The Roman law evolved the principle that in the absence of evidence to the contrary it should be assumed that a person was born free. A humane principle, given the times, but no substitute for the principle that all persons are born free!

Lower Classes: Life in the Capital

In a number of ways Rome was a safer and more satisfactory place to live under the early Empire than in the late Republic. Augustus had divided up the city into fourteen regions, each with some minimal governmental forms. He had established the *vigiles*, the combination police-fire station for each two regions, and we know of a few substations, apparently established in especially troublesome areas. The city had plenty of water—most of it quite good water—brought in by a complex and growing system of aqueducts. Claudius had built two. The only area not well supplied in the first century was the Janiculum, across the Tiber from the city proper. In the next century, Trajan would remedy that with still another aqueduct. Sanitary drainage, though inadequate by modern standards, was as good as that of the major cities of the West more than a millennium and a half later.

The *vigiles*, as has been noted, could not make the city totally safe from fire or crime. It was best to avoid the unlit streets after nightfall. Juvenal's third *Satire*, on the city, explains why: some bully of a mugger would beat and rob the man who could not afford to have a retinue of servants along with him. Even at home one could not be safe:

When your house is shut, when bar and chain have made fast your shop, and all is silent, you will be robbed by a burglar; or perhaps a cut-throat will do you in quickly with cold steel.[2]

Moreover, other dangers lurked from the windows of the high apartments that lined the streets:

See what a height it is to that towering roof from which a potsherd comes crack upon my head every time that some broken or leaky vessel is pitched out of the window![3]

[2] Juvenal *Satire* 3. 302–305. Modified translation of G. G. Ramsay, in the Loeb Classical Library (Cambridge, Mass., 1959).
[3] Ibid., 269–271.

Destructive fires, as we have seen, on two occasions wrought major devastation in the century. We can imagine how many less destructive fires went unreported in our sources. Nero's plan for reconstruction after the great fire of his reign (in 64) meant wider streets, better distribution of water, and buildings better designed for fighting fires, but all this did not prevent the major fire of Titus' reign.

Safe or not, Rome was expensive. Rentals were high. Juvenal again provides us with a graphic example:

If you can tear yourself away from the games of the Circus, you can buy an excellent house at Sora, at Fabrateria or Frusino, for what you pay in Rome to rent a dark garret for one year.[4]

And the same poet tells what the cost of living could mean to a person of little means:

It is no easy matter, anywhere, for a man to rise when poverty stands in the way of his merits; but nowhere is the effort harder than in Rome, where you must pay a big rent for a wretched lodging, a big sum to fill the bellies of your slaves, and buy a frugal dinner for yourself.[5]

The poorest of the lower classes at Rome—if, indeed the welfare system was so managed as to select the most needy—were aided in their efforts to survive by the distributions of free grain. For centuries an average of about 200,000 persons received this dole, not merely as a privilege but as a hereditary right. Whatever they could gain from their labor would yet provide only miserable lodgings and a minimum of other necessities. Occasional largesse from the emperors or from officials or even private persons helped also.

The city was noisy. Traffic had long been a problem; Caesar, in fact, had forbidden vehicular traffic in downtown Rome during the daytime hours. In consequence, heavy freight deliveries were made at night. The grinding of iron wheels on protesting paving blocks and the swearing of the teamsters made the nights difficult for sleeping. The days brought other clangor and clamor. Many of the activities which in modern cities take place indoors were street-based in ancient Rome. Hawkers of goods, craftsmen, barbers, even butchers and bankers all used the streets. Add to this the crowds of people who were often outdoors simply because their living quarters provided little more than places to sleep and were inadequate for that, and one

[4] Ibid., 223–225.
[5] Ibid., 164–168.

can perhaps begin to get the feel for the sights, sounds, and noisome smells of the great metropolis.

Yet there were compensations: Rome was the most exciting place in the world, at least in the view of most of its inhabitants. Entertainments of varied sorts added spice to urban life. Great public baths provided, for a small fee, places for welcome afternoon baths and also served as social centers where Romans could play games, get a massage, buy hot food, or just talk with friends. Many lower-class Romans belonged to *collegia*—clubs of different types, some like craft guilds, others more specifically religious or social. (Those clubs with political tendencies had been banned by Caesar.) All the *collegia* helped to give some sense of identity within a social group. Most also provided some aid to members, at the least an arrangement for a proper burial, a thing that has seemed important to people in most times and places.

Lower Classes: Life in the Provinces

It would be impossible to generalize very much about the circumstances of the lower classes in provinces so diverse as, say, Egypt, where most families worked in serfdom for the state or great landowners, and Britain, where most workers probably toiled as independent small holders. Nor is there space for surveying conditions in each of the provinces. Earlier it was suggested that most of the lower classes found their lot under the Empire improved over their circumstances prior to absorption by Rome. That is, since peace has its blessings, since the Romans were mostly conscientious and orderly in their arrangements, and since local government was largely allowed to function as it had before Roman conquest, probably most lower-class provincials had as much freedom as before, with generally better economic conditions.

There were times, of course, when Roman subjects felt strongly their inferior political position. When the noncitizen found himself in confrontation with Roman citizens, especially Roman officials, he was at a certain disadvantage. Or if the provincial governor showed bad character or greed, there was little that could be done, in spite of the provisions for bringing suit in the admirable Roman court system. Perhaps there were few venal officials in relation to the total, but we know of several.

One particular area of abuse was the frequent bad treatment of the populace by Roman soldiers. John the Baptist, in the Bible, is reported to have told soldiers to be content with their wages, implying that they often were not and that they made up for it by some sort of extortion. The poet Juvenal—writing to a Roman audience, but the problem was universal—gives insight into the sort of incident that was common. His comments are in *Satire 16*, on the military. One benefit all soldiers had, he declared, was that civilians would never dare to attack one of them. If, on the other hand, a civilian was beaten up by a soldier, the former could not hope for redress. The reason? All such redress had to be sought within the camp, for no soldier could come before a civilian court. Even if the case should be heard by a centurion who was a strict disciplinarian, as many of them notoriously were, and he should decide in favor of the civilian, Juvenal says the complainant would simply have made an enemy of the soldier's whole cohort; he could expect even more brutal treatment in the future. Juvenal adds that it was easier to find someone to give false witness against a civilian than to find anybody to testify to the truth against a soldier. Yet, it will be remembered, army service was available to selected provincials, whose long enlistment in the *auxilia* brought citizenship, among other benefits, at discharge.

Public Entertainment: Games and Circuses

Emperors and kings have always found it prudent, especially when they rule from large capital cities, to try to keep the lower classes in their capitals quiescent and reasonably happy. Failure to do this has helped to bring about the fall of rulers from Nabonidus in Babylonia in the sixth century b.c. to Louis XVI in eighteenth-century France. To a degree the city plebs were useful to the principes. The capital was the backdrop to the imperial stage, and the urban plebs provided a sort of chorus for the imperial drama—or was it perhaps their role to serve as appreciative audience, applauding and cheering at proper intervals? No state would seem great and powerful without a chief who on occasion emerged in full panoply for some state occasion the success of which is pointed up by huge cheering crowds.

Great state occasions are not simply for show. They are warp and woof of the state. In Rome many of them had a religious connection. The success with which public spectacles are carried off does in some measure testify to the essential health of a regime. Nor had the great festivals of Rome been invented by the emperors; most were inherited from the Republic, along with the facilities. Two great circuses, the Circus Maximus and the Circus Flaminius, had existed long before the Caesars. Gaius, Nero, and Domitian all added new facilities. Nero's circus on the Vatican is now partially covered by the Basilica of St. Peter. A permanent stone theatre did not exist until Pompey built one in the first century B.C. Augustus added another, called the theatre of Marcellus, after his nephew, remains of which still impress tourists today. The great festivals carried over from the Republic lengthened and grew more elaborate. Others were added: Nero and Domitian both established quinquennial (five-year) games celebrating their own reigns; birthdays of the emperors tended to become festival days.

The major festivals in Augustus' reign, all of long standing, were those to Cybele, Ceres, and Flora in the spring; games in the summer to Apollo; and in the fall the Roman games and the Plebeian games to Jupiter and Hercules. Augustus added games to Venus Genetrix, tutelary deity of the Julian family. The total of such holidays reached about 77 under Augustus, increased to 87 under Tiberius (who added a festival dedicated to Augustus), and continued to rise until about 175 such days were marked in the official calendars of the fourth century A.D. Of course, it should not be assumed that all Romans could always be idle on holidays. If they did not work they got no pay. The workday began quite early and ended early; workers could labor a few hours and have time for some excitement after that. Moreover the hawkers, vendors, and others worked even harder on festival days.

In the first century the most entertainment time was allotted to theatrical performances, even though the classical theatre was actually in decline; more appealing to the crowds now were farces, mimes, and pantomimes. However, by far the largest crowds attended the horse and chariot races. The Circus Maximus could seat perhaps 150,000, with vantage points one way and another for perhaps 100,000 more. The factions had each a distinctive color, and the blues, the whites, the reds, and the greens all had their rabid partisans. For some reason the greens were dominant throughout most of this period. Those who have seen the motion picture *Ben Hur* can begin to appreciate the excitement of the chariot races.

Caesar began a practice occasionally followed by later rulers of putting on naval combats in an artificial lake he constructed along the Tiber. There were often boat races. Other types of performances included those seen in modern circuses: acrobats, jugglers, rope-dancers, fire-eaters, trained beasts, and the like. Animal fights or fights between men and animals (the men were usually condemned criminals) were often staged. Gladiatorial combat, later often thought to epitomize the Roman games, was not a part of public spectacle until late in the second century B.C. However, showings put on by private persons— earliest, at funeral games—had already become common and as is well known public showings increased steadily during the late

Republic and the early Empire. The emperor Claudius had a bloodthirsty streak in his character and exhibited many pairs of gladiators. He also put on a naval combat in grand style at the dedication of the works draining the Fucine lake. He brought criminals from all over the empire to serve in the crews—nineteen thousand men on each side, many of whom were slain.

Of the gladiators it should be said that while theirs was doubtless a demeaning, cruel, and bloody "sport" yet some attained notoriety and even wealth. The successful ones owned the finest decorated armor (probably not used in combat) and were frequently besieged by admiring women. Even freeborn men, on occasion of high social status, entered the gladiatorial ranks; others who did not still trained themselves in gladiatorial fashion. A few women are known to have fought in the arena. The practice reached a peak in the third century A.D. when numerous prisoners of war were available for combat.

As for length of celebration, the record was set for the first century by Titus, appropriately enough at the dedication of the Flavian amphitheatre, usually called the Colosseum, in 80 A.D. The games of all sorts went on for 100 days. Trajan's Dacian triumph early in the second century exceeded that, lasting 123 days.

The festivals and games no doubt permitted the crowds to let off steam and perhaps prevented general unrest (the argument is debatable, somewhat like the question of violence on television). Perhaps these crowd demonstrations to some extent substituted for the loss of the more orderly expressions of opinion in the now defunct assemblies. But there were frequent disturbances at the games, which required special coercive measures. The emperor Gaius, irritated one time when the noisy crowds began to enter the circus in the middle of the night, had soldiers clear the circus; a good many of the revelers were killed, several of equestrian rank. Activities on the fringes of the arenas and circuses required policing: gambling and sale of wine caused much trouble.

The emperors or their official representatives often made distributions of food and money at the festivals. It was probably Nero who first began the practice of throwing tickets into the crowd good for prizes and the like, sometimes valuable ones.

Italian and provincial cities, particularly in the West, imitated Rome in the matter of games as they did in government and architecture. As in Rome the crowds at the games were often rowdy. In Pompeii a few years before its destruction a gladiatorial contest brought on such riots that imperial authorities suppressed the games entirely for several years. This bloody affair is not only reported by Tacitus (*Annals* 14. 17), who

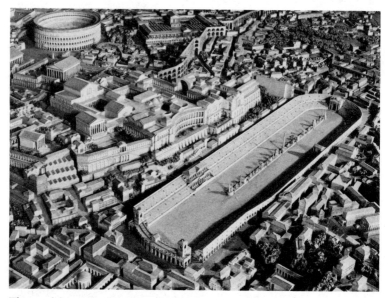

This model, a part of the city of Rome as it was about 200 A.D., shows the Circus Maximus, scene of the horse and chariot races; note the *spina* in the center. In the upper left is the Flavian Amphitheater or Colosseum; between is the Palatine Hill, with residences of the emperors.

dismisses it as "typical of such country towns," but it is also vividly portrayed in a wall painting from Pompeii that has survived the centuries. Puteoli was the scene of similar riots. Criminals were in many places routinely executed either by being forced to fight with each other to the death—after which the victor was killed—or by combat with starving and fierce wild animals. Whatever Christians may have done in and to the Roman Empire, their action in ending such bloody spectacles redounds greatly to their credit.

In many ways the second century was the greatest age of Rome. It is to be doubted that any nation in any age has managed by any selection process whatever to put into its highest office a succession of five men of higher caliber than the five "Good" Emperors who ruled between 96 and 180 A.D.: Nerva, Trajan, Hadrian, Antoninus Pius, and Marcus Aurelius. Competent, conscientious, and hard-working, they performed at a consistently high level. In unprecedented fashion they assisted systematically in the welfare of orphans and the poor; they organized the civil administration along rational lines; they controlled state expenditures carefully, most avoiding personal, extravagant show. Like their predecessors they too were absolute autocrats; indeed, that was the role they played in the system. But they acted with advice from the governing class and usually without the arbitrary coercion often characteristic of rule by one person. In their time the Empire would be "Principate," not "Dominate."

The Empire attained its largest size in this period, with boundaries on the East in Mesopotamia and on the West limited only by the Atlantic. There was almost uninterrupted internal peace; the wars on the frontiers were usually limited to necessary operations. Even the most warlike emperor of the five, Trajan, seems not to have been motivated by a personal greed for power. Though Christians occasionally endured persecution, the populace generally enjoyed considerable personal—though not political—freedom. We have the testimony of notable men of non-Roman stock singing the praises of these intelligent, urbane emperors and the empire they ruled. Conditions of life in Rome and cities all over the Empire—housing, sanitation, public facilities—were superior to those in the ages that followed until the nineteenth century.

THE HIGH EMPIRE: THE GOOD EMPERORS AND THE SEVERI, 96–235 A.D.

11

A Broadening Base of Participation in Government

Particularly notable in this period is a trend that began in the days of the Republic: the circle of active participants in government continually widened. In the last century of the Republic the Romans had extended the citizenship, and the concomitant right to hold the highest offices, to all Italians. By the time of the Flavian emperors, formerly Italian families held most of the dominant positions in government and society. In fact, the emperors themselves well illustrate the trend: first came the Julio-Claudians, drawn from older Roman families; then the Flavians, drawn from formerly Italian rather than old Roman stock; after them the Good Emperors, all but the first of whom also derived from Italian families which by then had been citizens for generations but had migrated from Italy to Spain or Gaul; finally, the Severi, of neither old Roman nor Italian stock, though citizens to be sure, and with roots in Africa and (through Julia Domna, wife of the first Severus) Syria. Most other emperors to the end of the Empire derived from provincial families. The evolutionary process produced a class of officials, particularly in the military but also in the central administration that, like the emperors, had ever less familial connection with Rome and Italy. Widening privilege continued in the gradual extension of the citizenship until, in 212 A.D., almost all free persons in the whole Empire became "Roman" citizens. It should not be inferred that this broadening circle of participants in government brought with it any democratization in governmental structures.

Romanization of the Provinces

Other continuing changes in the nature of the Empire naturally accompanied the gradual extension of privilege. One of these concomitants was the Romanization of the Empire. It does not really matter here whether one says these areas were Romanized because of the extension of privilege or that privileges were extended to areas because they became Romanized. In the East, where Greek culture had long been dominant, neither statement is quite correct. Everywhere else, most notably in Spain, the Gauls, the Danubian provinces, and in North Africa west of Egypt, the Latin language and Roman ways penetrated, outstripping and paving the way for the extension of citizenship and other privileges. The term "Romanization" may mislead. What developed in the provinces was a sort of hybrid civilization, a melding both of peoples and cultures in which an overlay of Latin language and Roman ways gave an appearance of Romanization.

Another concomitant to the broadened base of participation was a growing intimacy between the central government and the people in the provinces, leading inevitably to the gradual centralization of function—and power. More men were recruited for the larger armies; those who had the citizenship could of course now serve in the legions. The governing city councils found themselves more and more the agents of the central government, particularly in the collection of taxes. Service as local officials that brought great honor—in part because the citizenship often came with it—began gradually and increasingly to be viewed as a burden. In another century or two the burden would become so intolerable that men would flee to the countryside to avoid it. But we are looking beyond the High Empire.

Provincial Cities: Degrees of Privilege

The ways that local citizens in the provinces might enter government service and rise to hold positions of some importance depended on the nature of the municipalities where they lived. These municipalities did not all enjoy the same privileges, even when most or all of their citizens were also Roman citizens. Some cities were "free" and ran certain of their own affairs without much interference from the provincial governors. Some were "free" and "immune," so that in addition their citizens did not pay one of the two major types of taxes collected everywhere outside Italy. These were the *tributum soli*, a land tax, and the *tributum capitis*, a head tax based on property census, perhaps somewhat like a personal property assessment. Some few of the most favored cities had also the *ius Italicum*, with the same financial privilege as Italy itself, and paid neither of the two major taxes. Though not all communities given the title of *colonia* possessed the *ius Italicum*, probably all the true colonies of Roman citizens, usually veterans sent out to settle on land in the provinces, were granted this most coveted privilege, as well as a few favored municipalities elevated to colonial status.

The colonies of veterans seem to have provided the best opportunities for government service for their citizens. And like the cities that grew up about the major army camps, the colonies also did much to Romanize the areas where they were located. Even noncitizens recruited from the provinces, who received the citizenship only upon discharge, ordinarily acquired the Latin language plus, usually, a Romanized attitude in religion, dress, and general view of the Empire. By this time, these veteran colonies served as important recruiting grounds, since sons frequently followed fathers in the military career. Men of ability could rise, often quickly, in the army. It was there, in the military, in fact, that it first became easy for lower-class citizens of ability to move into lucrative civil careers.

Under the Severi the offices available to men who rose through the military increased in number at the expense of the senatorial aristocracy, which therefore faded in importance. As for the Senate itself, though it remained an important body under the Good Emperors, by the end of the Severan dynasty it was well on the way to becoming little more than a glorified city council for Rome. Imperial decisions made with the advice of the emperors' *consilium* and implemented by the praetorian prefects replaced senatorial decrees, which by then were no longer a major source of law. Roman senators continued as the aristocratic elite of the Empire; but careers were forged elsewhere. A senator out of office was little noticed.

Portent of Decline

This generally bright picture of the Empire under the Good Emperors renders all the more disquieting the apparent fact that, despite the best efforts of the superior leaders of the second century, the decline of Rome in some ways had already begun. Culturally, the signs are clear. In literature this century saw the end of the Silver Age of Latin literature and the arrival of what one scholar has acutely called the "Silver Plated" age.[1] Architecture reached a peak early in the period and began a slow decline despite certain technical advances. Roman law entered the so-called classical period of development—but this is also the age when the government deliberately began to apply the law unevenly according to social status.

Symptoms of decline seem quite noticeable in the economic sphere: deterioration at the center continued, with trouble also in several of the provinces. By the end of the period, state revenues could be made to cover necessary expenditures only with difficulty, and only with stress upon the provincial upper classes responsible for the collection of taxes. The coins continued to symbolize the economic strain: the silver coins were increasingly debased throughout the period. By the end of M. Aurelius' reign the denarius was worth only about 60 percent of its value in the age of Augustus; by the time of the last Severus, Alexander, it was worth about 50 percent at best.

The picture of decline is no less somber because economic and other signs of weakness appear in part as the result of circumstances no emperor could control, including a series of years of bad crops over large areas, owing to weather, plague,

[1] Tom B. Jones, *The Silver Plated Age* (Sandoval, N.M., 1962).

depopulation, and unwanted foreign wars. So strong an empire should have mustered sufficient economic and manpower reserves to endure more successfully a few bad years. There is almost no accounting for the failure of spirit, the slackening cultural response to what seemed even then a great age.

Nerva, 96–98 A.D.

After Domitian was assassinated in a palace conspiracy, the Senate moved quickly to name a successor; this was Nerva, a rich senator in his sixties, who had some knowledge of the law and considerable governmental experience. Though he lived to rule barely over sixteen months, Nerva certainly deserves to be classified with the Good Emperors. He might well have been only the first of another series of ephemeral rulers during a civil war, since neither the praetorians nor the army had a hand in his selection. The troops were temporarily mollified, however, as donatives were paid to the praetorians and probably to the whole army, as well as to the city plebs. In addition, a land scheme—passed as law, incidentally, by some body called an assembly of the Roman people, the last such ever held—provided a distribution of land to other lower-class Romans. Nerva was generous enough to help finance at least this latter measure with his own wealth.

He carefully maintained amicable relations with the Senate; he swore not to put any senator to death without judgment of his peers, an oath repeated by each of the next several successor emperors. He allowed open criticism, even by one of the consuls, who thought he was being unnecessarily lenient with wrongdoers under Domitian's reign. Indeed, the senators were in a vengeful mood: they passed the *damnatio memoriae* against Domitian, by which all official references to the former emperor were erased, literally, from monuments and the like. And they were eager to begin the prosecution of Domitian's lieutenants. Even the amiable Pliny the Younger made ready to prosecute the man who earlier had prosecuted Helvidius Priscus. But Nerva, wishing to put an end to bitterness, refused to permit such proceedings. He took care to honor the *damnatio* but had certain of Domitian's acts specifically reconfirmed to avoid awkwardness.

Nerva had no son. Thus there was no question of his establishing a dynasty—the sore point which had set the intellectual community against Vespasian. On the other hand, this made the choice of an heir apparent the more important, especially as Nerva was not young. Any selection that would vastly displease the army, the praetorian guard, or the Senate might again cause a crisis with two or three candidates backed by different armies fighting for the purple. Nerva did not even pick a relative. With excellent judgment he chose Marcus Ulpius Trajanus, a second-generation noble (his father had been elevated by Vespasian) who was not only a senator of note but also an excellent general. He was at the time governor of Upper Germany and therefore in command of one of the largest armies. All the powerful elements of Roman politics accepted the choice. Only three months later while Trajan was still in Germany, Nerva died.

Trajan, 98–117 A.D.

It was perhaps the younger Pliny, in his *Panegyric* delivered about 100 A.D., who first termed Trajan *optimus princeps*. He doubtless meant to imply specifically that here at last was the "best citizen" which the Stoic and other philosopher-opponents of the Flavians had argued should be sought out for the highest imperial office. The intellectual community indeed seems to have accepted the view, and the Senate as well. Trajanic coin types later bear the appellation as an official, honorific title. Like Domitian, Trajan was addressed as "dominus"; in the case of the latter, however, the "et deus" was left out. Trajan's origin in Italica in southern Spain seems not to have aroused any doubts.

The changed attitude of most Romans toward their emperor hinged almost altogether on personality and administrative style: Domitian had been hated and feared, as Trajan was respected and admired. There was no important constitutional alteration in the position of the princeps that gained for him the popularity that had eluded the last of the Flavians. Indeed, Trajan's power was as absolute as Domitian's and he used it in some ways, particularly in the provinces, that Domitian had not. However, Trajan did repeat the oath of Nerva never to put senators to death without trial by their peers, and what is more important, he treated them with respect, even deference, and made use of them both in formulating and in carrying out his policies.

Despite the good-humored courtesy and common sense displayed by Trajan—seen particularly in his replies to the letters sent him by Pliny when the latter was governing Bithynia (110–112 A.D.)—Trajan strongly desired efficiency in government and did not hesitate to take extraordinary measures to bring about improvement. Pliny furnishes a good example. Bithynia, in Asia Minor, was a consular province, senatorially controlled; but a number of its cities through bad management had got their financial affairs into disorganized states. Trajan got Senate approval and took over this senatorial province; he sent Pliny, a senator, with orders to intervene in the affairs of the city-states of the province in an attempt to restore financial order. The practice was continued both by him and by his successors. Moreover, Trajan sent "correctors" to various places, including even the free cities of Greece. This again was in the interest of efficiency, perhaps as well of sound government free of corruption. Yet it has been properly noted that freedom includes the freedom to make mistakes; and Trajan's interventions, though beneficial locally—as well as to the imperial treasury—meant enlarged power for the central government and a diminution of freedom in local matters. The tendency toward centralization of power, seen even under an enlightened princeps, seems, in retrospect, inevitable and relentless.

New Conquests: Extended Frontiers

For a good many years the tribes north of the Danube had tested Rome's defenses along that river, and occasionally had swept across it, bent on plunder. Domitian had strengthened the military contingents on that frontier and had even led campaigns in person. Twice he lost whole legions and parts of other units. He had eventually stabilized the area of the lower Danube by making Decebalus, king of Dacia (in modern Rumania), a Roman "ally" and giving him a subsidy. Trouble continued on the middle Danube, however, and Nerva campaigned against the Suebi there.

Trajan made war against Decebalus. Whether he failed to behave like an ally or whether Trajan simply felt that the arrangement made by Domitian was impossible is not known. In fact, for details for Trajan's Dacian wars of about 100–101 and 105–106 A.D., historians must rely on scraps of information and on the magnificent relief sculpture which spirals upward about the column that Trajan erected sometime later in a new forum in Rome. One scene shows the 3300-foot bridge the Romans built across the Danube, a wood superstructure on twenty great stone piers, some remains of which still withstand the swift currents of the river. The roadbed was destroyed after only a few years to prevent easy crossing of the stream by possible enemies. Though the accomplishment was Roman, the architect, Apollodorus, was a Syrian with a Greek name.

These major wars demanded extensive mobilization of men and resources. It was claimed that Trajan captured a great treasure in the war and that this, with other spoils and income from the Dacian gold mines, more than paid for the war. Gold does seem to have become gradually cheaper in relation to silver. If

The spiral reliefs of Trajan's column in Rome depict in successive scenes the beginning and the progress of the Dacian campaign. (*Alinari–Scala*)

truly a profitable war, it was probably the last such fought by Rome. After the first war Decebalus was left as king but his territory was reduced. He soon rebelled. After the second war he committed suicide. The territory now became the Roman province of Dacia, a kind of salient across the Danube, which prevented easy movement along the river for Rome's potential foes and divided them. This province—later subdivided—was, however, in an exposed position itself, and proved difficult to defend. By now nine legions with large numbers of auxiliary units were stationed along the Danube frontier.

Soon after the end of the Dacian war, Trajan moved into the Near East and took over the Nabatean kingdom on the death of one of its client kings. Trajan made part of the kingdom a separate province, called Arabia Petraea. This was approximately the Sinai peninsula, with some adjacent territories. Since he stationed a legion there, his motive in the whole venture may have been the defense of important trade routes connecting with the Arabian peninsula to the south.

Trajan took the name Dacicus, celebrated record-length games in Rome along with a triumph, and spent enormous sums on a donative for the urban plebs. He soon was engaged in extensive building projects, to be surveyed later in the chapter along with some of his economic measures and welfare projects.

After a time he again turned his attention to the East. There Rome had long had problems with the loosely constructed state of Parthia. Nero, it will be recalled, had sent his greatest general, Corbulo, to the East and, after a combination of campaign, maneuver, and diplomacy, had come to an enduring agreement. The chief difficulty then, as for Trajan later, was the Kingdom of Armenia. Since it was strategically located at a geographical pivot between the two spheres of influence, neither Roman emperor nor Parthian king could permit completely external control of that area. Nero's compromise had permitted a relative of the Parthian monarch to become king, but he received his coronation from Nero himself in Rome, with all that that implied.

When the Parthian king Chosroes put his nephew on the Armenian throne without consulting Rome, Trajan chose to regard it as a hostile move, sufficient to warrant, not merely a campaign, which through a demonstration of power might restore the Neronian compromise, but also a major war designed to both weaken Parthia and provide a permanent solution to the recurring problem of control over Armenia. After extensive preparations Trajan sailed east in 113 A.D.

During the next three years Trajan occupied Armenia; then he moved south into Parthia, captured Ctesiphon on the Tigris, a Parthian capital, and at one point penetrated all the way to the Persian gulf. He was aided by division within the Parthian dominions. However, there were no defensible frontiers and it was impossible to put Roman garrisons in all of the key points of such a vast area. The Parthian monarch kept up the fight in every way he could, from direct attack to guerrilla tactics to stirring up opposition in territories occupied by Romans.

The very elements conspired against Trajan, who was almost killed in a devastating earthquake at Antioch in the winter of 114–115. Rebuilding the city was to require great expenditure. Moreover, a serious Jewish rebellion demanded attention. Beginning in Cyrene and Egypt it spread to Cyprus and even to Roman-held sections of Mesopotamia. Gentiles were said to have been slaughtered by the hundreds of thousands; doubtless the figures can be discounted, but the toll certainly was appalling. Trajan of course took measures to put down the rebellion—if that is the right term to describe this bloody reaction to a long series of events that had goaded the Jews beyond endurance. Roman troops soon in turn were slaughtering the Jews in equally appalling numbers.

But Trajan did not live to see the end of either his Parthian grand venture or the Jewish revolt. He died in Cilicia, on the way back to Rome.

When teachers and textbooks must condense their history material to suit the needs of survey courses, they usually portray Trajan as the conquering imperialist and Hadrian as the peaceful builder—and so they were. Yet Trajan, in Italy at least, built as much as Hadrian did, and the latter gave close and continuing attention to the army. Hadrian did end the wars as soon as he could, even giving up territories that Trajan had won in the Mesopotamian region, and then adopted a generally defensive stance everywhere. A number of factors may have emphasized to Hadrian the need for such a course. In the East, the rebellions within Mesopotamia, the signs of Parthian revival, the difficulty of setting defensible boundaries, and the Jewish–Gentile struggle may all have indicated a need to draw back and consolidate much-contracted gains. Perhaps Hadrian saw that the costs of Trajan's campaigns had grown all out of proportion to any possible long-term benefits.

Hadrian's own rather uncertain position may have influenced him strongly: Trajan had acted as guardian to him; they were cousins and both of them came from Italica in Spain. Also, Trajan had favored Hadrian in several ways, using him as an important army commander in the Dacian wars and as governor of Syria, the logistical base for the Parthian war. But Trajan had never formally adopted him or otherwise specifically designated him as his successor until just before he died. There seems little reason to doubt the story told by Plotina, Trajan's wife, that the dying emperor did announce the adoption and intended succession. There was no other likely candidate; Hadrian was the nearest male relative of any importance; he had married Sabina, a grandniece of Trajan; probably Hadrian already had the emperor's signet ring, with all that that implies, before Trajan's illness. It is true that men told stories of attachment between Plotina and Hadrian; there seems to have been little love between Hadrian and his wife. The rumors caused mutterings and grumblings back in Rome.

The Senate had little to do with the choice of the new emperor. Some senators seem to have doubted Hadrian's legitimacy, either on the ground of improper dynastic succession or philosophical doubt that here was really another *optimus princeps*, the "best leader" for the post. A conspiracy led by some of Trajan's chief administrators and generals developed in 118 and was put down, with several executions, by Attianus, the praetorian prefect, a man also from Italica and earlier a second guardian for the young Hadrian. The executions of senators in the case, without the approval of the Senate, brought Hadrian much ill will. He disavowed any involvement in the executions, and replaced Attianus. Eventually the Senate accepted the new emperor and deified the dead one, but relationships between Hadrian and the Senate seem always to have been strained.

Static Frontiers

Hadrian abandoned most of Trajan's conquests in Mesopotamia, except for some territory in northern Mesopotamia, which would guard the flank of Armenia and provide some additional buffer area for Antioch, the important administrative and economic center in Syria. He set up additional forts to protect the north-south trade routes down to the Red Sea on the east side of the great rift that includes the Jordan valley; and he increased the legions in this sector of the empire to ten. He completed and strengthened the *limes*, a frontier collection of forts and walls, that linked the Rhine and Danube rivers across what is now mostly southern Germany. In Britain he built a wall twelve to twenty feet high, eight feet wide, and eighty miles long, across the entire island in the north. He improved the defenses of North Africa in various ways. Obviously, Hadrian had concluded that the days of expansion were over.

This peaceful policy, however, involved no weakening of the army. Hadrian reorganized the units, altered their tactical dispositions, and set up new training maneuvers, so useful that they were still in use at least a century later. He visited most of the units personally and shared their strenuous training. In several ways he improved the lot of the common soldier and saw to it that officers were not overly privileged. By now the legionaries were drawn mostly from the provinces; greater use was made of noncitizens in a larger number of auxiliary units. The legions now became more closely identified with a given area; replacements were usually enlisted locally; and legionaries could live a life somewhat like that of civilians. Ultimately this was to give the troops in an area a more homogeneous and localized character—perhaps a mistake. At any rate, Hadrian vigorously attempted to keep his army strong and battle-ready, something not easily done when decades went by without major combat. The troops worked regularly on building projects, roads, and combat exercises.

Hadrian and the Provinces

Hadrian traveled over all the vast extent of his empire more than any of his predecessors. He made two extended tours of four and five years besides other shorter journeys. These were not mere travels but inspection trips during which he visited the army posts and participated in training exercises. Every major city was the beneficiary of some public building or road or bridge or aqueduct, sometimes constructed in a sort of matching funds program, financed partly through local subscription.

For this emperor, the provinces were the Empire; the city of Rome was for him perhaps a bit more than a mere symbol, but his attitude was clear enough. Naturally the view did not endear him either to the Roman Senate or to the urban plebs: the latter actually had little reason to feel neglected, for Hadrian gave them the usual games and largesse, and engaged besides in huge construction projects in the capital. However, the real government traveled with the emperor, and nothing could more clearly indicate to the senators their subordinate role. Even when Hadrian was at Rome he was often out at his new villa near Tibur; this too was a center of government when he was there. Hadrian seemed to be able to get along quite well without the Senate—indeed, without the capital.

Centralization of Administration

Hadrian took a particular interest in improving the efficiency of government in all its phases; the result was a greater concentration of direction from the emperor and his staff. The emperor took care to consider the sensibilities of the aristocrats in the Senate in most things. Thus he carefully preserved the old treasury controlled by the Senate, the *aerarium Saturni*. But as much as any emperor before him he was responsible for accelerating the process by which the various *fisci* in the imperial provinces, the patrimonium, or personal holdings of the emperors, and the other imperial repositories of funds were gradually converted into a single treasury of overriding importance, the Fiscus. The old Treasury of Saturn had long been overshadowed by the various properties and sources of income controlled by the emperors. Hadrian appointed a special Advocate of the Treasury (*advocatus fisci*) to safeguard the legal interests of the Fiscus—possibly meaning all the imperially controlled repositories of funds—in court suits and the like. This action helped to bring about a single administration of imperial finances.

The civil bureaucracy was in general enlarged and rationalized. Fewer freedmen were employed in positions of responsibility, in accord with a trend going back to Vespasian; they were replaced by men of the equestrian class. The formalizing of ranks, salaries, titles, and the like also had its beginning with the Flavians and extensive development in Hadrian's reign. Careers now were organized according to specific patterns. One unfortunate addition deserves mention: Hadrian began to make use of a group of officials called *frumentarii*—whose primary duties had lain in procurement of supplies for the army, as the title implies—to collect confidential information on officials, provinces, and the like. This was the origin (though in some form it must have existed before) of the secret police of eventual infamy.

The imperial properties all over the empire got attention from Hadrian. Important even in the reign of the first emperor, the patrimony must have grown to immense size by the second century. Nero had confiscated a large number of properties; for example, six large landowners were said to have controlled half of the province of Africa, and Nero took all their holdings. Confiscation of private property, in fact, was one of the standard ways by which the more improvident emperors balanced a budget that was out of control. The income from these properties was a most important component of the imperial revenues. To insure their efficient management, Hadrian appointed a new imperial procurator to that specific task. From this time there was doubtless a strong tendency to regularize practices on the various estates. Some scholars see in the developments of this period, particularly in the system of treating tenants on imperial estates called *coloni*, the growth of a system that led to medieval serfdom.

Italy itself, as the abode of a population still consisting mostly of citizens from old Roman and Italian families (except for Rome and its environs, where much of the population was of foreign origin), had to a degree resisted the centralizing pressures of the emperors. Caesar and Augustus to some extent had rationalized the hodgepodge of municipalities, colonies, and allied states that made up the peninsula. Hadrian undertook to reorganize its legal structure. He divided Italy into four parts and placed officials over them for judicial administration. The officials were senators—consulars, in fact—but the measure somehow disturbed the Senate. Moreover, it infringed upon the autonomous character of some municipalities and offended them too.

In Rome itself Hadrian did not hesitate to lay hands on the legal machinery. Praetors had for centuries issued an annual edict that governed law and legal procedure. Hadrian in 131 employed expert jurists under Salvius Julianus to come up with a "perpetual" edict. Promulgated by himself and presumably changed only with imperial consent, it symbolized the imperial encroachment upon prerogatives and the decline of power of the old republican officials, and thus of the Senate itself. The actual change in the edict, which had been carried down from year to year in such a way that it was virtually perpetual in nature already, surely was unimportant. One other consequence of this reform was that praetorian prefects, as representatives of the emperor, began to do some of the work previously done by the praetors. Jurists gained new status (and new salaries) and sat regularly on the emperor's *consilium*. After this time praetorian prefects were often jurists. Some of the greatest of them held this position under the Severi.

Hadrian's Last Years

Hadrian's final years were unhappy ones. He felt increasingly the tension between himself and the Senate, deriving from his

The Roman Forum, view from the Palatine Hill. In foreground, columns of the temple to Castor and Pollux; on left, remains of Caesar's basilica; above left, the arch of Septimius Severus; above right, the curia or Senate-house. (*A. Devaney, Inc., New York*)

distant personality, his long absences, his greater—or more open —exercise of power. There was a conspiracy among some of his relatives, it seems. To make matters worse, in the East the Jews once more broke out in rebellion against Roman rule.

The conspiracy, in 136, involved two of Hadrian's relatives, a ninety-year-old brother-in-law and his eighteen-year-old grandson. We know little about it. It is likely that the older man attempted to get the grandson designated successor to the sick Hadrian and, failing that, tried more direct action. Hadrian forced the two to commit suicide and threw others—some of them senators—into prison and seems to have intended to execute them. The Senate was furious, feeling that Hadrian had broken the vow—usual since Nerva—not to put senators to death without trial of their peers.

The Jewish rebellion was partly Hadrian's fault and partly the operation of the same factors that had made Palestine the most difficult of Rome's provinces to govern from its acquisition. When the emperor was traveling in the East about 130 A.D. he decided to rebuild Jerusalem and plant a Roman colony there called Aelia Capitolina. The site of the ruined temple, he apparently decided, should be the location for a temple to Jupiter. The inevitable reaction, a rebellion, broke out in 132 under the leadership of a man calling himself Bar Kochba, Son of the Star. The slow but methodical repression decimated the Jews. Survivors were banished from Jerusalem and surrounding areas.

Hadrian's first choice as successor died before he did; he therefore chose another, known to us as Antoninus Pius; and he designated the young man called Marcus Aurelius as successor in the second generation. On his death, the Senate wanted to pass the *damnatio memoriae;* Antoninus dissuaded them and even got the usual decree deifying the dead emperor.

Antoninus Pius (138–161 A.D.)

Though born in Italy, Antoninus came from a family that had long resided in Nîmes, in southern France. Perhaps his ancestors were original members of the colony of veterans that Augustus had established there. Antoninus had risen to the consulate and had served as one of the four consulars in charge of the judicial districts that Hadrian set up in Italy. Antoninus got his surname, it seems, by his strong filial defense of the dead Hadrian and insistence on the latter's deification.

For information on the reign of Antoninus we are reduced to a very bad biography (in the *Historia Augusta*), scraps of literary information, as in the letters of Marcus Aurelius, evidence drawn from legal materials, and miscellaneous inscriptions, coins, and the like, plus, of course, some remains turned up by the archaeologists. (The literary evidence is almost as sparse for Trajan and Hadrian.) The most remarkable feature of the evidence for Antoninus is not its unfortunate paucity but its uniform tone of praise: almost nothing that could be called criticism or complaint survives. Even the Christians, who have some just complaint about others of the Good Emperors, find little bad to say about Antoninus.

The interest in judicial affairs evident in Antoninus' earlier career carried over into his reign. Our limited information tells us that he was concerned with the courts in the provinces; he emphasized that provincial governors must be accessible. Further, in the interests of foreign residents, he reorganized, at least in one province but probably more, the administration of the courts at the judicial levels below that directly supervised by the governors. In Italy he used important jurists, for example Salvius Julianus, in his council and he personally intervened in court cases that seemed to establish important precedents, always in a direction that moderns would find enlightened. One instance may be noted: the principle that in cases of doubt as to the status of a person, he should be considered free. To conciliate the Senate, Antoninus did change the judicial system in Italy set up by Hadrian; in the next reign it was restored.

Restraint characterized the man also. He showed this in his life style, in his methods of administration, and in his principles. Not only did he live economically, but he was also the sort of man who would labor along with a group of workers in the first of the vintage and then join with them in their simple meal. Young Marcus Aurelius, from whom we learn this bit of information, was much impressed with the modesty, restraint, and yet firmness in the right that Antoninus displayed.

The emperor found it unnecessary to engage in any serious warfare, though there were a few difficulties, as in Britain, where he attempted to push the frontier a bit to the north and then built a new wall, this one of turf, some thirty miles long, less than half the length of Hadrian's wall. Hadrian had traveled incessantly, benefiting the provincial towns where he traveled, perhaps, but also no doubt seriously burdening them with the expenses of entertaining him and his court. Hadrian had also offended the Senate by his peregrinations; they seemed to show a contempt for that body if not for the very city of Rome itself. Antoninus traveled little, to the gratification of the Roman grandees. His motives may have been partly to save on court expenses. Antoninus did not skimp on games and circuses for the Roman plebs; none of the emperors were likely to do that any more.

One thing Antoninus did for Italy was to remit the "crown gold," an accessions tax which had developed from an original practice of giving gifts of golden wreaths to the new emperors. Possibly he was able to reduce taxes somewhat even for the provinces. Those were fortunate days, with long periods of peace on the frontiers, under a sensible and frugal emperor. Antoninus could leave a well-filled treasury to his successors.

Marcus Aurelius (161–180 A.D.)

The well-known Stoic propensities of Marcus Aurelius illustrate how different was the position of intellectuals in the time of the Good Emperors. In the previous century, Nero, Vespasian, Domitian, all had executed some prominent philosophers and exiled others. Now came an age in which such men were not only officially tolerated but even encouraged. For Marcus, such philosophers were his mentors and heroes, and he exemplified their teachings in his own life. One of his teachers, Rusticus, was a descendant of the Stoic of that name done to death by Domitian. Marcus was greatly influenced also by Epictetus, the former slave and Stoic teacher whom Domitian exiled. Perhaps he learned of Epictetus only through his admirers, who wrote down the simple but powerful teachings of the freedman. As a quite young man Marcus studied with the Stoic Apollonius and learned from Sextus of Chaeronea, nephew of the great Plutarch. Marcus' own *Meditations*, written toward the end of his troubled reign, mark the emperor as a philosopher in his own right, though the work hardly qualifies as one of the more important Stoic documents of antiquity. Through the centuries the *Meditations* have been read by many for their moral and inspirational value. The work portrays a serious, contemplative, and hardworking man who saw himself as, above all, a public servant.

Associated with Marcus Aurelius as co-ruler was Lucius Verus, son of the man who was Hadrian's original choice as successor; he had requested Antoninus to adopt Lucius along with Marcus. Antoninus apparently intended to leave Marcus alone on the throne, but the latter insisted on equal power for Lucius. The sources indicate a strong contrast between the two co-rulers; Lucius seems to have loved luxury and the banquet hall more than duty. It was perhaps fortunate for the Empire that he died in 168.

Marcus Aurelius would have preferred a reign like Antoninus', wherein full attention could be given to internal matters. But possibly Antoninus had been too peaceful: all along the frontiers, tribes and peoples seem then as always to have awaited only signs of weakness before they burst across the borders in search of easy spoils or a permanent home within the Empire. (It should be noted that there was an almost continuous, peaceful, small-scale immigration.) Marcus was forced to fight a long war against the Parthians in the East (Lucius was the first commander in this war, though little inclined to active generalship), an even longer series of wars against a multitude of tribes along the Danube frontier, most important of which were the Quadi and Marcomanni, and other less serious wars in Spain and Egypt. Each conflict began with serious losses and ended with success, but only after hard fighting and heavy casualties.

The Parthian struggle was heralded when the Parthian king, in the manner of two of his predecessors, attempted to acquire full control over Armenia. A major mobilization, strong reinforcements, and actual invasion of Parthia finally forced a solution satisfactory to Rome. By that time serious irruptions along the Danube frontier required still more recruiting and reinforcement. Marcus commissioned at least two new legions and several auxiliary units. He ultimately determined to establish new provinces north of the Danube, with mountain ranges marking the new frontiers in place of the river. If he had lived to carry through his plan, the frontier would have been shortened considerably, and the history of the later Empire might have been different. But he could not complete his task and his son abandoned the effort.

Perhaps the plan was too grandiose for the resources, human and economic, of the Empire. The recruitment problem was even more troublesome than usual, for troops returning from the Parthian war had brought back some sort of plague. The unreliable literary sources unanimously proclaim this a devastating blow to the Roman world, indicating losses of as much as a third or one-half the population in some areas. Recent studies based on epigraphical army records do not seem to corroborate any such disaster. Yet it is probably wrong to discount too much the testimony of the ancient writers; doubtless they wrote in hyperbole, but the plague must have taken many lives in many places, a serious matter in an empire already underpopulated in some rural areas where lands were abandoned.

Of course the great military effort was expensive. Marcus Aurelius dramatized the degree of sacrifice called for; he displayed a large number of imperial treasures, from jewelry to gold-threaded dresses of his wife, Faustina, in the Forum of Trajan and then put them up for sale in a kind of auction.

Against all challenges Marcus struggled valiantly, despite some sort of physical affliction that affected his chest and stomach. He had trouble sleeping. From his personal physician, the famous Galen, he got a prescription, which seems to have been opium; predictably he became dependent upon it. There does not, however, seem to be any clear evidence that it seriously affected his ability to perform his tasks, before death, possibly from plague, overtook him in 184 A.D., on the Danube frontier.

Commodus and the End of the Principate (180–192 A.D.)

Commodus, son of Marcus Aurelius and emperor at age 18, has been termed Aurelius' greatest mistake or his greatest tragedy. Marcus probably expected his young son to mature into a more stable personality. Besides, he could only have excluded Commodus from the succession by killing him, and that is expecting a great deal of a father. Toward the end of his life, Marcus seems to have realized both that Commodus was inadequate to his task and that his own death was approaching, yet he did not attempt anything that might have preserved the traditions of the previous century. No doubt he expected that his advisors and administrators would help Commodus to govern effectively. He did ask Commodus not to give up the plan to enlarge the northern empire and improve the frontiers.

Despite his dying father's request, Commodus immediately negotiated a settlement of the northern war. And it may not have been a mistake: the effort was great for an empire reeling under blows from wars, plague, and the widespread drought and famine of these years, which we hear about so much. For some decades there was little trouble along the affected frontier. Marcus Aurelius' campaigns were not wholly wasted.

Our sources uniformly portray Commodus in a bad light. He was too much influenced by personal servants and favorites; he allowed his praetorian prefects who functioned as prime ministers to tyrannize over the Senate, Rome, and the Empire, while waxing rich; and he did not control the Praetorian Guard itself, which grew dissolute and insolent along with its commanders. When anything went wrong, however, and there was public outcry, it was Commodus' technique to sacrifice the prefect. He wanted nothing to disturb him in his own extravagant and depraved life. The young emperor was not given much of a chance to mature in his duties. In his third year he was nearly assassinated in a conspiracy that included Lucilla, his sister, and a number of senators, most of whom were executed in a style quite unlike the age of the Good Emperors. It is interesting that at this point two future emperors, both then serving in Syria, were relieved of their posts but not otherwise mistreated. These were Pertinax, the govenor, and Septimius Severus, a legionary commander. Both were given new positions after the fall of the prefect Perennis.

What Commodus did to the Senate—or allowed his prefects to do—was probably the worst feature of his reign. He permitted his personal servant Cleander to sell offices, even the consulate. In 190 there were twenty-five consuls. Thus the highest office held by senators was reduced to a mockery. However unbalanced the partnership, the Senate had previously served as a sort of constitutional check upon the power of the emperors—or *principes*. Commodus exposed the senators' utter powerlessness by administering as he pleased without reference to the Senate, and so vastly reduced the body's prestige and usefulness. The first of the Severi would be able to ignore it or manipulate it almost with impunity. Confiscated properties helped to finance Commodus' continued extravagances.

Another conspiracy succeeded, this one involving Marcia, Commodus' concubine (a Christian, it was said), and others. Commodus, who was big and strong, fancied himself Hercules; he had had himself sculptured in stone with appropriate garb, the lion-skin and club; and he had participated at public games as Hercules and in several other capacities. At last he planned to appear as consul on January 1 in the costume of a gladiator. But his wrestling partner, bribed by the conspirators, strangled him on new year's eve, 192 A.D.

The Severi: The Military Monarchy

The troubled situation on January 1, 193, threatened to dissolve into civil war, just as in the months following Nero's assassination in 68. The successor, Pertinax, chosen by the Senate, was much like Nero's successor, Galba, the right man at the wrong time. Pertinax, the son of a freedman, had forged an extraordinary career, rising to become consul. An able administrator and general, he was noted as a disciplinarian. Money was a problem for him as emperor. He did not give the praetorians all they expected—"only" 12,000 sesterces per man—and even worse tried to discipline them. After a few weeks they turned on him and killed him. Then they brought two would-be emperors at the same time to different gates of the camp, and got them bidding for the guards' support. The winner, Didius Julianus, bid 25,000 sesterces per man, several years' wages. The amount was not really so extravagant: Marcus Aurelius and L. Verus had paid 20,000 as a gift upon their accession—though that was disgraceful enough. But the virtual auction of the imperial office repulsed both the Senate and the Roman people. The city mob began to riot. Somehow a kind of appeal was made to the governor of Syria, Pescennius Niger, to come to Rome to straighten out matters and presumably to become the new emperor. Naturally the situation produced other claimants, supported by other armies. Besides Septimius Severus, governor of Upper Pannonia, the eventual winner, there was a third major candidate, Clodius Albinus, governor in Britain.

Septimius made some sort of deal with Albinus, recognizing him as "Caesar" and apparently adopting him. Then he moved on Rome with his army (of the major armies, his was nearest the city), posing as the avenger of Pertinax. The Praetorian Guard, which had already executed Julianus, surrendered and was completely discharged; the former guardsmen were forbidden to stay within a hundred miles of Rome. A new guard was formed from legionaries, and doubled in size. One of the regular legions was stationed in the Alban Hills just south of the city. Senate and people were generally complaisant, and Septimius was soon ready to move east to meet the most important threat to the new regime, that of Niger. With support from the other Danubian and the Rhine armies, Septimius confined some of Niger's forces in Europe within the fortress-city of Byzantium. The next year he defeated Niger himself decisively at Issus in north Syria, site of a battle five hundred years earlier between Alexander the Great and the Persians. He made a sweep across the Euphrates as a warning to the Parthians, and ended with a long siege of Byzantium. Meanwhile the Senate voted a triumphal arch for Septimius, which was eventually completed, and still stands in the Roman Forum.

By this time, to legitimize his rule Septimius had arranged for the dead Marcus Aurelius to "adopt" him, and he now styled his oldest son, Bassianus, Marcus Aurelius Antoninus. History knows him as Caracalla, from a Gallic cloak that he liked to wear. The pseudo-adoption perhaps implied that the new emperor would follow in the steps of the Good Emperors; preserving such a line would reassure many persons, including senators. However, Clodius Albinus saw a dynasty in the making that left him out. He crossed the Channel and mobilized all the troops he could command, in central Gaul. The eventual struggle was decided near Lugdunum (Lyons), where Septimius' victory meant that the Empire was his (February 197).

If Severus posed as the successor of the Antonine emperors he did not find it possible or profitable to act like them. For example, when he got back to Rome he executed a good number of senators who had perhaps favored Albinus. And he executed others on later occasions. Nor did the Senate any longer serve even as a symbolic focus of the governing aristocracy. The imperial family, with army backing, dominated the political scene as never before. Septimius broke with tradition by using equestrians who rose through the army for many high military and administrative positions previously reserved for senators of certain rank. Moreover, judicial powers of the Senate soon were largely transferred to the (now two) praetorian prefects. The results of these administrative changes were social as well as political. The core of upper-class society, no longer formed by the Senate, lay in the government and in the army. In this Septimius perhaps only recognized reality and refused to continue what the senatorial aristocracy had found a pleasant fiction. But the change made it clear that the era of the Principate, of any sort of partnership between ruler and Senate, had come to an end. Historians have termed this the beginning of the Military Monarchy.

The Severan Dynasty

From an early date Septimius made it clear that he would be succeeded by his sons. Caracalla was made consul at age 13; Geta, the second son, had to wait until he was 15. By then both were "Caesars," a term that had come to indicate an heir apparent. The certainty of his intentions perhaps served to keep down conspiracies; there was a problem, however, with the praetorian prefect Plautianus, who exercised tremendous power for several years and was often in conflict with Septimius' wife, Julia Domna. But eventually he went too far and was killed, perhaps by Caracalla's machinations. At Septimius' death in 211 while on campaign in Britain, there was nothing to prevent the peaceful succession of the two brothers. He is supposed to have advised the brothers to stick together, take care of the armies, and to worry about nothing else.

The first part of his admonition was a vain hope. Caracalla and Geta hated one another and the elder brother had perhaps attempted to kill Geta even before the death of their father. In fact, there were stories that he tried to hurry off Septimius himself. Their mother Julia tried to keep them reconciled but Caracalla soon killed Geta and ruled alone.

Caracalla has a bad reputation, somewhat like that of Nero or Domitian, and on the whole it is probably justified. Aside from his vagaries and occasional tyrannical behavior, he is remembered on the positive side chiefly for his tremendous baths, the vast ruins of which still impress the traveler to Rome, and for his action, probably in 212, which gave Roman citizenship to almost all free persons in the Empire who did not already have it. The sources are unkind enough to suggest that he took the latter step because he wanted a larger accession tax, which was paid only by citizens. But it could have simplified imperial administration, especially of legal matters. It certainly did not equalize the legal treatment accorded to all: that was apportioned with a bias that rested on social and economic status, all citizens being classified as *humiliores* or *honestiores,* approximately lower class and upper class. Not so very different from the administration of justice almost any time in history, but officially recognized then.

Caracalla went east toward the end of his five-year reign. He visited Egypt, was in some way incensed at a public demonstration by the Alexandrians—who had the reputation of being almost totally ungovernable—and killed many of them. He then prepared for a Parthian war, apparently seeing himself as a reborn Alexander. Caracalla had executed Plautianus' successor, Papinianus, one of the great classical jurists. His new prefect, learning that he also was to be liquidated, assassinated the young emperor in 217. This was Macrinus, the first equestrian to seize the throne. He did not show much aptitude for the position, but for a time there was no particular focus of opposition. Julia Domna's sister, Julia Maesa, eventually engineered an upset.

The Severan Women

The Julias had come from the city of Emesa in Syria, of a family of high priests to the god Elagabalus, the local Baal. Julia Domna enjoyed many years of influence during the reigns of her husband and sons, initially, perhaps, because Septimius was impressed with her horoscope, but later because of her abilities

On the left is Julia Domna, first of a series of powerful women in the Severan dynasty. Her husband, Septimius Severus, perhaps hoped she would be a restraining influence on his son, Caracalla, on the right. If so, it was a vain hope.

and the force of her personality. Unfortunately, soon after the overturn of Caracalla by Macrinus, she herself died, apparently of cancer. Her sister, Julia Maesa, had two grandsons by her daughters, Julia Soemias and Julia Mamaea; the older of these, son of Soemias, was Bassianus who, though in his early teens, held the hereditary high priesthood. It was decided to give him an aura of legitimacy by claiming his illegitimacy. Accentuating his resemblance to Caracalla, his mother Soemias said that he was really the son of the former emperor. The ruse worked, less perhaps because of any merit than because Macrinus was disliked and no other successor appeared in the vicinity of the army. Bassianus, whom we know as Elagabalus (the name of his god), was hailed as emperor by some troops and after a battle, Macrinus was killed. It was said that Julia Maesa herself rallied the soldiers at a critical moment and led the victorious charge. The Senate accepted the third emperor in a year, sight unseen.

Elagabalus turned out bizarre. He brought an image of the Emesan Baal, a sun god, to Rome with him and "married" the god to the moon gods of Carthage. Meanwhile, the Syrian priest displaced the pontifex maximus in rank. Elagabalus himself turned to debauchery. He was bisexual, with quirks that offended even the tolerant society of the times. He "married" males and females, including one of the Vestal virgins. His male sexual partners he installed in high office. He offended the all-important soldiery by appearing in public wearing rouge and various other sorts of female adornment. Julia Maesa was unable to control him at all and simply took the best way out: she prepared her other grandson to take over when, inevitably, Elagabalus was assassinated, along with his mother, in 222, after a rule of four years.

Severus Alexander, as the last member of the dynasty is known to history, was the son of Julia Mamaea. Since he was a mere stripling of thirteen or fourteen years at his accession, there would obviously have to be some sort of regency. This was accomplished through a kind of cabinet of the Senate, dominated by Julia Maesa until her death in 226, and then by Julia Mamaea. These remarkable women as nearly approached imperial office as any women in Roman history. And the administration began well; the great jurist Ulpian, for example, became the praetorian prefect. If the army could have been persuaded to put up with this arrangement for any extended period, the government might have functioned well. However, since the reign of Marcus Aurelius there had been a rather continuous series of wars. Probably these were easily within the capacity of the Empire to control, but they required strong military leadership. Julia Maesa could conceivably have played even the role of general, as she supposedly had in the charge against Macrinus near Antioch in 218. But she died early in the reign—and was consecrated a goddess. Alexander attempted to command the armies personally, but without great success. His mother helped as much as she could. They fought against Ardashir, the Persian founder of the new Sassanid dynasty which had replaced the Parthians in about 227, but with only partial success. Called back west to a new threat from across the Rhine, they and their advisors chose to negotiate rather than fight. Many of the army officers showed disgust with Alexander and with female influence over the army; Mamaea had presented herself not only as "Mother of Augustus" but also "Mother of the [army] camps and of the Senate," and finally "Mother of all human kind." The generals, then, in 235 engineered the assassination both of Alexander and the queen mother. Ulpian had been murdered earlier. Half a century of virtual chaos was to follow.

The Economy in the High Empire

Earlier in this chapter some of the disquieting indications of decline were considered; but the economy of the Empire in its greatest age deserves a longer treatment. Interpretation of the scattered evidence left to us is extraordinarily difficult. In the rare statistics available, as for example on income from land, we often can ascertain nothing of the land's quality, whether the figures given deal with gross or net profit, and so on. Yet certain trends seem to stand out rather clearly.

As might be expected, the political centralization of authority in the period brought a correspondingly greater control over economic matters. We have seen this tendency before, both in Trajan's financial "correctors," whom he sent in to stabilize certain provinces, and in the special authority of Pliny the Younger, as governor of Bithynia, to examine the financial affairs of cities and on that basis decree necessary improvements. Hadrian's *frumentarii*, the prototype of the secret police, as they traveled about the Empire, naturally sent back information on which central decisions were made affecting all. Imperial financial officials, the procurators in charge of the emperors' affairs in the provinces, tended to encroach on the powers both of the provincial governors and local officials (with some consequent friction), naturally contributing to the trend toward centralization.

By the middle of the second century, if not earlier, the central government began to take over the operation of state-owned mines in the provinces—in Noricum, for example—instead of auctioning off to the publican companies the privilege of working them for private profit, as in the past. By the time of Marcus

Aurelius the state also began to collect customs duties in the ports directly instead of through the publican companies. In each instance the motive was, of course, greater efficiency, with a more direct, larger profit for the state. Yet the publican companies, despite the bad reputation some of them earned and doubtless deserved (so well known from stories in the New Testament), in general had served the state well. One need not be a hidebound conservative to doubt that the government bureaus set up to take over the mines and the customs functioned more efficiently in the long haul. Initially there was probably a benefit to the central treasury.

In the cities the emperors—notably the Severi—exercised a greater control over small industry, as well as over the artisan class, by restricting the old corporations (*collegia*) of workers and in some places requiring the formation of new ones; this movement paralleled the reduced freedom of the *coloni* in the countryside, whose status was degenerating toward serfdom.

The more intense, state-controlled exploitation of the silver and gold mines not only reflects concern for the growing metal shortage in terms of an adequate money supply but also points to a clearly established inflationary trend, gradual during the period of the Good Emperors, but sharper after the death of M. Aurelius. Prices seem to have gone up on staple items at least 75 percent from about the middle of the first century to 235 A.D., at the end of the Severan dynasty. Wages, as usual in the ancient world, lagged a bit; even the soldiers, whose pay had been doubled by the time of Septimius Severus (as compared to the first century before Domitian) found their wages buying less during much of the second century. The occasional huge donatives (as at accessions) more than redressed the balance, however.

There was, at the same time, a gradual cheapening of the silver coinage, with some lightening of the gold as well. Nero, it will be recalled, initiated the process, adding lead to the nearly pure silver and reducing the weight both of gold and silver. From that point on, at periods difficult to determine, since there is some normal variation in weights and composition, silver coins were slowly debased further. As has been noted, by the end of the reign of M. Aurelius the standard silver denarius contained perhaps 60 percent as much silver as in the early empire; by the time of Alexander Severus the comparable figure is about 50 percent. The latter ruler also reduced, again, the weights of the gold coins. In the chaotic period following, the debasement was to accelerate wildly.

It is not proper to assume, however, as so often happens, that the debasement of the coinage exactly corresponds with a real cheapening of the currency. The problem is not that simple. The debased coins may have been actually almost as valuable as before. Part of the reason for the lessened quantity of silver in each coin, it seems certain, is that the production of silver declined, at least relative to needs, and the bullion became relatively more valuable in terms, for example, of the amount of basic foodstuffs it would buy. Gold declined in value as compared with silver. Perhaps the gold of Dacia may help to explain that. It would be more accurate to say that silver outstripped gold in the inflation race.

Large quantities of silver, as well as gold, were exported to purchase imported goods. Probably the largest quantities went to the East, especially India, as the price for such items as spices and silk cloth. Rome had few exports acceptable to the eastern traders—except precious metals—and there was, thus, a considerable imbalance of trade. It involved not only the East: much precious metal was also exported to Germany and other areas across the Danube, where it was hoarded as wealth rather than used as currency. So long as the Spanish, British, and other mines produced an adequate quantity of precious metals, this adverse balance of trade meant little. But when silver and gold came into shorter supply the effect was more serious. Moreover, the international traders would not accept the debased coins; they insisted on the older, pure silver ones—or upon bullion (which was weighed, as probably the silver coins also were)—and this no doubt meant that the imports, already expensive, became relatively more costly still. The shortage was compounded by the inevitable hoarding both of the better coins and of bullion; doubtless the use of precious metals for statues, jewelry, and other art objects contributed to the problem.

It appears, however, that the degree of debasement of the silver coins was greater than was called for by the rising market value of silver bullion. Thus the value of the actual silver in a coin of Alexander Severus was less than the value of the greater amount of silver of a coin of Augustus, even allowing for the increased value of the metal. This means that during the intervening period there had been a gradual, artificial expansion of the money supply, no doubt to meet the current, growing expenses of government and the defense of the frontiers. This trend led to a mistrust of the currency, a psychological attitude that caused some to refuse to accept it at face value, just as the international traders refused to accept it at all.

Inflation must always be paid for by somebody. In this case it would not be—for long—the army; the soldiers were too necessary. Nor would it be paid for by the government workers; they could protect themselves and gain a sympathetic ear from the administration. The economic victims were primarily the small farmers and tenant farmers. City laborers also were hurt. Prices for their labor and for manufactured products rose, but not in proportion to the rise in prices of the commodities they had to buy.

Even early in the second century, under Trajan and Hadrian, we hear of agricultural land going out of production. Possibly it was fringe land, and likely it was land that had declined in production through overcropping, especially of cereals. But it was a serious problem. In some places Hadrian offered the land free to anyone who would occupy it and bring it back into production, and granted remission from taxes for a period also. Yet the problem remained, and it must mean (1) that the prices of products that farmers had to buy inflated more rapidly than the prices of farm products; and (2) that these lands were so depleted as to make them unprofitable; or (3) that the exactions of the tax collectors or absentee landowners made farming impossible at times. Perhaps there was usually a combination of the three factors.

Imperial budgets during most of this age must have been manageable; but when, especially in times of war, they became intractable, excesses of expenditures over income were usually paid for through debasement of the currency. Confiscation of property of rich opponents was an occasional alternative in the later decades of this period. A major part of the reason for larger costs was increases in the size of the army, from the time of Marcus Aurelius on throughout the period. Another factor was the continuing growth of the imperial administration—the burgeoning bureaucracy. The latter problem looms as large in the twentieth century as it did in ancient Rome. It often seems necessary to create new departments of administration: it never seems possible to dissolve them.

Italy: State-Supported Welfare and the Economy

So long as Rome was the center of government, there was always an artificial stimulant to the Italian economy. Not only was a great deal of money put in circulation from salaries paid to government employees and to the guardsmen; many of the emperors also took a special interest in the well-being of the peninsula through special enactments. Trajan, for example, was responsible for passing a measure requiring candidates for high office to have a third of their wealth in Italian real estate. For a time at least, this meant that all property close to Rome increased in value. The Campagna, the country around the capital, had been in decline but now revived somewhat because of this measure. Wealthy Romans who owned estates in the resort areas about Naples and Puteoli, the port city to the west of Naples, spent large sums on elaborate villas and the like. This seems to have maintained the prosperity of that part of Italy despite the shift of a considerable segment of the import trade to the artificial ports built by Claudius and Trajan at Ostia.

The emperors of this period also favored Italy in the establishment and development of the *alimenta*. The Alimentary Institutions were first conceived and put into practice by private persons; Nerva and Trajan brought the government into the picture on a regular basis. We know of fifty such institutions in Italy and there must have been many more. They worked like this: the government furnished a capital sum, which was loaned, within the territory of the town concerned, to major property-holders. The interest on the loans was used to support, in perpetuity, needy children—sometimes specifically orphans. The capital sums loaned to the landowners may occasionally have been needed for improvements to the land, which increased productivity in some instances. However, it seems that in other instances the larger landowners (who got most of the money) were pressured into taking it. The loan remained as a permanent obligation on the property, reducing its value, naturally. In any case the system continued to expand within Italy and on a private basis in some of the provinces. Boys were ordinarily preferred in the *alimenta*, but girls were accepted also in some places. The original intention was probably to bolster future military manpower, but obviously the goals became broader in time. The chaotic period after the death of the last Severus destroyed many such auxiliary programs, but some lasted at least to the end of the third century. The widespread building programs (of Hadrian especially) throughout the Empire and the establishment of the *alimenta* in Italy perhaps served, somewhat like the so-called "pork barrel" legislation of the United States Congress, to spread out government expenditures more evenly, with attendant beneficial economic effects.

The general picture of the economy in Italy away from Rome is spotty. In the central and southern portions some of the ills which later plagued the economy had begun to be felt even earlier, as already noted. Deforested uplands were eroding; the erosion had begun to do secondary damage by choking up river mouths, producing swampy lands that harbored malaria-producing mosquitoes. Some of the land lost fertility through overcropping of cereals. There was never enough manure for fertilization and although crop rotation was understood, it was imperfectly practiced throughout the Roman history. There seems to have been a decline in the slave-operated large farms in favor of tenant farming; absentee landlordism with its evils continued as before.

The Po valley, with its enormously productive soil, continued prosperous. The close connection with several of the economically developing frontier provinces such as Noricum and Raetia immediately to the north and the Pannonian provinces to the northeast gave the area's producers and merchants opportunities which they were not slow to develop. The trade was two-way; but the army payrolls always made it possible for the frontier provinces to buy more than they sold.

Industry in the Po valley also continued to grow throughout the period. This was not the case in central Italy. In Etruria, Latium, and Campania, the metal goods, glassware, and ceramic manufacturers gradually lost out to new entrepreneurs in the western provinces. These imitated the Italian products—already mentioned, for instance, is the famous Arretine ware, a type of red pottery with relief decorations made at Arretium—and undersold their Italian competitors so drastically that Gallic pottery was exported even to Italy.

Though Italy was noted for its wine, here too competition grew apace. Italian olive oil to a considerable degree likewise gave way to imported products. The competition in these areas came especially from Spain, which must nearly have dominated the Roman market. The wine and oil came by ship—the only long distance means of transportation that was at all feasible—in cheap, mass-produced amphorae. The pots, not worth keeping, were thrown away, and broken sherds piled up near the docks area on the Tiber at Rome until they formed a hill (Monte Testaccio) that covers so many acres at Rome that it has never yet been adequately investigated archaeologically. Enough sherds have been surveyed to show that most of the amphorae arrived full from Spain and that the flood of such imports began early in the period we are considering.

The decline in Italian agriculture and industry, though it must have affected the economy of the peninsula even in the palmy days of the Good Emperors, was masked by the artificial stimulus of state income so long as Rome was the effective center of government. In the third century and after, however, the decline would be more marked.

Buildings and Construction in Rome and Italy

As we have seen, there were signs of economic deterioration in the Empire particularly affecting Italy in this period. One should not overemphasize the decline, however. True, Marcus Aurelius chose to auction some imperial treasures to finance the northern wars, and the fractional debasement of the coinage continued even under this careful emperor. However, the coinage was still generally sound and the debasement may have been largely owing to the decline in silver production and its consequently higher bullion value. Moreover, Marcus' auction perhaps was intended primarily as a gesture to emphasize the need for sacrifice. He later bought back all the items sold to purchasers who wanted their money back. And in spite of the costs of the wars, there is no indication that he left an empty treasury to his son. He found it possible to pay enormous bonuses to his troops and to stage lavish games for the Roman populace.

One of the indications that the Empire continued generally prosperous despite some economic weak spots is the tremendous amount of construction of all sorts which the emperors and private builders of the period managed to finance, especially in Rome and Italy.

Trajan's forum and the market complex or shopping center built in conjunction with it constituted one of the grandest building projects—perhaps the largest single one—ever carried through in the capital. The magnificently conceived forum contained an open area bordered by colonnades between great semicircular porticoes; a magnificent basilica used for the courts; a Greek library and a Latin one; a temple and of course the famous column with its spiral reliefs that picture the great general's Dacian campaigns. The top of the 127-foot column was in later antiquity supposed to mark the crest of the hill that had been removed to clear the site. This is now known to be wrong, but certainly it was a tremendous earth-moving project. Adjacent to the forum itself Trajan constructed a new shopping center, hundreds of shops on four levels; altogether, a monument worthy of Rome and of this great princeps. Credit also should go to the architect, the Greek Apollodorus of Damascus, who designed and supervised not only the forum but also most of the works of Trajan described below. The architect was haughtily disdainful of Hadrian's work later, and Hadrian first exiled and then executed him.

Trajan built the city's tenth aqueduct, to bring water to the Janiculum, across the Tiber. Some of its substructures underlie the present building of the American Academy in Rome, and its water still supplies a fountain built by Pope Paul V, in 1605, high on the brow of the hill overlooking the city, at night the most beautiful of the many fountains in modern Rome.

Outside Rome Trajan constructed extremely important works also. At Ostia, where the artificial harbor built by Claudius was proving inadequate, he spent a tremendous sum to excavate a new, hexagonal, inner harbor, connected to the Tiber by a canal. The dock facilities there, surrounded by covered colonnades, must have been as attractive as any ever built. Similarly, to the north of Rome along the coast, Trajan formed another artificial harbor at Centumcellae, modern Civitavecchia. A third such facility, this one portrayed in relief sculpture on the emperor's column, was constructed across the peninsula on the Adriatic, at Ancona. Like so many Roman building projects, these testify as much to Roman engineering ability as to architectural genius.

Hadrian's extensive building activity in and about Rome is well known: some of it is still eminently visible. The Pantheon, though originally built by Augustus' lieutenant Agrippa, was completely reconstructed after it was destroyed by lightning and fire in 110 A.D. and thus is really the work of Hadrian. The interior is an elevated hemisphere; the distance from wall to wall, about 144 feet, is about the same as the distance from the floor to the twenty-seven-foot aperture in the dome, which admits light. It is still one of the largest masonry domes in existence. Hadrian's mausoleum, called by the Italians the Castel Sant' Angelo, across the Tiber not far from the Vatican, still

The mausoleum of Hadrian (modern Castel Sant' Angelo) from a Tiber bridge. Originally the circular structure sat atop a cube. Part of the present building dates from the Middle Ages, when it was used as a fortress. (*Louis Goldman from Rapho–Guillumette*)

wears the military accretions of the wars of the middle ages. It was intended not alone as the tomb of Hadrian but for the imperial family for many years. The mausoleum Augustus had erected in the Campus Martius on the city side of the Tiber, also impressive, had filled up. A third great structure in Rome conceived and built by Hadrian was the temple of Venus and Roma. Placed between the Colosseum and the Forum on a platform large enough to contain three football fields abreast, it was a double-apsidal building of great size, in the Greek style though not in classic proportions.

Out toward Tibur and the Sabine hills Hadrian constructed a whole governmental center ("Hadrian's villa"), noted earlier in this chapter. This was a tremendous complex of buildings of all sorts, which took years to complete. So much constant building about Rome of course contributed materially to the economic well-being of the city. No wonder that huge brickyards grew up about the city. It is a curious fact that ownership of brick- and tile-making plants was considered quite respectable for Roman aristocrats, who in general felt that any occupation in business was demeaning. The reason apparently was that brick-making grew up in connection with farming; and as an essentially agricultural industry in its origins, it retained a kind of respectability that other manufacturing did not possess.

The other emperors continued to embellish the city with buildings. Marcus Aurelius put up a large temple in the Forum in honor of Antoninus and his wife Faustina; and his column with spiral reliefs like that of Trajan still stands in the Piazza Colonna, along the Via del Corso (ancient Via Lata). Septimius Severus, among other things, put up most of the complex of the imperial palace on the Palatine, the ruins of which loom over the Circus Maximus in the valley below. He also brought an aqueduct over to the Palatine; the earlier lead pipes evidently had been unable to take the pressure necessary to force the water up so high. And southeast from the Circus Maximus Caracalla built the massive baths that his father had planned, with their tremendous barrel vaults and cross-vaulting. Later, even in decline, Rome continued to amass structures. The most impressive of these doubtless were the baths of Diocletian and the great basilica in the Forum started by Maxentius and completed by Constantine.

Anyone today who visits the ruins of Rome, studies the plans of the public fora and buildings, and perhaps tries to imagine himself in perspective while gazing at a scale-model reconstruction, can catch a glimmer of the feeling that the old Romans must have had for their city and the empire it symbolized. The words most often used are magnificence, grandeur, permanence. No wonder the Romans called theirs the "Eternal City."

Building Construction in the Provinces in the High Empire

Though Rome and Italy were relatively favored in the building of cities and harbors, there was nonetheless a tremendous amount of such construction throughout the Empire during the high period, financed by emperors, local governments, or private persons. Roads, especially, important to the political, military, and even social welfare of the Empire, radiated outward in a total network of scores of thousands of miles. In Roman Britain, a province of only moderate size and importance, more than 5,000 miles of Roman roads have been identified.

These roads were built along natural routes, of course, and often over preexisting roads. But Roman engineers straightened many of the old routes and laid out numerous new ones. The roads naturally varied in the quality and permanence of construction. In most cases the Romans favored deep and careful preparation, both for retaining the roadbed and for drainage. The crowns were usually finished off with paving stones and curbed; along the route stood permanent milestones, which were important to systematic maintenance as well as informative to the traveler. In difficult mountain routes the Romans did not hesitate to drill tunnels through solid rock; in marshes they elevated roadbeds on causeways. The major routes were those arteries both militarily significant and critically important to the imperial post system. The official post maintained way stations for officials and imperial messengers, making possible rapid communications, all-important to such a huge and sprawling empire.

The high roads were usually 20 or 24 feet wide, narrowing in mountain areas. The narrower routes in the mountains reflect not merely the greater difficulty of construction but also the undoubted fact that most of the traffic over them involved asses or mules with back-packs rather the wheeled vehicles used in the lower elevations. Such mountain roads were often only eight feet wide.

The most extensive network of roads was in Europe. A single route about 1600 miles long connected the Danube and Rhine frontiers from the Black to the North seas. Another continuous road of about the same length stretched from Rome to Gades in southern Spain. A traveler could select from a considerable number of variant routes how he might go from the Bosporus to Gibraltar, the Pillars of Hercules in ancient terminology. A route of around 3000 miles stretched along the coast of North Africa; several branches useful both for trade and for the military extended south into the Sahara. Though improved, many miles of these roads were not paved. In Egypt east of the Nile a road—the name Via Hadriana indicates the prime mover —linked Berenice, a port on the Red Sea, with Alexandria. This was of course important in the eastern spice trade. The ancient coastal route still provided the main artery along the eastern Mediterranean coast, through Palestine, Phoenicia, and Syria. It was Trajan who began the interior road north from the Gulf of Aqaba that provided a more satisfactory alternate route for eastern trade in spices and other luxuries. From a sea terminus at Aqaba this road ran through the remarkable rock-cut city of Petra, on to Amman (Philadelphia in antiquity), then northwest to Damascus, or, on a more northerly course, to the great caravan city of Palmyra and then to the Euphrates river. Land routes to China and to the Persian Gulf fed into the trade centers along this road. Silk became a major import from China. The ancient routes on into Asia Minor through the Taurus mountains (there were alternate routes) were of course maintained and improved by the Romans—or on the Roman system, at least; local governments or private property owners were required to maintain some roads.

Hundreds of graceful bridges, causeways rising above marshes or atop retaining walls on steep slopes, and rock-cut tunnels along the mountainous routes marked the course of the roads system. The bridges, usually of solid rock, arched over the streams and chasms that obstructed convenient travel. Many of these bridges survive intact, and still more partially so, all over the Empire. The greatest number in one place is of course at Rome, where several arches of the eight ancient bridges survive, as the Milvian bridge to the north, arches on both sides of the Tiber island, and a span of the Pons Aemilius, which probably replaced the ancient, wooden Pons Sublicius, the oldest of the Tiber bridges. The most spectacular bridge anywhere was probably that described earlier, erected by Trajan, spanning the Danube just down from the Iron Gates in modern Romania. Only some of the piers survive. However, the same architect again, Apollodorus, built a similar bridge in Spain across the upper Tagus. Three arches still stand of the original eighteen; the bridge was some 1300 feet long. Another great bridge, across the Tagus at Alcántara, stands intact (though it was torn down and then rebuilt during the Spanish civil war in this century). The six soaring arches, ninety feet in diameter, stand 158 feet above the river. The total length of the bridge, however, is only

Model of the Roman bridge at Alcántara in Spain; it is intact and used still. (*Alinari–Scala*)

640 feet. In the East there are other notable bridges; in Syria, north of Antioch, fourteen arches (of twenty-four) still remain of the one that spanned the Adana. It was about 1000 feet long.

Sometimes the Romans combined bridges and aqueducts, as in the much-visited Pont du Gard north of Nîmes in southern France. The aqueduct, lifted on arches superimposed on a lower tier that supports the bridge, is no longer in use; the bridge still serves local traffic. A similar combination, equally graceful, spans a stream near Barcelona. Surviving arches of the aqueducts themselves are yet found in many of the provinces. Most notable is perhaps the Augustan one at Segovia in Spain carried on lofty tiers of granite arches, superimposed one above the other, across one of the main streets of the present city; it still carries water —through modern pipes—into the city. Other fine remains of aqueducts in Spain stand near Tarragona and at Merida.

The aqueduct that supplied the Roman city of Trier (Augusta Treverorum, French Trèves) was about fifty miles long, as was that at the colony founded by the Romans on the ancient site of Carthage. Roman officials, imperial and local, worked assiduously throughout the first two centuries A.D. to meet the needs of all the important cities of the Empire for communications, a water supply, and public buildings such as the arenas, theaters, temples, and basilicas, ruins of which are found by today's tourists scattered from Bath in England to Palmyra in Syria. North Africa—even in areas today desiccated—still shows impressive remains of structures of all sorts built during the Roman occupation, especially in the first and second centuries. Septimius Severus, a native of the city of Leptis Magna, built a whole new precinct there, including a forum and a basilica.

Herodes Atticus, Private Benefactor

A number of major public buildings of the period were put up with money raised partly or wholly from private sources. Rich citizens underwrote the costs of some quite munificent structures. Perhaps the best known benefactor of the sort in this age was Herodes Atticus, the rich Athenian Sophist. Atticus possessed a vast family fortune acquired mostly by his grandfather Hipparchus, it seems. This worthy seems to have made his money in various ways, including industry, trade, and land. Somehow he came under the condemnation of the emperor Domitian, who executed him and confiscated his lands. Still, it seems, a considerable amount was left—or perhaps Nerva may have restored the lost property. Hipparchus' son, the father of our subject, also called Herodes Atticus and also a Sophist, entered the Senate (under Nerva?)—as a good many Greek and other provincials did in the early Empire—and was given praetorian status, then made legate of Judaea; this was followed by the consulship, possibly in 104. The younger Atticus, born about the turn of the century, lived until 177 or 178; he was a friend of Hadrian and was one of the teachers of both Lucius Verus and Marcus Aurelius.

Atticus erected several public structures in his home city, Athens, more or less carrying on where Hadrian had left off. Best known of these is the Odeion, a magnificent concert hall, the remains of which may still be seen near the Acropolis. Buildings financed by him in several other cities are known, among them an aqueduct with nymphaeum at Olympia and a reconstruction of the stadium at Delphi. The tradition, illustrated in the life of Herodes Atticus, of financing some public service or building—along with imperial confiscations, especially of Gaius, Nero, and Domitian in this period—somewhat ameliorated the bad consequences of a system wherein otherwise the rich might have become ever richer at the expense of the poor.

Almost all the emperors from Augustus through Severus Alexander, as we have seen, built something of note in each of the provinces: if not a triumphal arch or bridge or aqueduct, then at least a series of milestones, testifying to the continual building and rebuilding over long centuries. These enduring monuments, even in ruins after the neglect of nearly two millennia, still evoke, in those who contemplate them, feelings of respect and admiration, or perhaps a kind of nostalgic sadness for what might have been.

One theme of the historian M. I. Rostovtzeff in his great work *The Social and Economic History of the Roman Empire* (though stated only at the very end in what one feels are rhetorical questions) is that higher civilization can be disseminated widely to the common people only at the expense of its unhappy dilution and decay. Almost no one in modern America wants to accept such a thesis, but there is something to be said for it. It does seem true that in the high period of the Roman Empire, at a time when the upper-level system of education was reaching its peak, with well-paid professors and polished lectures; when more Romans than ever before were highly educated, cultured persons; when the city of Rome was the most cosmopolitan and sophisticated city in the world—the greatest age of Roman culture, as of Latin literature, was already past; that is, it was in decline.

Perhaps the loss of political freedom for the governing, educated classes (this is the real distinction between the Republic and the Empire, stated baldly) brought with it a concomitant loss not only of intellectual freedom, but also of intellectual vitality. The best literature produced in the High Empire was that which somehow permitted writers to protest against the times; in a work of history, it might take the form of a comparison of some great emperor such as Trajan with a predecessor such as Domitian. Dissidence was more easily expressed through satire. What this literary decline seems to suggest is that even though stability and general prosperity made possible a broader education and a more numerous intellectual elite, there was something culturally stultifying about the Roman Empire at its height.

It is not easy for scholars to say exactly what caused the stagnation of culture in the second century (much less to reach a consensus in the matter.) The increasingly monolithic form of government, with its dependent social structures, must surely have

THE HIGH EMPIRE: CULTURAL VICISSITUDES

12

played a role. Direct repression or censorship from on high was, to be sure, not frequent; however, all of government and society was subject to a great deal of informal pressure toward conformity. An upper-class person who had any hope of a career or even of continued high social status could hardly afford to offend the powers above by patronizing some free-spirited author. The prevailing rhetoric, characterized by eloquence rather than substance as a means of persuasion, was most suited to the times. It was far better, at parties or salons, to laugh at satire directed at misfits or women or pompous men of little influence than to abet biting political satire like that of Lucilius two centuries earlier. Yet this may be only a small part of the explanation. Wellsprings of culture at times in history have seemed to run dry for no discernible reasons; originality fades, to be replaced by mediocre work whose chief characteristic may be only that it is different in some superficial way. Perhaps the brightest minds gave their attention to something other than literature. Problems of decline and fall are nearly always so complicated as to defy simple explanation.

Education: From the Days of the Republic

During the Republic, Roman parents themselves undertook a major portion of their children's education. Even when, by the second century B.C., well-to-do Romans often acquired tutors and pedagogues for their children in imitation of Greek practices, they did not deliver their progeny completely into the care of such educated slaves or hired teachers. The elder Cato had insisted on teaching his son personally; however, in spite of his low opinion of Greeks as a group he had his son taught by Greek tutors and even sent him, with many warnings, to Athens for further instruction. Conservative as he was, Cato would not subject his son to corporal punishment. We have seen that in the second quarter of the second century B.C. Terence could present a play (*The Brothers*) at Rome, the thesis of which was that a permissive education and upbringing might well turn out a better human being than the old rigorous and suppressive discipline. Though Romans made greater use of tutors and teachers of various sorts as time went on, it remained true throughout history that Roman parents—both of them—ordinarily assumed personal responsibility for the education of their offspring.

A second noteworthy feature of Roman education in the Republic—but with less and less importance in the Empire—was the extent to which sons of important Romans learned in the Forum from their fathers as well as from eminent orators, jurists, and administrators there, or in the army from the generals. This was more than the mere habit of adolescent Roman boys' observing closely everything that went on in the Senate, the assemblies and other gatherings of the people, the law courts, or military campaigns. A promising boy would be formally accepted as a sort of high-level apprentice (*tirocinium fori* or *militiae*), as Mucius Scaevola accepted and instructed young Cicero—doubtless along with others. A strongly pragmatic element in the education of Roman boys of high family thus continued, even after greater emphasis was placed on rhetoric in higher education toward the end of the Republic, and on into the Empire, when a career might depend more on the favor of the princeps than on attracting public attention through some sort of public service.

These basic elements in the education of a Roman are seen also in the lower social classes. The poorest Roman children were taught by their parents, as best they could, to read, write, and figure. The boys would most likely learn the occupation of the father in much the same way that a son of Cato might emulate his father's political methods and speaking style. We must assume a considerable degree of near illiteracy at these levels; yet the graffiti of Pompeii in the first century A.D. are often addressed to mule drivers or potters or to other groups not likely to have had the advantage of formal education. Most persons must have been able to read, write, and figure at an elementary level.

The Roman system of education followed the Greek, but only in part. For example, Romans chose not to adopt a system of state-supported elementary education (though some municipalities seem to have done so). For a society not very democratic and dominated by a typically aristocratic outlook, the goals of education were mainly to develop obedience, character (virtue), and the means—and desire—for useful public service. To the oligarch, service to the state and to the *nobilitas* were equivalent. Where better could these ideals be learned than in the home and in the Forum? Thus the schools quite deliberately were relegated to a secondary position in the educational system, and there they stayed, even though they did grow in relative importance as time went on.

The schools (*ludi*), then, were private, and they varied enormously in quality and cost. At the lowest levels, some schools, perhaps in charge of slaves who hoped to make enough to purchase their own freedom, might be so inexpensive that even sons (rarely daughters) of laborers might attend for a time. The better schools—which also might be taught by slaves or freedmen—cost much more. Affluent families were more likely than poor ones to send their daughters to be educated along with their sons. Such parents would of course have a *paedagogus*—a sort of general guardian—to look after their children and to cooperate in their education; and some of them would engage tutors. In some cases tutored children would not go to these *ludi* at all; more often, it seems, the upper classes preferred a combination of tutoring and elementary schooling for their children.

By the first century B.C. the upper-class youngsters of ability customarily went on to higher level education. They might take instruction in music or mathematics or other subjects; but most boys studied language, literature, and oratory under a *grammaticus* and later a *rhetor*. Under each master they would also get some history, philosophy, and science. The early linguistics teachers and the rhetoricians were Greek, and they naturally tended to use the same sort of curriculum and methods that characterized Greek education.

Many Romans stubbornly resisted the new teaching. The Greek rhetoricians especially seemed to conservative Romans to emphasize form without content or character—a speaking style designed to persuade through polished rhythms and stylized techniques more than through solid content: a far cry from old Cato's methods. He had said that good oratory was "a good man speaking" and he emphasized the acquisition of a mass of factual knowledge; the words would come, he said. The censors of 92 B.C.—not unenlightened men: one was L. Licinius Crassus, a leading orator and statesman—issued an edict against the Latin *rhetores*, who were imitating the Greeks, saying that young men were wasting their time with them, that what they taught was contrary to the *mos maiorum*. Possibly they took a less harsh view of the Greek *rhetores*; it was important for Romans to achieve facility in reading and speaking the Greek language. But when the Latin rhetors tried to prepare Roman young men for a career in the Forum by applying Greek techniques, the whole thing seemed subversive to them. There is no evidence that this censorial edict was enforced for long, if at all. Latin rhetoric, pretty much in the Greek style, continued to evolve as an essential part of higher education.

The Roman teachers did, however, emphasize pragmatic, substantive matters in their upper-level educational system. In the late Republic there was no greater influence than Cicero; and he argued strongly for content. The study of oratory he felt should include not only the typical foundation in language and literature; it should also require training in history, law, philosophy, and the sciences. And he stressed the traditional, direct learning from Roman statesmen in the Forum.

Education in the Period of the Empire

Lower-class education was probably not much affected by the transition into empire. Since the city of Rome was a world capital into which flowed enormous sums of money for one reason or another, the consequent general prosperity may have made it possible for a larger number of children of this lower stratum to get an education. Scattered references to children of the middle group in society indicate that the sons and daughters knew, certainly, how to read and calculate—some could rise to affluence as Petronius' Trimalchio did—but they seem to have learned little of the gentler arts. Their training fitted them for the marketplace, rather than the Forum. This level of education, designed for boys who would be merchants, traders, small manufacturers, and the like, is becoming better known. There exist—mostly unpublished and untranslated—handbooks that must have been used in such schools, designed to teach how to write letters, for example, or to calculate at a practical level. Some of the early Christian letters follow the pattern of the handbooks, and imply this sort of middle-class educational background for the writers—though not, of course, acquired at Rome.

Upper-class education at Rome did undergo change. Along with a greater sophistication in the social sphere and a more complex system of social and political relations went an emphasis in education on polish and elegance—as on what would later be referred to as the liberal arts. A proponent of the concept of liberal education in the twentieth century will find it hard to criticize the trend; surely any life is enriched by an introduction to arts and letters. But in the Roman Empire these changes seem, somehow, to reflect the decline of the old order. What critical need now for the old system, with upper-class sons the formal pupils of statesmen and jurists, poring over the course of Roman history, the development of the constitution, the law? Great decisions were now made in the emperor's *consilium* or in the even narrower confines of the emperor's own chambers, where only a few trusted advisors were brought into the ultimate decision-making process—or in some obscure office, by anonymous bureaucrats. Important speeches might still be made in the Senate relating to trials or even conspiracies, but they could only seem trifling as compared to the great orations out of the past still preserved and read. Rhetoric designed to produce the polished gentleman became thus more important, the most pragmatic elements of earlier education less important. Education might now turn out a sophisticate whose wit and learning would make him a welcome member of any social group. Incidentally it might, yet, help him toward a career in public affairs.

The change must not be overstated. Scions of members of the expanded aristocracy of the Empire still observed in the Forum, made notes, discussed them, as the great historian Tacitus informs us in his *Dialogue on Oratory*. The most important of the Latin rhetoricians now brought Latin authors into their courses of training; and any study of Vergil necessarily brought with it exposure to the older ideals. Moreover, some rhetors still followed Cicero, as we may see in the work of Quintilian, a Roman of Spanish background, the most important teacher at Rome in the first century A.D. And much depended on the students themselves. Probably the most serious of them were the sons of former Italian families or of old but undistinguished Roman stock. Opportunities opened to such families in the new order, and fathers, ambitious for their sons, doubtless pressed hard for a proper education for them.

One of the latter, from a previously obscure family, became emperor in the person of Vespasian. He had himself been given a good education by his parents; certainly he had studied Latin and Greek literature, though he seems not to have been much exposed to philosophy—or at least he had little taste for it. Under Vespasian more than ever before careers were opened to men of ability; a proper education got them off to an early start and presumably sharpened the qualities that brought them to the attention of the emperor. Vespasian also first began the practice, extended under his successors, of paying state salaries in what we may term chaired professorships of both Latin and Greek literature. Quintilian, appropriately, was the first to receive such an appointment, at the excellent salary of a hundred thousand sesterces per year.

It is notable that, just as the emperors in the second century came mostly from families that had settled in the western provinces, so several of the rhetoricians and literary lights of the Early Empire came from those areas. Among those from Spain besides Quintilian are the elder Seneca, rhetorician and historian, his son, the minister of Nero and a Stoic philosopher, and his grandson by the latter's brother, Lucan the poet, all of Corduba, and the poet Martial. From the elder Seneca and later sources we learn that educational trends in the provinces followed those at Rome. Rhetors there, as at Rome, emphasized the practice of declamation upon invented, sometimes fanciful topics (*controversiae*). Probably the schools in the Gauls and Spain were good enough; but it was the practice for those who could afford it and who were ambitious for their sons, to send them to Rome for a year or two of finishing there.

During the second century Hadrian and other emperors increased the subsidy for professorships, and some were established even outside Rome, as at Athens. Possibly local funds in some sort of matching arrangement helped pay salaries in such cities. Hadrian also arranged retirement benefits for teachers, and he built an athenaeum at Rome for the rhetoricians. Antoninus Pius upgraded the status of rhetors, grammarians, philosophers, and physicians by granting them immunity from certain taxes. The rules applied all over the Empire, but there were limits on the number of persons in a given city who could receive such benefits.

M. Cornelius Fronto, whom we have seen as the teacher of Marcus Aurelius, may illustrate for us the continuing trend. He was born in Numidia, and combined his teaching with a political career; he rose even to the consulate. He must have been a sound scholar to have retained the respect and affection of his star pupil; yet Marcus Aurelius turned away from his field for philosophy. And it is apparent from their correspondence that Fronto, like the rest, chose to emphasize language and style much more than content. Neither Cicero nor Quintilian would have approved.

Upper-level education in the High Empire, then, put much stress on rhetoric and declamation. The older teaching of subject matter doubtless continued, however, and ambitious young men yet learned in the Forum or on military campaign. If the case of young Marcus Aurelius is not atypical, the total educational experience of promising young men must have included a sampling at least of more than one school. Perhaps one might study rhetoric and practice declamation, then later attend lectures in philosophy under some (most likely Greek) master. Then one might also attend one of the law schools. These latter were now more formally organized. Gaius in the second century and Paulus in the early third both wrote *Institutes* or textbooks designed for formal teaching of law, and all the great jurists taught, whatever else they did. Other instruction was available in architecture and engineering, as in music, mathematics, and language. It was possible, in second-century Rome, to get a broader education under more competent masters than ever before (except perhaps in oratory); and yet, as noted above, somehow there had been a qualitative decline. Perhaps higher education had become more an end in itself than a preparation for life: the most highly educated persons were qualified more for professorships than for anything else.

It seems worthwhile to mention that the most highly educated Christian apologists of the period received their training in the usual system. It is true that the earliest of the Christian writings owe little to the Greco-Roman educational curriculum. Paul the apostle, however, had an interesting variety of training, a combination that included upper-level Greek and Jewish education and also, doubtless at an earlier age, work in the middle-level, practical educational system mentioned earlier. More typical of the well-educated Christian publicists were Apollos (mentioned in the New Testament), the hellenized Jewish Christian of Alexandria, the same cosmopolitan city that produced the Jewish scholar Philo, and the later second- and third-century Christian writer-scholars Clement and Origen.

In the west, the best example of an educated Christian writer in the High Empire is Tertullian. Born and educated in Carthage in the broad manner in law, philosophy, and rhetoric, once converted he turned his training to the production of high-flown and occasionally turgid apologetic works in which he attacked pagan culture rather effectively. Later Christian writers in the West, through Jerome, Constantine, and beyond, all owed something to the educational structure painstakingly put together by Greek and Roman mentors over a period of centuries and essentially preserved through the third-century barbarian invasions, civil wars, plague, and financial collapse.

In the chaotic third century some imperial edicts are known the purpose of which was to safeguard the rights of teachers; but probably they testify only to the crumbling of the special benefits that had come to the profession during the High Empire. After the restoration of order by Diocletian, the emperors continued their interest in educational affairs; apparently it became usual for them to make the appointments to the chaired professorships all over the Empire, as Constantius Chlorus is known to have done at Autun. Julian, in the middle of the fourth century, attempted through strict controls to exclude Christians from important teaching posts, holding that they could not possibly have a sympathetic understanding of the literature they thought pagan. We happen to know that Theodosius, later in the century, set up a sort of university at Constantinople, with a staff of thirty-one. Justinian, in the sixth century, in an excess of Christian zeal closed down all the famous old schools at Athens, including those of Plato and Aristotle—the Academy and the Lyceum.

Later Silver Age Authors

We have noted above that, as the Empire reached and passed its peak, the quality of Latin literature declined—even under such a ruler as Hadrian. The degree to which this state of affairs was caused by the political system is quite uncertain. Even a radically different political form might have meant little to literature.

On the one hand there was in this age a practical aspect of Latin literature, as one would expect, and surely this was little affected by the constitution or by the current ruler, whether princeps or tyrant. Thus Columella, the Roman of Spanish birth who continued the tradition of agricultural writing during Nero's reign, surely was safe from the sort of stricture which that jealous emperor visited upon Lucan. One of the twelve books of the *De Re Rustica* was in verse—not good enough to excite jealousy; it was mainly an agricultural handbook: there was a rural calendar, with sections on trees, vines, beekeeping, and the like. Similarly the *Natural History* which the elder Pliny dedicated to Titus in 77 and to which we have earlier referred, was not likely to give offense to any emperor at all. Not that Pliny's compendium was totally practical—for example, he gives the color of the eyes of five emperors—but the emphasis was on facts of nature and Pliny's various excursuses deal with uncontroversial matters. So also Frontinus, writing mostly in Domitian's reign after a military career that saw him governor of Britain under Vespasian, was unlikely to give offense even to the imperious Domitian. He wrote a book on land surveyors (we have only excerpts), another on military affairs (lost but used by Vegetius, a writer probably of the late fourth century), and another military work, the *Strategematica*. Under Trajan, he served as director of the waterworks. The Latin, *curator aquarum*, makes the job seem much more important, as indeed it was; the title was first held by the eminent Marcus Agrippa under Augustus; besides the city distribution system there were scores of miles of aqueducts outside the city to be seen to. Based on this experience, he wrote *De Aquis Urbis Romae*, which is a major source of information still.

Another category of literature was totally safe because it was so purely literary that it had little to do with the real world. Seneca's tragedies might be mentioned here—unless, contrary to most scholarly views, the *Octavia*, dealing with the daughter of Claudius who was Nero's unfortunate wife, was indeed one of Seneca's plays. His tragedies are based on common stories out of Greek myth or legend. They seem designed for reading at Nero's salons rather than for performance; and mostly they seem dull except to historians of literature or linguists. In the history of literature they are quite important, owing to their great influence on later writers, as the great masters of Elizabethan England, centuries later.

Nero's repressive measures following the conspiracy of Piso, which brought death to Lucan, Seneca, and Petronius, doubtless suggested caution. Writers in the years immediately following, and especially those publishing in the reign of Domitian, often seem quite inconsequential. The poetry of Valerius Flaccus in his epic, the *Argonautica*, written under Domitian, is perhaps some of the best of the age; but Jason and the golden fleece were romantically long ago and far away. Statius' poetry of the same period is by and large not bad even if much influenced by rhetorical style; it is highly polished and sometimes quite pleasing. The epics, the *Thebaid* and the *Achilleid* deal mostly with the world of heroes and gods in the manner of Valerius Flaccus; other poems—especially the major extant work, the *Silvae*—sometimes actually treat of real-life events, and are thus of some value to the social historian. A notable aspect of Statius' work is the flattery of Domitian. Flattery had long been a part of Roman literature from Cicero's speeches (if not earlier) on; but one feels a kind of unlovely insincerity here: Statius alludes to planned works on Domitian which one feels he never really intended to write.

It might be expected that the work of Silius Italicus, the *Punica*—an epic treatment of the history of the second Punic war—would perhaps deal with somewhat more sensitive matter. It, too, was written under Domitian. It follows Livy closely, but with inoffensive rhetorical embroidery. The longest surviving Latin poem, it is often tedious, with its long speeches in the style of the time. It would not have survived, of course, without some merit. Interestingly, the work begins with Hannibal's oath, and the Carthaginian emerges as more of a hero than Scipio.

Martial and the Social Set

The social and economic historians find a mine of information in the *Epigrams* of the poet Marcus Valerius Martialis. A native of Bilbilis in Spain, he came to Rome in the reign of Nero and spent about the last thirty-five years of the first century there. He was received into a group that included several participants in the conspiracy of Piso, and perhaps was saved from involvement only by his relatively recent arrival. He turned to poetry, mostly epigrams, but some longer poems also, and became quite popular. His often salacious and obscene quips, masterfully crafted so that the whole point often is delivered with sudden impact in the very last word, did not require any intellectual effort on the part of the reader. He was not rich, and had to get along any way he could at Rome—which was not bad as compared to most Romans, but miserable as compared to the upper class with whom he hobnobbed. Around the turn of the century, thanks to the generosity of the younger Pliny and some Spanish patron, he was able to return to Spain and a comfortable retirement.

Martial bemoaned the lack of a latter-day Maecenas who

might adequately subsidize him; some of his patrons did send substantial annual gifts—an important facet of Roman social life. Still, he lived from hand to mouth and at times had to scrounge dinner invitations or hint for a new toga. He found it necessary to play the role then expected of clients: he came at dawn, sometimes cold and shivering, to his patron's house, and rather ungratefully received the small cash payment (*sportula*) that had become customary. This was a sum, perhaps a *denarius* or five *sestertii*, a sort of largesse of the rich to their less important clients, that helped to keep bread, cheese, and cheap wine on the table. Falernian wine, for such a client, was beyond reach— except when on some special occasion a dinner invitation was also forthcoming.

The *sportulae*, both cash payments and special feasts, became an important feature of upper-class society not only in Rome but also in the major provincial cities. Rich leaders occasionally gave *sportulae* to all the citizens of a town, the amounts varying according to status—decurions, for example, receiving three or four times as much as common citizens. The emperor Claudius referred to games he gave to the populace as *sportulae*, and indeed the games and circuses were, in effect, the benefice of a sort of superpatron to a huge mass of clients.

Martial could hope to make some money from the sale of his books. However, there were no copyrights, and he wrote that some of his works had even been read at a salon or dinner party by a host who himself claimed authorship. The poet's complaints about his low income as compared to others reminds one of plaints of intellectuals of our own time: a cobbler who pleased his customers and so got included in some of their wills had ended in a more comfortable situation than he; and the winner of a race in the circus got more in one day than he might receive in a year.

Martial's satirical and sarcastic epigrams could have the kind of punch that he sought only in treatment of themes that lend themselves well to such style. This means that he reflects not the usual, but the unusual, or even the bizarre. Many of his poems deal with sex—every imaginable variety, very explicitly set down, sometimes naming names—and he leaves the impression that heterosexual monogamy had almost disappeared from the lives of the social set at Rome. Fortunately, we have the works of the younger Pliny and others to partially offset this undoubted exaggeration. Still, an indelible impression of moral decadence emerges from Martial's lines.

Martial wrote quite a lot about food. Obviously dining sumptuously had become one of the chief ends of life. The poet gives whole menus; from such works modern scholars have compiled Roman cookbooks, and some of the dishes appeal to modern tastes. Sow's udder, cooked rare with the milk, however, one of the gourmet entrées for fancy dinners at Rome, seems not to have caught on with twentieth-century palates. One whole book of Martial's epigrams consists of couplets on specific food items, from beans to truffles.

Martial flattered Domitian shamelessly. The lines may reflect a genuine attitude; that emperor gave way to the cruel streak in his character only at the end of his life, after conspirators tried to kill him. The poet later hailed Nerva and Trajan, but spoke of the end of Domitian's reign only as a hard and difficult time. Certainly Martial bears witness to Domitian's popularity at one point in midreign (probably) when the emperor gave some games and received a prolonged ovation.

One can almost see some of the Romans whom Martial portrays—the pretty fellow, depilated and smelling of balsam, who was an idle sophisticate and gossip, or the magister of the elementary school, bawling at his poor pupils even before dawn, waking the sleepy poet nearby. The baths, great social centers, come alive too, not in the technical details of operation, but through the characters with their intrigues and idiosyncrasies.

It is not easy to determine the poet's attitude toward women nor to be confident that his verses seriously reflect his or anyone else's views. The incidental remarks may demonstrate real views more than the specifically directed verses. For example, when Martial writes that he likes best the woman who is a prostitute, always willing, and cheap besides, he is probably only trying for laughs. He seems generally to accept women as social equals; wives, however, he implies should accept a secondary sex role, not complaining about concubines or youthful man-slaves. To be sure Martial would, with typical jest, grant wives equal opportunity to cheat on their husbands. One rather enigmatic epigram on the subject may be worth quoting:

Let the matron be subject to her husband, Priscus;
In no other way do woman and man become equal.[1]

Tacitus, Pliny, and Career Upper-Class Politicians

Tacitus and Pliny the Younger not only present to us in their writings much of what we know of the nature, feelings, and aspirations of upper-class Romans of the age; they are also themselves specimens—perhaps not altogether typical—of their

---

[1] Martial *Epigrams* VIII, 12; translation of Walter C. A. Ker, Loeb Classical Library edition (Cambridge, Mass., 1968).

class. Both came of old Roman stock, though not of the older aristocracy, from families that had migrated to north Italy (or, in the case of Tacitus, perhaps Narbonensian Gaul); both probably got their early education in their home cities but came to Rome for finishing, Pliny under the famous Quintilian, Tacitus under Marcus Aper and Julius Secundus. They were of similar age: Pliny was born in 61 or 62 and Tacitus about five years earlier. Each developed a considerable ability at oratory to advance his career. Tacitus first held important office under Vespasian, Pliny a bit later; and both managed to advance their careers under Domitian, whom they came to hate. The consulate came to each at the end of the century. They were friends; some of Pliny's letters are addressed to Tacitus. Their writings, however, are vastly different. Tacitus is remembered primarily as a historian, though he wrote other works, as for example, *Dialogus de Oratoribus*, a sort of chronicle of the decline of oratory that must have been used by the rhetors in their schools despite its pessimistic tone. Pliny is noted for his *Letters,* carefully composed in polished, literary style, and for his *Panegyric* of Trajan.

Without specifically criticizing the principate, Tacitus in his *Dialogus* deplored the petty themes of the speeches of his own day, in contrast with the great orations on public policy or war or important legislation of the late Republic. This sort of ambivalence about the Empire saturates Tacitus' other works as well—chief of which (in order of composition) are his *Histories* and *Annals*, which, in inverse order, covered the period from the death of Augustus to the death of Domitian. Tacitus thought it possible, even with the loss of independence under the Empire, for men of his class to act with courage, determination, and moral integrity. His model was his own much-admired father-in-law, Julius Agricola, memorialized in a biography that elaborates the theme. Tacitus' other major work, the *Germania*, an important source of information on the Germans, holds up the primitive virtues of these half-civilized tribesmen as an example to his own decadent age.

Moralizing on sex, the historian contrasted the behavior of Romans of his age to that of the Germans:

Their life is one of close modesty, with no seductions of arena-spectacles, no provocations at dinner feasts to corrupt them. They know nothing of secret billets-doux between men or women. . . . No one there laughs at vice, nor dismisses it . . . as the spirit of the times.[2]

[2] Tacitus *Germania*, 19; translation of W. Peterson, Loeb Classical Library edition (New York, 1914).

Tacitus admired any people who would fight for their freedom; with overtones for his own age, he wrote,

The German fighting for liberty has been a keener enemy than absolutism of Arsaces [the Parthian king.][3]

Tacitus looked with jaundiced eye at what the Empire had developed into after Augustus, and displayed not only bitterness but unreasonable bias against Tiberius and his successors, reaching a kind of crescendo with the "monster" Domitian. None of the imperial butts of his sharp phrases were as bad as he said; and it is inexcusable that the historian pretended even to understand what Tiberius thought, without any evidence whatsoever. However, Tacitus' virtues as a historian were many: he used his sources well and was accurate in his presentation of facts; his psychological insights impress one; and his compressed style often produced epigrammatical sentences that compare favorably with those of Martial. One of the more famous such remarks is this summary characterization of Galba: "All would have agreed that he was capable of ruling—if he had never ruled." [4]

Some of the thinking of Tacitus—and of others of his class —seems clearly reflected in a speech that the historian put into the mouth of Galba, on the occasion when that emperor adopted a man expected to be his successor (see *Histories* I, 16). The speech acknowledged that the Empire could never return to a republican form: the need remained for a *rector* or *princeps*. But the principate had been handled as if it were a "sort of heritage" (*quasi hereditas*). Now, however, emperors begin to be selected, and that is a sort of "substitute for freedom" (*loco libertatis*); the new system is expected to turn up the "best" persons for the job. Written in the reign of Trajan, this passage and others show that Tacitus agreed with Pliny, who, as we have seen, termed the new ruler *optimus princeps*. In the same book (I, 1) the historian spoke of that "rare and happy time when you can feel what you wish and say what you feel."

Tacitus thus shared some of the views of the philosophers who had opposed Vespasian and Domitian because the hereditary principle had resulted in the formation of a new dynasty. But the martyred Helvidius Priscus, though admired by the historian, was not his ideal. He favored men who spoke out, who acted, not those who opposed in passive silence. And despite his longing for the old freedom, in essence forever lost, he approved the Empire and shared Vergil's conviction that Rome had a

[3] Ibid., 37.
[4] Tacitus *Histories* I, 49.

destiny to rule men well. Further conquests he doubtless approved as a fruit of the old military virtues. Freedom could not really be reconciled with empire; all Tacitus and the others could hope for was a succession of good emperors who would respect the independence of the ruling class. Had the historian lived to be a centenarian, he would not have been displeased.

While Tacitus, in semiretirement, was writing his *Histories* and later the *Annals*, Pliny continued on his political career. He served as prefect of two of the imperial treasuries and sat on the Emperor's *consilium*. Then, as an imperial legate, he set out to govern the province of Bithynia, about 110 A.D., and died there in service a couple of years later. From the tenth and last book of his letters we learn much of the imperial governance of provinces, of the uses of the imperial post, of the financial disorder and bad planning in the province. And, incidentally, we learn of the large number of Christians in the area and how they were treated. The earlier books of his letters tell us of social life to some degree, and of the various problems, requests for letters of recommendation and the like that a man in his position faced. Pliny talks much of his land holdings and income—or lack of it, for in the manner of some of the well-to-do he continually deplores the low return from his farms. He also set up in his home town, Comum, one of the alimentary institutions discussed in Chapter 11. Altogether, the reader gets a very favorable impression of Pliny and his class—and he surely planned it that way. The letters avoid the seamy side of life; they give quite a different impression than the works of Martial—or of Juvenal, to whom we now turn.

Juvenal: Satirist as Social Critic

Decimus Junius Juvenalis, born in the latter years of Nero's reign at Aquinam, was a friend of Martial and must have been influenced by him. Like Martial, he lived hand-to-mouth as client of important Romans. Juvenal's sixteen *Satires* were published in the reigns of Trajan and Hadrian, after Martial had returned to Spain. Rhetorical, moralistic, and pessimistic, the *Satires* present a somewhat sordid picture of an upper class in decline, and like Martial's epigrams, on occasion describe the vices of upper-class Romans in such detail that they must at times have been read more out of morbid interest in the prurient content than for any moral benefit.

One of the most quoted sections of *Satire* 10 comments sadly on the state of the *populus* in Juvenal's day:

*What of the mob of Remus? . . . the people who once bestowed
everything—imperium, the fasces, the legions—now anxiously
content themselves with just two things—bread and circuses.*[5]

In the poet's view, the one thing that ruined the Roman people
was luxury.

*We endure the evils of long peace: luxury, more savage than
war, has laid its hand on us, the revenge of a vanquished world.*[6]

The overwhelming influx of foreigners, attracted by the new
wealth, had flooded the city with corruption; Greeks attracted
especially caustic criticism. They were all comic actors, Juvenal
said, splitting their sides at your jokes, given to totally insincere,
outrageous flattery.

Everywhere Juvenal saw decadence. He excoriated the glut-
tons who squandered whole fortunes on delicate viands, the
aesthetes who must have the most diaphanous silks for their
tender skins, the husbands and wives who cheated on each other
(Juvenal seems not to have known many stable marriages), the
male prostitutes and male marriages, poisonings, murders, informing. The satirist held a somewhat Stoic conviction that
crime takes its own toll, inflicting punishment through a psychic
guilt that cannot be evaded.

Some of Juvenal's blackest pessimism he reserved for
women, whose depravity he depicted in *Satire 6*. Chastity
among women did once exist, he said—in the days of cavemen!
Will Hibernia be satisfied with one man? No more than she
would be with one eye. Censennia brought her husband a large
dowry: it is her license to carry on as she wishes before her
spouse's face (if he divorced her he would have to return the
dowry). If one finds a wife of good family, she taunts her poor
husband interminably with her hauteur. While the mother-in-
law lives a husband can expect no peace; she will aid and abet
her daughter's extramarital amours. The satirist somberly reported on savage women who took out their frustrations on their
slaves, and portrayed one cruel wife who had some minor mis-
creant beaten half to death while she made up her face. One
curl out of place could bring a flogging. Rich women, Juvenal
said, would not endure having children: they could afford the
fees and the strong drugs of the abortionist.

The poet told of a burlesque of the mysteries of the Bona
Dea (Good Goddess) at which the women burned with passion,
and another at which some females ended by urinating upon the
statue of Chastity! It is at this point that Juvenal made his

[5] Juvenal *Satire* 10, 72ff.
[6] Ibid., 6, 293–294.

A noble matron of the
Flavian period.
(E. Richter–Roma)

famous remark on the suggestion of some that wives be kept at
home with doors locked. "Who will keep watch over the guards?"
he asked.[7]

The satirist also condemned the feminist types who "boldly
go about the whole city, interfering in men's affairs, talking with
the generals," anxious to be the first to learn any news from
China or Parthia; and, incidentally, gossiping about the smallest
domestic matters. The woman who dominated an intellectual
conversation at dinner Juvenal could not stand. A little jealousy,
perhaps?

The satire is brought to a climax with the story of one
Pontia, who poisoned her two children and when confronted,
admitted the crime, saying she would have done the same if
there had been seven of them. Only once did Juvenal sound a
really sympathetic note for women: in *Satire* 2 he put into the
mouth of the prostitute Laronia an amusing speech in which she
defended herself against the twits of her male competitors.

Obviously Juvenal is not to be taken at face value. Moreover, at times, as when he tells of the activities of some women

[7] Ibid., 345ff.

and of foreigners, it may be that the poet unintentionally be-speaks a climate of relative social freedom that by twentieth-century standards can only be adjudged good. It is fortunate that we have Statius and Pliny to reflect for us a healthier society than that portrayed by Martial and Juvenal. But it is impossible to read the satirists of this age without retaining an impression that prosperity, power, and a centralized government, often domi-nated by persons who set sad examples—the Gaiuses and Neros and Messalinas and Agrippinas—had indeed profoundly affected for the worse Romans of all stations, but particularly the upper classes.

Suetonius: Reflecting a New Age

Though born only a few years after the younger Pliny, who was his friend, Gaius Tranquillus Suetonius, the Latin biographer, seems to reflect a new age. For him and his generation the ex-cesses and the tendencies toward tyranny of some of the Julio-Claudian and the Flavian emperors were curious and fading history, not a bitter and personally resented immediate past. Suetonius' *Lives of the Twelve Caesars*—Julius Caesar through Domitian—came out about 120 A.D., though of course the work had been in preparation for several years. Less mordant than Tacitus, but also less penetrating, Suetonius is entertaining, objective, less judgmental as he discusses in rather stereotyped form the early lives, influences, and omens or prophecies for each of the early emperors, and then recounts the major events in the lives of his subjects. His critical acumen suffers by com-parison with Tacitus', but the biographer does supply frequent quotations from the basic sources—for example, letters of Au-gustus to Livia asking what they are to do about poor, handi-capped young Claudius—that make it possible for modern historians to do something more than criticize an interpretation based on facts unknown to us, as one must often do when using Tacitus.

The younger Pliny took a friendly interest in Suetonius, and obtained for him one of his early appointments. Suetonius held three secretaryships under Hadrian, including the important *ab epistulis*, in charge of correspondence, and must have had access to the official archives. Even after he was fired for some breach of manners toward the Empress Sabina, Suetonius may still have been able to use the imperial files. Hadrian was not really fond of Sabina—he much preferred his young friend Antinoüs until the youth's untimely death—and surely he was more concerned with proper form than anything else: it seems unlikely that he took any further action against his cabinet officer. This doubtless explains why the biographer was able to use such documents as Augustus' letters.

The new generation, impressed with the superiority of the more recent emperors, was ready to believe the worst about the rulers past. The stories that Suetonius tossed in liberally, almost casually, of the errant sexual excesses of these emperors must have derived from confidential memoirs, perhaps set down years after the facts, rather than on any official records. Though human behavior in this area in our jaded age tends to make it easy to believe rather sordid tales, it is yet difficult to accept Suetonius' picture of Tiberius' alleged lewd and disgusting behavior during the years of retirement in old age on the island of Capri or of Agrippina allegedly seducing her own son, Nero. Yet Suetonius mostly wrote as a man who did much research in good sources. His works have a mixed effect: on the one hand the emperors are humanized, shown to be individuals who struggled with difficult tasks; on the other, many of the twelve seem bizarre and the Empire lucky to have survived.

According to Pliny, Suetonius was slow to publish. Yet he wrote a number of works, and must have lived to the reign of Antonius Pius. Besides the biographies of the Caesars we have only some sketches remaining from his *Lives of Illustrious Men;* the subjects are grammarians, rhetoricians, and poets, among whom are Terence, Vergil, and Horace. Suetonius himself was something of a grammaticus, as we can tell from the titles of some of his lost books; and he wrote in Greek as well as his native Latin. The lost books would have added much to our scanty information of the middle-second century, especially those on Roman manners and customs, and on the festivals.

With Suetonius' death comes the end of the Silver Age of Latin literature; there follows a decline both in quantity and quality of literary output. Yet Suetonius was much imitated in following years, by other biographers like Marius Maximus, whose works have mostly disappeared. Still later, the author (or authors) of the *Scriptores Historiae Augustae,* biographer(s) of several emperors beginning with Hadrian, followed a similar format. Christian writers also used Suetonius as a model; so too did Einhard in writing the life of Charlemagne in the ninth century; and Suetonius' influence continued, like that of Cicero, Seneca, and others, into the Renaissance and the Modern Age.

Apuleius

Another Latin writer of the later second century is Apuleius, who was born in Africa and received his early education in Carthage. He studied also in Athens and Rome, and had some pretensions as a philosopher and rhetorician. The most important of Apuleius' works is a sort of novel, the *Metamorphoses*, commonly called *The Golden Ass*. It is the story of a young man who dabbled in black magic with the help of his girl friend and accidentally turned himself into an ass. He could be changed back only by eating fresh roses—but didn't manage to get any before the season was past. He therefore remained an ass for about a year, which was chock-full of amusing and sometimes unbelievable adventures. He was beaten, petted, feasted, and starved, before the goddess Isis brought about his restoration.

The social historian—and the religious scholar—can find much in Apuleius of interest. He describes everyday scenes from the lives of the rich and the poor: for the palates of the rich, imported fish dishes garnished with fine sauce, marinated beef, or peppered fowl, with fine wines; for the poor, barley fried with cheese or only a crust of bread. The rich sleep on beds with down bolsters and coverlets of linen dyed with Tyrian purple or cloth of gold; one poor man sleeps on straw under a rough

Old market woman. (*The Metropolitan Museum of Art, Rogers Fund, 1909*)

lean-to, even in winter. The rich wear fine linens or diaphanous silks; the poor, cast-off, torn, and patched coarse mantles. The stories themselves are of course fantasy, but the settings often have the impress of reality: townspeople, aroused by the arrival of a large company of travelers in the middle of the night, assuming they are a company of thieves and setting dogs on them; slaves mistreated at a sweatshop bakery; local officials giving traditional and expected largesse to the citizenry.

Apuleius describes several of the gods in the form and costume in which they were conceived and popularly portrayed. The reader can almost be a spectator at a couple of religious processions, so well are they pictured in words. With some scorn the writer tells of one band of "priests" of the Dea Syria, little better than beggars, who went about bearing the image of the deity, beating drums, clanging cymbals, playing flutes, wearing painted faces and elaborate vestments, pounding on doors, demanding gifts. On the other hand, Apuleius presents the goddess Isis (with her consort Osiris) as omniscient and benevolent, a sort of composite of all the major female goddesses; some of the well-known male divinities, as Mithra, for example, are only her lieutenants. The emphasis on a female deity hardly implies any generally enlightened attitude toward sex, however. Apuleius mostly presents women in traditional roles, and regularly refers to them as the "weaker" sex.

Several writers of the first and second centuries compiled interesting and occasionally significant stories or anecdotes, probably intended as source books for orators and rhetors. One such, in the second century, was Aulus Gellius, whose work, in Latin, is mostly extant, and called *Attic Nights* because it was composed in Attica. Amusing as the work is, it nevertheless symbolizes the decline of Latin literature. It is a haphazard, motley collection, even though it is put together with pleasant style.

Greek Authors of the High Empire

Greeks who wrote about Rome—at least those whose writings have survived—tended to be rather enthusiastic about the dynamic, brash state that had risen to conquer the world, perhaps in natural response to the Roman tendency to admire all things Greek. Even in the second century B.C. Polybius had been impressed with the Roman state—its constitution, that is—and he wrote about it at some length. In the latter first century B.C. Dionysius of Halicarnassus, who lived and wrote at Rome after about 30 B.C., was similarly admiring of the Romans. His *Roman Antiquities*, written mostly to explain Roman history to a Greek audience, parallels Livy, yet diverges at times and provides a useful supplement. Diodorus of Sicily lived and wrote about the same time. His *World History* emphasizes the eastern civilization much more than that of the newcomer, Rome, and displays less regard for that state, which had subjected Sicily to so much bad government during his century.

The major Greek writers of the High Empire mostly felt themselves a part of the universal state that was Rome, as indeed they were, not only intellectually but, for many of them, politically as well. It is therefore artificial convention to treat of the Greek writers as if they were in a totally different category from their Latin colleagues. They did indeed have a somewhat different background, but in manner of education, training, and outlook they belonged to the same cosmopolitan group.

Surely the most popular biographer who ever lived was the Greek, Plutarch, who lived from the middle of the first century into the middle years of Hadrian's principate. His *Lives*, mostly presented in pairs, a Greek and a Roman with similar careers, has been influential down to modern times. Shakespeare, for example, used North's translation of Plutarch as the basis for his plays on classical themes, and the moving spirits both of the French and American revolutions were obviously familiar with his work. Napoleon's early orientation toward the East seems to reflect his fascination with Plutarch's life of Alexander the Great. In his own time, Plutarch's other works—the extant ones are grouped together in a collection usually called the *Moralia*—may have been more popular than the *Lives*. The parallelism in the biographies symbolizes the cultural and intellectual partnership of Greece and Rome.

Though Plutarch spent most of his life near his home in Chaeronea, he did travel to Rome, where he lectured and studied. He made close friends among Romans in high places and may have been given an official post in his home province, Achaea. The works give the impression of a very civilized person. His biographies show that he was more interested in people than in politics; in consequence, modern historians often bemoan the lack of detail on political history or chronology. But Plutarch remains a mine of information on people, religion, philosophy, and other social and cultural topics.

Greek writers important in the High Empire include three historians who might be described as Greco-Roman. Appian of Alexandria moved to Rome and wrote Roman history organized by foreign wars, except for the most important *Civil Wars*, dealing with the internal history of Rome from the Gracchi to 36 B.C. The chief remaining work of Arrian of Bithynia is the best account of Alexander the Great (second is Plutarch's life) remaining to us from antiquity. And Dio Cassius, also of Bithynia, who became a senator late in the second century and under the Severi in the next century was twice consul, wrote a history of Rome from its beginnings to his own time. Dio's narrative is rhetorical in style and as history is inferior to Livy—and Appian. The extant portions nevertheless provide us with important information at critical points where otherwise there would be gaps in our knowledge.

A compiler, like Gellius, who wrote in Greek was the Hellenized Egyptian Athenaeus; his work, the *Deipnosophists*, contains the sort of anecdote or story, amusingly composed, that might have been the subject of conversation at banquets or symposia. It is important for its wealth of quotations from earlier authors, mostly of comic playwrights and poets, but also from historians and others. Athenaeus published his work about the turn of the third century. Another second-century writer (in Greek, though his native tongue was probably Aramaic) deserving of brief notice is Lucian of Samosata. A sort of latter-day Sophist, his satires, mostly in the form of dialogues, have been so much admired in our own age that some of them have been included in Great Books courses.

This survey is by no means a complete list, even of authors of the High Empire whose major works are mostly extant. A great many technical writers flourished, authors who specialized, as for example, Galen, a second-century native of Asia Minor, who wrote philosophical and, most importantly, medical works in Greek. Galen studied in Smyrna, Corinth, and Alexandria, both philosophy and medicine. He was a physician for gladiators in Pergamum. About 162 he went to Rome and by a consular was introduced into Roman society. On the outbreak of plague, he returned to Pergamum, but came back to Rome in 169, and later became court physician to Marcus Aurelius. He engaged in scientific research, particularly in anatomy; he dissected apes, apparently, and added much to human knowledge of the circulatory system.

Great jurists—a few of whom will be discussed under the heading of law—were busy writing digests and histories in the period. And Christians wrote works some of which deserve the name of literature; Tertullian's works are rhetorical, and in some ways typical, products of the age. But these, too, are reserved for discussion elsewhere.

Religion in the High Empire

In the second century B.C. Polybius had said that Romans were the most religious of all peoples; and Romans themselves felt that this religiosity had contributed much to their political success. In the Empire, the emphasis continued; some of the oldest, most primitive deities were remembered dimly; others were worshiped with archaic ceremonies of almost forgotten meaning. The state gods, neglected during the civil wars of the late Republic, again received official attention, and a variety of new gods, brought in mostly from the Hellenistic East, replaced the earlier ones no longer worshiped. An observer, seeing the multiplicity of temples, shrines, festivals, priestly colleges, liturgies, sacrifices, and private devotions, would have thought that Romans were as religious as of old.

Historians familiar with the tendency of imperial states of the earlier Near East to promote the worship of their major gods in step with their political expansion might have expected the Romans to require their chief deity, Jupiter Optimus Maximus of the Capitol, to be worshiped with Roman rites all over the world. Arnold Toynbee noted as characteristic of universal states that they produce a universal religion. Yet even after attaining unchallenged power in the Mediterranean, the Romans were slow enough about this, despite the seriousness with which they took their religion. Probably the reasons for this failure are the same as the reasons why Latin literature did not immediately sweep through the cultures of the eastern Mediterranean: those cultures were older and more developed. Moreover, the process of religious syncretism characteristic of the Hellenistic world had already produced composite deities; the Roman gods simply fit in with the system there developed. Jupiter thus was also Zeus, was also the Egyptian Ammon, and so on. The peculiarly Roman features of Jupiter's worship could have no great impact on the world.

Ultimately the Romans did advance one cult, which took on some of the characteristics of a universal religion and became a political tool in the interest of stability—a symbol of loyalty to the state and its rulers. This was, of course, the imperial cult, the worship of the emperor-as-god. The concept of the hero-become-god had roots that went back at least to the legendary Sumerian king Gilgamesh in the third millennium B.C. From Alexander the Great onward, deification had become usual in the Hellenistic world. Great men among both Romans and Greeks often traced their ancestry back to deity. It was, thus, not so remarkable a matter that Julius Caesar, who claimed as his ancestors Aeneas, son of Aphrodite, and Romulus, son of Mars, should have been exalted by his followers, doubtless with his approval, as in some sense divine.

Augustus, as we have seen, made much of his "divine" father-by-adoption, Caesar, and he permitted some temples and shrines to be constructed both in the eastern and the western provinces where subjects venerated Augustus also, along with Roma. Augustus was officially deified at his death; this became the standard practice; there were only occasional exceptions, as when Caligula and Domitian in the first century and Commodus in the second demanded recognition as deity in their lifetimes. The provincial councils, made up of upper-class men, gave much attention to the imperial cult; so also did the Augustales, priestly colleges of freedmen; other priestly colleges included rites to the emperors in their regular observances; and the army made much of it, as in oaths and observance of birth dates. The imperial cult thus touched the lives of many persons in all the social strata. As in the case of other state cults, the proper observance of its ceremonies became a symbol of patriotism, as well as of piety.

From earliest times Romans embraced—eagerly, at times— foreign gods and rites; and during the Republic, their religion changed under the impulse of Etruscan and Greek influence. In the late Republic and early Empire, as we have seen, a host of new gods and goddesses associated with eastern mystery religions came into the city. These new deities came in mostly with immigrants, and probably did not find many devotees among native Romans and Italians at first, as the archaeological remains seem to indicate. In an early period foreigners, especially of Greek origin, tended to settle in social enclaves on the Aventine Hill. Indeed this location may have had some sort of official sanction. Later, in the early Empire, the Janiculum received social colonies of immigrants of all sorts; on the slopes of that hill and in the Trastevere nearby remains are found of temples to their gods. Inscriptional remains indicate that the foreigners sometimes organized themselves in clubs. Among the various groups on the Janiculum, the Jews seem to have been quite numerous; two synagogues at least have been found there.

The new mystery gods included Isis, the Egyptian goddess who was especially looked to by women in connection with childbirth, and her consort, Osiris; the Dea Syria; Cybele (brought in at the end of the Second Punic War), and her male consort, Attis; and Mithra, of Persian origin. Mithra penetrated the Mediterranean world through Asia Minor; particularly important in the army, the god was venerated along the frontiers at the major army posts. In general these deities were served with initiation ceremonies and rites involving mysteries known only to the initiates, usually with some sort of purification process and bringing a hope of life beyond the grave. Each, it seems, developed a code of ethics. Devotees were caught up in a relationship with the deity much more personal than in the older

Roman religion except, perhaps, for the family and household gods. In any case, since these religions were not monotheistic it was easy to hold on to the old and add the new.

Christians: Aliens in the Empire

Christianity was obviously the most important Hellenistic import into Rome, where it flourished despite sporadic repression, finally to become the official state religion—the universal religion of Toynbee's thesis—displacing all the rest.

The roots of the Christian religion lie in Judaism, where it was born; its immediate antecedents are to be sought in those sects of the Pharisees and Essenes which produced the Dead Sea scrolls. John the Baptist, Jesus himself, his apostles and other disciples, all their earliest converts, were Jews or Jewish prose-lytes, and they thought they were somehow fulfilling the Hebrew law, not breaking away from it. But the new teaching caught on best with the Hellenized Jews and proselytes outside of Palestine, so that it was perhaps inevitable that the emphasis soon should be on converting gentiles.

The Christians wanted, for a time, to be considered Jews: the Jewish religion was *licita* (officially recognized), with certain distinct privileges—as, for example, exemption from army ser-vice. But after the Jewish revolts in 66–70 A.D. and in the reigns of Trajan and Hadrian, Christians preferred to emphasize their distinction; the gulf between the two groups by then was virtu-ally unbridgeable, anyhow. Christian leaders had already decided years before, in a conference at Jerusalem, that converted gentiles would not, in effect, have to become Jews in order to be Chris-tian. There was peril, however, for members of an unapproved (*illicita*) religion; as we have seen, possibly by the time of Nero, certainly by the time of Domitian, it had become fixed Roman policy that to be guilty only of the name Christian—that is, having committed no crime other than to join the sect—was to incur the death penalty. Pliny's letters to Trajan from Bithynia, where there were many Christians, and Trajan's reply show that this was long established policy, though Trajan wanted no wide-spread campaign to enforce it.

Yet Christianity spread. Strongest for a century or so in Asia Minor and Greece, it also took hold in Rome itself and in the western provinces. In some ways the other Hellenistic reli-gions had helped to pave the way. The similarity made Christian-ity acceptable. Many found it in several ways superior. Central in it was Jesus, a historic, not a mythical figure, who was enor-mously appealing. His teachings as presented in the books soon known as the Gospels (Greek, *Evangelia*) attracted many. Complete well before the end of the first century, these were in tone and content elevated—though written in the language of the people and in a style the rhetors could sneer at.

Even Stoicism may be said to have prepared many for acceptance of Christianity. The new religion contained much of the best in Stoicism but without its sternness and with the added message of love and forgiveness. The Christians sometimes made specific appeals to Stoics; this can be seen as early as the speech of the Apostle Paul to the Athenians (*Acts* 17). An early intellectual apologist for Christianity, Justin (c. 100–167), himself originally a student of several philosophical schools, made such appeals through comparison with Stoic doctrine and an attempted harmonizing of views; he did the same for Platonism. He moved to Rome and taught there, but was denounced to the authorities by a jealous philosopher-rival and tried before the urban prefect Q. Junius Rusticus, ironically a Stoic himself, and a teacher of the reigning Emperor, Marcus Aurelius. Rusticus recognized in Justin a broadly educated person and urged him to reject his Christianity. Justin refused. Imperial policy had not changed; to be a Christian—and to refuse to recant—was worthy of death. Justin has henceforth been known as Justin Martyr. At Lugdunum (Lyons) a decade later in Marcus Aurelius' reign, a considerable number of persons were tortured and executed in various ways, as by wild beasts. In the latter instance a general public outcry against the Christians caused the unusual, widespread persecution. Even a Rusticus, even a Marcus Aurelius would not reconsider the question of whether the existing law and policy were just; they would only enforce them.

By the time of Tertullian, toward the end of the second century A.D., Christian literature began to be composed in the style of those trained in rhetoric. Still, it remained difficult for highly educated people to become Christian. St. Jerome (who lived in the latter half of the fourth and the early fifth centuries A.D.) confessed that his first exposure to the Jewish prophetical literature—and doubtless the Christian works as well—repelled him, as he compared them to the incomparable, polished style of Cicero, whose works he loved. Moreover, there was a spiritual gulf between Christian and pagan: much in the Roman world repelled the dedicated Christian. The pagan religion inseparably intertwined all sorts of daily events; the festivals, the games and circuses, the theater, all involved ceremonies the Christian could not be a part of. So strongly did the associations carry over that some Christians averred that flute music in itself was sinful! Everywhere they saw obscenity, aberrant sex morals, philosophical materialism, skepticism, or just uncaring hedonism. Some Christians retreated into social isolation. The separationist tendency went back to Jesus; though he advocated obedience to authority and taxpaying, his emphasis was on something beyond: the kingdom of heaven. Later authors of the books that ultimately comprised the New Testament continued the emphasis. Christians "are not of the world," John quotes Jesus as saying.

Yet the early Christians in some ways not only tolerated the Empire; they approved of it. Jesus had taught men to "render unto Caesar the things that are Caesar's." Paul was quite clear on this point, and proud of his Roman citizenship. He advocated complete obedience to the imperial and local authorities. In many ways devout Christians must have been excellent citizens. Yet intellectually, culturally, socially—and religiously, of course—Christians were in some important ways aliens. "We have not here a lasting city: but we seek one that is to come," wrote the author of the *Epistle to the Hebrews*. After Nero, largely of necessity, Christians began to set up a sort of state within a state, made up of people who did not believe in the gods, did not bow down to the emperor or his image, would be inclined not to participate in important governmental institutions —including, for some at least, the army—and who thus generally rejected the whole social and cultural undergirding of the state. Tertullian might complain all he wished about Christians being convicted though not guilty of any real crime. To the Roman governing classes they seemed a threat to the whole order of things. And ultimately, indeed, they were.

Roman Law: The Classical Period

Just as Roman society from an early period was saturated with religion, so also it was suffused throughout with the law. Literary sources for the period of the kings, even though suspect in detail, indicate that there was great development of law in that age; the XII Tables, traditionally dated to the middle-fifth century B.C., show the centrality of law to the state then. One of the central features of the patron–client system, a social structure that antedated the Republic, illustrates the importance of law even for the lower classes: the major duty of the patron to his client was to represent his interests at law. So familiar were Romans with legal terms and usages, that the comic playwrights of the second century B.C., Plautus and Terence, could make puns —understood by the common people, one assumes—based on rather obscure legal terminology.

In the centuries after the XII Tables, as Rome evolved into a republican empire, a system was developed (see Chapter 5) that permitted flexibility and growth to fit the changed situation. The sources of law, besides statutes and, informally, sena-

torial decrees, included the edicts of the various magistrates—
the two praetors in Rome, the urban and the peregrine praetors,
being the most important—and also new rulings made possible
by the evolution of the formulary system. Roman contact with
the laws of other states, especially in the provinces, but even
in Rome itself, brought modifications as well. This is illustrated
for us by Roman commercial law, which developed mostly from
Hellenistic models.

In the Empire the sources of law inevitably changed along
with the structures through which it was applied; and its theo-
retical development took new channels, as well. The emperor
influenced the law directly and indirectly. Through his consilium,
for example, he could indirectly control most of what came to
the floor of the Senate. That body became a primary source of
new law, since the princeps now enforced its decrees as law:
they were, after all, mostly his decrees. The assemblies withered
both as elective and as lawmaking bodies, both of these activities
being taken over by the Senate. From the time of Augustus, the
policy decisions made for those provinces which the emperor
directly controlled tended to be applied also in the consular
provinces; by the second century if not earlier, the princeps or
his agents really controlled all the provinces and a degree of
uniformity existed. Imperial opinion—reached with the aid of a
growing imperial staff, of course—had the force of law. Imperial
edicts became increasingly important in the High Empire. The
famous Constitution of Caracalla in 212, which gave citizenship
to all free persons in the Empire, was an edict.

Praetors gradually waned in importance as formulators
and supervisors of the law and of the courts. By the time of
Hadrian, jurists who were imperial advisors influenced the development of the law more than praetors. By the end of our
period, as we have seen, the praetorian prefects in many ways
controlled the legal machinery—which explains why several of
the prefects were renowned jurists. The edicts, completely stabilized from the time of Hadrian on, were changed only on authority of the emperor. Even outside the imperial bureaucracy,
the influence of the principes can be seen. Thus the opinions of
certain, named jurists were designated by them as authoritative.
This practice continued; however, when the procedure was re-
formulated in the Theodosian Code (438 A.D.), the jurists named
as authoritative were then men long dead.

Some of the classical jurists turned out by the two major
(private) schools of law deserve mention. Salvius Julianus was
the distinguished lawyer whom Hadrian asked to compile the
permanent praetorian edict; Gaius, who flourished in the middle
of the same century, drew up a textbook, the *Institutes*, which

was tremendously influential then and later, both among Greek and Roman jurists. Papinian (Aemilius Papinianus) capped his legal career with the office of praetorian prefect, which he held from 203 until 212, when he was executed by Caracalla because he did not approve of Caracalla's murder of his brother Geta. Papinian seems notably to have been governed by humanitarian concerns, as indeed were many jurists of the period. It seems ironic that these great men were formulating legal principles governing universal human rights at a time when the political structure of the Empire was sinking toward absolutism.

Two understudies of Papinian, who seem to have been praetorian prefects at the same time, were Paul (Julius Paulus) and Ulpian (Domitius Ulpianus). Ulpian is usually considered as the last of the great, classical jurists. Paul's voluminous writings made him famous in his own time. Ulpian had a greater reputation in later times. He is the most quoted of the jurists in the Justinian digest (see below); about a third of it comes from his works. Both of these jurists were perhaps less original than Papinian; their primary work was that of synthesis—but that is quite important in the ordering of the law.

The great edifice of the law was to be, perhaps, the most important of Rome's bequests to the later world. Most influential in western Europe after the fall of Rome was the Theodosian Code of the early fifth century. But the most imitated and studied code of law in history is the formulation by a group of lawyers headed by Trebonian under the emperor Justinian. The *Corpus Iuris Civilis*, as it is called, issued in 534 A.D., contained a *Digest* of opinions of jurists, the *Institutes*, a textbook based on Gaius, the *Code* itself, and the *Novels*, newer additions. Studied in medieval and early modern times to the present, this code served as a direct model for many of the nations of western Europe in the modern age and also for South Africa, Japan, and portions of Canada and the United States. Indirectly the principles of the Roman law, though perhaps not the procedures, have also strongly affected the development of the Anglo-Saxon Common Law, which is the direct basis of the legal systems in most English-speaking nations.

The classical period of the development of Roman law came at the very end of the High Empire, when economic and political deterioration was already insidiously at work. When Ulpian was assassinated by some praetorians in 233 A.D. the Romans had only two more years of relative peace before the onset of crisis and near-chaos that wracked the Roman world for half a century. The structures of law and government that had been so painstakingly erected in the previous centuries were to suffer grievously; yet they stood strong enough to prevent complete collapse; Diocletian and his immediate successors were able to shore up the battered foundations so that the Empire could exist for yet another two hundred years. The law, naturally, did not cease to develop; and indeed much of the actual legislation of the Justinian Code is of later date. But the great age of development based on analysis and formulation based on the values inherent in the law, was over.

Doubtless it can be said of every human institution that has failed, that it contained the seeds of its own decline. So of the Roman Empire. Its establishment had meant the destruction of freedom—not for all, since not all were free—and the concentration of great power at one center, Rome. The system made almost inevitable still greater restraints on freedom, constant new accessions of power by the central government at the expense of local and regional freedom and power. Such a state becomes increasingly top-heavy and inflexible, less able to respond to crises of any sort. Indeed, it might eventually collapse of its own weight.

So long as the Roman Empire defended the frontiers and maintained internal peace the price, considering the alternatives, may not have been excessive. But the system not only made it easy, eventually, to mount civil rebellion, it also made it easy for such civil strife—ordinarily led by military men—to make early headway; no longer were there large numbers of strong and loyal local government units that might check conspirators. The brief civil wars after the deaths of Nero and Commodus had been difficult enough to contain; the convulsions which began with the demise of Severus Alexander, complicated by frontier incursions, went on fitfully for half a century. The new, Sassanid Persian state that controlled all the territories contiguous with Rome's easternmost provinces presented a series of challenges to Roman rule. The new state was infused with two concepts straight out of the Persia of Darius the Great, 700 years before: Zoroastrianism and imperialism. The Sassanids wanted all that had once been Persian—and that included Roman Asia Minor, Roman Syria, and Roman Egypt. Other peoples, less civilized but no less determined, awaited only an opportunity to flood across the Roman frontiers on the Danube and the Rhine.

The political, economic, social, and

FINAL CENTURIES: A WORLD IN DECLINE

13

cultural consequences of these internal and external problems changed the Roman world. Diocletian and Constantine managed to restore peace and recover some of what had been lost. And curiously, most of the Roman world yet saw its best destiny in this centralized government; none of the occasional rebellions that still came seem to have had the character of national uprisings. After Constantine the Empire became Christian and that in turn changed many things, some profoundly. But the patched-up structure could not, after the fourth century, withstand increasing barbaric invasions; the Empire broke in two, and at length into several pieces. Some of these long remained important, especially in the East; in the sixth century Justinian, from his base at Constantinople, almost managed to reunify the whole; but it was too great an effort. In the West, during the fifth and sixth centuries, the structure collapsed, changed, dissolved—or reappeared in new forms. At any rate, eternal Rome, mother of the nations, was no more.

In this chapter we can sketch only some of the more important of the events, and discuss broadly the concomitant social, economic, and cultural changes.

A Half-Century of Distress and Disorder (235–284 A.D.)

Most Romans—certainly those in the larger cities, those who lived near the great roads, and those who lived along the northern or eastern frontiers—must have felt their world falling apart in the years following the assassination of the last of the Severi. An unending succession of generals sought and gained transient power through civil wars; invasions from without disrupted the frontiers; trade virtually collapsed; farming activities declined over broad expanses; inflation turned rampant; and social structures bent to accommodate the new conditions of life.

Many of the more deleterious trends that were a marked feature of this chaotic age had their roots in the earlier Empire; the period of disorder merely accelerated the growth. Centralization of power in the emperor, a part of the principate from the beginning, during this period approached absolutism: military emperors, when they were in control, tended to rule the administration with the same authority that they used toward their soldiers. The center of government was located wherever they moved. There was no time to confer with senators far away in Rome even if they had been so minded.

The routine, civil affairs of government were dealt with by the bureaucracy, which not only survived, but flourished. It was headed by a class of officials completely dependent upon the emperors, but in many ways it functioned as an almost independent entity. The bureaucracy encroached upon the power of the aristocracy, and it was not always responsive to imperial officials who headed its departments.

Septimius Severus had made a drastic change at the top when he gave over to the Equestrian Order—purely military men, mostly—positions previously reserved for the senatorial nobility. A culmination of this trend may perhaps be discerned in an action attributed by one source to the emperor Gallienus (259–268 A.D.), of debarring senators from any military command. Actually, it seems, the change was gradual. Though it still meant something to be a Roman senator, by the end of this period the most important positions went to others.

Financial problems that became acute in the recurrent crises of this age to some degree existed earlier, as we have seen. The abandonment of land by tenants, a problem of the times, was also a feature of an earlier age, for example, though the reasons then surely were only taxes and exactions of landlords, whereas in this age deserted lands must often have resulted from the depredations of ill-supplied Roman soldiers on the march, and the even worse depredations of invading semibarbarians. Art, architecture, literature eclipsed in this time of troubles; nevertheless, they had begun to decline a century before. What all this adds up to, doubtless, is a truism: problems, including weakness of structure, always exist and always are accentuated by crises, such as civil disorder or foreign war.

Of the "Barracks-room Emperors," as the rulers from Maximinus "Thrax" the Thracian (235–238) to Diocletian (284–305) are called, we know enough about fifteen of them to write short biographies; thumbnail sketches can be put together of about that many more emperors or would-be emperors of this period. But there were yet other claimants to the throne, one of whom is known solely from coins he struck. Several of these were quite competent and might have enjoyed long reigns in a more peaceful time; and a few were, as well, men of culture, fit to have served in the High Empire as princeps, "first citizen," rather than as absolutists. We shall look at only a few of these often ephemeral emperors, with their problems, as typical of the whole.

In the seven-year period 238–244 A.D. there were seven major claimants to the throne, including Maximinus, his son Gordian I, the latter's son, and also his grandson. The last four were all proclaimed emperor in 238. Gordian III was only thirteen years old at the time. Maximinus campaigned against the Alamanni east of the Rhine, and against the Dacians and Sarmatians on the Danube frontier. He was killed in 238 before he could respond to a Persian incursion into Roman territory.

Internally, he faced financial problems which he solved in part through the familiar tactic, confiscation of opponents' property; and he initiated a persecution of Christians, possibly because Alexander had rather favored them.

Gordian III (238–244), under some senatorial influence, attempted to reduce somewhat the power of certain imperial administrators, especially the procurators. With the help of a capable praetorian prefect, Timisitheus, he defeated the Persians and coped with other crises. But Timisitheus died and his replacement, a general called Philip the Arab—he was the son of an Arab sheik—killed Gordian and himself assumed the purple.

Typically, Philip (244–249) was a thorough Roman in spite of his birth. He gave his son the title of Augustus also; and the empress, Otacilia, who figures prominently on the coinage, seems to have been important in his administration. Philip celebrated in 248 A.D. the completion of a thousand years since the founding of Rome. It was not an auspicious year. The general who had been sent by Philip to deal with the Goths in 249 killed the emperor and himself took over.

The new emperor was Decius (249–251). All the major problems of the age faced him in his short reign: internal administrative difficulties; financial decline with uncontrollable inflation; invasion, by the Goths in particular; a series of events that would mean the loss of Armenia to Persia; and plague, which again made inroads upon the already depleted population. Decius also was reviled by Christians because he was the first emperor to decide that they represented such an internal threat, such a mass of potentially disloyal citizens, as to require empirewide persecution. Everywhere all citizens had to appear before local officials, swear sacred allegiance to the emperor, and carry with them signed statements in proof of this obeisance Those who refused to submit were mostly Christians. Punishment for noncompliance varied with the attitudes of local officials. Christians rejoiced when Decius was killed by the Goths in warfare on the lower Danube.

Overwhelming problems continued to dog the emperors of the next three or four decades. Valerian and Gallienus, father and son, of distinguished family, highly educated, generally competent, faced both a barbarian thrust into Asia Minor that reached even to Ephesus, where the famous temple to Artemis, one of the so-called Seven Wonders of the Ancient World, was destroyed, and a Persian invasion under the energetic King Sapor, that penetrated to Antioch, possibly twice. Valerian lost a large army in upper Mesopotamia, and was actually captured (260 A.D.). The Persians made much of the coup: the image of

Valerian on his knees before Sapor appeared on coins and was also engraved on rock-face reliefs.

Gallienus, in the West, could do nothing about the Persians. In 258 the Alamanni had broken even into north Italy. In succeeding years he confronted eighteen challengers for the throne (that we know of) and new incursions of Goths, who overran Dacia and parts of Macedonia and Greece, ravaging Delphi and Athens.

An official of the trading city of Palmyra in the East, Odenathus, given the title of *dux* by Gallienus, did organize an offensive against Persia, it seems. But soon he called himself king, and gained control of about the eastern third of the Empire. After his death his widow, Zenobia, continued to rule as queen. In the West a general named Postumus had earlier detached a considerable portion of the western Empire (Gaul, with Britain and Spain). When Gallienus was assassinated (267 A.D.) the Empire lay in three fragments. Gallienus' successor, Claudius, guided the war against the Goths to victory, earning the surname Gothicus, but died of the plague which was still endemic, before he could restore the unity of the Empire (270 A.D.).

Aurelian (270–275 A.D.), of Danubian peasant stock, through heroic effort did reunify the Empire and gained the title Restitutor Orbis. It is astonishing how much action he packed into five short years of power. Twice he campaigned against the beautiful Zenobia, finally bringing her back captive to Rome

This coin, an *antoninianus* (perhaps a double *denarius*) shows the progress of debasement; its silver content was quite low. The head is that of Aurelian.

(she was allowed to live out her life in comfort at Tivoli); twice or three times he repelled invasions across the Danube; he checked a threat within Italy again; and finally he recovered the western "Gallic Empire" for Rome. The wall he built about Rome, portions of which still stand, testifies of dangers that threatened the capital itself. For the first time an emperor permanently abandoned an imperial province, Dacia. He had plans for military reconquest in Mesopotamia, but these were cut short by his assassination.

Political and Military Recovery Under Diocletian and Constantine

Diocletian (284–305 A.D.), a competent Illyrian, at long last managed to bring the generals under control and to establish lasting rule throughout the Empire. Though he was not a great military commander, he had a certain charisma, a strength of personality, that brought him to the top. Probably most citizens, high and low, realized that the near anarchy of the previous half-century simply could not go on if the Empire was to survive in any form, and it helped that there was somewhat less pressure on the frontiers for a time.

Diocletian held power and survived by making himself an absolutist, not only by use of his armies, but symbolically through ceremony, court practice, and even dress. He was rather inaccessible except to trusted subordinates, whom he treated well, giving them great authority and honorific titles. His chief lieutenant, Maximian, was made a partner and given the name Augustus; he controlled much of the Empire. Each of them then had a second in command called a Caesar; these men, Constantius Chlorus for Maximian and Galerius for Diocletian, also had separate courts and areas of command. Administratively, the Empire was split in half: He and Galerius held the eastern half, while Maximian and Constantius held the West. Each of the tetrarchs had his own administrative center; none of them ruled from Rome. Diocletian's headquarters was at Nicomedia in Asia Minor; Galerius chose Sirmium in Pannonia; Maximian, Milan in north Italy; and Constantius, Trèves in northeastern Gaul. The two praetorian prefects did everything but lead the armies; they provided the money and supplies, controlled the bureaucracies, supervised the administration of justice.

Diocletian reorganized the army, much enlarging it, perhaps from necessity; also of necessity, he used more men originating outside the Empire as soldiers. The cavalry contingents had grown and now comprised a much larger proportion of the military than in earlier ages. Frontiers were much strengthened; the legions, reduced in size, now were stationed farther back from the frontiers for defense in depth. The provinces were increased in number by a reduction in size. Only a few—the oldest, and Italy itself—now were ruled by senators. The reorganized provinces were grouped together in dioceses under vicars—thirteen of them. The centralizing tendency continued even though the power at the top was divided among the tetrarchs. Thus the local government units lost the functions of road-building and recruiting for the army; perhaps gladly. Yet the larger army and the increased central functions—along with the four separate and expensive courts of the tetrarchy—required more money. A reorganized financial and tax structure met the needs.

Diocletian's tetrarchy seems to have been designed with three goals in mind: first, to make possible quicker response to threats across the frontiers; second, to prevent—or quickly eliminate—pretenders to the throne; and finally, to provide for an orderly succession. In the first two purposes the structure proved fairly successful. In the last—the perennial problem of the succession—the structure failed, in the end.

Diocletian must have astonished the Roman world when he decided to retire, in 305, and forced Maximian to retire with him. The two Caesars, Constantius and Galerius, as planned, became Augusti. But instead of allowing each of them then to choose a Caesar, Diocletian permitted Galerius, his trusted second-in-command, to choose both. Galerius left out Constantine the son of Constantius and Maxentius the son of Maximian. A short period saw the following changes: Constantius died and his troops hailed his son Constantine as Augustus; Maxentius seized power, calling himself Augustus, and Maximian came out of retirement to help him; a pretender arose in Egypt who of course called *himself* Augustus, not Caesar, and the two Caesars appointed by Galerius, Maximin and Licinius, named themselves Augustus also. There were now no less than seven "Augusti" and no "Caesars" at all! At one point Diocletian came out of retirement and settled the competition by force of his personal authority, but soon after, arms again prevailed. By 313 only two Augusti remained, Constantine, in the West, and Licinius, now controlling the East. Galerius had died of disease in 311; the rest had been eliminated. Constantine defeated Licinius also in 324, and until his death in 337 controlled the whole Empire. The end of the tetrarchy did not mean an end to the division of authority in the Empire. Constantine created four praetorian prefectures and each prefect exercised civil and judicial powers on delegation from the emperor.

In social and economic policy, as we shall see, Constantine followed Diocletian and some of his predecessors. Like them he kept a tight rein on finance, effecting some reforms; he retained and extended restrictions on careers of private persons, further restricting class mobility. However, in other ways Constantine appears as an innovator whose actions foreshadow the future. His religion, of course, is a case in point. As early as 312 he was said to have seen a vision instructing him to use the Christ-symbol, the Chi-Rho (χ or χ) in the battle of the Milvian bridge. He followed the victory with a declaration of tolerance. Though he retained the pagan trappings of tradition—he was still pontifex maximus—he gradually identified himself with Christianity and became the effective controller of church affairs, even intervening in doctrinal disputes.

In some of his political moves Constantine also set a new pattern. The powers of the praetorian prefects were trimmed and some of their functions given to palace officials closer to the emperor. The new titles sound like the middle ages: masters, counts, chamberlains. It was Constantine who first settled large numbers of the semibarbarian tribesmen, Sarmatians and Goths, in Roman territory—though on a smaller scale, of course, this had been going on for centuries. And Constantine's new city, Constantinople, in the East on the site of ancient Byzantium, seems to symbolize the coming demise of the West as well as the continuation of the eastern Empire, with the new capital its headquarters.

It is not difficult to find the reasons for Constantine's decision to find a new site for his second capital. Rome had not really served as a political and military capital for years; it no longer suited, geographically. Moreover, in that city—now more like a museum than the center of the Empire—the past no longer served to instruct the present and to make men wise for the future. Rome's past was pagan, and it lay over everything like a web, obstructing, deadening. Constantine was never happy there, though for some years he built within the city, notably the basilica begun by Maxentius, and various Christian churches, including the first St. Peter's. But the aristocracy and the urban crowd both disliked him, in part because of his religion. When he refused to carry out the time-honored ceremonies to Jupiter Optimus Maximus, it seemed to the Romans, most of them still pagan, that he profaned and displayed unpatriotic disloyalty to the greatness of Rome past, and perhaps even endangered the city and the state. Constantinople was geographically better sited for rule and for defense, and also it was a place that Constantine could mold into a capital of his liking, with his stamp—and of his building.

The Economy: From the Severi to Constantine

Unending civil struggles compounded by barbarian invasions and other wars, as with the Persians, plus plague and a whole series of connected problems produced a most serious effect upon the Roman economy.

It is often not understood on what precarious foundations the ancient economy rested, how small dislocations might produce profoundly depressing effects. The class of the rich was always quite small. The great majority of persons, whether rural or urban, lived at the subsistence level. Most of their income went for food; most of the rest for rent. Any considerable drop in production for any cause, naturally producing higher prices for basic commodities, would immediately wipe out any "extra" buying power the ordinary person might normally have. All available money would have to go for food; there would be none left over to buy other necessities, let alone anything like luxuries. Thus, only a small percentage increase in food prices reacted upon the rest of the economy. In antiquity, war often stifled agricultural production and forced up prices. That explains the familiar pattern: war, famine, pestilence.

A modern example of the same sort of depressing effect on the economy is seen in the sudden raising of oil prices by the oil exporting states in the 1970s. In an industrialized society oil is in many ways a necessity, not a luxury; it must be purchased; if, therefore, its price rises sharply, less money is available for purchase of other things (and costs rise for myriads of manufactures); thus the higher cost of this single commodity reverberated in all phases of the economy.

Businessmen and traders of all sorts also suffered in the often chaotic situations of the third century. Even earlier, trade had dropped off somewhat because of restrictions and a growing network of customs stations. There was no new policy; the network was expanded as a means of shoring up declining revenues. The rich were less affected than the poor, of course, by rises in food costs, since only a small percentage of their income went for basic foodstuffs. They were adversely affected financially, nonetheless, by other economic problems. Rich landowners often suffered along with the small holders, especially those with villas along the great military roads. Marching armies, often ill-equipped "requisitioned" food for their needs—and perhaps "liberated" a few other choice possessions at the same time. These requisitions were obligations upon the state and technically legal (more or less), but in this age seldom paid. Rostovtzeff saw in the depredations of the soldiers deliberate class warfare, the lower-class soldiers intentionally preying on the rich. Probably that is wrong; but the effects were the same. This sort of ravaging of farms is particularly to be noted in the case of the provinces along the Danube but it occurred in some other places as well. On the other hand, those lucky enough to be living in provinces relatively unaffected did well. Africa, for example, seems to have declined little in its economy. In fact, higher prices for farm products may have actually made it possible for farmers there to do better, for a time. Even in the affected provinces, the state kept certain basic activities going: the iron mines in Noricum, for example, continued to work busily—for obvious reasons. That province was, however, less disturbed militarily than others in the Danube region.

The problem of abandonment of land, alluded to earlier, intensified in this period. The passage of armies, friendly as well as unfriendly, partly accounts for the mounting seriousness of this problem; repeated depredation would discourage anyone. Some land, long mistreated by overcropping without rest, manuring, or crop rotation, or by deforestation followed by erosion, lapsed into unproductiveness. Actual underpopulation may also have been a factor. The government, over two or three centuries, tried to deal with abandonment in several ways. Sometimes tax advantages were offered to those who put such land back in production, or individuals were given land not theirs if they farmed it. Landowners with contiguous holdings occasionally were forced to cultivate some of the deserted acreage. Decurions of nearby towns might be saddled with the burden of seeing to it that abandoned lands were worked.

The large farms, now more and more centered upon the villas of the landowners, tended out of necessity to become more self-sufficient. This tendency, too, had affected rural life for a century or more. Even earlier, on the great slave-manned farms of the late Republic and early Empire, operations had begun to be diversified somewhat, in order to make more efficient use of slaves—who had to be fed, clothed, and housed year-round. Now, however, in a development that would extend into medieval times, the great farms grew still more self-sufficient, not only in farming and local manufacturing, but also in self-protection. Large landowners sometimes managed to withdraw their lands from the jurisdiction of the local city-states that were the imperial administrative units. This contributed to the economic and political debilitation of the urban centers. By the end of the third century—it was a question of survival in a time of invasions and despoliation—many towns, especially in the northern provinces, had begun to move from the valleys to the hilltops. Such fortified towns would be characteristic in the centuries to follow.

Accelerated Debasement of the Coinage

The most conspicuous evidence for the financial distress of the Empire in the third century is the coinage. Here, too, the first steps of decline are earlier—in Nero's reign. He first debased the silver and lightened both the silver *denarii* and the gold *aurei*, as we have seen. And we have noted that there was some further debasement of the silver and lightening of the gold coins even during the palmy days of the second century. At the beginning of the civil wars in 235 B.C. the *denarius* contained no more than half the silver that it had from the Second Punic War to Nero; and the *aureus* by now also contained only fractionally more than half the gold. A new coin, the *antoninianus*, issued by the Severi, from the beginning contained less silver in proportion to the *denarius* than its face value, which was apparently two *denarii*.

The emperors of the third century were forced to debase the money rapidly. By the time of Gallienus, a few years after the middle of the century, the *antoninianus* contained only about 5 percent of silver, and before the end of the century it had only a silver wash—extremely thin plating—on it. Often one must look carefully at surviving specimens with a magnifying glass to see the particles of silver still clinging, in protected places, to the base metal. "Gresham's law"—bad money drives out good— seems to be one of the most unrepealable of principles; it cer-

An *antoninianus* of the emperor Decius, the first ruler to persecute Christians throughout the whole Empire. He wears a radiate crown, symbol of the sun-god.

tainly applied in this period. At the same time, there was a loss of confidence in the whole monetary structure; the result was rampant inflation and a return to barter, that is, payment in goods instead of money, in many areas all over the Empire. This situation naturally compounded difficulties for traders, businessmen, moneylenders, and the government as well, even though the government was in one sense responsible.

Part of the reason for debasement of the coinage was a shortage of silver and gold bullion (as we have seen, this may have been a problem even in the High Empire); not enough existed any longer to make possible a volume of currency equal to the money-supply demands of government and the economy. We have little data, but it would seem that the Spanish and other mines no longer produced precious metals in the quantities of earlier centuries. The wars and attendant disorders may also have reduced the output of the mines.

One might well think that what happened to the coinage (as in the High Empire) was not inflation so much as a simple rise in the price of the precious metals in relation to, say, the prices of basic foodstuffs. And there is some truth in this. A coin with 5 percent of silver was worth more in the late third century than a coin with a similar content of silver by weight a century earlier. But this is no complete explanation, for, as nearly as we can determine, prices rose more than can be accounted for by the decreased value of the metals in the coins. Still, it is possible to overemphasize the runaway inflation by failing to take into account this shortage of precious metals and the consequent increase in their value. As noted earlier, the *antoninianus* dropped from about 50 percent to about 5 percent silver in fifty years; much of the drop occurred in the last five or ten years of that period. Though that reduction seems enormous, it represents a rate of annual inflation that many governments today would find "acceptable."

There was a genuine, sharp inflation, then, and the immediate reason for it was the practice of each short-lived ruler to try to solve some of his financial problems by melting down old coins and producing a larger number of new ones with the same face value, but with less metal value. The inflation reflects the fact that people all over the Empire refused to accept the money at previous face value—in the market place, at any rate; to refuse an agent of the emperor accompanied by a squad of soldiers or even to refuse a soldier, required more courage. In our own twentieth century, though the concept of fiat money is accepted, its value drops when there is a lack of confidence in the government or the economy. In antiquity the public would accept the smaller bronze or copper coins as fiat money, but insisted on intrinsic value in the basic currency. Some of the evidence on relative values of gold and silver in that age seems almost incomprehensible. Gold seems to have been driven out of circulation. Yet the Price Edict of Diocletian and other information indicates a price ratio of 1 to 6 for gold and silver as compared to about 1 to 12 in the early Empire. Perhaps the continuous attempt to overvalue the silver in the coins through debasement was more successful than is sometimes thought. That is, the "silver" coins circulated at a face value far above their intrinsic value, despite constant change.

Economic Recovery

Heroic efforts made in the age of recovery under Diocletian and Constantine did much to restore the economy and the coinage; however, the economy benefited more from internal peace and a restoration of the frontiers than from any economic measures taken by the emperors. Some serious wars continued to be fought and, in the years of Constantine's rise to power there was again internal civil conflict; yet nothing like the chaos of the previous century returned. Breathing spells allowed economic revival between crises.

The absolutist character of the policies intended to stabilize the shattered Empire has already been pointed out. Diocletian attempted price and wage controls, as seen in his famous edict of 301 A.D.; this seems to have been promulgated, however, only in the eastern half of the Empire. We may doubt that this attempt to put ceilings on prices and wages was very successful, in view of the ineffectiveness of similar measures in our own century, with our vastly improved communications and law enforcement—and there is some evidence that indeed it did not work. Yet it may have had some effect, even if only to stem what we now term an "inflation psychology." Diocletian also reorganized the tax structure. A new assessment method was devised for lands and crops—again used particularly in the eastern part of the Empire—employing new land-production units called *iuga*. The size of each *iugum* varied with the quality of the land and its use, whether it was planted to crops, vineyards, or orchards.

Diocletian introduced a new coinage system, based chiefly on gold coins weighing sixty to the Roman pound; there was also a new silver coin a little lighter than the denarius of the High Empire. The term *denarius* continued to be applied to the copper coins with a silver wash, of two or more sizes with face values of two and five denarii. To be sure, smaller bronze coins were minted also. Testimony that Diocletian could not find enough gold and silver to effect a return to a money economy is seen in the tax system: taxes could be paid in kind and apparently were indeed collected in goods rather than money in many sections of the Empire.

Since Diocletian also reorganized and enlarged the army, and since his political system, involving multiple courts under the two Augusti and two Caesars must have been considerably more expensive than before, there was continued pressure for higher imperial taxes and for required services of all kinds from the provincial citizens and towns. Some later legislation would seem to imply that Diocletian, in spite of his fairer tax system, went about the business of tax collection in the usual inexorable fashion: we hear of imprisonments, lashings, and tortures— which, of course, may have been common in earlier ages.

Constantine in general followed Diocletian's economic policies. He managed to mint a gold coin called the *solidus*, at seventy-two to the pound (as well as fractional gold), in sufficient quantity to make it the basis of the monetary system, as it was for centuries. Some bullion Constantine got from confiscated temple treasuries—one of the benefits of a Christian viewpoint? He issued silver coins rated at one-twenty-fourth of the *solidus*. Constantine also came up with new taxes, imposing one on the nobility and another, collected only on special occasions, on most groups in the cities. Landowners, who paid taxes on their land, did not pay this latter tax, and there were some special exemptions: teachers, for example. But most others, including even prostitutes, were liable. Though our information is fragmentary, it appears that the state increasingly controlled directly many things in the economic sphere that formerly were contracted out. These included mining, collection of customs duties, construction of storage facilities, and actual manufacture as well as distribution of uniforms to the armies. Constantine's income was sufficient, as already implied, to permit him to continue the military and political changes begun by Diocletian, to build the city of Constantinople, and to put up numerous large churches and other structures in many places.

Society: From the Severi to Constantine

The rule of the military emperors during the middle-third century caused some social changes and hastened others. The senatorial nobility, which had declined in prestige under the Severi, became even less influential; as we have seen, important military commands were no longer open to them, and they now governed only a few of the oldest provinces. Yet vestiges of the old power remained, and in the next century Constantine would find it useful to revive the order to a degree. Perhaps, like Augustus in an earlier age, he had either to revive and use the older aristocracy or to create a new one, to help him administer the Empire. The equestrian class during the third century became virtually a military nobility, and increased vastly in numbers and importance. Its members held the military commands once the preserve of the Senate. But the group was diffuse and hardly constituted an Order in the old sense. Promotion from the ranks, at least the ranks of the centurions, possible even in the early Empire, now was common, and such men could reach higher office—even the throne itself, if things worked out right.

Almost everywhere in this age of disorder, the local nobility, the class that furnished the decurions (or *curiales*) for the city-states that were still the component units of the Empire, suffered badly. Service in city offices and on these city councils once had brought great prestige and if some expense was involved was yet worth it because of the honor. But formerly voluntary contributions to the local town or city—indeed, the offices themselves—became obligatory; so did service as decurions. The imperial duties of these councillors grew and became most onerous: theirs was the responsibility for collecting the taxes, furnishing recruits for the armies (until Diocletian; they could collect cash as a substitute, in the case of Jews and some others), and performing other tasks. Members of the decurion class—the list of eligibles was drawn up according to a property qualification varying from region to region—began to try to escape service in every possible way. There were official exemptions for all those in the higher service of the state, for most private entrepreneurs who bid in state contracts, and for certain professionals such as teachers and physicians. Some escaped by entering these ranks. Others moved away to areas where they might not be listed in the census, at least for a time. Laws and decrees attempted to deal with the situation. Under penalty for infraction, the decurions were forbidden to move from their home city-states. The rank, with its inherent obligations, was made hereditary. As a group, then, this class suffered heavily and diminished in numbers.

On the other hand, the class of large, rural landholders grew in importance and influence. The great landholders had once been mostly city inhabitants, absentee landowners. Now many removed themselves from the cities and established themselves as a rural nobility of the country-squire sort. This tendency, the student will recognize, was to continue into the Middle Ages.

What of the lower classes? The age of disorder ruined many traders, great and small; but in some places they could continue as before. Such men were resilient; even in troubled areas they might serve an imperial purpose by supplying the armies, and by purchasing spoils from the soldiers or furnishing them with personal supplies. With the return of peace under Diocletian their numbers would soon increase. They might, as compared to the earlier Empire, continue to be hampered by more and higher customs, collected by venal lower level officials who looked out for themselves. And much of the old international trade doubtless was gone. Still, this group seems to have made a reasonable recovery with the return of order.

Naturally, many of the lower classes found opportunity in the larger armies of this period and of the Empire ever after. Even in the High Empire a large percentage of those who enlisted in the auxiliary units came, not from the lowest classes in the provinces, but from the middle group of the fairly well-to-do; in an age that saw soldiers increasingly privileged, the tendency must have been accentuated. Perhaps the lowest class youths now enlisted in the ethnic units, which served with the Roman armies as mercenaries. Such units, hired by Julius Caesar and perhaps some earlier generals, were increasingly employed by the emperors.

Many lower class people found their freedom restricted in various ways. Social mobility had been a characteristic of the early Empire, as indeed the Christian New Testament well enough indicates. Restrictions had begun to appear by the time of the Severi, and Diocletian and Constantine stiffened them: membership in the craft guilds, once voluntary, became obligatory; as noted earlier, men were "frozen" in their occupations and their children had to be trained in their fathers' crafts. Mobility was drastically reduced.

Much is heard of a new class—the half-free *coloni*—that was not so new really; it was made up of tenants who worked the great farms all over the Empire. Tenancy had always existed, even in the early Republic, and when great farms became common, in the middle to late Republic, tenancy was an alternative for the large landholders to slave-manned operations. Though no quantitative study seems possible, it appears that, after a time of relative stability, considerable numbers of landlords had begun to turn increasingly to tenants and away from slaves from the second century onwards. A possible reason was a decreased availability of relatively cheap slaves suitable for rough labor on the land; in an early period, these had come in mainly as captives from the semicivilized areas that bounded the Empire on the east and north. Later, slaves were kidnaped and sold— illegally—in the Roman markets. Slaves of course were bred also, but these were likely to be given at least a minimal education and trained for high level positions; they were too valuable for farm labor. Tenancy may also have been attractive because it required less capital investment; but then it may also have produced less profit, depending upon the quality of the *vilicus* or manager of the slave-manned farms. To sum it up, for whatever reasons, there was a gradual increase in the use of tenants in place of slaves on the land.

It is necessary to point out another facet of tenant farming frequently overlooked: tenants often were in worse economic condition than slaves, who had to be kept healthy if they were to be profitable. Tenants had to look out for themselves. Nor were tenants always altogether free before the development of the *coloni*. Tenant farmers in all ages tend to get in debt, either (most commonly) to the owner of the land, who demands all he can get, and in bad years perhaps more, or to someone else—in the southern United States a few decades ago, perhaps to the owner of the country store (who was, sometimes, also the land-lord). Once in debt, the tenant is no longer really free. In the Roman Empire the laws of debt, more severe than our own, made sure that a debt-ridden tenant worked for his landlord until he paid the last *denarius*, which, often, was never. So grew the nucleus of the "new" class, the *coloni*. Some freeholders in an uncertain age voluntarily bargained away their own property in return for protection and for some guarantee of specific rights in connection with the land, rights that were hereditary. The *coloni* are thus immediately recognizable as the forerunners of the serfs of the Middle Ages.

One should not assume that the *coloni* all at one time or in one century, became everywhere the dominant rural lower class. But an extensive beginning was made in this troubled age. Nor should one assume that what was really a very complicated and various development has been fully explained above: for example, nothing has been said of the great imperial estates on which much of the development occurred. But perhaps these paragraphs will give some indication of the evolution of this important change in rural society.

Religion in a Time of Troubles

In retrospect we know that one of the more significant developments of the period of the middle and late Roman Empire was the rise of Christianity. Since it grew most rapidly as the Empire declined, in the third century and after, it has often been suggested, first by contemporary pagans, that Christianity was a partial cause of the decline. If not overplayed, the point has some validity. Many Christians found it possible to be comfortably a part of "Eternal Rome." But others felt themselves aliens in a world of false gods; their loyalty was to the church and not to the Empire. Though not revolutionaries, many felt that God would bring an end to wicked Rome, and they were hardly distressed at the prospect. Some of them refused to serve in the army; all of them struck at the essential fiber of the Empire when they refused to worship the state gods and rejected the very basis of Greco-Roman education and culture.

The causes of imperial decline, however, were many, and Christianity seems to have played only a relatively minor role. Civil wars, famine, plague, and barbarian invasions—no complete list—had little to do with Christianity. Indeed, it may be that these tended to cause Christianity to flourish in an "age of anxiety," as it has been called, rather than vice versa. The age brought with it a wave of pessimism, of disillusionment with the Empire if not the world itself, a felt need for a safe retreat for mind and spirit. Even in philosophy such a trend may be seen. Marcus Aurelius' *Meditations* express devotion to duty, but without optimism and without hope. Plotinus, who in the third century advocated a sort of mystic system called Neoplatonism, saw man as a microcosm of all that is, including God or the One or the Good, in Plato's term; and for him, unification with the Good, achieved—but rarely—through education, training, and exercise of the will, was the highest human attainment. Nothing in the physical world deserved such attention and effort.

Paganism too changed in the time of troubles. New gods from the East, often combined syncretically with the older deities, attained high status. In the early third century the emperor Elagabalus united the sun god of Emesa, after whom he took his own name, and all the other major deities connected with the sun, into one cult. Basically the same Syrian god, Sol Invictus, became the chief deity of the state—though not exactly displacing Jupiter—by action of Aurelian and succeeding emperors of the latter half of the second century. Closely connected was Mithra, most popular in the army. In this age Mithraism was spreading perhaps as rapidly as Christianity. The most appealing religions of this time abounded in mystery and mysticism.

As always in the pagan cults, the new deities could be worshiped along with the old; they were not exclusivistic. Devotees did indeed speak of Mithra as the "only god," but everyone understood that they meant only that all the gods were somehow comprehended by the concept; no one could be offended. Modern scholars often profess to find that paganism was in a dying state and that efforts somehow to combine similar gods or to form a kind of unified pagan religion indicate that decline. But this

Cult statuary of the Mithraic religion. Mithra killing the sacred bull, from which he created the earth and all life. (*Alinari–Scala*)

would be difficult to demonstrate from contemporary evidence. The disordered age did cause a search for new gods and new ways of finding inner peace; several of the pagan cults seem, however, to have been well adapted to meet those needs.

It has already been noted that the third century saw the instigation of great, empirewide persecutions aimed at wiping out Christianity, root and branch. Begun by Decius in mid-century and continued with varying intensity by most of the following emperors until just before the death of Galerius, 311 A.D., the campaigns harried, hounded, and sometimes slew Christians for their beliefs. The reasons are mostly known. Christians were misunderstood in some ways: they were accused of cannibalism, especially of eating babies, a distorted view of the Communion service; they were called atheists (as in a sense they were), haters of mankind; they were labeled as skulking, hiding, and secretive; people said that they dishonored the emperor. And, perhaps most important, they were blamed for all the evils that wracked the state. Tertullian, the Christian apologist of the second century, had noted even then how ready Romans were to shout, "Christians to the lions!" when any sort of disaster hit the state, from the flooding of the Tiber to earthquake or drought. In this time of troubles there were plenty of reasons for men to view with dark suspicion any group that might have displeased the gods and so brought down their wrath.

Thoughtful intellectuals by the late second century had begun to attack Christianity, though earlier such persons had given little attention to a cult they thought insignificant. Celsus in the second century and Porphyry in the third are examples of pagan intellectuals who launched full-scale attempts to tear down the new religion by reason and ridicule, pointing out inconsistencies, contradictions, or impossibilities, as they saw them. Christian intellectuals answered in kind. Origen of Alexandria (c. 185–254), in particular, not only replied; far more than Justin a century before, Origen provided a sort of rational-philosophical basis for the Judaeo-Christian view. In any case, these attacks by pagan scholars and the responses of Origen and others were relatively unimportant to the growth of Christianity. It appealed, after all, primarily not to intellectuals, even though some were included in its ranks, but rather to the lower classes. Some of the latter, indeed, were relatively well-educated, but in a pragmatic, not an academic sense. Most citizens paid little attention to the high-level polemics of either side. Those who accepted the new religion did so because the relatively simple message of sin and salvation touched their hearts.

Celsus and Porphyry saw the evolving structure of the Christian church as a dangerous state-within-the-state; they leveled a charge of divided loyalty that would continue to plague the Christian church in its relations with civil authorities for centuries after it became a religious monopoly in Europe. Neither of these learned opponents of the Christians sought persecution. But there was a strong popular aversion to Christians, a demand for suppression, as seen in the persecution in Lugdunum (Lyons) in the 170s, when an angry crowd might have wiped out all the local Christians had there been no control. What happened there with official sanction was bad enough. Besides all the reasons already mentioned for hating Christians, one might add that Christian intolerance of pagan beliefs tended to breed retaliatory intolerance of Christianity.

One other factor may be suggested here. The emperors of the High Empire, along with their officers and advisors, might indeed deplore what they considered the ignorance and obstinacy of the Christians; yet they would not seriously think them responsible for the natural or other disasters that came upon the state, nor initiate any sweeping, fierce persecution. Many of the military emperors of the troubled third century, however, by no means aristocratic intellectuals, came of the same stock as the superstitious pagans who cried out for the blood of the Christians at Lyons. Some of those emperors may really have believed that that terrible age of disaster upon disaster, which never seemed to end, might reflect the wrath of the gods for some great affront—perhaps by the Christians. Such emperors might feel duty-bound to free the state of so sacrilegious, blasphemous, and dangerous a group.

The persecutions did not succeed, as we know, although there may have been times when even the beleagured Christians thought that they would. The task was by then impossible: there were too many Christians, some of them in positions to protect the rest. And, as the Christian historian Eusebius said later, the blood of the Christians was the seed of the church. At length came surcease and then the first Christian emperor, Constantine.

With official recognition, Christianity found different problems. Already there had been schisms and heresies. Tertullian had succumbed to one of these, Montanism. Gnosticism, in various forms, now often divided the Christian communities. Constantine attempted, at the Council of Nicaea in 325, to settle one of the most difficult of numerous controversies over the nature of Christ, with only partial success.

The history of both the growth of the church in structure and doctrine and the changes that came with the recognition of Christianity as the official state religion under Theodosius the Great towards the end of the fourth century—all this belongs more properly to the study of the Middle Ages than of Rome. In some sense the reign of Constantine marks the end of the Roman period. The Christianized Greco-Roman culture that followed characterized the Middle Ages, and to some extent forms the somewhat disordered core of western civilization today.

Collapse of the Empire in the West

After the death of Constantine the Great the Empire was for a time ruled by his three sons: the familiar pattern of the general who gained power and established a dynasty thus continued. A nephew, Julian, who ruled 360–363 after the death of the last son, was termed the Apostate by the Christians because he attempted to restore a united and rather Neoplatonic paganism; moreover, in some ways he reduced the privileges of Christians, who, for example, were forbidden to hold professorships on the grounds that they could not possibly understand and teach the traditional literature and culture. But the setback was temporary and under the general-become-emperor Theodosius (the Christians called him "The Great"), 379–395, Christianity became the official religion. Christians now often became persecutors of pagans; they destroyed or made churches of temples; sometimes they destroyed synagogues as well. The growing influence of churchmen in the West is well illustrated by the power that Ambrose, Bishop of Milan, exercised over Theodosius. Twice he excluded the emperor from the privileges of the church until he should repent of acts Ambrose disapproved of.

All during the fourth century there was constant pressure on the northern frontiers. In 378, at the fateful battle of Adrianople, in Thrace, the heavy-armed cavalry of the Goths inflicted disastrous defeat upon the Roman legions, and killed Valens, the emperor who was leading them. The ultimate consequence was reorganization of the Roman army over a long period, with greater dependence upon heavy cavalry—again a portent of the Medieval future. Goths now settled within the bounds of the Empire in large numbers, unassimilated and occasionally moving about, to the distress of the local population and the government, particularly in the West. Franks had earlier been allowed to settle west of the Rhine.

SEQUEL:
HERITAGE

At the death of Theodosius the Empire was divided—it was to be a permanent division now—between his two sons. Under Honorius in the West it was found necessary to withdraw the legions from Britain, which was cast adrift, in order to defend Italy from a mixed group of invaders. Ironically, the general who conducted the defense in these years—at times, brilliantly—was Stilicho, himself of German descent, as many of the soldiers by now were. He was actually the effective ruler. Honorius established his administrative capital at Ravenna, more easily defended than Rome or Milan. Rome itself was taken and sacked during his reign by the Visigoths under Alaric, in 410 but, fortunately, the city was not ravaged. Almost exactly 800 years had passed since Rome had last fallen.

In this century much of the West was taken over by the invading or simply immigrating barbarians, who settled down and established kingdoms in the former provinces. In Britain, the Picts, Scots, Angles, Saxons, and Jutes soon were in substantial occupation. The Vandals moved across Gaul, into Spain, and finally into North Africa. They were besieging Carthage as St. Augustine, Bishop of Hippo, was writing the last of his *City of God*. His disintegrating universe surely influenced his theology. The Visigoths first occupied southern Gaul and then moved into Spain. From Africa, under Genseric, the Vandals descended on Rome by sea in 455 and sacked it again, this time brutally and thoroughly. The government had been neither passive nor altogether ineffective against the flood of invasions. The general

Mosaic from Carthage, depicting a Vandal horseman. (*Copyright British Museum*)

Aëtius, under Valentinian III (assassinated just before the Vandal capture of Rome), had achieved a spectacular victory against odds over the Huns at Chalons in Gaul in 451. But the resources of the western Empire in money and especially men were no longer equal to the overwhelming task. Franks, Burgundians, and others moved into Gaul and the Ostrogoths into northern Italy. The date of the takeover of the western Empire by Odoacer, 476 A.D., often is taken as the end of the Roman Empire, and that date serves as well as any, though the German general was Romanized and surely a more effective emperor than the last of the "Roman" emperors, the shadowy Romulus Augustulus, whom he replaced. Even Theoderic, the Ostrogoth who took over as king of Italy after killing Odoacer in 493 (with the approval of Zeno, emperor of the eastern Empire at the time) was hardly a barbarian; he had been exposed to Greco-Roman culture at Constantinople as a youth.

The eastern Empire yet stood, and would flourish, with vicissitudes, for another millennium, until Constantinople would at last fall to the Turks in 1453. One of the eastern emperors we should note, Justinian (527–565 A.D.), the codifier of the Roman law, made a valiant attempt to reconquer the West and for a time held Italy and large parts of North Africa and Spain. He, too, eventually found the effort too great; the successor kingdoms, dominated by Vandals, Visigoths, Franks, Ostrogoths, and others, continued. Each of these adopted many Roman ways and institutions in modified form. The concept of a unified great state lived on, seen ideally as embracing all Christendom. Thus Charlemagne saw himself in 800 when he took the old title, Emperor of the Romans; so did his successors in the "Holy Roman Empire" until Napoleon put an end to that particular conceit in 1806.

Assessing the Decline and Fall

In modern times Rome has interested all sorts of persons, not only historians. Poets, columnists, and politicians have been powerfully stirred by the crumbling of this great Empire. The most famous historical examination of the demise was composed by Edward Gibbon, in his renowned *Decline and Fall of the Roman Empire*. Though he took into account a number of factors, his basic conclusion was that the Empire's fall was a "triumph of Christianity and Barbarism." In the two centuries since Gibbon many other factors have been suggested as the primary cause of the collapse. It has been laid to climatic change; to soil erosion or exhaustion, coupled with the rise of malaria in the choked mouths of rivers; to manpower shortage owing to plague and various other disasters; to a leveling process in education that diluted the product; to a failure of nerve and a decline in essential patriotism; and, in the 1970s (by a scientist and a sociologist), to the decline in production of precious metals and to lead in the diet from water pipes and wine vessels (which in theory caused sterility, so that the population did not reproduce itself). The interested reader can find convenient summaries containing extracts[1] for all except the last two factors mentioned—though this list is not complete. Thoughtful persons today might wish to consider one more factor not listed here but implied elsewhere: the inevitable tendency of bureaucracies to become ever larger, more cumbersome and intractable, and more expensive.

The reader of this volume will understand that the total problem of Rome's fall is very complex; no simple explanation exists and much must be taken into account. Moreover, he or she will be able to discount the frequent, groundless predictions of impending doom that are inevitably based on a partial, biased, or even ignorant view of Roman history. But doomsday prophets notwithstanding, the reader of Roman history is also acutely aware that great states do indeed decline and fall.

The Roman Heritage

Every educated person is at least somewhat aware of the importance of Roman ideas and ways for the modern world. Much that originated in the Near East or in Greece was passed on to later civilization through Rome and, indeed, the greatest contribution of the Romans may be a matter of transmission. But original contributions there were, as well as refinements of older achievements. The Latin language not only provided the basis for all the "Romance" languages (Italian, French, Spanish, Portuguese, Romanian), but also at least half the vocabulary for English, the single most important modern tongue. Any survey of the great literature of the world would surely include some selections from the Latin. The Roman legal system, surviving in the eastern Roman Empire, in the successor states in the West, and in the canon law of the Roman Catholic Church, has powerfully influenced legal systems in much of the modern world. Political structures swayed not only Charlemagne and his successors in the Holy Roman Empire, but many others as well: the founding fathers

[1] D. Kagan, *Decline and Fall of the Roman Empire* (Boston: D. C. Heath, 1962); M. Chambers, *The Fall of Rome* (New York: Holt, Rinehart and Winston, 1963). For a convenient summary of the process of decline see S. Katz, *The Decline of Rome* (Ithaca, N.Y.: Cornell University Press, 1955).

of the United States of America were conversant with and influenced by the Roman political experience. Some of Rome's architectural and engineering know-how disappeared in the Middle Ages, but much continued, especially in the design and building of the great Medieval churches that developed from the Roman style of basilica. Until only a few years ago, most large public buildings erected in the United States (and elsewhere in the western world) included Roman features. Christianity, though near eastern in origin, was much influenced, particularly in organizational structure and to some degree in outlook, by the Roman experience.

The world today—Europe, the Americas, and much of the rest—would be a very different place if the Mediterranean basin had been dominated not by Rome but by, say, the Carthaginians or an eastern empire such as the Parthian or the Sassanid Persian, or even by an empire of Alexander the Great, held together and dominant in the western Mediterranean as well as in the Near East. But Alexander died young, before he could satiate his boundless ambition or firmly establish the empire he conquered; and the Carthaginians too long failed to see that the Romans were to be their indomitable foes. So by chance, good fortune, design, and resolve—all the kaleidoscopic elements Roman history comprises—it was the Romans who became our direct cultural ancestors. And so it is that now every citizen of the United States somehow encounters Roman influence in every day of his life.

SELECT
BIBLIOGRAPHY

General Works, Period Studies, Area Studies

BALSDON, J. P. V. D., ed. *Roman Civilization*. Baltimore, 1969.

BARFIELD, L. *Northern Italy Before the Romans*. New York, 1972.

BOREN, H. C. *The Gracchi*. New York, 1969.

BRAUER, G. *The Age of the Soldier Emperors: Imperial Rome*, A.D. 244–284. Park Ridge, N. J., 1975.

BROUGHTON, T. R. S., ed., T. Mommsen, *The Provinces of the Roman Empire*. Chicago, 1968.

CASSON, L. *Travel in the Ancient World*. London, 1974.

COOK, S. A., ADCOCK, F. E., AND CHARLESWORTH, M. P., *The Cambridge Ancient History*, vols. vii–xii. Cambridge, 1928–1939.

EARL, D. C. *The Age of Augustus*. New York, 1968.

FINLEY, M. I. *Aspects of Antiquity*. London, 1968.

GARZETTI, A. *From Tiberius to the Antonines; a History of the Roman Empire*, A.D. 14–192, trans. J. R. Foster. London, 1974.

GRUEN, E. S. *The Last Generation of the Roman Republic*. Berkeley, 1974.

HAMMOND, M. *The Antonine Monarchy*. Rome, 1959.

———. *The City in the Ancient World*. Cambridge, Mass., 1972.

JONES, A. H. M. *The Cities of the Eastern Roman Provinces*, 2nd ed. Oxford, 1971.

———. *The Later Roman Empire, 284–602; a Social, Economic, and Administrative Survey*, three vols. Oxford, 1964.

MacKENDRICK, P. L. *The Iberian Stones Speak; Archaeology in Spain and Portugal*. New York, 1969.

———. *The Mute Stones Speak; the Story of Archaeology in Italy*. New York, 1960.

———. *Roman France*. New York, 1972.

———. *Romans on the Rhine; Archaeology in Germany*. New York, 1970.

MacMULLEN, R. *The Roman Government's Response to Crisis* (A.D. 235–337). Leiden, 1976.

MAGIE, D. *Roman Rule in Asia Minor to the End of the Third Century After Christ*, two vols. Princeton, 1950.

McKAY, A. G. *Ancient Campania*. Hamilton, Ont., 1972.

MILLAR, F., with D. BERCIU, R. N. FRYE, G. KOSSACK, AND T. T. RICE. *The Roman Empire and Its Neighbours*. New York, 1967.

MOORE, R. W. *The Roman Commonwealth*. London, 1942.

NASH, E. *Pictorial Dictionary of Ancient Rome,* 2nd ed., two vols. New York, 1968.

PETIT, P. *Pax Romana.* English translation J. Willis. Berkeley, 1976.

ROSTOVTZEFF, M. I. *Social and Economic History of the Roman Empire,* 2nd ed., two vols. Oxford, 1957.

ROWELL, H. T. *Rome in the Augustan Age.* Norman, Okla., 1962.

SCARBOROUGH, J. *Roman Medicine.* London, 1969.

SEAGER, R., ed. *The Crisis of the Roman Republic.* Cambridge, 1969.

SHERWIN-WHITE, A. N. *The Roman Citizenship,* 2nd ed. Oxford, 1973.

SMITH, R. E. *The Failure of the Roman Republic.* Cambridge, 1955.

STARR, C. G. *Civilization and the Caesars; the Intellectual Revolution in the Roman Empire.* Ithaca, 1954.

STEVENSON, G. H. *Roman Provincial Administration.* New York, 1939.

SYME, R. *The Roman Revolution.* Oxford, 1939.

TRUMP, D. H. *Central and Southern Italy Before Rome.* New York, 1966.

WHEELER, R. E. M. *Rome Beyond the Imperial Frontiers.* London, 1954.

Architecture, Construction

BLAKE, M. E. *Ancient Roman Construction in Italy from the Prehistoric Period to Augustus.* Washington, 1947.

————. *Roman Construction in Italy from Tiberius Through the Flavians.* Washington, 1959.

———— AND BISHOP, D. T. *Roman Construction in Italy from Nerva Through the Antonines.* Philadelphia, 1973.

BOETHIUS, A. AND WARD-PERKINS, J. B. *Etruscan and Roman Architecture.* Harmondsworth, 1970.

BROWN, F. *Roman Architecture.* New York, 1961.

McKAY, A. G. *Houses, Villas and Palaces in the Roman World.* Ithaca, 1975.

Biography

AFRICA, T. W. *Rome of the Caesars.* New York, 1965.

BALSDON, J. P. V. D. *The Emperor Gaius.* Oxford, 1934.

————. *Julius Caesar.* New York, 1967.

BIRLEY, A. *Marcus Aurelius.* London, 1966.

————. *Septimius Severus; the African Emperor.* London, 1971.

BOWERSOCK, G. W. *Augustus and the Greek World.* Oxford, 1965.

CHARLESWORTH, M. P. *Five Men; Character Studies from the Roman Empire.* Cambridge, Mass., 1936.

GELZER, M. *Caesar; Politician and Statesman,* English translation. Cambridge, Mass., 1968.

GRANT, M. *Julius Caesar.* New York, 1969.

————. *Nero, Emperor in Revolt.* New York, 1970.

HADAS, M. *Sextus Pompey.* New York, 1930.

HENDERSON, B. W. *Five Roman Emperors.* Cambridge, 1927.

————. *Life and Principate of the Emperor Hadrian.* London, 1923.

JONES, A. H. M. *Augustus.* London, 1970.

Momigliano, A. *Claudius*, 2nd ed. Oxford, 1961.
Seager, R. *Tiberius*. Berkeley, 1972.
Smith, R. E. *Cicero the Statesman*. Cambridge, 1966.
Warmington, B. H. *Nero: Reality and Legend*. London, 1969.

The Decline

Brown, P. *The World of Late Antiquity; A.D. 150–750*. London, 1971.
Downey, G. *The Late Roman Empire*. New York, 1969.
Grant, M. *Fall of the Roman Empire: A Reappraisal*. New York, 1976.
Haywood, R. M. *The Myth of Rome's Fall*. New York, 1958.
Jones, A. H. M. *The Decline of the Ancient World*. New York, 1966.
Katz, S. *The Decline of Rome and the Rise of Medieval Europe*. Ithaca, N.Y., 1955.
Vogt, J. *The Decline of Rome*, trans. J. Sondheimer. New York, 1967.
Walbank, F. W. *The Decline of the Roman Empire in the West*. Rev. Ed. Toronto, 1969.

The Economy, Economic Policy, Crafts

Badian, E. *Publicans and Sinners; Private Enterprise in the Service of the Roman Republic*. Ithaca, 1972.
————. *Roman Imperialism in the Late Republic*. Pretoria, 1967.
Brown, D. *Roman Craftsmen and Their Techniques*. London, 1974.
Burford, A. *Craftsmen in Greek and Roman Society*. Ithaca, 1972.
Chilver, G. E. F. *Cisalpine Gaul; Social and Economic History from 49 B.C. to the Death of Trajan*. Oxford, 1941.
Coleman-Norton, P. R., ed. *Studies in Roman Economic and Social History in Honor of Allan Chester Johnson*. Princeton, 1951.
Duncan-Jones, R. *The Economy of the Roman Empire*. Cambridge, 1974.
Finley, M. I. *The Ancient Economy*. Berkeley, 1973.
Frank, T. *An Economic History of Rome*, 2nd ed. Baltimore, 1927.
————, ed. *An Economic Survey of Ancient Rome*, six vols. Baltimore, 1933–1940.
Heichelheim, F. M. *An Economic History of the Ancient World*. Leiden, 1959.
Heitland, W. E. *Agricola. A Study on Agriculture and Rustic Life in the Greco-Roman World*. Cambridge, 1921.
Jones, A. H. M. and Brunt, P. A. *The Roman Economy: Studies in Ancient Economic and Administrative History*. Cambridge, 1972.
Miller, J. I. *The Spice Trade of the Roman Empire 29 B.C.–A.D. 641*. Oxford, 1969.
Paul-Louis. *Ancient Rome at Work; An Economic History of Rome from the Origins to the Empire*. London, 1927.
Sutherland, C. H. V. *Roman Coins*. London, 1974.
Toutain, J. *The Economic Life of the Ancient World*, trans. M. R. Dobie. U.S. ed. New York, 1951.
White, K. D. *Roman Farming*. Ithaca, 1970.

History, Literature, Drama

BREHAUT, E. *Cato the Censor "On Farming."* New York, 1933.
BUTLER, J. H. *The Theatre and Drama of Greece and Rome.* San Francisco, 1972.
DOREY, T. A., ed. *Latin Biography.* New York, 1967.
————. *Latin Historians.* London, 1966.
DUFF, J. W. *A Literary History of Rome from the Origins to the Close of the Golden Age.* 3rd ed. London, 1953.
————. *A Literary History of Rome in the Silver Age, from Tiberius to Hadrian.* London, 1927.
FRANK, T. *Life and Literature in the Roman Republic.* Berkeley, 1930.
GRANT, M. *Roman Literature.* Cambridge, 1954.
JONES, T. B. *The Silver-Plated Age.* Sandoval, N.M., 1962.
LAISTNER, M. L. W. *The Greater Roman Historians.* Berkeley, 1947.
SHERWIN-WHITE, A. N. *The Letters of Pliny; a Historical and Social Commentary.* Oxford, 1966.

Philosophy, Education, Rhetoric

ARNOLD, E. V. *Roman Stoicism.* London, 1911.
CLARKE, M. L. *Higher Education in the Ancient World.* Albuquerque, 1971.
————. *Rhetoric at Rome; a Historical Survey.* London, 1953.
————. *The Roman Mind.* London, 1956.
GWYNN, A. *Roman Education from Cicero to Quintilian.* Oxford, 1926.
KENNEDY, G. *The Art of Rhetoric in the Roman World 300 B.C.-A.D. 300.* Princeton, 1972.
SANDBACH, F. *The Stoics.* London, 1975.

Religion

ALTHEIM, F. *History of Roman Religion,* trans. H. Mattingly. New York, 1938.
BARNES, T. D. *Tertullian; a Historical and Literary Study.* Oxford, 1971.
CUMONT, F. *The Oriental Religions in Roman Paganism.* London, 1911.
DODD, C. H. *The Founder of Christianity.* New York, 1970.
DODDS, E. R. *Pagan and Christian in an Age of Anxiety.* Cambridge, 1965.
FOWLER, W. W. *The Religious Experience of the Roman People from the Earliest Times to the Age of Augustus.* London, 1911.
————. *The Roman Festivals of the Period of the Republic.* London, 1899.
FREND, W. H. C. *Martyrdom and Persecution in the Early Church.* Oxford, 1965.
GLOVER, T. R. *The Conflict of Religions in the Early Roman Empire.* London, 1909.
GOUGH, M. *The Early Christians.* New York, 1961.
GRANT, F. C., ed. *Ancient Roman Religion.* New York, 1957.

Grant, M. *The Jews in the Roman World.* New York, 1973.

Heyob, S. *The Cult of Isis Among Women in the Graeco-Roman World.* Leiden, 1975.

Leon, H. J. *The Jews of Ancient Rome.* Philadelphia, 1960.

Lewis, M. W. H. *The Official Priests of Rome Under the Julio-Claudians.* Rome, 1955.

Markus, R. *Christianity in the Roman World.* London, 1975.

Momigliano, A. *The Conflict Between Paganism and Christianity in the Fourth Century; Essays.* Oxford, 1963.

Ogilvie, R. M. *The Romans and Their Gods in the Age of Augustus.* New York, 1969.

Rose, H. J. *Ancient Roman Religion.* New York, 1948.

Sherwin-White, A. N. *Roman Society and Roman Law in the New Testament.* Oxford, 1963.

Taylor, L. R. *The Cults of Ostia.* Bryn Mawr, 1912.

———. *The Divinity of the Roman Emperor.* Middletown, Conn., 1931.

Witt, R. *Isis in the Graeco-Roman World.* London, 1971.

Society, Law

Abbott, F. F. *Society and Politics in Ancient Rome; Essays and Sketches.* New York, 1909.

Arnheim, M. T. W. *The Senatorial Aristocracy in the Later Roman Empire.* Oxford, 1972.

Auguet, R. *Cruelty and Civilization: The Roman Games.* London, 1972.

Balsdon, J. P. V. D. *Life and Leisure in Ancient Rome.* New York, 1969.

Barrow, R. H. *Slavery in the Roman Empire.* London, 1928.

Bertman, S., ed. *The Conflict of Generations in Ancient Greece and Rome.* New York, 1976.

Boak, A. E. R. *Manpower Shortage and the Fall of the Roman Empire.* Ann Arbor, 1955.

Brunt, P. A. *Italian Manpower 225 B.C.–A.D. 14.* Oxford, 1971.

———. *Social Conflicts in the Roman Republic.* London, 1971.

Cameron, A. *Circus Factions in the Roman Empire.* Oxford, 1976.

Carcopino, J. *Daily Life in Ancient Rome.* New Haven, 1940.

Cary, M. and Haarhoff, T. S. *Life and Thought in the Greek and Roman World.* London, 1940.

Casson, L., *The Horizon Book of Daily Life in Ancient Rome.* New York, 1975.

Cowell, F. R. *Everyday Life in Ancient Rome.* New York, 1961.

Crook, J. A. *Law and Life of Rome.* Ithaca, 1967.

D'Arms, J. H. *Romans on the Bay of Naples: a Social and Cultural History of the Villas and Their Owners from 150 B.C. to A.D. 400.* Cambridge, Mass., 1970.

Dilke, O. *The Ancient Romans: How They Lived and Worked.* London, 1975.

Dill, S. *Roman Society from Nero to Marcus Aurelius.* London, 1904.

DUFF, A. M. *Freedmen in the Early Roman Empire*. Cambridge, 1958.

FOWLER, W. W. *Social Life at Rome in the Age of Cicero*. London, 1899.

FRANK, T. *Some Aspects of Social Behavior in Ancient Rome*. Cambridge, Mass., 1932.

FRIEDLANDER, L. *Roman Life and Manners Under the Early Roman Empire*, English translation, 7th ed., four vols. New York, 1908–1913.

GARNSEY, P. *Social Status and Legal Privilege in the Roman Empire*. Oxford, 1970.

GELZER, M. *The Roman Nobility*, trans. R. Seager. Oxford, 1969.

HANDS, A. R. *Charities and Social Aids in Greece and Rome*. Ithaca, 1968.

HARRIS, H. A. *Sport in Greece and Rome*. Ithaca, 1972.

HILL, H. *The Roman Middle Class in the Republican Period*. Oxford, 1952.

JOLOWICZ, H. F. *Historical Introduction to the Study of Roman Law*, 3rd ed. Cambridge, 1972.

LEFFINGWELL, G. W. *Social and Private Life at Rome in the Time of Plautus and Terence*. New York, 1918.

LINTOTT, A. W. *Violence in Republican Rome*. Oxford, 1968.

MACMULLEN, R. *Roman Social Relations 50 B.C. to A.D. 284*. New Haven, 1974.

PERCIVAL, J. *The Roman Villa*. Berkeley, 1976.

SCHULZ, F. *Classical Roman Law*. Oxford, 1951.

SHERWIN-WHITE, A. N. *Racial Prejudice in Imperial Rome*. Cambridge, 1967.

SMALLWOOD, E. M. *The Jews Under Roman Rule from Pompey to Diocletian*. Leiden, 1976.

TREGGIARI, S. *Roman Freedmen During the Late Republic*. Oxford, 1969.

WATSON, A. *The Law of the Ancient Romans*. Dallas, 1970.

WEAVER, P. R. C. *Familia Caesaris: a Social Study of the Emperor's Freedmen and Slaves*. Cambridge, 1972.

WHITE, K. D. *Country Life in Classical Times*. London, 1977.

WILSON, A. J. N. *Emigration from Italy in the Republican Age of Rome*. New York, 1966.

WISEMAN, T. P. *New Men in the Roman Senate, 139 B.C.–A.D. 14*. London, 1971.

YAVETZ, Z. *Plebs and Princeps*. Oxford, 1969.

Women

BALSDON, J. P. V. D. *Roman Women; Their History and Habits*. London, 1962.

KIEFER, O. *Sexual Life in Ancient Rome*. London, 1934.

TURTON, G. E. *The Syrian Princesses: The Women Who Ruled Rome, A.D. 193–235*. London, 1974.

INDEX

Farmers, farming, 59–60, 67, 80–84, 86, 105, 133–34, 287–88; *see also* Agriculture

Final Decree, 86, 89, 107

Fiscus, 156–57, 220

Flaccus, Marcus Fulvius, 86

Flamininus, Titus Quinctius, 52, 71

Freedmen, 127, 160, 178, 188, 201

Freedom, 150, 247, 279

Frontiers, 158–59, 161, 183, 215–16, 219

Gaius, emperor, 173–76, 205, 207, 245, 264

Gaius, jurist, 253, 275–76

Galba, emperor, 181–82, 229, 260

Games, 11, 69–70, 129–30, 171, 177, 203, 205–8

Gaul, Cisalpine, 108

Gaul, Narbonensian, 109

Gaul, provinces of, 158, 191

Gaul, Transalpine, 109–11

Gauls; *see* Celts

Germans, Germany, 158, 161, 191, 219, 259

Gladiators, 11, 206–7; *see also* Games

Gracchus, Gaius Sempronius, 66, 85–86, 90, 105

Gracchus, Tiberius Sempronius, 60, 82–86, 127, 133

Grain distribution, 116

Grain supply, 83, 85, 156, 189

Hadrian, emperor, 209, 218–24, 233, 236, 239–41, 252, 261, 264, 274

Hannibal, 48–50, 59

Helvidius Priscus, 197–98, 213, 260

Herculaneum, 185–86

Herodes Atticus, 245

Horace, 78, 164–66, 265

Illyria, province of, 56

Income, state; *see* Confiscations, Indemnities, Patrimonium, Publicans, Taxation, Tribute

Indemnities, 48, 50, 53–54, 58, 82, 95–96, 100

Industry, 169–71, 238

Inflation, 58, 193, 234–36, 287, 289–90

Intellectuals, 194–98

Italians, Italian allies, 32, 49–50, 89–92, 105–6

Italic Right (*ius Italicum*), 159, 211

Italy, local government, 187–88, 221, 234

Jews, Jewish state, rebellions, 45, 101, 175, 180, 183–84, 191, 217, 223, 272

Jugurtha, Jugurthan war, 86–87, 145

Julia, daughter of Augustus, 166

Julia Domna, 210, 230–31, 232 (fig.)

Julia, granddaughter of Augustus, 161, 166

Julia Maesa, 231–32

Julia Mamaea, 232–33

Jus Italicum; *see* Italic Right

Juvenal, 197, 202–3, 205, 261–65

Land, distributions, 28, 84

Latifundia, 82, 167

Latins, Latin allies, 32–34, 39, 49–50, 89

Law, 21–22, 77–78, 145–47, 201–2, 221–22, 274–76
Livia, 161, 200, 264
Livius Andronicus, 73
Livy, 7–8, 70, 142, 163–64
Lower classes, 57, 61–62, 67, 132–35, 151, 199–205, 251, 287–88, 293–95
Lucan, 180, 197, 255
Lucilius, 78
Lucullus, Lucius Licinius, 98, 100–101, 141

Macedonia, province of, 43–44, 52–56, 158
Maecenas, Gaius, 165–66
Marius, Gaius, 87–89, 93–94, 105, 107–8
Martial, 78, 256–58, 260, 265
Middle class, 62, 136–41, 170
Migrant workers, 67
Minerals, mines, mining, 2, 12, 35, 42, 50, 109, 169, 177–78, 190, 233–35, 288, 290
Mithra, Mithraism, 271, 296–97 (fig.)
Mithridates, Mithridatic War, 92–96, 98
Monarchy, 9
Money, 92, 96, 191–94; see also Coinage
Moneylenders, moneylending, 57–58, 99, 110, 115
Morals, 70–71, 76, 151–52, 258–59, 261–62, 273
Mos maiorum, 72, 83, 143, 151, 250

Naevius, 73
Navy, 160
Nero, emperor, 179–81, 193, 196–97, 199, 205, 207, 225, 229, 245, 255, 261, 264
Nerva, emperor, 209, 213–14, 237

New Man, Men, 24, 80, 88, 101–2
Nobles, nobiles, nobility, 24, 58–59, 62–64, 102, 139, 161–62, 212, 249, 281, 292–93; see also Upper classes
Numen, numina, 3
Numidia, 50–51, 86–87

Octavius, Octavian; see Augustus
Optimates, 84, 98
Otho, emperor, 182
Ovid, 165–66

Panaetius of Rhodes, 73
Parthia, Parthians, 217–18, 226, 231
Patricians, 3, 14, 19–21, 23–25, 63, 163
Patrimonium, 156–57, 185, 220
Patron, patron–client system, 14–15, 64, 80, 106, 147, 257
Pax Romana, 149, 199
Perseus, 54–55, 72
Persians; see Sassanids
Pertinax, emperor, 228
Philip V of Macedonia, 52–54
Philosophers, philosophy, 71, 142–44, 196–98, 245, 296
Pietas, 152–53 (fig.)
Plautus, 74–76, 274
Plebeian assembly, 20–21, 25
Plebeians, 3, 14, 19–21, 23–24, 127, 129
Plebs, urban, 19, 61, 67–68, 80, 85, 105, 127–30, 234, 236
Pliny the Elder, 198–99, 255
Pliny the Younger, 213–15, 233, 258–59, 264–65
Plutarch, 225, 268
Pompeii, 185–87, 249
Pompey, 74, 96–98, 100–103, 108, 112–15, 127, 141, 196, 205–6

10 11 12 13 14 15 16 17 18 19